Scholar, author, former editor and minister, **Arun Shourie** is one of the most prominent voices in our country's public life and discourse. He is the author of over twenty-five bestselling books.

Praise for *Two Saints*

'A stellar contribution.'

– LiveMint

'Arun Shourie may not be a saint. But he is a genuine seeker ... in *Two Saints*, he launches a relentless neurological reduction of consciousness, in particular, "religious experience" or "mystical" experiences to tricks of the brain. As always, the breadth of his reading and the numerous footnotes to scientific literature are truly daunting and impressive ... The book is subversive, but perhaps also an act of tough love.'

– The Indian Express

'[An] intriguing and, often, fascinating journey into the minds and lives of two particularly revered saints in India – Ramakrishna Paramahamsa and Ramana Maharishi.'

– Deccan Chronicle

By the same author

Does He Know a Mother's Heart?
Self Deception—India's China Policies
We Must Have No Price
Where Will All This Take Us?
The Parliamentary System
Falling Over Backwards
Will the Iron Fence Save a Tree Hollowed by Termites?
Governance, and the Sclerosis That Has Set In
Courts and their Judgments
Harvesting Our Souls
Eminent Historians
Worshipping False Gods
The World of Fatwas
Missionaries in India
A Secular Agenda
'The Only Fatherland'
The State as Charade
These Lethal, Inexorable Laws
Individuals, Institutions, Processes
Indian Controversies
Religion in Politics
Mrs. Gandhi's Second Reign
Institutions in the Janata Phase
Symptoms of Fascism
Hinduism: Essence and Consequence
Anita Gets Bail

Two Saints

Speculations Around and About
Ramakrishna Paramahamsa and Ramana Maharshi

ARUN SHOURIE

HarperCollins *Publishers* India

First published in hardback in India in 2017 by
HarperCollins *Publishers*
A-75, Sector 57, Noida, Uttar Pradesh 201301, India
www.harpercollins.co.in

First published in paperback in 2018

2 4 6 8 10 9 7 5 3 1

P-ISBN: 978-93-5277-923-9
E-ISBN: 978-93-5264-505-3

The views and opinions expressed in this book are the author's own
and the facts are as reported by him, and the publishers
are not in any way liable for the same.

Arun Shourie asserts the moral right to be identified
as the author of this work.

Typeset in 11/14 Sabon Roman at
SÜRYA, New Delhi

Printed and bound at
Thomson Press (India) Ltd

For my mother and father, for Malti Shukla,
who gave up so much for us

For Anita, who has borne so much with unimaginable fortitude

For our Adit, who bears his travails with Ramana-like equanimity

Karti hai gauhar ko ashkbaari paida
Tamkeen ko mauj-e-bekaraari paida
Sau baar chaman mein jab tadapti hai naseem
Hoti hai kali pe ek dhaari paida

Contents

Their mesmeric power

The Master has been praying to the Devi, and weeping and wailing before her to send him disciples who will carry forth the work. He has visions in which he has seen some of the young men who will come to him; in particular he has seen and come to know facts about one young boy, Narendra, who is rebellious, independent-minded, agnostic. By a series of happenstances, along with some friends, he starts visiting the Master at Dakshineswar. On seeing them, in particular Narendra, the Master is joyous as can be.

Narendra visits Dakshineswar with a friend. He concludes that the Master is a 'monomaniac'. Yet, a few days later he decides to trudge from Calcutta to Dakshineswar again. He is exhausted by the time he gets there—he had never thought the place was that far. He goes directly to the room of the Master. The latter is sitting on a small bedstead near his bed.

> I saw him sitting alone, merged in himself ... There was no one with him. No sooner had he seen me than he called me joyfully to him and made me sit at one end of the bedstead. I sat down but found him in a strange mood. He spoke indistinctly something to himself, looked steadfastly at me and was slowly coming towards me. I thought another scene of lunacy was going to be enacted. Scarcely had I thought so when he came to me and placed his right foot on my body, and immediately I had a wonderful experience. I saw with my eyes open that all the things of the room together

with the walls were rapidly swirling and receding into an unknown region and my I-ness together with the whole universe was, as it were, going to vanish in the all-devouring great void. I was then overwhelmed with a terrible fear; I had known that the destruction of I-ness was death and that death was before me, very near at hand. Unable to control myself, I cried out loudly and said, 'Ah! What is it that you have done to me? I have my parents, you know.' Giving out a loud laugh to hear those words of mine and touching my chest with his hand, he said, 'Let it then cease now; it need not be done all at once; it will come to pass in course of time.' I was amazed to see that extraordinary experience of mine vanish, as quickly as it had come when he touched me in that manner and said those words. I came to my normal state and saw inside and outside the room standing still as before.

The experience causes what Narendra is to later describe 'a revolution' in his mind.

Narendra comes a third time. There is a crowd at the temple. The Master asks him to accompany him for a walk in the garden and a house that abuts the temple. They enter a room of the house and sit down. The Master enters into ecstasy. Narendra is observing the change in the Master. Suddenly, the Master approaches and touches him. Narendra becomes 'completely overwhelmed at that powerful touch. He lost consciousness completely that day, not partially as had happened on the previous occasion.' When he regains awareness after some time, he finds the Master passing his hand on his chest...

Weeks pass. One day, standing in the veranda outside the Master's room, smoking, Narendra and a friend are mocking what they have heard from the Master about everything in the world being God. 'Hearing Narendra laugh, he [the Master] came out of his room like a boy with his cloth in his arm-pit, and coming to them smiling, said affectionately, "What are you talking about?"' He goes into ecstasy, and touches Narendra. Narendra experiences 'a complete revolution'—'I was aghast to see actually that there was nothing in the whole universe except God.' He remains silent, to see how long the experience would last. 'But that inebriation did not at all diminish that day...' Indeed, it lasts for days. When he comes back to his normal state, he feels that he has experienced non-duality: 'Since then I could never doubt the truth of non-duality.'

Narendra is drawn more and more into the circle. But he remains sceptical, argumentative, questioning.

His father dies. The family is thrown into penury. There is not enough to eat. At mealtimes, Narendra often makes out that he has to go to a friend's house for the meal. It is just pretence—he does not want to eat the little that there is at home so that his mother and siblings have a little more to eat. Those well-to-do friends who used to flock around him shun him. He goes from pillar to post looking for a job. He finds none ... Hunger, helplessness, anger, disillusionment follow one after the other...

The summer has passed. Rains are upon the province. As on so many days, Narendra has been roaming the whole day looking for a job. He is utterly exhausted, so exhausted, he tells his associates later, that he could not place a single step further. Drenched, 'I lay like a log of wood on the open veranda of a nearby house. I cannot say whether I lost consciousness altogether for some time; but I remember that thoughts and pictures of various colours, one after another, arose and vanished of themselves in my mind...' And questions that have been assailing him erupt again: 'Why are there malign forces in the creation of the Benign? Where is the harmony between stern justice and the infinite mercy of God?' 'I was beside myself with joy,' he said later. 'Afterwards, when I resumed my walk home, I found there was not an iota of fatigue in my body and that my mind was filled with infinite strength and peace. The day was then about to break.'

He becomes 'absolutely indifferent' to praise and blame. And he becomes 'firmly convinced' that he has not been born to earn money, to serve his family, to live a life of the world. He starts getting ready 'secretly' to renounce the world—as his grandfather had done.

Let us follow in his own words what happens:

When the day for starting on my itinerary was fixed, I heard the news that the Master would come to a devotee's house at Calcutta that day. I thought this was very good; I would see the Guru before I renounced home forever. As soon as I met the Master, he importunately said to me, 'You must come to Dakshineswar with me today.' I offered various excuses, but he was inexorable. I had to drive with him. There was not much talk in the carriage. After reaching Dakshineswar I sat with others in his room for some

time, when the Master entered into ecstasy. In a moment he came
suddenly to me and, taking my hand in his, began singing as tears
flowed:

Katha koite dorai, na koileo dorai...
I am afraid to tell you, and equally afraid not to tell you
I fear I might lose you forever...

I long kept back the surge of the strong emotions of my mind but
could no more check their force. My breast too was flooded with
tears like that of the Master. I was quite sure that the Master knew
everything. All the others were astonished to see that behaviour of
ours. Some asked the Master the reason for this after he came back
to the normal state when he smiled and answered, 'It is something
between ourselves.' Afterwards, sending away all others, he called
me to him at night and said, 'I know you have come to the world
for Mother's work; you can never live a worldly life. But remain
in your family for my sake as long as I live.' Saying so, the Master
immediately began shedding tears again with his voice choked with
emotion.

Narendra gives up his idea of renouncing the world. But the troubles
of his mother and brothers continue. Poverty, hunger, the humiliation
of going from person to person looking for a job, *any* job that would
enable him to earn a little for feeding his mother and brothers. Alas,
to no avail. Dejected, he goes to the Master and implores him to
ask the Mother to help his family. 'My child,' the Master tells him,
'I cannot say such words, you know. Why don't you yourself pray?
You don't accept the Mother; that is why you suffer so much.'
Narendra told him, 'I have no knowledge of the Mother; please pray
to the Mother yourself for my sake. Pray you must; I will not leave
you unless you do so.'

'I prayed to Mother many times to remove your sufferings. But
as you do not accept the Mother, She does not grant the prayer,'
the Master tells him. 'Well, today is Tuesday, a day especially
sacred to Mother. Mother will, I say, grant you whatever you ask
for. Go to the temple tonight and bowing down to Her, pray for
a boon. My affectionate Mother is the Power of Brahman; She is
pure Consciousness embodied. She has given birth to the universe
according to Her will; what can she not do which She wills?'

Narendra is now convinced that all their sufferings will now certainly come to an end, that the Mother *will* grant his prayer—as the Master himself has assured him of that. Three hours into the night, the Master asks him to go to the temple and ask for the boon.

A firm conviction gripped me that I would actually see Mother and hear Her words. I forgot all other things, and became completely merged in that thought alone. Coming into the temple, I saw that Mother was actually pure Consciousness, was actually living and was really the fountainhead of infinite love and beauty. My heart swelled with loving devotion; and beside myself with bliss, I made repeated salutations to Her, praying, 'Mother, grant me discrimination, grant me detachment, grant divine knowledge and devotion, ordain that I may always have an unobstructed vision of you.' My heart was flooded with peace. The whole universe completely disappeared and Mother alone remained, filling my heart.

Narendra returns to Sri Ramakrishna's room. 'Did you pray to the Mother for the removal of your worldly wants?' the Master asks Narendra. Startled at the question, Narendra answers, 'No, Sir, I forgot to do so. So, what should I do now?' The Master asks him to hurry back, and ask for the boon. He rushes back, 'and coming to the Mother's presence, became inebriated again. I forgot everything, bowed down to her repeatedly, and prayed for the realization of divine knowledge and devotion before I came back.' 'Well, did you tell Her this time?' the Master asks him. Narendra describes what has happened a second time, and how he forgot to pray that their difficulties come to an end. 'What is to be done now?' 'Silly boy, could you not control yourself a little and make that prayer? Go once more if you can, and tell Her those words. Quick!'

I started a third time; but as soon as I entered the temple a formidable sense of shame occupied my heart. I thought, 'What a trifling thing I have come to ask of Mother! It is, as the Master often says, just like the folly of asking a king, having received his grace, for gourds and pumpkins. Ah, how low is my conceit!' Overpowered with shame and aversion I bowed down to Her over and over again, saying, 'I don't want anything else, Mother; do grant me divine knowledge and devotion only.'

It is only when he comes out of the temple that it occurs to Narendra that 'it certainly was the play of the Master, otherwise how was it that I could not speak the words though I came to pray to Her as many as three times?' He returns to the Master and insists that as 'it is certainly you who made me intoxicated like that,' he, the Master, must now ensure that his mother and brothers would not lack food and clothing. In the end, the Master observes, 'Well, they will never be in want of plain food and clothing.'[1]

We know Narendra as Swami Vivekananda. The Master, of course, is Sri Ramakrishna. Time passes, with a myriad of exceptional happenings. A community of devotees and direct disciples forms. That Sri Ramakrishna looks upon Narendra with exceptional affection and hope is manifest to all.

Months pass ... Cancer seizes Sri Ramakrishna's throat. In spite of the most devoted efforts to arrest it, to alleviate the pain, Sri Ramakrishna's condition continues to worsen. The devotees shift him to a house within the city so as to be near medical care. Then they shift him to an airy house with a five-acre garden in a suburb. He is lodged in a room on the first floor. The devotees, Sarada Devi and others stay on the premises. The boys sleep in a small room on the ground floor. They take turns to keep vigil through the night.

Narendra begs Sri Ramakrishna to let him experience the ultimate state. Sri Ramakrishna keeps putting him off—I will do so when I get well, he tells Narendra. But what if you die? What would I have got then? Narendra lets out. Sri Ramakrishna is startled to hear that—'What is he saying?' he exclaims, as if to himself. He scolds him also—for wanting something for himself when he has come to help so many others in the world. But one evening, as he is lying down and meditating, Narendra suddenly begins experiencing a strange state, he feels that a bright light has been placed at the back of his head ... He loses all awareness of everything around him, he experiences his soul ascending, it merges into the Absolute ... As he regains some awareness, he can't apprehend his body; his head, he can, but his body? He can't perceive it. He cries out to an elderly devotee who is meditating in the same room, 'O Gopal-da, where is my body? Where is my body?' Gopal tells him that it is very much there. He tries to make Narendra feel it. But Narendra is lying prostrate, rigid, as if lifeless. Gopal shouts for others. They are unable to bring Narendra to his senses. Is he dead? What has happened to him? they ask each other. Alarmed, they rush to Sri Ramakrishna. The Master is calm, as if, sitting in his room, he knows what is happening in the room below. 'Let him be, let him be,' he tells the anxious young men. 'He has teased me long to reach that state.'

Once he comes back to a semblance of normality, Narendra goes to see Sri Ramakrishna on the first floor. Looking deeply into his eyes, Sri Ramakrishna says, 'Now, then, Mother has shown you everything. Just as the treasure is locked up in the box, so will this realization you have just had be kept under lock, and the key remains with me. Now you have work to do. When you have finished my work, the treasure-box will be again unlocked; and you will know everything even as you have just known.' After a while, Sri Ramakrishna turns inward and prays to Mother, 'O, Mother! Keep this realization of Advaita-*Jnana* covered up in Noren! I have much work to be done by him!'[2]

Sri Ramakrishna's illness continues to worsen. He is hardly able to speak. He is no longer able to swallow solid food ... One day, he makes Narendra sit in front of him, and, gazing at him, he goes into samadhi. Narendra feels a shock penetrating his body, and he too loses consciousness. When he returns to normal consciousness, he sees that Sri Ramakrishna is weeping. The Master tells him that he has given him, Narendra, everything he had and has now become a fakir...[3]

Sri Ramakrishna passes away. Narendra is the natural, and by the hand of Sri Ramakrishna himself, the anointed leader of the small band of young men who have resolved to carry forth the work of Sri Ramakrishna—of revitalizing and saving our religion and, through it, our country. And yet the tug of giving everything up, of devoting himself entirely and exclusively to spiritual realization erupts again and again. Once again he is in mind of giving everything up, and seeking deeksha at the hands of a renowned yogi, Pavhari Baba, whom he has met. He journeys to Ghazipur. Every day, he goes to Pavhari Baba to advance in spiritual realization. He is being torn between continuing the work assigned to him by Sri Ramakrishna and surrendering himself to Pavhari Baba. The inner tussle becomes a torment. Finally, he rises to go to the cave of the Baba, which is nearby. But '...something held him back. His feet refused to move; his body became heavy. A great wave of sadness came over him. He felt heart-sick.' It was as if he was betraying the dear one ... He sinks back into the ground...

'He made the stern decision; but at the very thought his eyes filled with tears: his throat was as if choked. And it was as if ague had seized him.' Sri Ramakrishna appears before him, 'looking intensely into his eyes, saying nothing' ... He is filled with remorse for having been disloyal. His eyes fill with tears ... 'The form of the Master was still there looking with an expression of sadness into his eyes. Two or three hours passed in the vividness of this vision. Not a word issued from the Swami's lips. His body was in a sweat of suffering; his mind was as though pounded...'

He decides, 'No, it must be Ramakrishna.' The struggle continues for twenty-one days. The vision and the experience occur again and again ... Vivekananda is confirmed in the calling of his life...[4]

Scores and scores of such experiences of Sri Ramakrishna's mesmeric influence can be recounted. In the foreword that he wrote to Swami Nikhilananda's *The Life of Ramakrishna*, Mahatma Gandhi observed, 'The story of Ramakrishna Paramahamsa's life is a story of religion in practice. His life enables us to see God face to face...'

THE APPREHENSION OF THEIR POWER

In the same way, to be in the presence of Sri Ramana was to fall under a spell. Learned persons would go with questions, deeply felt conundrums which were gnawing away at their beings; so many would go with bundles of clever questions which they were certain would expose the inconsistencies of the Maharshi. But as they entered the hall where Sri Ramana used to sit, everything would seem so clear, the questions so trifling that many would forget even to ask them. Here is a typical instance involving a name that most readers would recognize instantly:

Somerset Maugham, a well-known English author, was on a visit to Sri Bhagavan. He also went to see Maj. Chadwick* in his room and

---

*Major Chadwick was an Englishman who had given up everything and was living at the Ashram.

there he suddenly became unconscious. Maj. Chadwick requested Sri Bhagavan to see him. Sri Bhagavan went into the room, took a seat and gazed on Mr. Maugham. He regained his senses and saluted Sri Bhagavan. They remained silent and sat facing each other for nearly an hour. The author attempted to ask questions but did not speak. Maj. Chadwick encouraged him to ask. Sri Bhagavan said, 'All finished. Heart-talk is all talk. All talk must end in silence only.' They smiled and Sri Bhagavan left the room.[5]

I never had the great good fortune to have seen Sri Ramana, though I still remember as a child his benign photograph in my maternal grandparents' house in Jalandhar. My grandfather had travelled all the way to Tiruvannamalai for the Maharshi's darshan. And for long, everyone in the family remembered that one day our grandfather had the strong feeling that something very big had happened—later it was learnt that that was the day and time when Sri Ramana had passed away.

Many years later, I had a shiver of an experience of how magnetic his presence and influence must have been. As I became interested in and began writing about public affairs of our country, I was naturally drawn to Gandhiji, and would spend days reading the *Collected Works*. Years later, I began to read about and became enamoured of Ramana Maharshi. I learnt of the deep, deep regard that the two held for each other: when a new issue of Gandhiji's journal arrived, I heard, it would be read avidly at Sri Ramanasramam; when anyone in Gandhiji's circle was in distress or disturbed, Gandhiji would send him to spend a few days at Ramanasramam. This being the case, one thing began to puzzle me. Why is it that Gandhiji himself never went to meet Ramana Maharshi? The question was compounded when I came across a few most uncharacteristic comments made in passing by Sri Ramana.

The entry is of 27 January 1946 in Devaraja Mudaliar's *Day By Day With Bhagavan*. A devotee, Krishnaswami, had gone to Madras to see Gandhiji. The diary entry proceeds:

K. said there were huge crowds in the train and that he had to stand all the way from here to Madras, that there again there was a crowd of more than a lakh, that there was an ocean of cars parked at one corner, that anyhow through the kind offices of some of our friends he sat quite near Mahatma Gandhi with a 6-rupee ticket, that later all the crowd rushed in breaking the gates, that Gandhi refused to speak in any language except Hindi, and so on. Bhagavan said, 'You have seen Gandhi. Now you know and have enjoyed the pleasure to be got out of such trips,' and so saying he gave back the ticket with the remark, 'Keep it safe. It is worth six rupees.'

A hint there, if not of disapproval, at least of dismissal? The conversation drifts to other matters. Krishnaswami returns to the subject of Gandhiji:

K. also told Bhagavan, 'Some of our friends wished to suggest to Mahatma Gandhi that he should visit our *Asramam*. But when they consulted Mr. O.P. Ramaswami Reddi, he said: "Here none of us has any access to Mahatma Gandhi. Rajaji alone has influence."' Bhagavan thereupon said, 'He won't be allowed to come to such places'...

The remark that followed went further:

About a week ago, Bhagavan was mentioning that once the Mahatma came to this place, was near the cattle fair site (a furlong or less from our *Asramam*), finished his business there in less time than the time fixed for it, collected a purse and left the place. K. also brought news that the Mahatma told people that he was frequently thinking of Bhagavan and had great reverence for him. Bhagavan said, 'Yes. Yes. That may be so. Whenever anybody tells him he has no peace of mind, he packs them off here, telling them, "Go and stay at Ramanasramam for a time." They come and tell us.'

Could the explanation be as simple as was implicit in the remark of Sri Ramana—'He won't be allowed to come to such places'? Gandhiji was a very strong-willed person. If he had wanted to go up to Arunachala, who could keep him from doing so? But it was what followed that was completely uncharacteristic of Sri Ramana—that Gandhiji had come to a cattle fair nearby—just a furlong from the Ashram—finished his business there, and, even though there was time to spare according to the programme, Gandhiji had collected the purse, and left the place.

As it was unthinkable that Sri Ramana thought that not visiting him was in some sense lese-majesty, was there a trace of disappointment?

The next day's entry was sharper:

> One Gokul Bhai, who was here recently, has written that he tried to bring Gandhiji here, but he found that Gandhiji peremptorily ordered that nothing at all should be added to his programme which was already too crowded. Bhagavan added, 'They can't find time for all this.'[6]

As I read more and more about the two of them, the question became all the more puzzling. I asked Ramachandra Gandhi—he had been my senior at college; a philosopher, he was Gandhiji's grandson; and in those days he used to spend a lot of time at the India International Centre in Delhi, so it was easy to get to him. He thought for a moment and said that Sri Ramana was a Shaivite and many of Gandhiji's followers were Vaishnavites, and Gandhiji might have felt that were he to visit Sri Ramana, the followers would get offended.

But that didn't sound right at all—after all, Gandhiji was sending persons who were disturbed or agitated to the Ramanasramam for peace and solace.

Later, I came across a more benign response of Sri Ramana. The occasion and response were described by Nagamma Suri in her *Letters*. Writing to her brother, she recorded:

> Yesterday, Harindranath Chattopadhyaya* showed a photo of Mahatma, and said, 'It is a pity that there was never any meeting between Gandhi and Bhagavan.'
>
> Sri Ramana said, 'Some time ago, he came to Tiruvannamalai. A meeting had been arranged for him to be held on the road around the hill, beyond the Ashram. People here thought that he would come to the Ashram on his way back, but owing to the pressure of the crowds it was impossible, and he went away direct

---

*Brother of Sarojini Naidu.

to the station. It seems that he very much regretted this afterwards. Shankarlal Banker was very keen on bringing him here, and in 1938, when Rajendra Prasad and Jamnalal Bajaj came here and saw Skandasramam, they wanted to induce the Mahatma to stay there for some time. But it did not happen. If at Sabarmati, or at Wardha anyone said that he was mentally depressed, the Mahatma used to say, "Go to Ramanasramam and come back after a month's stay there." When Ramaswami Reddiar went to see the Mahatma immediately after taking office as Chief Minister, Madras State, the Mahatma, it seems, asked him for how long he had been going to the Ramanasramam. When he answered that he had been going there for over thirty years, the Mahatma said, "Is that so? I have tried thrice, but so far have not been able to go there." What could he do? How could he come here when he was not left alone for one moment?'[7]

That was certainly more benign than the somewhat curt remarks of the Maharshi that had been included in other accounts. But, really speaking, it did not answer the question. After all, Gandhiji was quite firm about being alone when he wanted to be. Recall his retreating to his ashram. Recall his maunavrata days: whoever came, howsoever pressing the matter at hand, Gandhiji would not break his silence. So, could it just be that he could not go to see Sri Ramana because he was not left a moment to himself?

Sometime later, I happened to be in Madras, and had gone to meet a close acquaintance, the erudite civil servant, S. Guhan. His uncle, Professor K. Swaminathan, had edited and brought out Gandhiji's *Collected Works*. He was also a devotee of Sri Ramana—that I knew from the biography he had written of the sage. I mentioned the question to Guhan and inquired if I could meet Professor Swaminathan through him.

Guhan and Mrs Shanta Guhan, his wife, took me to him one day. The professor was quite elderly by this time and was leading a retired life. He was consideration itself.

But suddenly a strange thing happened, something that threw me off balance.

When I asked the professor why Gandhiji had not met Sri Ramana even as he was sending persons in distress to him for solace, the professor looked at me as if struck; he was silent for a

few moments; his eyes became moist ... I was taken aback. Had
I said something wrong? Had I offended him in any way? Had I
transgressed? I apologized, 'Sir, I am so sorry if I have said something
wrong.'

'No, no, young man. You have pierced my heart. You see, I was
a follower of the Mahatma. And I was a devotee of Ramana. It was
my life's ambition to bring the two of them together. And did I try!
But there was always one so much cleverer than all of us—whenever
we tried, he did something to make sure that the meeting wouldn't
take place.'

'Who?'

'Rajaji, of course. Rajaji knew that the country needed Gandhi.
He must be there to lead the freedom movement. But if he went up
the Hill,* he may never come down—that was Rajaji's apprehension.
And the country would have suffered a terrible loss. That is why,
whenever we contrived some plan, he would outwit us and derail it.'

Talk of mesmeric power, indeed of the apprehension of mesmeric
power!

Their Himalayan Influence

The presence, the teaching of the two saints had the most far-reaching
consequences. Bengal was being swept off its moorings. Our religion
had become, in the eyes of many, something to be ashamed of.
Idol worship had come to be regarded as something primitive. The
missionaries, and even missionary scholars like Max Müller had
come to repose great hope in Keshab Chandra Sen and the Brahmo
Samaj—they felt that in Keshab Chandra they had found the lever to
lift India into Christianity.[8]

Sri Ramakrishna by his manifest holiness, by his manifest
simplicity, by his magnetism, by his spiritual attainments turned
all this upside down. He made idol worship and other practices of
our religions respectable. He awakened Indians to the fact that it
is their religion that had gleaned the great truths, that it was in no
way inferior to religions—Islam and Christianity—that had come
to be associated with conquerors. He pulled adherents of different

---

*Arunachala, the hill on which Sri Ramana spent fifty years.

sects out of their prejudices against one another. And, far from fulfilling the conquest that the missionaries had set their hearts on, Keshab Chandra Sen became an ardent devotee of his! Because of Sri Ramakrishna, as his biographer, Swami Nikhilananda notes, tantra was purified, and, because sadhus from all over the country, and from all sects flocked to him, his insights came to illumine and pull back on to the right course several strands of our religious tradition. He located, nurtured, trained, impelled a group of disciples to carry the task forward.

Sri Ramana's impact was just as profound. In particular, it encompassed all the dimensions that Sri Ramakrishna's example and teaching had illumined. He awakened thousands and thousands to the great spiritual truths that our forefathers had uncovered. His teaching stripped away the dogma and philosophical rigmarole in which our religious and philosophical discourse had got ensnared. He lifted us out of sectarian disputations. In fact, he lifted anyone who went to him, or even came across his teaching second-hand, out of disputation all together. While he studiously kept away from active participation in any non-spiritual endeavour, he was the solace and reassurance and beacon for many who were involved in the freedom movement, to confine ourselves to just one example.

So Different, So Similar

To try and grasp Sri Ramakrishna is to try and gather quicksilver in a sieve! Sri Ramana, on the other hand, is the textbook embodiment of Achaan Chah's 'clear forest pool' to whom all sorts come to quench their thirst.[9] For us ordinary persons, he is a bit distant though. He teaches by silence. Sri Ramakrishna is always mesmerizing those around him with tales and parables, with his sparkling similes and metaphors. A careless word never escapes Sri Ramana's lips. Sri Ramakrishna teaches, he tells jokes—sometimes naughty ones: 'I don't give these young men a strictly vegetarian diet!' he exclaims. When the devotees are around for his darshan, Sri Ramana hardly leaves the bedstead on which he is reclining. Sri Ramakrishna weeps, he sings, he dances. Having moved to the Arunachala Hill in 1899 at the age of twenty, Sri Ramana almost never leaves it till he passes away in 1950—once for six months during an outbreak of plague;

and when he circumambulated the hill. Sri Ramakrishna gets into
a carriage ever so often—to visit houses of his devotees, to attend
festivals, to see plays; once he even ventures on a pilgrimage to
Benares, Vrindavan, Mathura and Allahabad. Sri Ramana transports
the blessed with a gaze from a distance. Sri Ramakrishna comes
close, he touches; he places his foot on the chest of the young and
sceptical and rebellious Narendra, and Narendra goes into a swoon,
and the argument is ended.[10] The serenity with which Sri Ramana
bears the excruciating pain and cancer that are devouring him itself
places him on a mountain top far out of our reach. The childlike
reactions of Sri Ramakrishna as his throat burns from cancer, and as
he loses physical strength are recognizable.

Their approaches differ, rather their assessment of what we
ordinary folk are capable of differs. Sri Ramakrishna feels that in Kali
yuga, jnana marga, the path of knowledge is well-nigh impossible
for us. He counsels us to plunge into devotion. Sri Ramana teaches
that true bhakti is well-nigh impossible for us ordinary folk, that
the direct path is the one that is most accessible—of inquiring what
the 'Self' is that permeates us, that is there whether we are awake or
asleep, conscious or unconscious.

And yet they are so similar—even in their teaching. When
we take his scathing asides against mere learning and reason too
literally, Sri Ramakrishna teaches us that what he is counselling
against is obsessive reasoning; but one must reason, he says, and
learn to discriminate between the Real and the unreal, between the
Everlasting and the ephemeral … When a visitor parades his mastery
of books, Sri Ramana pulls him up in words that might as well have
been spoken by Sri Ramakrishna.

As for approaches, who says,

> He who is an *Acharya* has to know different things. One needs a
> sword and shield to kill others; but to kill oneself, a needle or a
> nail-knife suffices.
>
> One ultimately discovers God by trying to know who this 'I'
> is. Is this 'I' the flesh, the bones, the blood, or the marrow? Is it the
> mind or the *buddhi*? Analysing thus, you realize at last that you are
> none of these. This is called the process of '*Neti, neti*', 'Not this,
> not this'. One can neither comprehend nor touch the Atman. It is
> without qualities or attributes.

Words we would associate with Sri Ramana, though they are what Sri Ramakrishna spoke to his devotees as he was explaining the differences between and the ultimate identity of God-with-Form and God-without-Form.[11]

Both were the soul of consideration—both would alter their emphasis according to what the listener who was seeking guidance actually needed: an aspirant who was tilting to unreflective blind devotion would be reminded of the need for discrimination, examination, jnana; one obsessed with bookish knowledge would be chastised about the futility of what is written in books.

Both discouraged questions about reincarnation, and the rest, questions that are so often used by us—unwittingly, unconsciously— to dodge the spiritual task at hand. Both were against bookish learning—Sri Ramakrishna in more colourful words: mere Pandits are like diseased fruit, he said; they are reputed to be wise, but they are attached to 'woman and gold'. 'Like vultures, they are in search of carrion...'; 'Mere knowledge of Advaita!' he exclaims to the Divine Mother, 'I spit on it!...'; 'Mere dry reasoning—I spit on it! I have no use for it,' he tells devotees; mere study of books will avail you nothing, he warns devotees—one may recite the written part of the drum glibly, but to play the drum is exceedingly difficult; he scolds even such a prodigious scholar as Bankim Chandra Chatterjee in the sharpest terms ... Not just bookish learning, Sri Ramakrishna had no time for books themselves—not even for scriptures: get the essence of the scripture, he told devotees, what is the point of going on and on with them? Scriptures are like the almanac, he said. The almanac forecasts rain for the year, but you won't get a drop by squeezing its pages...[12] Sri Ramana, of course, would cut short academic disputation even before it had commenced! And while writing this book, I am all too aware of their admonishing!

Both were explorers of the inner world. And in exploring, both personified the essence of our tradition of inquiry—that is, delving from one layer of truth to the next, deeper layer through personal experience. Neither of them had read the texts. Both plunged into the lab, so to say, with just one compass—their own, direct experience. When the texts were read to them or when, as in Sri Ramana's case, he happened to read them much later to answer the query of an aspirant, both were to say that they then learnt that the scriptures contained or validated what they had themselves, directly experienced.

More important than anything else, both testified to the same effulgent experience. They lived the same truth.

2

The real miracle

In *Does He Know a Mother's Heart?* I set out the explanations that
our sacred books give for suffering. To say the least, the explanations
were such that they would not stand a moment's scrutiny. They put
God in a very bad light, indeed. Therefore, I sought to find out what
three persons whom I revere—Sri Ramakrishna Paramahamsa, Sri
Ramana Maharshi and Mahatma Gandhi—said to persons who
had suffered the blows of fortune and had turned to them for
solace. Gandhiji's explanations—for instance, for the devastating
1934 earthquake that killed almost 30,000 in Bihar, and for the
unspeakable horrors that were rained down on Jews in Europe by
Hitler—in effect blamed the victims. For believers like him, nothing
happens, not a leaf moves but by the will of God; God in turn is all-
powerful, all-knowing and compassionate; hence, the suffering that
befalls us—a collective like the Jews or an individual like our Adit or
a natural calamity like an earthquake or a tsunami—is just reward
for what the victims have done. These explanations—which Gandhiji
reiterated many times over—bordered on the embarrassing. And yet
they were explanations to which a believer in God is inevitably led.
So I turned even more diligently to what Sri Ramakrishna and Sri
Ramana had said to those in distress. And how had they explained
their own illnesses and accidents? Sri Ramakrishna's health was
always frail. Once, to his consternation, when he was in samadhi
he broke his teeth, once as he leaped to grasp the vision of Lord
Jagannath, he broke his arm. Sri Ramana suffered from customary

18

ailments, including sciatica. In any case, how did they explain the cancers that felled them in the end, and caused them terribly painful deaths? Their explanations also turned out to be no more reassuring.

But the search had one incidental effect: my fascination and reverence for Sri Ramakrishna and Sri Ramana grew manifold. On every count, their goodness, their lives, their compassion, their mesmeric power, the difference they made to the lives of thousands upon thousands, and to the course of our country were of a Himalayan scale. I, therefore, got hold of all the accounts in English about them that I could, and immersed myself in them.

Quite naturally, everyone who reads about them wants to learn about their unique experience—the mystic or 'peak' experience. But I soon learnt that they said little about it. On the contrary, what they said was that the experience could not be described. Sri Ramakrishna often gave the simile of 'the salt doll' to drive home the point. One day, a doll made of salt decided to find out how deep the ocean was, he would say. So, it dived into the sea. Long before it could reach the bottom, it dissolved into the ocean. No doll, no account of how deep the ocean is!

On the other side, the human brain is rightly said to be the most complex entity in the known universe. Furthermore, advances in neuroscience in the last fifty years, in particular the better and better technologies for observing what is happening inside our skulls, suggest that even simple experiences—like seeing a landscape—implicate many complex networks of many components of the brain. One can, therefore, reasonably assume that many, many networks connecting myriad parts of the brain, often at great distances from each other, would be activated when a person has such an overarching, engulfing experience as the mystic one. While several models have been advanced as possible hypotheses about which networks among which parts are liable to 'light up' during a peak experience, it is, in spite of the enormous advances in neuro-imaging over the last fifty years, too early to say anything definite about that ultimate experience. Moreover, even if what are called the 'neural substrates' of the mystic experience get to be observed, could one stop there and maintain that the activation of those networks is the 'cause' of the peak experience any more than one can say that the pneumonia that he caught day before yesterday is the 'cause' of the death of the ninety-year-old patient who had been enfeebled over the year by a terminal illness? The answer depends on how far back one chooses to go. True, the networks 'light up' as one is transported into the peak experience. But what lit them up? Years and years of prior practice? The guru's blessing? What the practitioner thought is going to happen once he receives the guru's blessing? Divine intervention?

So, the pearl remained out of reach. But the peak experiences were not the only remarkable ones that were reported about the two saints. There were so many other experiences that were only a little less fascinating for us, uninitiated persons. These were peripherals. But given the way we are in India, often these incidental experiences are the ones around which legends grow. They are taken as evidence of the saintliness, indeed, in the case of both Sri Ramakrishna and Sri Ramana, of their divinity.

This book is about those peripherals, rather about what psychologists and neuroscientists are liable to say about those peripherals.

What psychologists and neuroscientists have to say on a matter arising out of one of the peripherals—let us say the visions that Sri Ramakrishna used to have—is often of interest in itself. It bears directly on our mundane lives. Consider an instance. Sri Ramakrishna subjected himself to extreme, in fact to incredible austerities for *twelve years*. In the case of Sri Ramana, this period of sadhana lasted *three-and-a-half years*. We read every other day of how the body influences the mind—a toothache changes our view of the world! Just as several studies have established how we can change our bodies, including our brains, by working on and with our minds, others have shown how working on our bodies can help us change our minds, and through that our brains.

For instance, piles of studies show that connections between neurons get altered, even the cubic space that is devoted to a particular function gets altered, by what we do and even by the way we think repeatedly over a period of time. Sometimes, when, for instance, the activity has great emotional salience, this 'period of time' turns out to be very short indeed—just weeks or even days; a single traumatic blow of chance, taking no more than an instant, may alter them perceptibly.

That would seem to suggest a question. Would the years and

years of sadhana that our mystics undergo not have altered their brains and its networks? Did these alterations in turn cause the peak experiences that they had? Or at the least, the visions that they saw or the anahata sound, the cosmic sound that they heard?

The question, therefore, was whether the long years that the two saints spent practising such extreme austerities would have so altered their brains and minds as to predispose them to the sorts of experiences that they had later. I could have just referred to a few studies that showed the effect that working on the body has on the brains and minds of the persons concerned. But the question is of direct interest in itself irrespective of what it may suggest about the experiences that Sri Ramakrishna and Sri Ramana had. Each of us has to contend with illnesses that originate in the brain—I have had to do so every day since our son, Adit, was born forty-two years ago and we were told that he had suffered a severe brain injury; and for the twenty-three years in which Anita, my wife, has had Parkinson's disease. In such a circumstance, Ramakrishna or no Ramakrishna, each of us wants to know whether working on the body will help alleviate the symptoms that plague one's dear ones. For this reason, when considering the effect of the body on the mind, and how it may be used to alter the brain and the mind, I have summarized somewhat more of the literature than would have sufficed for speculating about the experiences of the two saints. I have included accounts of studies and instances that may be of interest of their own, and may even be of use to the reader as they have been to me.

Or consider the question of hypnotism, of self-hypnotism in particular. Sri Ramakrishna placed the greatest emphasis on *longing*, on shedding attachments to everything of this world, and instead longing for God—one must long for God as a man whose head is being held forcibly in the water longs for breath, he would say. Unless you long for God to that extent, He will not appear, the saint would tell his devotees, but if you do, He will surely appear. In his own case, the Goddess Kali was, of course, a constant presence. But from time to time, Sri Ramakrishna would start wanting to have a vision of some other deity—of Sri Hanuman, of Sri Krishna or Radha; once he longed to have a vision of Jesus, on another occasion of Prophet Muhammad. In these periods, everything about him would change. He would wear clothes that were different—a woman's clothes and ornaments when he wanted to see Sri Krishna as Radha saw him; clothes worn by Muslims when he wanted to have a vision of the Prophet. The food he ate, his gait, his facial expressions, everything would change. When he wanted to have a vision of Sri Hanuman, his gait changed to such an extent that instead of walking, he would hop from step to step, he would eat raw vegetables ... he even said that his tailbone had grown by an inch during that time. And sure enough, he would soon have the precise vision for which he had been longing.

Does longing to this extreme degree have an element of self-hypnosis? That was the question. But the fact that hypnosis is used as an aid in curing patients by some of the leading hospitals of the world, that in Belgium it is used even as a substitute for anaesthetics in surgery, is of interest in itself. Could it be used, instead of yet another medicine, to help rid a Parkinson's patient of hallucinations?

It is for this reason that I have included material that, strictly speaking, goes beyond the questions that arise out of the experiences of the two saints.

But once you start reading about any of these matters 'in itself', you soon discover that the literature is just overwhelmingly vast. Therefore, while from the point of view of questions that relate to the two saints, some of the material is more than what is required; from the point of view of what is available on the subject, it is too little. Where I have been confronted by this superabundance of riches, I have not tried to provide a summary, much less a review of all the studies on that subject. I have given glimpses of a few of the studies depending on where the balance of the argument seemed to me to lie. That is why in the section on near-death experiences, for instance, I have not referred to the extensive writings of, say, Raymond Moody or Kenneth Ring, two of the principal persons in the field. I would hope that in such instances, the little that I have reported will propel the reader to examine the subject in greater detail. By contrast, in regard to the studies that seemed to me to better reflect the balance of the argument as it stands today, I have done the opposite: I have resisted the temptation to reduce the paper to two or three sentences; instead, I have devoted a good deal of space to setting out what the study has shown and how. I sincerely hope that the reader will find the propositions of these authors and the evidence that they adduce for them as interesting as I did.

The point is especially relevant because of the way this book is organized. Consider a symptom. A devotee is going to perform puja at his home. He is very, very keen that Sri Ramakrishna bless the puja and his home by his presence. Sri Ramakrishna is happy to go. But the person who looks after the affairs of the Dakshineswar temple at which the saint is the priest—though himself a protector and ardent devotee of Sri Ramakrishna—says 'No'. The devotee is distraught. Sri Ramakrishna consoles him: Don't worry, he tells the devotee; you perform the puja in such and such a way, and I will be there. When some days later the puja is being conducted, lo and behold, the devotee sees that Sri Ramakrishna is present; he doesn't just see, he *feels* the presence. But everyone knows that that day Sri Ramakrishna never left the premises of the temple. Such incidents are common occurrences in the lives of saints.

Or take another instance that is even more directly relevant. Sri Ramakrishna told his devotees that during that period of sadhana, when he sat down for meditation, a young man who looked very much like him would emerge from Sri Ramakrishna's own body, seat himself in front of Sri Ramakrishna and guide him.

We can, of course, dismiss these accounts as the imaginings of devotees or, in the latter case, of Sri Ramakrishna. But there is a parallel, and that may offer an alternative explanation. Recall that this is a phenomenon well known among mountaineers and explorers. The great explorer, Sir Ernest Shackleton himself experienced the presence of a fourth man as he led two companions to bring help for his shipwrecked and freezing crew. Not just that, the fourth man is the one who guided Shackleton and his companions through treacherous landscape and murderous weather. We are told that Reinhold Messner, said to be the greatest climber ever, could summon the presence at will. There are manifest differences, of course: Shackleton and the mountaineers who felt the presence of a guide were in life-threatening situations; Sri Ramakrishna was not. But such was his longing that for him too, advancing towards the goal of enlightenment was literally 'a matter of life and death'. Could such intense longing trigger the same experience as the life-threatening situations did?

Consider yet another example. Sri Ramakrishna would be sent into a trance by all sorts of triggers: the passing allusion to the Mother or to Radha in a conversation, two prostitutes standing in a doorway as Sri Ramakrishna was being driven in a carriage to Calcutta, the sunset over the Ganga, the sight of Benares—anything could set off the trance. Ever so often it was music: the young Narendra singing a hymn, singers passing by a house singing about Krishna ... Again, there is a parallel: musicogenic epilepsy is a well-known condition as readers of Oliver Sacks's *Musicophilia* will know—a note, a song, a tune on the radio triggers a seizure.

Does that mean that Sri Ramakrishna had musicogenic epilepsy? There is no medical evidence to that effect at all. Among doctors of the kind who attended on Sri Ramakrishna, the neural correlates of conditions like seizures had not been traced, conditions like 'musicogenic epilepsy' had not been identified or labelled. Moreover, no medical records are available—after all, Sri Ramakrishna lived from 1836 to 1886, and that too in a village, and later in a temple that was at a considerable distance from the city; a period during which and places in which compiling systematic medical records would not even have been heard of. Sri Ramana, of course, lived till 1950. But for years he lived like a hermit in the wilderness, in a cave with just one or two lay companions; almost the only contact he had was with the occasional passer-by, with some curious folk who had heard of the young swami, with an elderly lady who would bring food up the hill to the mendicants. Even for the later years, even for the final years when he was being subjected to medication and surgery for cancer, no medical records are available—or at least so I was told when I made inquiries from the Ramanasramam. However, in his case, we do have a statement from Sri Ramana himself that he suffered from fits.

But to get back to musicogenic epilepsy, and the way this book is organized. In the book, we first get to see the two saints as they live and move about, and notice some symptoms. And then we learn a bit about parallel conditions in which those sorts of symptoms occur. And later, what neuroscience says about those symptoms today.

Sri Ramakrishna's condition may have been as far removed from musicogenic epilepsy as can be, we just do not know. The key is in the word 'parallel' that I used in the preceding paragraphs. In dictionaries the word has either of two meanings:

parallel:/*adj* **1a:** extending in the same direction and always being the same distance apart ... **4a:** analogous or comparable...

parallel *noun* **1** somebody or something equal or similar in all essential particulars; a counterpart **2** a comparison to show resemblance...

So, the parallels may show that the two sets of experience are entirely different, 'always being the same distance apart', or that they are 'something equal or similar in all essential particulars'. Each of us will decide for himself.

A Few Things We May Gain

And yet, much can be gained by looking at parallels. True, as the great brain scientist David Marr observed, 'there is no way to understand how a wing of a bird works by studying its feathers'.[1] But maybe we will learn a bit about the feathers.

Second, the work done by neuroscientists, psychologists and others that we learn about is most absorbing in itself—to chance upon the innovativeness and simplicity of the experiments of neuroscientists, for instance, is sheer delight. Third, it may be that the experiences that the saints had and the experiences of others in different circumstances may hold clues. For instance, as we shall see, a series of sensations erupted when points in the cortex were stimulated after the skull had been opened for surgery. These have an uncanny resemblance to experiences that we will be reading about— hearing heavenly music, the sensation that one is floating away, that one 'is half here and half there', the feeling that he is talking to his friends in South Africa when, in fact, the person is lying on an operating table in Montreal ... Yes, the circumstances are wholly different. But could it be that, being so similar, the experiences of the saints and of these patients undergoing surgery were triggered by or implicated the same components of the brain?

Fourth, descriptions of those alternative conditions may be of use to us. Take just one instance with which I am personally familiar. As I just mentioned, persons suffering from Parkinson's disease often start having auditory and visual hallucinations; information about these disturbing imaginings and what can be done about them is of direct use. In such instances, in the accounts that follow, our saints become what they were to thousands when they were alive—they lead us to cures, they become healers.

And, finally, learning that the symptoms that we have been taking to be marks of sainthood occur in other circumstances also, that they occur to ordinary mortals also, helps sift incidentals about the saints from the core. Legends about the incidentals often distract us. We take the fact that Sri Ramakrishna used to go into a trance at the mention of Radha or upon hearing a hymn as a mark of his 'God-inebriation'. We take the apparition that would appear from his own body and guide him as he sat at meditation to be the doing of the Mother to prepare him for the purpose that She had in mind. We take his being seen at two places at once as evidence of his divine powers. But in the case of both Sri Ramakrishna and Sri Ramana, their goodness was the miracle. Their insights into life, the acuity of their observation, the transformation they brought about in the lives of thousands, the sparkling words of Sri Ramakrishna, the communicative silence of Sri Ramana—these were the wonders. The acme of their attainment was the mystic state. By learning that the incidentals can occur in other circumstances, that they can occur to other, ordinary persons, we will learn to set them to one side, and to concentrate our reverent gaze on the core of these saints—their goodness, their overflowing kindness, their deep insights into the human condition—and on their core experience—the mystic state.

The Only Assumption We Need

The only premise we need is that when we encounter a person whose deeds or claims, or claims by others about whose deeds, run counter to the laws of nature, we should first look for the natural explanation before leaping for the supernatural explanation. Before insisting that our festivals are divinely ordained, should we not examine whether they have to do with the cycles of seasons, whether they have to do with the cycles of sowing seeds, and tending shoots, and reaping harvests?

We do not have to presume that natural explanations— explanations that seem to account for a phenomenon in the light of current knowledge—explain everything; nor, indeed, that they explain everything about the phenomenon at hand. The rationalist's plea is more restricted: all he is saying is: 'When trying to understand a phenomenon, let us see how far natural explanations will carry us before we jump on to a supernatural one.' An example will illustrate what that means.

Sri Ramakrishna had a very tender body. His devotees attributed this to the extreme austerities to which he had subjected himself for twelve long years. He often suffered from dysentery, gas. Once, as he saw Lord Jagannath in a vision and tried to embrace him, he broke his arm as any of us might do. Eventually, he developed cancer in his throat—this resulted in a torturous and very painful end.

Today, when we read,

> The Master smoked tobacco a few times a day, using a hubble-bubble that he kept in the southwest corner of his room. He sometimes offered smoke to his visitors. After meals he would chew betel rolls. Holy Mother would prepare them for him, and his lips would become crimson from chewing them...[2]

our instinctive reaction is to link these habits—smoking tobacco, chewing betel leaves—to the cancer that erupted in his throat. But in those days, everyone—Sri Ramakrishna himself, Sarada Devi, his devotees—invoked supernatural explanations: that the cancer had erupted because, out of compassion, he had been taking on the evil karma of others; that it had erupted because once, when his brother was ill and when, in spite of the doctor forbidding the brother from taking anything, he had tried to drink water, and Sri Ramakrishna had snatched the glass away from him, the brother had cursed him that a day would come when *he*, Ramakrishna, would find it difficult to swallow anything; that the cancer had erupted and the extreme pain had been inflicted on him so as to move his consciousness from the saguna to the nirguna; that the cancer had been visited upon him so that genuine devotees may be sifted from the others. While someone at that time might have linked the cancer that afflicted his throat to the tobacco he had been smoking or to whatever may have been mixed in the betel rolls, I have not come across the account. The closest that I have come across to a physiological explanation is in Swami Saradananda's *Sri Ramakrishna, The Great Master.* He too recounts the supernatural causes—taking on the sins of others, the curse, etc.—and at one point he traces the disease to overexertion by Sri Ramakrishna in instructing anyone and everyone who was thirsty for spiritual progress, and to his not sleeping adequately as a result.[3]

Of course, it is entirely possible that tobacco and the things in the paan did not account for the cancer—there may have been other triggers. But our instinct today would be to first examine how far this proximate, natural explanation carries us in accounting for the cancer before invoking the supernatural explanations that struck Sri Ramakrishna and others at that time—explanations that, in fact, struck them as being so 'natural'.

Can the Commonplace Fell God?

That even today most of us proceed by the opposite sequence is, of course, not just a matter of analytical preference. We are loath to believe that such a commonplace, mundane thing as smoking tobacco or chewing paan could have felled God—for that is who Sri Ramakrishna, also Sri Ramana for that matter, was and is to his devotees.

Sri Ramakrishna and Sri Ramana themselves were so much more realistic about these matters. Sri Ramakrishna delighted in puries; rice pudding; ice cream; 'some of that stuff—a little sour, a little sweet—that begins to fizz when you push down the cork' as he put it to a devotee when he asked him to bring a bottle of it—that is, lemonade; he loved fish of all kinds; he occasionally ate goat meat. He could always make room for jalebis, a sweet. Once at the house of Keshab Chandra Sen, the leader of the Brahmo Samaj, Sri Ramakrishna had had his fill. When someone asked him whether he would want more, he said, like the child he was, 'My stomach is full, but if you give me a *jilipi* I shall eat it,' adding in his impish way, 'During the fair the roads are jammed and overcrowded. At that time it is difficult for a man to pass through. But if the Viceroy's carriage comes along, all other carriages make room for his to pass. Similarly, the stomach makes room for *jilipis!*' He liked khichdi—so much so that Swami Vivekananda 'introduced this *khichuri* offering to the cosmic form of the Master...'[4] Did these childlike desires diminish him in any way? Indeed, do they not endear him all the more to us ordinary folk?

The same goes for their illnesses. They talked often about these. Sri Ramakrishna, as I just mentioned, had a very frail constitution: he often suffered from ailments common to those times, and to so many of us—dysentery, gas, fever, cold, cough and the rest. His 'skin was so soft and sensitive that he could not be shaved with a razor. The barber would simply trim his hair and beard with a [pair of] scissors.' His feet were so delicate that they would suffer from walking on a rough surface.[5]

Similarly, Sri Ramana slipped and his shoulder bone cracked. His back and his sides were afflicted by eczema. He suffered from severe rheumatic pains in his feet, his knees, his back. As the sciatica pain increased, he came to find walking very difficult. His eyesight deteriorated...

In the end, both were struck by cancer. And both died excruciatingly painful deaths.

Do these illnesses diminish them in any way? On the contrary, do they not raise them higher? That in spite of so much that is the lot of all of us, they ascended to such unimaginable heights? As I type this, I am reminded of passages that I read as a schoolboy in Panditji's *The Discovery of India*:

> It has always seemed to me a much more magnificent and impressive thing that a human being should rise to great heights, mentally and spiritually, and should then seek to raise others up, rather than that he should be the mouthpiece of a divine or superior power. Some of the founders of religions were astonishing individuals, but all their glory vanishes in my eyes when I cease to think of them as human beings. What impresses me and gives me hope is the growth of the mind and spirit of man, and not his being used as an agent to convey a message.
>
> Mythology affected me in much the same way. If people believed in the factual contents of these stories, the whole thing was absurd and ridiculous. But as soon as one ceased believing in them, they appeared in a new light, a new beauty, a wonderful flowering of a richly-endowed imagination, full of human lessons ... I have often wondered what manner of men and women they were who gave shape to these bright dreams and lovely fancies, and out of what goldmine of thought and imagination they dug them out.
>
> ... Many Hindus look upon the *Vedas* as revealed scripture.

This seems to me to be particularly unfortunate for thus we miss their real significance—the unfolding of the human mind in the earliest stages of thought. And what a wonderful mind it was![6]

The point of our exercise is not to undermine faith, the point is to help understand faith better. True, as they say, faith can move mountains, it can bring persons back from the brink of death. But when a terminally ill person, one who believes with all his heart and soul that his ishtadevata, that his guru *has* the power to save him, and that his god and his guru *do* rush and save their devotees, when such a person gets well, is it the power of that god or guru that has saved him or his faith that they have that power?

Similarly, the point of the exercise is not to debunk miracles. But to help sift a miracle—something contrary to the known laws of nature—from what we take to be a miracle. After all, to stay with what Panditji wrote, the miracle may not be that our rishis had the antenna to take down what Brahma dictated. The miracle may well be that human beings—beings made of the same flesh and bones as you and me—could soar so high, that, with none of the instruments of modern science, they could, for instance, glean so much about our mind and its workings. In the specific case of our saints, the point is not to insist that they had no special powers or attributes. The point is to sift their genuine attainments and powers from what Sathya Sai Baba used to call their 'calling cards'—in his case, his producing vibhuti and gold lockets and watches.

PROFANING THE DIVINE?

What goes for saints goes for the experiences they had, and even more so for the experiences that their devotees had about them or in their presence. What are we to make of these experiences when similar experiences can be triggered by stimulating points on the cortex with electrodes, when even the peak experience can be induced by such stimulation? What are we to make of the experiences when we read the account of a young neuroscientist about what she went through as she had a stroke, an account that is indistinguishable from a description of the peak experience? How are we to distinguish accounts of devotees who affirm in all sincerity that they saw and felt the presence of the saint after he passed away from accounts given by persons who have recently lost a dear one? How is it that when a saint sees a ghost, it proves that ghosts exist; and when suggestible persons feel the presence of ghosts in houses that have the reputation of being haunted, that just proves that they have feverish imaginations?

If thinking about the saints in these ways ruffles us too much, think of ordinary devotees: how is it that devotees of one God—Vishnu, say—when they have a vision, never have a vision of some other God—say, Shiva; or how devotees of one Master, Sri Ramakrishna, never have a vision of another Master, Sri Ramana? Why is it that Tibetans do not have visions of the Khizr as a Muslim might, or of the Virgin Mary as Christians do? And the particular form that the Virgin Mary will take for an Ethiopian Christian will be very different from what a European Christian will see. Why go that far: the particular form in which we today see Sri Rama or Sri Krishna in the north is so different from the particular form in which devotees see them in the south: the figures that we in the north envision are probably the products more of calendar art than of any historical description just as the figures that they envisage in Tamil Nadu are more the result of south Indian bronzes. The forms in which we 'see' the gurus today are almost entirely the result of Sardar Sobha Singh's paintings, certainly more so than of any reliable accounts in writings that the Sikhs hold sacred. Or is it that the fact that one person has visions of Amitabha Buddha, the other of Khizr, and the third of the Virgin Mary, or the form in which Sri Ramakrishna sees Rama and Krishna, Radha and Kali is just incidental, that we can readily concede that it is influenced by the culture and time in which one has been brought up; but that underlying the specific and disparate emanations is a reality, the universal phenomenon, and that is 'the essence of the visions'?

But to get back to the experiences of saints and ordinary folk. We are loath to view the two sets of experiences through the same prism. For us, *everything* about the saint is extraordinary. When Sri Ramakrishna likes khichdi, the disciple does not see him just liking khichdi. He is at once reminded of the fact that a specific food was particularly liked by every avatar—rajbhog by Sri Rama, butter and kshir by Sri Krishna, phainta by the Buddha, flattened rice mixed with sweet curd and fruit by Sri Chaitanya...[7]

That is an almost inseparable constituent of devotion. Of course, the experience of a person who is himself treading the path may well have convinced him that, say, the peak experience is indeed beyond our capacity to examine it, and so he would scotch every attempt at examination as futile. But there is also another side to it—a trace of apprehension. And on two counts. One, that unless the saint is perceived as superhuman *in every respect*, the entire edifice of devotion would crumble. And, two, a subliminal apprehension about what the inquiry might turn up: we are nervous lest scrutiny suggest other explanations, and thus knock the bottom out of our raft, the saint.

I experienced this first-hand. I was looking for a list of accounts of Sri Ramakrishna's life that senior monks of the Ramakrishna Mission themselves regard as absolutely authentic, and for this purpose had gone to meet the head of one of the principal institutions of the Mission. As he had not yet returned from another part of the building, I was ushered into the office of another senior monk. When in answer to his question, I mentioned that I wanted to learn whether anything could be known about the neural substrates of the mystic experience, he reacted with such firmness that I was taken aback. 'You are profaning a divine experience,' he admonished me. The vehemence with which he reacted threw me off balance completely. Even though the reaction of the head of the institution was quite different, when I left the institution the admonition of that senior monk is what stayed in my mind.

An Open Mind, Confidence in Our Tradition

Now, such a reaction is the exact opposite of, say, the way the Dalai Lama has approached the matter. He has strained hard to persuade the great Tibetan adepts to make themselves available to neuroscientists for study. He has helped set up and nurture the Mind and Life Institute, which has been at the forefront of examining mind–body relationships. He is constantly encouraging and himself participating in dialogues between meditation adepts, Buddhist scholars and scientists—ranging from physicists to neuroscientists.

I remember him giving a set of discourses on a Buddhist meditation text. A monk would read out a passage, and the Dalai Lama would elaborate and comment on it. The monk read out some passages that dealt with the universe, its evolution, and the rest. The Dalai Lama leaned away from the monk in mock-horror! 'Buddhist theories of cosmology,' he said with his characteristic chuckle, paused, and continued, 'such a disgrace. Must throw them in the waste-paper basket...' And he laughed.

In his book, *The Universe in a Single Atom*, the Dalai Lama recalls a 'disturbing conversation' with an American lady—she had been married to a Tibetan. She disapproved of the Dalai Lama entering into dialogues with scientists. 'She told me that history attests to the fact that science is the "killer" of religion,' he writes, 'and advised me that it was not wise for the Dalai Lama to pursue friendships with those who represent this profession.' He did not heed her counsel! And for a fundamental reason. In the book the Dalai Lama continues, 'My confidence in venturing into science lies in my basic belief that as in science so in Buddhism, understanding the nature of reality is pursued by means of critical investigation: if scientific analysis were conclusively to demonstrate certain claims in Buddhism to be false, then we must accept the findings of science and abandon those claims.'[8] He says that science too may learn a few things as a result of engagement with spiritual traditions; in any case, that these traditions will learn, on that there is no doubt: 'It may be that science will learn from an engagement with spirituality, especially in its interface with wider human issues, from ethics to society, but certainly some specific aspects of Buddhist thought—such as its old cosmological theories and its rudimentary physics—will have to be modified in the light of new scientific insights.'[9]

Of course, the Dalai Lama is not saying that whatever science is saying at this moment is gospel truth—scientists themselves do not claim it to be so. While quoting the initial passage, Evan Thompson reminds us of what the Dalai Lama's interpreter, Thupten Jhumpa, says, namely, that the Dalai Lama always adds 'a caveat' to that observation—that even as we study what science has proven, we must in effect remember that 'the absence of evidence is not evidence of absence'; that science has not found any proof that there is rebirth does not entitle us to conclude, 'Science has proven that there is no rebirth.'[10]

'Buddhism must face facts,' he counsels often. And while Tibetan

Buddhists regard him almost as divinity incarnate, he always refers to himself as an ordinary Tibetan monk. Indeed, he goes out of his way to condition the Tibetans to look upon him as just an ordinary, mortal human being—with his jokes, with his informality, with his well-practised forgetfulness: 'The teacher must have ten qualifications ... One ... two ... seven ... What was the eighth? O, the Dalai Lama forgets!'

This open-mindedness truly is an example for us. It has five components—each of which demands humility as well as confidence:

- We must not cling on to some 'fact' just because that is what is written in some ancient text, much less because that is what some current guru or saint has said. We must examine the 'fact' in the light of logic, reason, of our own experience, and, in particular, in the light of the current discoveries of science.

- A concept does not become more valid, nor a word clearer just because it is put in Sanskrit. Nor if it is capitalized: 'Ishwar' is no clearer than 'Allah'; 'God' is no clearer than 'god'. Nor does the meaning become clearer by mere repetition: in a single book of a great mystic you will find 'the true truth', or 'a more perfect perfection', repeated again and again; but the words are not clearer than the more humble 'truth' or 'perfection'.

- Listening to our godman, reading his tract, we must always remember how easy it is to string together high-sounding words: 'Infinite', 'Eternal', 'soul'—or better still each with a capital letter, 'Soul', 'Bliss', 'Consciousness-force'— 'maya', 'lila', 'Cosmic Gnosis', 'Cosmic Light', 'Cosmic Being', 'Essence', 'Reality', 'the living Real', 'the Spirit', 'the Supreme', 'the divine Absolute', 'the Absolute Divine', 'the Time Spirit' ... and to throw in a Sanskrit expression or two—satchidananda, Prakriti–Purusha—now and then. The person using them may be a genuine seer or one of our contemporary fakes.[11]

- The rationalists have to bear in mind that what is currently held by science to be the fact may be overturned by some new discoveries tomorrow.

- On the other hand, those steeped in religion and spirituality have to realize the tenuousness of basing their beliefs on what science has *not* been able to prove thus far—the fragility, to use the current expression, of a God-of-the-gaps. New discoveries are always turning up, and the floor may be pulled from under our certainties tomorrow.

That is obviously the case in regard to notions about the creation and evolution of the cosmos, of life. But it is equally true of chakras, of various practices, about the peak experience itself. It is almost impossible to believe that the rapid advances in neurosciences will leave every proposition about the mind and the spiritual experiences intact. It is entirely possible that fifty years from now, the neuronal regions and processes that trigger even the mystic experience will have become known. It will then be possible to induce even peak experiences in completely controlled ways. What will be left of our faith if we have kept our heads in the sand all the while?

On the other hand, it is entirely possible that were we to keep up with these advances, we may learn a good deal more about the spiritual experiences too—and that is especially so because the great practitioners and masters have time and again declared that the experiences are ineffable, incommunicable.

In short, we must open our minds to facts, we should be less protective of our gods and saints—in the fullest confidence that the goodness and compassion and wisdom of our saints will always shine, that they will always remain a beacon.

'MEDICAL MATERIALISM'?

In the very first of his famous Gifford lectures, the lecture titled 'Religion and Neurology', William James warned against 'medical materialism'—the presumption that every spiritual experience could be reduced to operations of the physical brain, indeed to dysfunctions of the physical brain. The peak spiritual experiences that he was going to talk about 'we can find only in individuals for whom religion exists not as a dull habit, but as an acute fever rather,' he wrote.

But such individuals are 'geniuses' in the religious line; and like many other geniuses who have brought forth fruits effective enough for commemoration in the pages of biography, such religious geniuses have often shown symptoms of nervous instability. Even more than perhaps other kinds of genius, religious leaders have been subject to abnormal psychical visitations. Invariably they have been creatures of exalted emotional sensibility. Often they have led a discordant inner life, and had melancholy during a part of their career. They have known no measure, been liable to obsessions and fixed ideas; and frequently they have fallen into trances, heard voices, seen visions, and presented all sorts of peculiarities which are ordinarily classed as pathological. Often, moreover, these pathological features in their career have helped give them their religious authority and influence.

'Scientific theories are organically conditioned just as much as religious emotions are; and if we only knew the facts intimately enough,' he warned, 'we should doubtless see "the liver" determining the dicta of the sturdy atheist as decisively as it does those of the Methodist under conviction anxious about his soul.' Religious opinions, like scientific ones, must be tested 'by logic and by experiment, no matter what may be their author's neurological type,' he wrote. 'Their value can only be ascertained by spiritual judgments directly passed upon them, judgments based on our own immediate feeling primarily; and secondarily on what we can ascertain of their experiential relations to our moral needs and to the rest of what we hold as true.'

Accordingly, he admonished us, 'by their fruits ye shall know them, not by their roots', and, having advanced his reasons, concluded, that we 'will all be ready now to judge the religious life by its results exclusively, and I shall assume that the bugaboo of morbid origin will scandalize your piety no more'.

'Immediate luminousness, … philosophical reasonableness and moral helpfulness are the only available criteria,' he said.[12]

Three observations are in order. I do not think that we in India are put off by psychological peculiarities of our saints. We routinely take the saints to be exceptional, to be so exceptional indeed that normal norms of conduct and being do not apply to them. Few would need to be warned against getting obsessed with 'the bugaboo of morbid origin' of the saint's experiences.

James justifiably told us, 'In the natural sciences and industrial arts it never occurs to anyone to try and refute opinions by showing up their author's neurotic constitution. Opinions here are invariably tested by logic and by experiment, no matter what may be their author's neurological type. It should be no otherwise with religious opinions.' Precisely—and that is the second point. At that time many were rejecting religious notions out of hand—James cited examples of a priori and derisive rejection of propositions advanced by religious figures. And so, he was right to emphasize that religious propositions must be examined in the same way—by logic and experiment—that propositions of the natural sciences are examined. Today, and specially among us in India, the resistance is the other way round: notions advanced by religious figures—say, in regard to the nature of reality—are said to be beyond the reach of scientific methods. This is certainly the case in regard to the mystic experience. The mystics themselves affirm that it is ineffable.

The overwhelming proportion among us would also not be 'medical materialists' in the sense that we would scoff away the exalted experiences of a Ramakrishna or a Ramana on the ground that they were just manifestation of some pathologies. But, and this is the third point, we should also not shy away from seeing how far merely medical explanations carry us. Indeed, William James himself urged as much—his classic work, *The Varieties of Religious Experience*, was itself an endeavour in this direction. Does the mystic experience provide 'a warrant for truth of the twice-bornness and supernaturality and pantheism which it favors?' he asked, and wove his conclusions around three facets:

1. 'Mystical states, when well developed, usually are, and have the right to be, absolutely authoritative over the individuals to whom they come.
2. 'No authority emanates from them which should make it a duty for those who stand outside of them to accept their revelations uncritically.
3. 'They break down the authority of the non-mystical or rationalistic consciousness, based upon the understanding and the senses alone. They show it to be only one kind of consciousness. They open out the possibility of other orders of truth, in which, so far as anything in us vitally responds to them, we may freely concur to have faith.'[13]

'But I now proceed,' he continued, 'to add that mystics have no right to claim that we ought to accept the deliverance of their peculiar experiences, if we are ourselves outsiders and feel no private call thereto. The utmost they can ever ask of us in this life is to admit that they establish a presumption...'

For one thing, the reports of mystics differ. Moreover, several of the experiences they report are too close to the experiences of persons who are known to have been touched:

> [In the 'lower mysticisms', we encounter] The same sense of ineffable importance in the smallest events, the same texts and words coming with new meanings, the same voices and visions and leadings and missions, the same controlling by extraneous powers; only this time the emotion is pessimistic: instead of consolations we have desolations; the meanings are dreadful; and the powers are enemies to life. It is evident that from the point of view of their psychological mechanism, the classical mysticism and these lower mysticisms spring from the same mental level, from that great subliminal or transmarginal region of which science is beginning to admit the existence, but of which so little is really known. That region contains every kind of matter: 'seraph and snake' abide there side by side. To come from thence is no infallible credential. What comes must be sifted and tested, and run the gauntlet of confrontation with the total context of experience, just like what comes from the outer world of sense. Its value must be ascertained by empirical methods, so long as we are not mystics ourselves.[14]

Nor is this imperative—of distinguishing the higher mysticism from what James called 'diabolical mysticism, a sort of religious mysticism turned upside down'—the only reason for gauging how far 'medical materialism' will carry us. Religious practices offer a ready example. It isn't that religions have done us no good, certainly not that the spiritual quest does us no good. The religious impulse has, even organized religions have, given birth to sublime art and music, to magnificent edifices, to the most poignant literature. They gave impetus to inquiry, and, therefore, as William James reminded us, even 'primitive religions' were in a sense the incubators of 'primitive science'. Even the appurtenances of religion—rituals, for instance—have made contributions of the highest order: they have provided solace to the stricken, the belief in their curative powers—the belief that I will be cured if I were to undertake that pilgrimage—would have helped countless numbers; they have welded communities together.

Therefore, it isn't that religions and religious practices are all and entirely useless. But we must learn to sift the kernel from the chaff. Yes, rituals help weld us into a community—to recall Diana Eck's evocative words, 'India has been defined by the footfalls of its pilgrims.' But rituals can also become, even the form of dress can become, a device to distance us from the rest: recall the insistence of the Prophet that the faithful wear their pajamas no lower than their ankles because the pajamas of the unbelievers run past their ankles; that the faithful shave their moustache and let their beards grow as the unbelievers shave their beards and let their moustache grow ... What difference does it make to the poor lamb whether it is butchered one way or another, whether or not some words are uttered before it is killed? And yet these distinctions are used to set one community apart from another...

The Real Test

As he came to list the conclusions to which his classic survey of the literature on mystics had led him, William James listed as the very first conclusion, 'When we survey the whole field of religion, we find a great variety of thoughts that have prevailed there; but the feelings on the one hand and the conduct on the other are almost always the same, for Stoic, Christian, and Buddhist saints are practically indistinguishable in their lives. The theories which Religion generates, being thus variable, are secondary; and if you wish to grasp her essence, you must look to the feelings and the conduct as being the more constant elements...'[15]

At the level of the individual, the effect of the religious life, of the spiritual quest, as William James pointed out, and as we see when we contemplate the lives of Sri Ramakrishna and Sri Ramana Maharshi, is saintliness. That eventual result is preceded by various specific experiences, experiences that later become part of the nature of the saint:

A feeling of being in a wider life than that of this world's selfish
little interests; and a conviction, not merely intellectual, but as it
were sensible, of the existence of an Ideal Power ... A sense of
friendly continuity of the Ideal Power with our own life and a
willing self-surrender to its control ... An immediate elation and
freedom, as the outlines of the confining selfhood melt down ...
A shifting of the emotional center towards loving and harmonious
affections; towards, 'yes, yes' and away from 'no', where the claims
of the non-ego are concerned...[16]

Each of these has immediate, palpable, practical consequences that
set the persons apart:

Asceticism: a deep pleasure in it as measuring and expressing the
degree of the aspirant's loyalty to the higher power ... Strength of
soul: personal motives and inhibitions become too insignificant to
notice; in their place, new reaches of patience ... Extreme sensitivity
to any inner inconsistency ... And from these 'an ardor of sacrifice,
for the beloved's sake, of everything unworthy of him'.[17]

In Sri Ramakrishna and Sri Ramana Maharshi, we will see living
examples of these effects.

And who can say what their eventual contribution shall be? Sri
Aurobindo maintained that the mystic experience is the next, logical
stage in our evolution. As we come to love life more, we come to
fear death all the more. We try one potion after another to postpone
this catastrophe. We busy ourselves with works, with great causes,
we identify ourselves with institutions, communities, countries that
live longer than us. We build great monuments that will stand
for centuries. Nothing works. As Woody Allen remarked, 'I don't
want to achieve immortality through my work; I want to achieve
immortality through not dying. I don't want to live on in the hearts
of my countrymen; I want to live on in my apartment.' And so, the
dread of death continues to grip us. But the mystic experience is so
transformative, it fills the experient with such certainty that death
is not destruction, that it vaults him over this dread. Maybe that is
the evolutionary role that the mystics will eventually discharge—we
come to love life, they vault us over the dread of death...

3

'O, the state in which I was...'

One of the problems is that most accounts of saints like Sri Ramakrishna and Sri Ramana Maharshi, even if we exclude those that are written after they had passed away, were written after they had become well known, and devotees had started gathering around them. Generally speaking, little is known of the vital period of hardship that they went through before they came to stabilize in the state which we associate with them. It is as if they just alighted as perfected beings. This is compounded by the central belief of their devotees. For the devotees, these great saints were incarnations of God, they were avatars, in fact they were God Himself. Therefore, it would border on the blasphemous to entertain the idea that they required to ripen into the exalted state. Even the first, overwhelming experiences—the trance into which the ten- or eleven-year-old Gadadhar falls as he sees the white swans fly across the dark clouds; the 'death experience' that the sixteen-year-old Venkataraman has as he sits alone upstairs in his uncle's house—are seen as mere *confirmations* of the godhood of the sages. The experiences are not looked upon as having been instrumental, as having borne results that may not have occurred but for the experiences. The difficulty is compounded by what the saints themselves said on occasion. Sri Ramana, for instance, said many times that the very first experience had been conclusive, that after that he never had any doubt that he was not the body. But the experiences to which he testified in later years were not just what passed through his mind in that one episode

41

as he lay himself on the ground that day. The experiences—which led him to conclusions about reality, for instance—were much more encompassing. And these occurred, and his conception of reality and the rest were stabilized during three-and-a-half years.

Because we do not go beyond our premise that the saints were avatars, we miss a matter of central importance—that the extreme austerities and prolonged periods of immersion these saints went through must have caused the deepest psychological and psychic changes; of course, they would in addition have entailed the most fundamental changes within their brains, and, indeed, in every particle of their peripheral as much as their central nervous systems.

From what they themselves remarked later—and the occasions were rare indeed—what can we glimpse of the states into which Sri Ramakrishna and Sri Ramana were plunged during the years in which they were baked to perfection?

'O, THE STATE IN WHICH I WAS...'

Sri Ramakrishna had his first trance when he was ten or eleven: He is walking along paddy fields; dark clouds envelope the sky; a row of swans is flying across; Gadadhar, the young lad, is so overwhelmed by the contrast that he goes into a trance and falls unconscious. Villagers find him in that condition. They carry him back to his alarmed parents ... It is Shivaratri. A play has been arranged at the village, centred around Lord Shiva. At the last moment, the actor who is to play the part of the Lord falls ill. Gadadhar is chosen to play the part instead. Shiva's dress and accoutrements are put on. He is led to the stage. He becomes motionless and absorbed. 'Moreover, incessant streams of tears were flowing down his cheeks,' we learn. 'Some time passed, but Gadadhar did not speak or move. Then the proprietor and one or two elderly men of the village went to the boy and saw that his hands and feet were insensitive and that he had no external consciousness at all. The noise then doubled...' But he cannot be made to respond. He is carried home. In spite of efforts through the night, he regains consciousness only at sunrise the next day; in some accounts, he regains consciousness three days later, Swami Saradananda tells us.[1]

From then on, such instances become more and more frequent. Gadadhar loses interest in studies. He is forever spending his time with itinerant sadhus who wander through the village, listening to their experiences, to the tales they recount from our epics, singing devotional songs to the women in the village ... He as well as his family finds a respectable way to enable him to pursue his preoccupation—he joins a drama troupe. 'Gadadhar was in his element,' his biographers narrate; he frequently falls into a trance during the performances.[2]

We will recall elsewhere the sorts of visions he had. The point to note here is the *extreme* nature of the austerities that he went through during the following years.

The 'state of divine intoxication', as his biographer calls it, lasted *twelve years*. During half of this period—*six years*—we have it on Sri Ramakrishna's own testimony, he did not sleep a wink. Sri Ramakrishna told devotees later that he passed through states which an ordinary body could not have survived even if a fourth of them had occurred. He told them that he survived because he remained preoccupied with some vision of the Mother or the other for most of the day and night. 'I had no sleep at all for six long years,' he said. 'The eyes lost the power of winking; I could not close the eyes in spite of all my efforts. I had no idea of the passing of time and was not at all conscious of the body. When the attention turned from Mother to the body, even if a little, I felt apprehensive, thinking, "Am I on the verge of insanity?" I stood before a mirror and put my finger into my eyes to see whether the eyelids closed; I found the eyelids were even then equally incapable of winking; I became alarmed and wept, complaining to Mother, "Mother, is this the result of calling on Thee?..."' In the end, he would abandon the course of things to Her: do what You will, just do not abandon me, just let me attain Your vision. 'At that time, for want of proper care, my hair was matted,' Sri Ramakrishna narrated years later. 'Birds would perch on my head and peck the grains of rice left there during the time of worship. Often snakes would crawl over my motionless body—and neither I nor the snakes knew it. Oh, what visions flitted past my eyes, day and night...'[3]

His formal duty is to attend to the worship of the image at the Dakshineswar temple. In fact, he is lost in meditation and prayer and weeping for hours on end. What is today the Panchavati garden used to be full of pits and ditches and low lands; 'a deep jungle, thick with underbrush and prickly plants ... Used at one time as a burial ground, it was shunned by people even during day-time for fear of ghosts.' Sri Ramakrishna would go there, day and night, and be lost to the world for hours and hours. 'He almost gave up food; and sleep left him altogether.'[4]

Guides turn up. One of them is 'the Bhairavi Brahmani'. She guides him through many austerities and practices, including the tantric disciplines. Another is Totapuri, an itinerant sadhu, who leads Sri Ramakrishna to the Advaita vision of the non-dual. Years later, Girish Ghosh, a scandal-prone actor towards whom Sri Ramakrishna was most indulgent, teases him, 'Why did you have to practise spiritual discipline?' he asks. Sri Ramakrishna, seeing the mischief in the question, smiles and answers, 'Even the Divine Mother had to practise austere *sadhana* to obtain Shiva as Her husband. She practised the *panchatapa*. She would also immerse Her body in water in wintertime, and look fixedly at the sun. Krishna Himself had to practise much *sadhana*. I had many mystic experiences, but I cannot reveal their contents. Under the *bel*-tree I had many flaming visions. There I practised the various *sadhanas* prescribed in the Tantra. I needed many articles—human skulls, and so forth and so on. The Brahmani used to collect these things for me. I practised a number of mystic postures.'[5]

His behaviour becomes more and more erratic. As he was to say later, the outward behaviour of a man in such a state is sometimes like that of a madman—'he laughs, weeps, dances, and sings', 'Now he dresses himself up like a dandy and the next moment he goes entirely naked and roams about with his cloth under his arm'; sometimes his behaviour is like that of a five-year-old child—'guileless, generous, without vanity, unattached to anything, not under the control of any *gunas*, always blissful'; sometimes like that of a ghoul—'he doesn't differentiate between things pure and impure; he sees no difference between things clean and unclean'; and sometimes like an inert thing—'staring vacantly, he cannot do any work, he cannot strive for anything'.[6]

He longs for the Mother, and weeps and weeps at not seeing Her. 'His chest appeared constantly reddish and his eyes became suddenly filled with tears...' Swami Saradananda wrote. A passage from what he told disciples years afterwards about this period, and the moments preceding his first vision of the Mother will give us a glimpse of his condition at the time:

> I felt as if my heart were being squeezed like a wet towel. I was overpowered with a great restlessness and a fear that it might not be my lot to realize Her in this life. I could not bear the separation from Her any longer. Life seemed to be not worth living. Suddenly my glance fell on the sword that was kept in the Mother's temple. I determined to put an end to my life. When I jumped up like a madman and seized it, suddenly the blessed Mother revealed Herself. The buildings with their different parts, the temple, and everything else vanished from my sight, leaving no trace whatsoever, and in their stead I saw a limitless, infinite, effulgent Ocean of Consciousness. As far as the eye could see, the shining billows were madly rushing at me from all sides with a terrific noise, to swallow me up! I was panting for breath. I was caught in the rush and collapsed, unconscious. What was happening in the outside world I did not know; but within me there was a steady flow of undiluted bliss, altogether new, and I felt the presence of the Divine Mother.

'On his lips when he regained consciousness of the world was the word "Mother",' his chronicler tells us.[7]

After this vision, he is forever restless, forever yearning to have constant vision of the Mother. People surround him as he passes into states of abstraction and unconsciousness. He is unaware of them, and, when dimly aware, is unaffected by their gazing at him, by the commotion they stir up.[8]

His health deteriorates. Thinking that a change will do him good, his minders take him back to his village, Kamarpukur. His mother is alarmed to see him. She consults an exorcist. The latter tries, but fails to improve Sri Ramakrishna's ways or condition. A spirit is brought to bear on him. The spirit, however, tells the exorcist that no spirit has taken possession of Sri Ramakrishna, that his condition is that of a God-inebriated man ... Sri Ramakrishna now spends almost the entire day and much of the night worshipping and praying in a cremation ground.[9]

The stay in his village—he stays there for a year and a half, and is 'married' to the young Sarada Devi—helps restore his health somewhat. He returns to Dakshineswar. His teachers—first the 'Bhairavi Brahmani', a woman ascetic, and Totapuri, a wandering Advaitin—put him through further privations. One instance will suffice to illustrate the disciplines they imposed. Totapuri—Sri Ramakrishna refers to him as 'Nangta', the naked one, as he had forsaken clothes—is steering him through mental and psychological mazes to realizing the Absolute, formless Brahman. Here is how Sri Ramakrishna described the penultimate phase:

'After initiating me,' said the Master, 'the naked one [Totapuri] taught me many dicta conveying the conclusion of the Vedanta, and asked me to make my mind free of function in all respects and merge in the meditation of the Self. But, it so happened with me that when I sat for meditation I could by no means make my mind go beyond the bounds of name and form and cease functioning. The mind withdrew itself easily from all other things but, as soon as it did so, the intimately familiar form of the universal Mother, consisting of the effulgence of pure consciousness, appeared before it as living and moving and made me quite oblivious of the renunciation of names and forms of all descriptions. When I listened to the conclusive dicta and sat for meditation, this happened over and over again. Almost despairing of the attainment of the *Nirvikalpa Samadhi*, I then opened my eyes and said to the naked one, "No, it cannot be done; I cannot make the mind free from functioning and force it to dive into the Self." Scolding me severely, the naked one said very excitedly, "What, it can't be done! What utter defiance!" He then looked about in the hut and finding a broken piece of glass took it in his hand and forcibly pierced with its needle-like pointed end my forehead between the eye-brows and said, "Collect the mind here to this point." With a firm determination I sat for meditation again and, as soon as the holy form of the divine Mother appeared now before the mind as previously, I looked upon knowledge as a sword and cut it mentally in two with that sword of knowledge. There remained then no function in the mind, which transcended quickly the realm of names and forms, making me merge in *samadhi*.'[10]

Sri Ramakrishna remains completely absorbed in samadhi for three days, we are told. Totapuri tries to bring Sri Ramakrishna down to the plane of relative consciousness. He touches and prods him. The body is like a corpse. 'Is it really true?' Totapuri cries out in astonishment, we are told. 'Is it possible that he has attained in a single day what it took me forty years of strenuous practice to achieve? Great God! It is nothing short of a miracle!' With the help of Totapuri, Sri Ramakrishna's mind is finally brought down to the relative plane, Swami Nikhilananda tells us. As Sri Ramakrishna comes around, Totapuri 'answered the worthy disciple's prostration by locking him in a warm embrace'.[11]

And the sequel? Totapuri usually did not stay in a place for more than three days, Swami Nikhilananda writes. He stays at Dakshineswar for eleven months. After Totapuri left, Sri Ramakrishna remained continuously in a state of Nirvikalpa Samadhi for six months. Swami Saradananda sets out the Master's own description of his condition and symptoms during this period:

I was for six months in that state from which ordinary mortals never return; the body lives for twenty-one days only and then falls like a dry leaf from a tree. There was no consciousness at all, of time, of the coming of day or the passing of night. Just as flies enter into the nostrils and the mouth of a dead man, so they entered into mine; but there was no consciousness. The hair became matted on account of accumulation of dust. Calls of nature were perhaps answered unconsciously. Could the body have lived? It would have succumbed at that time. But a holy man came then. He had a small stick like a ruler in his hand. He recognized my state as soon as he saw it and knew that much of Mother's work was yet to be done through this body; much good would be done to many if only it could be saved. Therefore he would carry food in time and, by striking this body again and again, would try to bring it back to consciousness. The moment he saw signs of consciousness appearing he would thrust some food into the mouth. Thus on some days a little food found its way into the stomach and on others it did not. Six months passed that way. Then the Mother's command was heard, 'Remain in *Bhavamukha*; for the spiritual enlightenment of the people, remain in *Bhavamukha*.' This was followed by illness, blood-dysentery; there was wringing pain in the intestines and it was excruciating. It was after continually suffering for about six months that the mind gradually came down to the normal body-consciousness; before that it used to go up and reach that *Nirvikalpa* state ever and anon.[12]

Of course, the disciples took that itinerant yogi to have come by 'the direct will and power of the Divine Mother in order that the Master's body may be kept alive'.[13]

Sri Ramakrishna is completely lost to the world, as we can gather from remarks of his own years later. Krishnakishore, an ardent devotee of Lord Rama, one to whom Sri Ramakrishna would go to escape worldly talk of others and immerse himself in readings of *Adhyatma Ramayana*, asks him, 'Why have you cast off the sacred thread?' Recalling the incident years later, Sri Ramakrishna tells devotees, 'In those days of God-vision I felt as if I were passing through the great storm of Aashwin, and everything had blown away from me. No trace of my old self was left. I lost all consciousness of the world. I could hardly keep my cloth on my body, not to speak of the sacred thread! I said to Krishnakishore, "Ah, you will understand if you ever happen to be as intoxicated with God as I was."'[14]

'Oh, what a state of mind I passed through!' he tells devotees one day:

> When I first had that experience, I could not perceive the coming and going of day or night. People said I was insane. What else could they say? They made me marry. I was then in a state of God-intoxication. At first I felt worried about my wife. Then I thought she too would eat and drink and live like me.
>
> I visited my father-in-law's house. They arranged a *kirtan*. It was a great religious festival, and there was much singing of God's holy name. Now and then I would wonder about my future. I would say to the Divine Mother, 'Mother, I shall take my spiritual experiences to be real if the landlords of the country show me respect.' They too came of their own accord and talked with me.
>
> Oh, what an ecstatic state it was! Even the slightest suggestion would awaken my spiritual consciousness. I worshipped the 'Beautiful' in a girl fourteen years old. I saw that she was the personification of the Divine Mother. At the end of the worship I bowed before her and offered a rupee at her feet. One day I witnessed a Ramlila performance. I saw the performers to be the actual Sita, Rama, Lakshmana, Hanuman, and Bibhishana. Then I worshipped the actors and actresses who played those parts.

At that time I used to invite maidens here and worship them. I found them to be embodiments of the Divine Mother Herself.

One day I saw a woman in blue standing near the *bakul*-tree. She was a prostitute. But she instantly kindled in me the vision of Sita. I forgot the woman. I saw that it was Sita herself on her way to meet Rama after her rescue from Ravana in Ceylon. For a long time I remained in *samadhi*, unconscious of the outer world.

Another day I had gone to the Maidan in Calcutta for fresh air. A great crowd had assembled there to watch a balloon ascension. Suddenly I saw an English boy leaning against a tree. As he stood there his body was bent in three places. The vision of Krishna came before me in a flash. I went into *samadhi*.

Once, at Sihore, I fed the cowherd boys. I put sweetmeats into their hands. I saw that these boys were actually the cowherd boys of Vrindavan, and I partook of the sweetmeats from their hands.

At that time I was almost unconscious of the outer world. Mathur Babu kept me at his Janbazar mansion a few days. While living there I regarded myself as the handmaid of the Divine Mother. The ladies of the house didn't feel at all bashful with me. They felt as free before me as women feel before a small boy or girl. I used to escort Mathur's daughter to her husband's chamber with the maidservant...[15]

'It is not necessary for all to practise great austerity,' Sri Ramakrishna explains to devotees. 'But I went through great suffering. I used to lie on the ground with my head resting on a mound for a pillow. I hardly noticed the passing of the days. I only called on God and wept, "O Mother! O Mother!"' 'Oh, what a state God kept me in at that time!' Sri Ramakrishna told devotees on another occasion. 'One experience would hardly be over before another overcame me. It was like the movement of the husking-machine: no sooner is one end down than the other goes up. I would see God in meditation, in the state of *samadhi*, and I would see the same God when my mind came back to the outer world. When looking at this side of the mirror I would see Him alone, and when looking on the reverse side I saw the same God...'

He has long bouts of illnesses ... He goes to visit a pandit, well versed in the scriptures. It is afternoon by the time he gets into the carriage to return. 'As soon as Sri Ramakrishna got into the carriage he went into *samadhi*,' Mahendranath Gupta recorded. 'His physical frame was very tender as a result of the austerities he had undergone during the long years of his spiritual discipline and his constant absorption in God-Consciousness. The Master would suffer from the slightest physical discomfort and even from the vibration of worldly thoughts around him.'

Many come to look upon him as insane, even those closest to him—his nephew Hriday, his cousin Haladhari. Many are scandalized by his conduct at the worship of the Mother's idol at the temple. Sometimes he puts the garland meant for the Mother over his own neck, he touches it to his limbs, including his feet, and then drapes it over her neck ... On occasion he puts the food meant for Her to his own mouth and then offers it to her ... He feeds the offerings to a cat, and then offers them to the Mother ... Mathur alone, Rani Rasmani's son-in-law, ensures that he remains free to do what he will, and he warns people not to interfere with whatever he is doing ... Often, Sri Ramakrishna is himself plagued by doubts: Is his condition due to an illness? Has his mind got unhinged?

But he perseveres, and later comes to look upon the experiences as inevitable—'An elephant entering a hut creates havoc within and ultimately shakes it down,' he tells devotees. 'The elephant of divine emotion enters the hut of this body and shatters it to pieces...' And the physical and mental trials as necessary, as an unavoidable furnace through which the aspirant must pass: 'If an abscess is lanced before it is soft, the result is not good; the surgeon makes the opening when it is soft and has come to a head,' he tells devotees ... Can a man learn to feel the pulse in one day? he asks them. He must spend many days with a physician first ... 'You cannot make a pot without first carefully preparing the clay. The pot will crack if the clay contains particles of sand and stone. That is why the potter first prepares the clay by removing the sand and stones...'[16]

Sri Ramana Maharshi

Right from his childhood, Venkataraman has a trait—of going into a sleep so deep that he just cannot be roused from it. We are in May 1946. One afternoon, a young relative of his, Sesha Aiyar, comes. Sri Ramana is reminded of an incident that reveals a trait that is significant in the light of our present concern:

Seeing you reminds me of something that happened in Dindigul when I was a boy. Your uncle Periappa Seshaiyar was living there then. There was some function in the house and all went to it and then in the night went to the temple. I was left alone in the house. I was sitting reading in the front room, but after a while I locked the front door and fastened the windows and went to sleep. When they returned from the temple no amount of shouting or banging at the door or window could wake me. At last they managed to open the door with a key from the opposite house and then they tried to wake me up by beating me. All the boys beat me to their heart's content, and your uncle did too, but without effect. I knew nothing about it till they told me next morning.

Devaraja Mudaliar who recorded these remarks in his diary, asks, 'How old was Bhagavan then?' 'About eleven,' Sri Ramana says. And continues,

The same sort of thing happened to me in Madurai too. The boys didn't dare touch me when I was awake, but if they had any grudge against me they would come when I was asleep and carry me wherever they liked and beat me as much as they liked and then put me back to bed, and I would know nothing about it until they told me in the morning.

Mudaliar says, 'It would seem that even in those days Bhagavan's sleep was not ordinary sleep but some state like *samadhi*.' Sri Ramana is characteristically modest, 'I don't know what state it was, but that is the fact. Some who have written about my life have called it somnambulism.' Mudaliar persists: 'It was certainly not somnambulism; that is walking in one's sleep. This was more like *samadhi* or absorption in the Self.'[17]

A trait that is to take a different channel six years later? Or just a coincidental feature?

The young Venkataraman has had his first, and what will turn out to be decisive 'death experience'. He is just around sixteen. He has left home, and has reached Tiruvannamalai. For the next three to three-and-a-half years, he moves from place to place—sometimes he is carried unaware from one place to another; he goes through unimaginable physical privation; and even more unimaginable mental absorption. He does not set out to undergo austerities. He has had no formal training in meditation techniques. He has not read any of the classics on the spiritual quest. It is as if he were to fall into a lake, his mind were to totally lose itself in the waters, and that one of the consequences of the immersion would be that he would totally forget his body and its needs.

That decisive experience in his uncle's house has left him with the firm, unshakable conviction that he is not the body, that there is a 'Self' which is untouched. He is to say later that, as he was convinced of this, there was no need for sadhana, and that he never undertook any. 'The day before yesterday a learned man who came from Madras, began at 3 p.m. to question Bhagavan thus: "Was there a period at any time when Bhagavan did *sadhana*?" Nagamma Suri recorded in a letter on 23 August 1946, to her brother, D.S. Sastri, 'Bhagavan said, "*Sadhana*? *Sadhana* for what? What is there to do *sadhana* for? Sitting like this is itself *sadhana*. I used to sit like this always. I used to close my eyes then; now I keep them open. That is the only difference. What is now, was then also. What was there then, is also here now. *Sadhana* is necessary only if there is a thing other than 'I', Self. *Sadhana* is required only for one who does not look towards the Self which is permanent, but is deluded by looking at the body, etc., which are transitory and delusive; but not for one who sees the Self and so does not see anything else different. And what else is *sadhana* for?"'[18]

The young Venkataraman arrives at the town temple. He throws away the money—three-and-a-half rupees—that remains from his journey thus far; he throws away the sweets that a kind lady has given the hungry boy; a barber asks whether he wants his hair shorn, he agrees; he throws away his sacred thread. He has thus symbolically severed all contact with his past, and his identity. Over the next few days, he makes the 'thousand-pillared hall' of the temple his abode. 'He sat there during his period of *sadhana* without so much as a cloth, much less a mat, rug or shawl spread on the cold slabs,' Narasimha Swami was to write. 'His arm was his pillow; his palm was his plate; and the rag found by the way-side was his dress.'[19] One day, meditating in the mandappam of the temple, he finds stones being flung at him. They do not hit him, but he realizes that he will not be left alone if he continues to sit in the open. He moves to a dark and large pit in the mandappam. 'The dark pit, despite the sacred images in it, was never lit or swept or cleaned,' Narasimha Swami recorded. 'It was damp and full of insects. As the young *mouni* sat there, enjoying the bliss of his soul, scorpions, ants, mosquitoes, and other vermin ... attached themselves to the intruder's body and rejoiced in drinking his blood. The nether side of his thighs, and legs, as he sat there, were full of sores from which blood and pus issued...'[20]

Youngsters pursue him here also: they begin throwing stones and broken mud pots at him from the opening of the pit ... An elderly lady begins bringing some food. He is scarcely aware, and scarcely eats ... A man who has barely escaped the stones describes the frightful condition to another person at the temple. The two descend into the pit. They are appalled at the condition of the young lad. As he does not respond to their entreaties, they bodily lift the youth, carry him out of the pit, and deposit him in front of one of the shrines of the temple. 'The Swami still remained unconscious, his eyes closed; evidently he was in deep *samadhi*,' one of the persons states. 'We noted the large number of sores on the nether side of his thighs and legs, with blood and pus flowing from some of them, and wondered how anyone could remain unconscious of his body amidst such torture. Regarding it as irreverence, nay impertinence, to make any further noise in such presence, we bowed and came away.'[21]

The young lad remains in this condition. His body is beginning to show signs of utter starvation and neglect. A swami takes pity on him, and begins taking some of the mixture of milk, water, turmeric, sugar, plantain that is poured on the idol, and flows out through an opening, and feeding it to the young aspirant. The priest at the shrine takes pity at the sight, and directs that some of the milk offered at the shrine be given to this lad, without mixing it and diluting it with water. The youth remains immersed in samadhi for hours, so that food of even this kind 'sometimes had to be thrust into his mouth', he 'had to be vigorously shaken by the shoulders before he would notice and accept food and water which some devotee would bring him once a day...'[22]

Soon, he is shifted to a garden nearby. He remains lost in samadhi: often, he goes into that state under one tree only to become conscious under another, sometimes under one of the temple's ceremonial vehicles only to regain consciousness under another far away, not knowing when he had moved ... His 'residence' changes from the bottom of one tree to that of another, as he is harassed. 'One day, as he sat in *samadhi*,' records Narasimha Swami, 'a mischievous imp took the opportunity, when no one was in sight, of approaching him from behind and testing the intensity of his absorption. Liquid filth descended on the back of the Swami, thereby wetting his rags ... The young Swami was quite unaware of what had happened...'[23] He is shifted to the base of yet another tree. Even the codpiece has become a string of shreds ... It is time for the annual festival at the temple. 'Police from all over the district will be here,' an old Gurukal comes and admonishes him. 'They will arrest you and put you in jail if you are nude like this. So you must have a cod-piece.' 'So saying,' the Maharshi continued, narrating this incident in October 1946, 'he got a new piece of cloth, made four people lift me up and tied the cod-piece around me.'[24]

The young swami remains steeped in his absorptions. His body continues to grow more and more emaciated. It is the picture of neglect. 'The hair had got matted and woven like a basket,' Sri Ramana narrated one day, years later when the conversation turned to this period of his sadhana. 'Small stones and dust had settled down in it and the head used to feel heavy. I had also long nails, and a frightful appearance. So people pressed me to have a shave, and I yielded. When my head was shaven clean, I began to wonder whether I had a head or not, it felt so light. I shook my head this way and that to assure myself that it was there. That showed the amount of burden I had been carrying on my head.'[25]

He had by now become an object as much of reverence as of curiosity. People would be milling around. That began to tell on him. In 1897, he was shifted to Gurumurtham, a secluded *math* away from the temple. He was to stay here for more than a year and a half. His state continued as it had been: that is, he remained lost to the outer world; his body now began to show the cumulative consequences of extreme malnourishment and neglect. His nails grew so long that the hands could scarcely be used for anything. Ants and other insects roamed over his body and bit it freely. A mendicant who was looking after him—'looking after him' consisted of fetching that one minimal meal for the day and feeding it to him somehow—put a stool, placed its feet in utensils with water, and put him on it. 'He had no exercise and sometimes days passed before a slight relief was afforded to the distended bowels,' Narasimha Swami wrote. 'He would sit on the bench, mostly dazed, not knowing and not caring if it was morning or evening or one day or another of the week. He had just strength and clearness enough to retain his sitting posture and, if he tried to get up, he was unsuccessful. He would just lift himself some inches when, feeling giddy, would sink back into his seat again. He would try again but with no better result. Only after repeated efforts could he get up and get out...' Even as he was helped he did not know why—once when he remonstrated with the person holding him, he had to be told that he was being helped because he was about to fall, even though he was holding the door with both hands...[26]

This was the condition to which he had been reduced in 1897. Years later, when a picture of him taken around 1921 is shown to him and the devotee remarks how emaciated he looks, Sri Ramana says, 'That is because I was then living on one meal a day. For something like a year I was eating only one meal a day. But this condition of mine in the picture is nothing. You should have seen me at Gurumurtham. I was only skin and bone, no flesh anywhere. All the bones were sticking out, collarbone, ribs, and the hipbones. There was no stomach to be seen. It was sticking to the back, having receded so far. So this condition in the picture is not really so bad.'[27]

To prevent him from wandering away, as much as to keep visitors from disrupting his absorptions, Palaniswami, a Keralite, who was now attending on him—he had been praying to an image of Lord Vinayaka for long with indifferent progress when someone urged him to serve a living guru, the young Brahman Swami as Sri Ramana was then known—used to lock up the room in which Sri Ramana was seated when he would have to go out to fetch necessities.

Yet another move became necessary. He was shifted to a shed under a mango tree. We have him alluding to this place in a conversation set out by Nagamma Suri in a letter to her brother in April 1948. 'As you all know,' Sri Ramana told the devotees who were questioning him about his early life, 'I was in the mango grove next to Gurumurtham, for some time. At that time also, I had a small shed under a mango tree. They erected something overhead like a nest to prevent rain falling on me. There was however not enough space even to stretch my legs fully while sleeping. I used to be sitting almost all the time like a bird in its nest. Opposite my shed,

Palaniswami also had a small shed. In that huge garden, only two of us used to stay.'[28]

He soon has to shift from this shed also. He is moved to a small temple, Arunagirinathar. But within a month, he has to move again, this time to a temple on a spur of the Arunachala Hill ... His relatives trace him ... His mother herself comes and pleads that he return...

He continues his absorptions. And has to move from cave to cave on the hill. At last he reaches Virupaksha cave ... and his life begins to acquire a semblance of order and normality...

In any event, the three-and-a-half years are spent in almost uninterrupted, and uninterruptable, absorption. By now we know a good deal about the plasticity of the brain—how even an hour's engagement can alter the strength of connections within it; how prolonged use or disuse of some sensory areas can cause even the amount of 'real estate' devoted to specific tasks to be altered. Imagine the changes in the brain that would be caused by such total sensory deprivation brought about by such total, uninterrupted absorption over three-and-a-half years.

Even so gross an entity as the ego was completely overturned. Years later, when his fame has spread far and wide, and there is a constant stream of visitors and devotees to the ashram, at one point Sri Ramana starts begging for his food. Here is what he narrated about the liberating effect it had on him:

> You cannot conceive of the majesty and dignity I felt while so begging. The first day, when I begged from Gurukal's wife, I felt bashful about it as a result of habits of upbringing, but after that there was absolutely no feeling of abasement. I felt like a king and more than a king. I have sometimes received stale gruel at some house and taken it without salt or any other flavouring, in the open street, before great pandits and other important men who used to come and prostrate themselves before me at my *Asramam*, then wiped my hands on my head and passed on supremely happy and in a state of mind in which even emperors were mere straw in my sight. You can't imagine it. It is because there is such a path that we find tales in history of kings giving up their thrones and taking to this path.[29]

There is another significant point. The states that these chroniclers listed from the few occasions on which Sri Ramana alluded to them, and his early companions narrated them, are beyond the imagination of most of us, and to become so totally oblivious of one's body and its necessities must, in our way of thinking, require Herculean determination. Sri Ramana, however, thought nothing of the states. He did not set out to mortify his body, he explained more than once; he did not sit down to concentrate his mind on some spot. Others thought that he must be doing something of the sort, he said: 'I did not eat, so they said I was fasting; I did not speak, so they said I was observing silence.' Osborne puts the matter well:

When he first came to Tiruvannamalai he sat immersed in the Bliss of Being, utterly ignoring the world and the body. He would take food only if it was brought to his hands or mouth and even then barely enough to sustain the body. This has been described as *tapas*, but the word *tapas* covers a very composite meaning. It implies concentration leading to austerity, normally in penance for past indulgence and to root out all desire for its repetition and restrain the outgoing energy which seeks a vehicle in the mind and senses. That is to say that *tapas* normally means striving for realization by means of penance and austerity. In the case of Sri Bhagavan the elements of strife, penance and forcible restraint were completely lacking, since the false identification of the 'I' with the body and the resultant attachment to the body had already been broken. There was even no austerity from his point of view, since he had utterly ceased to identify himself with the body that underwent austerity. He intimated this in later years by saying, 'I did not eat, so they said I was fasting; I did not speak, so they said I was *mouni*.' To put it quite simply, the seeming austerity was not in quest of Realization but as a result of Realization. He has explicitly said that there was no more *sadhana* (quest or striving) after the spiritual Awakening at his uncle's house at Madura.[30]

That the absorption was so 'effortless', that it was, so to say, so spontaneous must show that it was so much deeper than can possibly be achieved by deliberate effort. And hence, the neurological changes that must have followed in its wake must have been much, much deeper as well as much more pervasive than the kinds of changes that we are today reading about in studies that have been conducted through brain scans of meditation practitioners.

CONSEQUENCES OF ONE OF THE AUSTERITIES

Even in these fragmentary descriptions of what they went through
during those twelve years and three-and-a-half years, respectively, we
see a series of elements: complete withdrawal from the world, total
immersion in what is happening in the mind, isolation, consequently
being cut off from all sensory inputs, starvation, sleep deprivation.

Now, each of these, carried to the extreme to which it certainly
was during the sadhanas of Sri Ramakrishna and Sri Ramana, is
bound to have major consequences for all three—the body, the brain
and the mind. Isolation and sensory deprivation, for instance, have
been documented to slow down one's sense of time. That complete
cessation of contact with others wholly alters one's sense of 'self'
also has been documented time and again. As for cutting off inputs
from the senses and focusing so completely on what is happening
inside oneself has even more drastic consequences: the brain remains
active even when sensory inputs are reduced to near-nil; soon it starts
weaving stories from and detecting patterns in both: the fragments of
sensory inputs that still make their way in—the odd sound, the bite
of a rat, the pangs from an empty stomach—and even more so, from
the spontaneous and random firings of neurons. We see this in our
daily, rather nightly, experience: when we narrate our dreams, we
talk of them as if they had been a movie; but they often are a story
that has been woven ex post out of random still images. But I will
not dilate on this consequence here as we will be running into it time
and again in the book. Instead, I will take up the consequence of just
one of the practices that both our saints said marked their years of
sadhana: sleep deprivation.

As you would expect, even the devotees noticed that the Master
was sleeping too little, and that this was affecting his health adversely.
While Swami Saradananda like others believed that, out of his
oceanic compassion, Sri Ramakrishna used to take on the sins of
others, and that this caused his cancer, he also traced the cancer to
his exerting himself unduly and to his sleeplessness. The passage is
worth attention:

> Besides the earlier devotees, new persons numbering five or six
> were daily seen to knock his door, thirsting for spirituality. It

had become a daily occurrence ever since Kesav had come to
Dakshineswar in the year AD 1875. Therefore, for the past eleven
years, the Master was often led away by his zeal for teaching the
people who came athirst, and was not able to keep regular hours
for daily bath, meals and the rest. Besides, he had very little sleep
owing to the impulsion of the *Mahabhava*. At the time, when we
were staying with him at Dakshineswar, we saw on very many
occasions that he got up shortly after he went to bed at 11 p.m.
and strolled in an ecstatic mood; he now opened the western door,
now the northern, and went out; again, though sometimes lying
quietly on his bed, he was fully awake. He left his bed three or
four times during the night and yet he rose daily as soon as it was
4 a.m., waited for the light of the dawn, remembering, thinking on,
and singing the glories of the divine Lord and would then wake us.
Is it surprising that his body should have worn out on account of
sleeplessness at night and his excessive labour in giving religious
instruction to many people during the day?[31]

And couple this with another effect of the twelve years that
Sri Ramakrishna spent in extreme austerities that Swami
Ramakrishnananda, a cousin of Swami Saradananda, recalled—an
effect that would certainly catch the eye of medical practitioners:

> Sri Ramakrishna had practised *pranayama* so much that he had
> formed a habit of remaining for long periods without breathing.
> Now and then he would stop breathing entirely. Even after we
> came to know him, he used to tell us, 'Whenever you see that I am
> not breathing, please remind me.' Sometimes when he was sleeping,
> we would see that his breath had stopped. Then we would wake
> him up and tell him, 'Master, you are not breathing.' 'Oh, thank
> you!' he would say and again begin to breathe.[32]

That is, of course, a condition that is familiar to doctors. It is known
as apnoea or sleep apnoea. It may be caused by obstruction of air
passages. It may also be caused by the dysfunction of the brain cells
that drive our respiration—this latter condition is known as central
sleep apnoea. Beyond a point, the condition can cause chronic
problems of the heart.[33] 'It is not rare,' Dr Asha Kishore[34] tells
me, 'and we see it quite often in our lab.' It can now be treated.
Central sleep apnoea may be congenital or it may be the result of

aging. The symptoms that the devotees set out would prima facie suggest apnoea. But we have no way of knowing. After all, there are manifest differences also. For instance, because a person affected by apnoea is constantly being pulled out of sleep, the quality of his sleep suffers and he is often drowsy during the day. Sri Ramakrishna was his sprightly self at all times.

But to get back to the years of sadhana, and not sleeping. When I first mentioned to Dr P.N. Tandon, one of the pioneers in neurosurgery in India, Sri Ramakrishna's statement that of the twelve years of his sadhana, he did not sleep at all, not one wink, for six years; and then narrated the accounts about Sri Ramana Maharshi having hardly slept during the three-and-a-half years of his sadhana, the distinguished surgeon exclaimed, 'That is just impossible. A person would die within a few months.'

Occasionally, we do read of persons who have not slept at all. There is the oft-cited case of the Vietnamese farmer, Ngoc Thai. In 1973, when he was around thirty-eight years, he developed fever. From that point on, he completely lost the ability to sleep. What is more, he seemed none the worse for it: when he was being written about in 2008—and by that time he had not slept for almost thirty-five years—he said that he was doing a normal day's work in the farm, that he could carry two 110 lbs sacks of rice over 2 miles to his house...[35] Most cases of this kind, however, including the case of this farmer, were not verified by medical experts, and, are, accordingly, not taken at face value in the literature. Some other reports in fact are said to have been contradicted by the subjects themselves.

But the course that some followed as they stayed awake has been documented. In 1959, Peter Tripp, who at the time was a well-recognized disc jockey in New York, stayed awake for 201 hours—eight days—to help raise funds for the 'March of Dimes'.[36] The event was staged in a glass studio in New York's Times Square. On YouTube, you can see a video in which the doctors who attended on him during the vigil recall the changes that overtook Tripp during the wake-a-thon of 201 hours.[37] He was his easy-going, genial, smiling self when the experiment began. Within two days he was, as the doctors recalled, abusing, cursing, insulting—in this instance—the barber he had known for long. His body temperature kept falling, and, the more it fell, 'the crazier he got'. When a doctor came to visit him, Tripp took him to be an undertaker who had come to take him away; frightened, he ran out into the street, and had to be brought back. Soon he began to see spiders in his shoes. The doctors noticed that the ninety-minute REM sleep cycle was being repeated—even though he was awake: the periods of lucidity and confusion began to alternate in accordance with this cycle. That is, he began 'dreaming'—these episodes took the form of nightmares and hallucinations—even though he was awake. During the last two days, he had to be kept awake with stimulants, and extra vigilance. By the end, a doctor who attended on him said, he was 'crazy as a loon'. It was a different individual from the one who had begun the vigil, recalled the doctor. When at last the experiment was over and he was allowed to sleep, he slept for twenty-four hours. In the subsequent period he felt normal; but his wife did not think so. Their marriage ended in divorce. His career plummeted.[38]

In any event, his record was soon bettered: to 260 hours. And then a seventeen-year-old high-school student, Randy Gardner, who heard of these wake-a-thons, decided to beat all existing records once for all. His feat—of going without sleep for 264 hours—eleven days—was also observed by doctors: it was a record, the longest period for which a person had gone completely without sleep under medical observation and without stimulants of any kind. Among the doctors who observed him was Dr William Dement, one of the foremost sleep researchers at the time. Eleven days is a wink compared to six years, but even in this relatively 'short period' the effects of going without sleep became palpable. The doctor from the US Navy to whom he had been brought for attention, and who wrote up the case study, had this to say about the progressive effects of not sleeping as the days wore on:

> During the *second day* of the vigil the patient noticed difficulty focusing his eyes. After the second day he stopped watching television for the rest of the experiment because his eyes were so extremely heavy and tired. At this time he also had mild astereognosis [impaired ability to differentiate objects]. By the *third day* he developed mood changes, ataxia [inability to coordinate muscular movements], difficulty saying tongue twisters, and marked nausea. During the *fourth day* he became irritable and uncooperative; he developed memory lapses, difficulty concentrating, the feeling of a

tight band around his head, and saw fog around the streetlights. About 0300 that night he experienced the illusion that a street sign was a person. A short time later he imagined he was a great Negro football player and resented statements made about his ability and the Negro race. By the *fifth day* his equilibrium was normal, but he had intermittent hypnogogic reveries, such as seeing a path running through a quiet forest and plants in a garden. On the *sixth day* ataxia, mild astereognosis, and dysnomia [impaired ability to name objects or retrieve words] were again present, and during the next three days slight irritability, mild uncooperativeness, memory lapses, and inability to concentrate reappeared. Intermittent slurred speech was evident on the *seventh day* and it continued to deteriorate to a soft, slow, slurred, mushy quality by the end of the wakeful period. By the *ninth day* he occasionally thought in fragments and frequently did not finish sentences. Also, blurred vision became more of a problem. During the *last two days* of the vigil he felt a certain radio entertainer on whose show he later appeared was trying to make him appear foolish because he could not recall certain specific facts about the vigil. The patient finally went to sleep after 264 hours of wakefulness (Jan 8, 1964) and slept for 14 3/4 hours. The reason for terminating the vigil was simply that the patient had achieved his goal.[39]

In other words, even during this relatively 'short' period of sleep deprivation, we observe effects on speech, comprehension, mood, vision; we have the person being gripped by illusion, delusion, hallucination ... In many ways, the student remained normal—in his posture and gait, for instance. But there were other effects in addition to the ones listed. 'He had considerable difficulty with serial sevens,' the doctor noted: in this a person starts from a number, say 100, and is to subtract seven at each step and speak out the result. The first time he stopped at 65, 'and stated he did not remember what he was doing. Upon continuing the test, he made four mistakes. On the second try he made two mistakes...' 'When asked to read a paragraph, he was only vaguely able to recall what he had read and details were absent,' the doctor recorded. Although his gait and posture were normal, and 'there was no evidence of involuntary movements', 'several examples of sudden clonic jerks of both upper extremities were felt to represent nocturnal jerks or what di Lisi described as "physiological hyponic myoclonias" appeared. Upon extending his arms in front of his body, tremulous finger movements were observed...'[40] The student returned to his normal condition very soon after resuming his normal hours of sleep.

Effects of this kind would not surprise neuroscientists. They know that sleep has restorative effects that are necessary for our bodies, and just as much for our brains. We read in textbooks that sleep replenishes glycogen levels. It helps in generation of new cells and the repair of ones that have suffered wear and tear during our normal waking activities. It gives time to 'clean away' the debris of by-products that accumulates as a result of the normal functioning of cells. It gives an interval for neurotransmitters to shut off and thereby for the receptors to 'rest and regain full sensitivity'. It enables us to work problems out—free of the constraints of logic and convention. The REM phase of sleep is said to help us consolidate memories. And so on.

As a mirror image, prolonged deprivation of sleep or even the accumulation of a 'sleep debt' because of inadequate sleep can impair our immune system—impaired sleep is said to increase the production of the hormone cortisol, and this in turn impairs our immune system. It can send the autonomic control systems that keep our temperature and other variables within a safe, narrow range to malfunction. It accelerates aging. Over long periods, even inadequate sleep, to say nothing of total deprivation of sleep, can predispose one to a series of ailments—from Type 2 diabetes to heart disease. Of course, the effects on our brain and mind are visible even sooner. Slackening alertness, attentional lapses, comprehension, longer reaction times, waning motor control—and thereby increased chances of performance errors and accidents ... all the way to a lessened ability to withhold automatic responses, and thereby a greater tendency to react inappropriately to emotional triggers, and to mood swings and psychosis; in those who are disposed to mania, lack of sleep may trigger it, the mania may in turn reduce sleep even further and thus push one into a vortex...[41]

Effects such as these have been documented in detail and for decades. No wonder that depriving a person of sleep is a common technique for ferreting information out of him, and for breaking him. Indeed, total deprivation of sleep over prolonged periods is reckoned among the methods of 'torture'.

Yes, there is a condition because of which one cannot sleep at all—a degenerative ailment known as *fatal familial insomnia*. But it is an extremely rare ailment—the rarest of rare, in fact. And, as the very name of the disease implies, it is generally inherited, and it is fatal: a person suffering from it dies within seven months to three years, the average being around a year and a half.

So, how are we to explain the six years during which Sri Ramakrishna said he did not sleep at all?

There seem to be at least five possible answers.

First, recent research highlights another group of persons who can do very well with much-less-than-normal sleep. The condition, or the asset if you prefer, is seen to run in families. These persons can do with just four or so hours of sleep, and it isn't that they are below par as a result. In fact, they are full of energy and bounce. Their brains and bodies are able to accomplish the repair and restoration work necessary—for instance, clearing out toxins and repairing cells in the brain that have got damaged during the day—in half the time than the majority of us take. Scientists have discovered one feature common to such persons—a slight mutation in a gene known as DEC2.[42]

The second possibility is 'sleep state misperception' or 'pseudo-insomnia'. The person genuinely believes and, therefore, insists that he has not slept at all, he may even be driven to deep exasperation by the fact that he cannot sleep at all—and this in spite of the fact that he does not feel fatigued or tired as he would if he had not slept. But when he is tested in a sleep lab, and recordings of his EEG, etc., are studied, they establish that he has slept just like most of us. The condition has been the subject of considerable research in the last forty years. The person having the misperception does indeed sleep, but his sleep has some distinctive features. Spectral analysis of the EEGs of the persons showed that, as they slept, alpha waves—associated with our being awake and which are normally recorded only in early sleep—seemed to 'intrude' into the periods of deep sleep. Moreover, the alpha waves turned out to have larger amplitude and that of the delta waves was correspondingly smaller. And 'fast waves'—the beta and gamma waves which are associated with being alert and even anxious—also kept 'intruding' into the periods during which the person was asleep, and, in a sense, shocking them into wakefulness only to have them fall asleep again, and then shocking them up again ... As a result of these differences, persons genuinely have the 'misperception' that they have not slept when, in fact, on all conventional measures, they have had full sleep.[43]

Third, there is 'micro-sleep': persons having piled a huge 'sleep debt' doze off for brief periods—ranging from ten-odd seconds to two minutes or so. Often they are not aware that they have fallen into and just come out of sleep.

The fourth possibility is more intriguing, and the cue comes from an array of mammals and fish—sleepwalkers, dolphins, some species of whales and sea lions, seals, manatees, a variety of birds, in particular, species of birds that migrate over distances so long that they just cannot afford to fall asleep the way we do. In each of these instances, the individual—that sleepwalker, the dolphin, the bird—is able to engage in a motor function even as it allows a part of its brain to, in effect, go to sleep. Some species can let one entire cerebral hemisphere fall asleep even as the other hemisphere continues in the awake state. The right hemisphere may be put to sleep, and the left eye may be shut; the left hemisphere may remain awake with the right eye open—you can see how useful this evolutionary ability would be in keeping a lookout for predators. This kind of sleep is known to neurologists, ornithologists and marine scientists as unihemispheric, slow-wave sleep. Dolphins can swim, they can rise to the surface and take in air, they can navigate, they can even swim in coordination with other dolphin while one hemisphere of their brains is asleep. Birds can fly, they can be disciplined members of the flock, they can—perhaps by occasionally opening their eyes— navigate their course over vast distances even as one hemisphere of their brains is in slow-wave sleep. Not just that: some species can switch between hemispheres—letting one side rest, and then, awakening this hemisphere, letting the other go to sleep.[44]

There is a fifth possibility—and it was put to me by Dr Ashok Panagariya, the much sought-after neurologist at Jaipur. The brain is hardly at rest when we sleep—indeed, during REM sleep its electrical activity seems just a shade less than when we are awake. By contrast, during meditation the wave patterns are certainly altered to what we exhibit when we are in a relaxed state. That entering into states of deep meditation has palpable restorative effects has been documented often; that even a brief period of yoga nidra relaxes one as much as longer periods of actual sleep would is also known. Could it not be that as they entered deeper and deeper states of absorption, Sri Ramakrishna and Sri Ramana, though untutored in yogic techniques, induced the relaxation of the body and brought about the restorative effects within the brain that normal sleep would have?

True. But if he had been restored so well in brief spells, how is it that his visage had changed to such exhaustion as he said, how is it that he was as restless, as worried at not being able to sleep?

4

A brief diversion

A point leaps at us at the very outset. We will not pursue it, but we must keep it at the back of our minds. As would have become evident even from these preliminary pages, we have to necessarily rely on the recollections of the principals themselves—Sri Ramakrishna Paramahamsa and Sri Ramana Maharshi—and the recollections of their immediate followers, those who had a chance to observe and hear the sages.

A heap of studies over the last forty years has shown that ever so often memory gets corrupted—even of the person who has himself undergone a deep experience—and that eyewitness accounts are notoriously unreliable. Furthermore, those false memories can be created—both inadvertently, and on purpose—and that this can be done with the greatest ease. The investigations of scholars like Elizabeth Loftus have been so persuasive on this count that courts in the United States, for instance, are now very cautious in basing a conviction on eyewitness accounts unless these are substantiated by other evidence.

'MEMORY IS NOT A VIDEOTAPE'

Experiments have demonstrated that the mere imagining of doing an act—'Shake the bottle', 'Break the toothpick'—creates a 'memory' of actually having done the deed. Furthermore, merely watching another person doing a thing—shaking that bottle or breaking that toothpick—can create a 'memory' in which one has oneself done that deed. So common is the tendency for such 'memories' to be created that they have been given names: the former goes by the name of 'Imagination Inflation', the latter by 'Observation Inflation'.[1]

Similarly, our memory of what we may have seen is modified by what we may in general associate with that kind of an event—the collision of two vehicles—or person—whether the terrorist who hurled a bomb in a crowded market had a beard or not; equally, by what we may have—even subliminally—heard or read about the event or the person subsequently. It has also been repeatedly shown that when details did not quite register in our brain, it—'the great interpreter' in the left hemisphere, as Michael Gazzaniga would point out—conjures them up. Loftus demonstrated that even the way a question is framed can affect what one remembers of an event: 'How fast were the cars being driven when they *smashed* into each other?' vs 'How fast were the cars being driven when they *hit* each other?' vs 'How fast were the cars being driven when they *grazed* each other?' Finally, scholars have demonstrated how easily 'memories' can be created of events that never happened—for instance, of having been sexually abused as a child—by a psychiatrist excavating the past so as to unearth 'the cause' for what an adult is feeling or doing decades later. And when we recall the event the next time, we are recalling not what we saw originally but the most recent 'memory' of that event, influenced as it has been by a host of factors.[2] Memory is not a videotape being replayed, we are cautioned. It is 'a dynamic act of creation', Leonard Mlodinow points out in his engrossing book, *Subliminal*. The unconscious does not just bring into awareness data that has been stored. It enhances it, it fills in the gaps—just as our brain fills in the part of the scene that is missing because of our blind spot. It interprets the data in terms of the context—the context in which the original event had occurred as well as the context in which it is being recalled. We hear the sound 'eel', he writes; if the last word was 'car', we hear it as 'wheel'; if it was 'sea', we hear it as 'eel'; if it was 'shoe', we hear it as 'heel'; if it was 'hospital' or 'wound', we hear it as 'heal'; if it was 'thief', we hear it as 'steal'. A 'bank' is the bank of a river one moment, and the place where your money is another. 'C' is a letter if it is followed by 'D', 'E'; 'see' if it is followed by 'scene'; 'si' if the speaker is from Spain ... Mlodinow illustrates the way memory gets varnished with the testimony of John Dean to the Senate Committee that was assessing whether or not the then President Richard Nixon should be impeached. John Dean had been legal counsel to Nixon and the White House. He had been fully aware of the cover-up; indeed, he had been a participant in it. His detailed statement about what had transpired (245 pages long), and the confidence with which and the detail in which he answered questions of the senators conveyed the impression that he had perfect recall; and, moreover, that he was being truthful—much of what he said implicated himself. In the literature on memory, Dean's testimony turned out to be an exceptional case—for, soon, the tapes of the actual conversations in the White House became available. In a telling lecture, Ulrich Neisser, then in the psychology department of Cornell University, compared what Dean had told the committee with what Nixon and Dean had actually said to each other. Neisser's analysis showed that Dean had been basically right—there *had* been a cover-up. But on his own role—both in regard to the extent of his culpability and in regard to how central he had been in the incidents—Dean's recollection was so off the mark that Neisser concluded that there had been 'systematic distortion'. The distortion subserved Dean's self-image, and may have also been influenced by what he had heard or read about the events subsequently or by how, in retrospect, the events cohered. He may or may not have been consciously lying—he *did* implicate himself, after all. He may have been stating what he genuinely recalled. And yet it was so very wrong.[3]

A Cautionary Experience

It isn't that one sets out to deceive, but that various factors alter the details and hues of what we remember about what had happened. Among the factors are our predispositions, and the hypotheses that we have already, albeit subconsciously, formed about that event or that kind of event or person. I myself had a vivid and cautionary experience while reading books and journal articles for this project. So many accounts of persons with neurological impairments or injuries tallied so closely with what had been written about the mystic experience that I had begun to wonder whether this experience was triggered by some similar neurological condition. I was swiftly pulled up by a first-hand 'confabulation', so to say.

In his lucid book, *Brain*, Michael Sweeney writes about a fascinating case, that of a young lady of Indian origin who had been in the US. It is a passage worth reading:

> She was a teenage girl of Indian origin in the 1970s. She had developed a malignant brain tumour. As the tumour grew, it began to press on her temporal lobe and her brain started to swell. She suffered a series of seizures. They grew increasingly frequent. However, whereas her initial seizures were intense grandmal convulsions, her new manifestations, localized in the temporal lobe, were weaker. She began experiencing dreamy states in which she saw visions of her home in India. Far from being unpleasant, they made her happy—'They take me back home,' she said. She remained peaceful and lucid during her episodes. The seizures killed her in a few weeks, but doctors often noted the rapt expression on her face as she moved deeper into her visions.[4]

When I first read the account, I took it to be another telltale incident that shows that the mystic experience, or at the least some elements of that experience—the calm, for instance, or the feeling of going home—or of what follows in its wake can be brought about by other brain conditions. I wanted to learn more about the case. I contacted neuroscientists. They could not find any description of Bhagwandi[5] in the case studies that were available in India. As usual, I turned to my friend, Philip Oldenburg. He Googled 'Michael Sweeney'. And lo and behold! The website even had his email address. I immediately wrote to him: Could he please lead me to a fuller description of Bhagwandi's case? He was so kind as to reply by return mail. He had written the book several years ago, he wrote, but would look up his notes to lead me to the original source of the information.

Soon, he wrote again to say that he had come across the case in Oliver Sacks's well-known book, *The Man Who Mistook His Wife for a Hat*.[6] To my chagrin, while I had read the book, I had forgotten this case. On rereading the account given by Sacks, I had to conclude—most reluctantly—that the accounts—actually, not the accounts, but my reaction upon reading Sweeney's account—

illustrated not what I had concluded—that the case suggested that elements of the mystic state could be brought about in other brain states—but an altogether different phenomenon, the 'Telephone Game', or 'Chinese whispers'. You tell your friend something over the phone—somewhat in a mumble—and ask him to tell that to a friend of his; who in turn is to tell it to a third friend ... and so on. By the time the story has reached the twentieth friend, it bears little resemblance to what you had said originally.

Please read Dr Sweeney's account again. And now let us see what Oliver Sacks had reported. Bhagwandi had developed a tumour in her brain when she was seven. The tumour had been excised. She had regained her functions fully. But the tumour had appeared again ten years later. She had been brought to the hospice at which Dr Sacks treated patients. She was having seizures. It was no longer possible to remove the tumour. Other approaches were tried. But no one was in any doubt that it would soon take Bhagwandi's life.

'She was, at first remarkably cheerful, seeming to accept fully the fate which lay in store, but still eager to be with people and do things, enjoy and experience as long as she could,' Dr Sacks reported. The seizures became more frequent. But these seizures were of a different kind: Bhagwandi would not lose consciousness; instead she 'would look (and feel) dreamy'. 'Do these distress you?' Dr Sacks and his colleagues asked her. 'No,' she said, with a peaceful smile, 'I like these dreams—they take me back home.'

These 'dreams' became more and more frequent, more and more vivid, and deeper: her relatives peopled them; she heard dances and conversations of her home; she was amidst fields of rice, and the low hills of her native place.

The concluding three paragraphs have to be read in full, to see how I had misled myself through a preconceived hypothesis:

Day by day, week-by-week, the dreams, the visions, came oftener, drew deeper. They were not occasional now, but occupied most of the day. We would see her rapt, as if in a trance, her eyes sometimes closed, sometimes open but unseeing, and always a faint, mysterious smile on her face. If anyone approached her, or asked her something, as the nurses had to do, she would respond at once, lucidly and courteously, but there was, even among the most down-to-earth staff, a feeling that she was in another world, and that we should not interrupt her. I shared this feeling and, though curious, was reluctant to probe. Once, just once, I said, 'Bhagwandi, what is happening?'

'I am dying,' she answered. 'I am going home. I am going back where I came from—you might call it my return.'

Another week passed, and now Bhagwandi no longer responded to external stimuli, but seemed wholly enveloped in a world of her own, and, though her eyes were closed, her face still bore its faint, happy smile. 'She's on the return journey,' the staff said. 'She'll soon be there.' Three days later she died—or should we say she 'arrived', having completed her passage to India?[7]

Acceptance. Calm. Even contentment. But not quite the calm that the mystics report. And yet I had inferred from Sweeney's account of what Sacks had witnessed and reported that Bhagwandi's tumour had resulted in a mystic-like state. Had Dr Sweeney not given me the source, had I not looked it up, I might have been telling friends that Bhagwandi's experience was yet another instance of a different brain state—in this instance, of a tumour having made its way into the temporal lobe—that had triggered the mystic experience.

'Believing is seeing,' they say. Here was, 'Expecting is spotting.'

FOUR SPECIFIC CONSIDERATIONS TO KEEP AT THE BACK OF OUR MINDS

Apart from these general reasons for caution, there are four specific factors that we have to keep at the back of our minds.

We have seen the extreme austerities that Sri Ramakrishna and Sri Ramana went through. To recall just one element of these, they hardly slept during their years of sadhana—a period that lasted three-and-a-half years in the case of Sri Ramana and twelve years in the case of Sri Ramakrishna. As we have noticed, the latter himself said that for *six of these twelve years* he did not sleep at all. Sridharan Devarajan of the Centre for Neurosciences at the Indian Institute of Science drew my attention to studies that show that 'sleep deprivation is known to impair consolidation of novel memories', and observed that this 'may have prevented these mystics from veridically recollecting particular incidents or aspects of their youth or early years'.[8]

Second, while a witness like Swami Vivekananda was of a sturdy disposition, while he was indeed far ahead of his times, indeed he shaped the times, others whose accounts we have necessarily to rely on were, like all of us ordinary folk are, affected by the temper of their time. To say nothing of Bengal 150 years ago, it is difficult for us to imagine today what that temper was even at the time of Sri Ramana, though he was amidst us just sixty-five years ago. The advances in understanding nature, in understanding the human mind, the extent of technological change, the shrinking of the world, the information that even lay persons have about the world and how things happen in it, all these have wrought a sea change in our beliefs and mores—to say nothing of what fakes have done to our faith even in good and saintly persons. The average recorder would today look with a very different eye at the events that happened and were recorded by the witnesses, in all likelihood he would place a very different construction on them.

There was another aspect in which the temper of the times would have impinged on our narrators. In the latter half of the nineteenth century, for instance, Bengal was in ferment—the received religion, beliefs, mores were all in flux, notions that had been commonplace were suddenly being looked upon as old-fashioned, as the superstitious delusions of the ignorant. That flux would have had an effect of itself on what should be reported and what should be left out: we will soon encounter, for instance, the hesitation with which Swami Saradananda includes Sri Ramakrishna's own account of his visit to the house of a devotee, and of his seeing two ghosts in the room: 'The Master saw a strange thing there at that time. We venture to state it here only because it was heard from the Master himself; otherwise we would have suppressed it...'[9]

Third, the devotees who wrote about these sages were *devotees*. We do not have to believe that they set out to write hagiographies, but we cannot shut our eyes to the fact that in their eyes the sages were not merely saints, they were avatars of God Himself, and that this could not but have had an effect of what they remembered as well as on what they inferred from incidents involving the sages. To take one instance, when he received materials on the life of Sri

Ramakrishna that he had requested Swami Vivekananda to help him obtain, Max Müller felt it necessary to screen out, from what he was going to write on the basis of this material, events and constructions on them which might have originated in what he called 'the Dialogic Process and the irrepressible miraculising tendencies of devoted disciples'.[10]

SWAMI VIVEKANANDA'S ADMONITIONS

Fourth, in the case of Sri Ramakrishna, we know that Swami Vivekananda urged that accounts of Sri Ramakrishna's life be written in a particular way. For instance, in a letter written on 3 March 1894 to a young associate—in which he sets out the basic beliefs of those who belong to the Order, and in which he urges the youngsters to henceforth carry the casket of jewels that he had been given to hand over to them—Swamiji says:

> Take thought, collect materials, write a sketch of the life of Ramakrishna, *studiously avoiding all miracles. The life should be written as an illustration of the doctrines he preached.* Only his—do not bring me or any living persons into that. *The main aim should be to give to the world what he taught, and the life illustrating that...*[11]

Swamiji despairs of 'Calcutta people'! He urges disciples in Madras to plough their own furrow. His counsel now is that narration of miracles, etc., be eschewed, and that as the language that Sri Ramakrishna used—earthy, direct, often with sexual similes and metaphors—will be misunderstood by people in the West, such expressions must be edited out. Here is what he writes to Alasinga, on 30 November 1894:

> ... We must organise our forces not to make a sect—not on religious matters, but on the secular business part of it. A stirring propaganda must be launched out. Put your heads together and organize.
>
> What nonsense about the miracle of Ramakrishna! ... Miracles I do not know nor understand. Had Ramakrishna nothing to do

in the world but turning wine into the Gupta's medicine? Lord save me from such Calcutta people! What materials to work with! If they can write a real life of Shri Ramakrishna with the idea of showing what he came to do and teach, let them do it, otherwise let them not distort his life and sayings. These people want to know God who see in Shri Ramakrishna nothing but jugglery! ... Now let Kidi[12] translate his love, his knowledge, his teachings, his eclecticism, etc. This is the theme. The life of Shri Ramakrishna was an extraordinary searchlight under whose illumination one is able to really understand the whole scope of Hindu religion. He was the object-lesson of all the theoretical knowledge given in the *Shastras* (scriptures). He showed by his life what the *Rishis* and *Avataras* really wanted to teach. The books were theories, he was the realisation. This man had in fifty-one years lived the five thousand years of national spiritual life and so raised himself to be an object-lesson for future generations. The Vedas can only be explained and the *Shastras* reconciled by his theory of *Avastha* or stages—that we must not only tolerate others, but positively embrace them, and that truth is the basis of all religions. Now on these lines a most impressive and beautiful life can be written. Well, everything in good time. *Avoid all irregular indecent expressions about sex, etc., because other nations think it the height of indecency to mention such things, and his life in English is going to be read by the whole world.* I read a Bengali life sent over. It is full of such words ... So take care. Carefully avoid such words and expressions. The Calcutta friends have not a cent worth of ability; but they have their assertions of individuality. They are too high to listen to advice. I do not know what to do with these wonderful gentlemen. I have not got much hope in that quarter. *His will be done.* I am simply ashamed of the Bengali book. The writer perhaps thought he was a frank recorder of truth and keeping the very language of *Paramahamsa.* But he does not remember that Ramakrishna would never use that language before ladies. And this man expects his work to be read by men and women alike! Lord, save me from fools! They, again, have their own freaks; they all knew him! *Bosh and rot.* ... Beggars taking upon themselves the air of kings! Fools thinking they are all wise! Puny slaves thinking that they are masters! That is their condition. I do not know what to do. Lord save me. I have all hope in Madras. Push on with your work; do not be governed by the Calcutta people. Keep them in

good humour in the hope that someone of them may turn good.
But push on with your work independently. 'Many come to sit at
dinner when it is cooked.' Take care and work on...[13]

The same day, he writes to the disciple in Madras he has mentioned
in the foregoing letter, 'Kidi', the name by which Mudaliar was
known:

> ... As to the wonderful stories published about Sri Ramakrishna,
> I advise you to keep clear of them and the fools who write them.
> They are true, but the fools will make a mess of the whole thing,
> I am sure. He had a whole world of knowledge to teach, why
> insist upon unnecessary things as miracles really are! They do not
> prove anything. Matter does not prove Spirit. What connection is
> there between the existence of God, Soul, or immortality, and the
> working of miracles? ... Preach Sri Ramakrishna. Pass the Cup
> that has satisfied your thirst ... Preach Bhakti. Do not disturb your
> head with metaphysical nonsense, and do not disturb others by
> your bigotry...[14]

Similarly, when in the conversation just mentioned, Max Müller
said that he would write a fuller account of Sri Ramakrishna's life
and teachings provided he got the necessary material,[15] Swami
Vivekananda immediately wrote to his fellow monk, Swami
Ramakrishnananda, to have such materials collected, with a
particular emphasis. Swamiji wrote,

> Max Müller wants all the sayings of Sri Ramakrishna classified,
> that is, all on Karma in one place, on Vairagya in another place, so
> on Bhakti, Jnana, etc., etc. You must undertake to do this forthwith
> ... *We must take care to present only the universal aspect of his
> teachings*...[16]

From Swami Vivekananda's point of view, such instructions were
entirely natural—he was founding an Order. On the other hand,
from the point of view of mere academics such instructions present
a problem—especially because, while Sri Ramakrishna was the
embodiment of humility, for all the other monks Swamiji certainly
was, and for generations since has been, an 'authority figure'!

From the point of view of a neurologist, such predispositions and instructions make things doubly difficult. To begin with, lay witnesses, even if they are not devotees, are no substitute for the eye of the trained neurologist, to say nothing of the video-EEG monitoring that is thought necessary in so many neurological conditions. As the devotees were not medical practitioners, they would not have recorded, they may not even have noticed symptoms that a neurologist would regard as telltale indices. And on top of that, either because of the 'temper of the times' and the anxiety not to give ground for readers to conclude that the Master suffered from mere human frailties, they may have censored what they noticed, and not reported it in their accounts.

That we do not have a record of symptoms which would have struck a neurologist, has an inevitable consequence. On occasion, we will have to extrapolate from the accounts that are available— 'generously extrapolate', some may say; we will have to construct a link from the symptoms that devotees or the saints recorded to the medical, psychological or psychosomatic condition that has since been identified. Provided we are careful to bear in mind that we are extrapolating, that we are constructing a speculative link, this is not as great a disability as may appear at first. The objective is to suggest possible parallels of the experiences, not to provide a diagnosis of the physiological or mental condition of the saints. The subtitle of this volume, advisedly, is, '*Speculations* around and about Sri...'.

These are weighty considerations. Even so, we will put them aside, and proceed—taking at face value the recollections of the sages themselves and the accounts of those who saw them and lived with them. The reason is that miracles, language, their universalist perspective are not of concern to us in this study. On the other hand, the narrators would have little cause to exaggerate or minimize the symptoms and manifestations that concern us in this study—with one possible exception: namely, the austerities that the sages went through. It may be that, to take one instance, Sri Ramakrishna did develop a sort of insomnia during his twelve years of sadhana, but that he did not stay awake for six years continuously. But there are other possibilities, as we just saw.

The two general caveats—that memory can get corrupted, that our expectations can colour what we infer from an event or an account of the event—of course, we must keep at the back of our minds. An additional precaution would stand us in good stead. We should not go by the details of what the witnesses or even the sages reported—as a forensic detective or a lawyer arguing in court would. Rather, we should go by the broad phenomenon that is being reported, and, perhaps, we should look for many reports of a phenomenon before taking it on board.

'We should look for many reports of a phenomenon before taking it on board,' I just wrote. But we must simultaneously remember the oft-repeated warning: Just because a 'fact' is reported in fifty copies of a newspaper does not make it fifty times more reliable! In the chapter of austerities, when I came to summarize what Sri Ramana had undergone, I relied on just four of the many accounts that report his own allusions to what his outward, physical state became during these years: the biography by Narasimha Swami to which Sri Ramana himself sometimes referred questioners—'That incident is set out in my biography'; the invaluable Munagala S. Venkataramiah's *Talks With Sri Ramana Maharshi;* the letters that Nagamma Suri wrote from the ashram to her brother, D.S. Sastri, who was to later compile and translate them—these cover the last five years of Sri Ramana's life; and A. Devaraja Mudaliar's diary. The other standard biographies, even those by the most earnest and scholarly devotees—for instance, Arthur Osborne's *Ramana Maharshi and the Path of Self Knowledge*[17] and K. Swaminathan's *Ramana Maharshi*[18]—more or less restate or reproduce passages, even pages from these four accounts. Thus, such confirmation that we seek is to be had from the four original volumes, the other accounts are best looked up for an occasional fact or expression. For the same reason, the comprehensive volume of Swami Saradananda is much more valuable than the later volume of Swami Nikhilananda—even though Gandhiji himself wrote the foreword to the latter.

There is a final consideration—from the other, medical side, so to say. Consider the proposition that is so often advanced in regard to several mystics—that the person suffered from epilepsy, from temporal lobe epilepsy in particular. In fact, there are so many conditions of co-morbidity—in which epilepsy may be occurring along with another ailment—that it would be rash, to say the least, to come to any definite conclusion that the symptoms—say, visions or hallucinations; or the tensing of limbs before the person goes into a trance-like state—prove that the person had epilepsy. And there is the other problem. It is well known that other pathologies may trigger epilepsy-type symptoms and thus lead to a mistaken diagnosis of the ailment as epilepsy. Or the symptoms of an epileptic condition may be so similar to symptoms of other ailments that they may mask the underlying epileptic condition.[19]

With that tentativeness in mind, let us proceed to glimpse an experience that was so often taken to be a special favour the gods were bestowing on the saints.

5

Deities, celestial beings, ghosts

The young lad whom we now revere as Sri Ramakrishna is six or seven years old (by some accounts, ten or eleven). Swami Saradananda recalls the incident as it was narrated to disciples by Sri Ramakrishna himself:

> I was then six or seven years old. One morning I took parched rice in a small basket and was eating it while walking on the narrow balks in the cornfields. It was the month of *Jyaishtha* or *Ashar*. In one part of the sky there appeared a beautiful black cloud charged with rain. I was looking at it while eating the rice. Very soon the cloud covered almost the whole sky, when a flock of milk-white cranes flew against that black cloud. It looked so beautiful that I became very soon absorbed in an extraordinary mood. Such a state came on me that my external consciousness was lost. I fell down and the rice got scattered near the balk. People saw this and carried me home. This was the first time that I lost external consciousness in ecstasy.[1]

That was a life-transforming experience, Sri Ramakrishna said as he recalled the event years later to his disciples. 'When I was ten or eleven years old and lived at Kamarpukur,' he told them, 'I first experienced *samadhi*. As I was passing through a paddy field, I saw something and was overwhelmed. There are certain characteristics of God-vision. One sees light, feels joy, and experiences the upsurge of a great current in one's chest, like the bursting of a rocket...' He recounted the event on other occasions also, so significant had it been. '... During my boyhood God manifested Himself in me,' he told the devotees. 'I was then eleven years old. One day, while I was walking across a paddy field, I saw something. Later on I came to know from people that I had been unconscious, and my body totally motionless. Since that day I have been an altogether different man. I began to see another person within me. When I used to conduct the worship in the temple, my hand, instead of going toward the Deity, would very often come toward my head, and I would put flowers there. A young man who was then staying with me did not dare approach me. He would say: "I see a light on your face. I am afraid to come very near you." But there is a state higher than this. When a man attains It, he moves about aimlessly, like a child...'[2]

A few months later, the young boy is accompanying a flock of women who are on the way to a temple of Goddess Visalakshi about two miles from his village Kamarpukur. He and the women are singing songs of gods and goddesses. 'The child stopped singing suddenly,' we learn. 'His body and limbs became stiff and benumbed. Streams of tears flowed incessantly from his eyes, and he did not reply to their repeated and affectionate calls as to what ailed him.' The women apprehend that he has had a sunstroke. They try to bring him round by calling out his name. He remains unconscious. One lady remarks that it would be better if they chant the name of Goddess Visalakshi. They do so repeatedly, beseeching her intercession. Eventually, the young boy returns to normality, bit by bit. He shows no fatigue or weakness. When they return home, and the incident is narrated to his alarmed mother, she thinks it has occurred because of some physical malady. But the young lad insists that it was because his mind had merged in the goddess.[3]

The young boy has heard how his father had had a vision of Sri Rama entering their house, and how after that their fields had begun to yield much greater quantities of paddy. He wants intensely to have the vision of that Lord Raghuvir. In his way, he begins worshipping Rama—and goes into savikalpa samadhi.[4]

After these initial incidents, the visions became increasingly frequent, and the boy is rapidly transformed.

At Every Turn, the Mother

Sri Ramakrishna lived amidst visions, so to say. He would go into samadhi again and yet again, even in a single day, or during a single outing to a devotee's house. A remark of his speaks of the frequency of the visions. His nephew, Hriday, is keen to have the experience in which Sri Ramakrishna revels. He follows him to the Panchavati forest. Soon he sees the Master's body disappear and become a luminous one ... He then experiences his own body acquire that luminosity. He is overjoyed. He begins shouting: 'O Ramakrishna, O Ramakrishna, we are not men—why are we here? Come, let us go from place to place and save people from their misery. You and I are of one stuff.' Sri Ramakrishna admonishes him to be quiet. He keeps shouting. Sri Ramakrishna touches Hriday's chest and puts an end to the experience. Hriday is disconsolate. Sri Ramakrishna exclaims, 'I only wished that you might be quiet now. I had to do it, as you raised such a storm over a trifling vision. *I see countless visions at all hours of the day,* but do I make a fuss over them? You are not yet fit to see them...'[5]

The visions become more and more frequent. As Swami Nikhilananda recorded in his 'Introduction' to Mahendranath Gupta's *The Gospel*:

Weeping bitterly during the moments of separation from Her, he would pass into a trance and then find Her standing before him, smiling, talking, consoling, bidding him be of good cheer, and instructing him. During this period of spiritual practice he had many uncommon experiences. When he sat to meditate, he would hear strange clicking sounds in the joints of his legs, as if someone were locking them up, one after the other, to keep him motionless; and at the conclusion of his meditation he would again hear the same sounds, this time unlocking them and leaving him free to move about. He would see flashes like a swarm of fire-flies floating before his eyes, or a sea of deep mist around him, with luminous waves of molten silver. Again, from a sea of translucent mist he would behold the Mother rising, first Her feet, then Her waist, body, face, and head, finally Her whole person; he would feel Her breath and hear Her voice. Worshipping in the temple, sometimes he would become exalted, sometimes he would remain motionless as stone, sometimes he would almost collapse from excessive emotion. Many of his actions, contrary to all tradition, seemed sacrilegious to the people. He would take a flower and touch it to his own head, body, and feet, and then offer it to the Goddess. Or, like a drunkard, he would reel to the throne of the Mother, touch Her chin by way of showing his affection for Her, and sing, talk, joke, laugh, and dance...[6]

The Mother becomes a constant presence. He sees Her during worship, of course, during meditation, of course. Soon, he sees Her even when he is not meditating or praying. He sees Her even as he retains consciousness of the outer world: 'His visions became deeper and more intimate. He no longer had to meditate to behold the Divine Mother. Even while retaining consciousness of the outer world, he would see Her as tangibly as the temples, the trees, the river, and the men around him...'[7]

Visions follow visions. In addition to the perpetual visions of the Mother, he has visions of various male figures like Bhairava and of celestial beings. The visions occur day after day ... He sees the serpent-power at the base of his spine awaken, and a 'celestial male figure' goes through the sushumna to each lotus centre; he makes them open by touching them with his tongue; as he proceeds from one lotus chakra to the next, the lotuses that were drooping, become erect and blossom...[8]

He yearns to see the deluding power of the Mother. Soon, a female figure 'of extraordinary beauty' rises from the waters of the Ganga and comes 'with dignified gait' to the Panchavati. She is in an advanced stage of pregnancy. 'A few minutes later,' Swami Saradananda tells us, 'he saw that she gave birth to a beautiful boy in his very presence and suckled the baby very affectionately; the next moment he saw that the same figure assumed a very cruel and frightful appearance and, taking the baby in her mouth, masticated it and swallowed it. She then entered the waters of the river whence she had appeared.'[9]

There is no limit to the number of forms in which he sees the Devi during this period, we are told. In each She is of incomparable beauty: 'I saw Her yesterday. She was clad in a seamless ochre-coloured garment, and She talked with me,' he tells a devotee. 'She came to me another day as a Mussalman girl six or seven years old.

She had a *tilak* on Her forehead and was naked. She walked with me, joking and frisking like a child. At Hriday's house I had a vision of Gauranga.[10] He wore a black-bordered cloth. Haladhari used to say that God is beyond both Being and Non-being. I told the Mother about it and asked Her, "Then is the divine form an illusion?" The Divine Mother appeared to me in the form of Rati's mother and said, "Do thou remain in *bhava*." I repeated this to Haladhari. Now and then I forget Her command and suffer. Once I broke my teeth because I didn't remain in *bhava*. So I shall remain in *bhava* unless I receive a revelation from heaven or have a direct experience to the contrary. I shall follow the path of love.'[11]

He sees maidens; they appear to him to be embodiments of the Divine Mother ... He goes to a performance of the Ramayana; the actors and actresses appear to him as the actual Rama, Sita ... He sees a woman clad in blue, standing near a tree; she appears to him to be Sita ... People are watching a balloon ascend; an English boy is leaning against a tree, his legs crossed; Sri Ramakrishna sees him as Krishna...

He is seated, and begins talking to the Mother, in a whisper, leading devotees to feel that She is nearby ... He is visiting a devotee's house. He proceeds to a couch, looks around as if he is seeing someone, and exclaims, 'Hello Mother! I see that You too have come. How you are showing off your Benarasi sari! Don't bother me now. Sit down and be quiet...' He is seated on a small couch and engaged in a conversation with the Divine Mother—'in a voice that would have melted even a stone'; he tells her, 'Mere knowledge of Advaita! I spit on it! You exist as long as You keep the ego in me. The *paramahamsa* is but a child. Doesn't a child need a mother?' ... He tells Mahendranath Gupta, 'I am shown everything beforehand. Once I saw Gauranga and his devotees singing *kirtan* in the Panchavati. I think I saw Balram there and you too...'

'HE CRACKED MY FINGERS'

He is on a pilgrimage to Mathura, Vrindavan and other places. 'The moment I came to *Dhruva Ghat* at Mathura, in a flash I saw Vasudeva crossing the Jamuna with Krishna in his arms' ... '*God talked to me*,' Sri Ramakrishna tells his devotees. 'It was not merely His vision. *Yes, He talked to me.* Under the banyan-tree I saw Him coming from the Ganges. *Then we laughed so much! By way of playing with me He cracked my fingers. Then He talked. Yes, He talked to me.*' Sri Ramakrishna elaborates: 'For three days I wept continuously. And He revealed to me what is in the Vedas, the Puranas, the Tantras, and the other scriptures ... One day He showed me the *maya* of *Mahamaya*. A small light inside a room began to grow, and at last it enveloped the whole universe ... Further, He revealed to me a huge reservoir of water covered with green scum. The wind moved a little of the scum and immediately the water became visible; but in the twinkling of an eye, scum from all sides came dancing in and again covered the water. He revealed to me that the water was like Satchidananda, and the scum like *maya*. On account of *maya*, Satchidananda is not seen. Though now and then one may get a glimpse of It, again *maya* covers It...'[12]

He is recounting his visions to Mahendranath Gupta:

Weeping, I prayed to the Mother: 'O Mother, reveal to me what is contained in the Vedas and the Vedanta. Reveal to me what is in the Purana and the Tantra.' One by one She has revealed all these to me.

Yes, She has taught me everything. Oh, how many things she has shown me! One day She showed me Shiva and Shakti everywhere. Everywhere I saw the communion of Shiva and Shakti. Shiva and Shakti existing in all living things—men, animals, trees, plants. I saw them in the communion of all male and female elements.

Another day I was shown heaps of human heads, mountain high. Nothing else existed, and I was seated alone in their midst.

Still another day She showed me an ocean. Taking the form of a salt doll, I was going to measure its depth. While doing this, through the grace of the guru I was turned to stone. Then I saw a ship and at once got into it.

The helmsman was the guru...

The guru was the helmsman in that boat. I saw that 'I' and 'you' were two different things. Again I jumped into the ocean, and was changed into a fish. I found myself swimming joyfully in the Ocean of Satchidananda.[13]

BRAHMA, BRAHMAYONI, GOD

The repertoire widens. He sees the ultimate cause of the universe as a huge luminous triangle, the Brahmayoni, giving birth every moment to an infinite number of worlds ... He hears the primal anahata dhvani, 'OM' ... He is describing his experiences of Brahman to the devotees:

> One day I had the vision of Consciousness, non-dual and indivisible. At first it had been revealed to me that there were innumerable men, animals, and other creatures. Among them there were aristocrats, the English, the Mussalmans, myself, scavengers, dogs, and also a bearded Mussalman with an earthenware tray of rice in his hand. He put a few grains of rice into everybody's mouth. I too tasted a little.
>
> Another day I saw rice, vegetables, and other foodstuff, and filth and dirt as well, lying around. Suddenly the soul came out of my body and, like a flame, touched everything. It was like a protruding tongue of fire and tasted everything once, even the excreta. It was revealed to me that all these are one Substance, the non-dual and indivisible Consciousness.
>
> Another day it was revealed to me that I had devotees—my intimate companions, my very own. Thereafter I would climb to the roof of the *kuthi* as soon as the bells and the conch-shells of the evening service sounded in the temples, and cry out with a longing heart: 'Oh, where are you all? Come here! I am dying to see you!...'[14]

'These are all deep mysteries,' Sri Ramakrishna says. 'What can you understand through reasoning? You will realize everything when God Himself teaches you. Then you will not lack any knowledge.'[15]

Mahendranath Gupta and Sri Ramakrishna's close disciples are seated around him. He asks whether there is any outsider present. Reassured that there is none, he narrates what happened a brief while earlier:

> The other day, when Harish was with me, I saw Satchidananda come out of this sheath.* It said, 'I incarnate Myself in every age.'

---

*Sri Ramakrishna's expression for his own body.

I thought that I myself was saying these words out of mere fancy. I kept quiet and watched. Again Satchidananda Itself spoke, saying, 'Chaitanya, too, worshipped Shakti.'

'The devotees listened to these words in amazement,' Mahendranath recorded. 'Some wondered whether God Himself was seated before them in the form of Sri Ramakrishna. The Master paused a moment. Then he said, addressing M.,* "I saw that it is the fullest manifestation of Satchidananda; but this time the Divine Power is manifested through the glory of *sattva*." The devotees sat spellbound...'[16]

During Meditation

The visions are an intrinsic element of Sri Ramakrishna's meditation. A representative account that he narrates to his disciples begins with the man with a trident whom we will soon encounter:

During my *sadhana*, when I meditated, I would actually see a person sitting near me with a trident in his hand. He would threaten to strike me with the weapon unless I fixed my mind on the Lotus Feet of God, warning me that it would pierce my breast if my mind strayed from God.

The Divine Mother would put me in such a state that sometimes my mind would come down from the *Nitya* to the *Lila*, and sometimes go up from the *Lila* to the *Nitya*.

Sometimes, when the mind descended to the *Lila*, I would meditate day and night on Sita and Rama. At those times I would constantly behold the forms of Sita and Rama. Ramlalla was my constant companion. Sometimes I would bathe Him and sometimes feed Him.

Again, I used to be absorbed in the ideal of Radha and Krishna and would constantly see their forms. Or again, I would be absorbed in Gauranga. He is the harmonization of two ideals: the *Purusha* and the *Prakriti*. At such times I would always see the form of Gauranga.

Then a change came over me. The mind left the plane of the *Lila* and ascended to the *Nitya*. I found no distinction between the

---

*That is, Mahendranath himself.

sacred *tulsi* and the ordinary *sajina*[17] plant. I no longer enjoyed seeing the forms of God; I said to myself, 'They come and go.' I lifted my mind above them. I removed all the pictures of gods and goddesses from my room and began to meditate on the Primal *Purusha*, the Indivisible Satchidananda, regarding myself as His handmaid...[18]

Women, an English Soldier, the Mother Tempt Him

Sri Ramakrishna is telling his disciples about the snares that arise during meditation:

> At the beginning of meditation the objects of the senses appear before the aspirant. But when the meditation becomes deep, they no longer bother him. They are left outside. How many things I saw during meditation! I vividly perceived before me a heap of rupees, a shawl, a plate of sweets, and two women with rings in their noses. 'What do you want?' I asked my mind. 'Do you want to enjoy any of these things?' 'No,' replied the mind, 'I don't want any of them. I don't want anything but the Lotus Feet of God.' I saw the inside and the outside of the women, as one sees from outside the articles in a glass room. I saw what is in them: entrails, blood, filth, worms, phlegm, and such things.[19]

Sri Ramakrishna continues his account: 'Sin' takes on the form of an English soldier, and tempts him with 'wealth, honour, sex, pleasure, various occult powers, and such things'. Sri Ramakrishna appeals to the Divine Mother to kill him ... On another occasion, the Mother Herself comes to tempt him. A disciple sleeping in Sri Ramakrishna's room finds him pacing the floor. 'At every turn he spat on the floor, remarking in a tone of utter disgust, "Fie! I spit on it! I don't want it, take it back, Mother! Don't tempt me with this trifle."' He regains some awareness, and tells the disciple what has been happening: 'At dead of night I suddenly awoke from sleep to find the Divine Mother approaching me with a basket in Her hand. She held it out to me and asked me to accept the contents, which were mine. At a glance I found that the Mother had brought me worldly honours. They looked so hideous that I turned my face in disgust and prayed to Her to take back Her allurements. Thereupon She disappeared with a smile.'[20]

Sri Ramakrishna is in samadhi. He is seated on a pillow, his feet dangling. The devotees are gathered around him. He begins talking to the Divine Mother. 'I shall take my meal now,' he tells Her. 'Art Thou come? Hast Thou found Thy lodging and left Thy baggage there and then come out? ... I don't enjoy anybody's company now. Why should I listen to the music, Mother? That diverts part of my mind to the outside world.'

'The Master was gradually regaining consciousness of the outer world,' Mahendranath Gupta records. 'Looking at the devotees he said: "Years ago I used to be amazed to see people keeping *kai* fish alive in a pot of water. I would say: 'How cruel these people are! They will finally kill the fish.' But later, as changes came over my mind, I realized that bodies are like pillowcases. It doesn't matter whether they remain or drop off."'[21]

PILGRIMAGE TO BENARES

As the boat approaches Benares, he has a vision of it as a city made of gold. Swami Saradananda explains this experience as symbolic: 'It [the vision of the city as being made of gold] was indeed a manifestation, in the present, of the invaluable golden mass of spiritual emotions of the hearts of holy devotees, deposited stratum after stratum and solidified through ages, so to speak, into this city.'[22]

Sri Ramakrishna is being taken in a boat on the Ganga. Passing the Manikarnika Ghat, he sees Shiva and Mahakali easing the way for the deceased:

I saw a tall, white person with tawny matted hair walking with solemn steps to each pyre in the burning-*ghat*, raising carefully every *Jiva* and imparting into his ear the *Mantra* of supreme Brahman. On the other side of the pyre, the all-powerful Mahakali was untying all the knots of bondage, gross, subtle and causal of the *Jiva* produced by past impressions and sending him to the indivisible sphere by opening with Her own hands the door to liberation. Thus did Visvanatha, the divine Lord of the universe, endow him in an instant with the infinite Bliss of experiencing non-duality, which ordinarily results from the practice of Yoga and austerity for many cycles. Thus did He fulfill the perfection of the *Jiva's* life.[23]

The vision takes a turn. 'I saw Shiva standing on that *Ghat*, embodying in Himself all the seriousness of the world. At first I saw Him standing at a distance; then I saw Him approaching me. At last he merged in me. Another time, in an ecstatic mood, I saw that a *sanyasi* was leading me by the hand. We entered a temple and I had a vision of Annapurna made of gold...'[24]

He has gone to the house of Balram, an ardent devotee. He tells the assembled devotees:

One day in the Kali temple Haladhari and Nangta* were reading the *Adhyatma Ramayana*. Suddenly I had a vision of a river with woods on both sides. The trees and plants were green. Rama and Lakshmana were walking along wearing their shorts. One day, in front of the *kuthi*, I saw Arjuna's chariot. Sri Krishna was seated in it as the charioteer. I still remember it. Another day, while listening to *kirtan* at Kamarpukur, I saw Gauranga in front of me.

At that time a naked person, emerging from my body, used to go about with me. I used to joke with him. He looked like a boy and was a *paramahamsa*. I can't describe to you all the divine forms I saw at that time. I was suffering then from indigestion, which would become worse when I saw visions; so I would try to shun these divine forms and would spit on the ground when I saw them. But they would follow me and obsess me like ghosts. I was always overwhelmed with divine ecstasy and couldn't tell the passing of day and night. On the day after such a vision I would have a severe attack of diarrhea, and all these ecstasies would pass out through my bowels.[25]

VISIONS OF EVENTS THAT ARE YET TO HAPPEN

Sri Ramakrishna did not just see visions of gods and goddesses. He often saw events before they happened. He often saw events happening faraway. He saw ghosts also. Just two or three instances

---

*Totapuri, a mystic, who led Sri Ramakrishna to the peak experiences of non-duality. As we noted earlier, he had renounced everything, including clothes. Hence, Sri Ramakrishna's name for him—'the naked one'.

and the circumstances in which they occurred will suffice to give us a glimpse of the range of visions, and what Sri Ramakrishna perceived through them.

The Dakshineswar temple where Sri Ramakrishna was a priest had been endowed by Rani Rasmani, a rich widow. Her son-in-law, Mathur Nath Biswas, looked after the affairs of the temple. He was most solicitous of Sri Ramakrishna. Indeed, it was only because of his protective hand, so to say, that Sri Ramakrishna was not removed from the Dakshineswar temple by people who could not comprehend what seemed to them his bizarre behaviour. By 1870, Mathur had begun to fall ill. In July 1871, one afternoon, the Master had been in Bhavasamadhi for two or three hours. He returned to normal consciousness around 5 p.m. He called Hriday and told him, 'Mathur got into a celestial chariot into which companions of the Divine Mother lifted him affectionately and his spirit went to the sphere of the Devi.' It transpired that Mathur did indeed pass away at 5 p.m.[26]

Sri Ramakrishna develops the desire to see the Sankirtan of Sri Chaitanya. He has a vision of this, and some faces in the multitude impress themselves on his memory. Later, when the would-be disciples come to him, Sri Ramakrishna recognizes them, and concludes that in a previous life they had been companions of Sri Chaitanya. Here is how Swami Saradananda describes the event—the account enables us to glimpse several facets at once: the way the Mother fulfils Sri Ramakrishna's desire; how he sees events happening faraway; how he sees what is to happen in the future:

> ... The Master then had a desire to witness the all-bewitching peripatetic *Sankirtan* of Sri Chaitanya. The divine Mother fulfilled that desire of his by showing it to him in the way described below: Standing outside his room, he saw wonderful waves of *Sankirtan* coming towards him from the direction of the Panchavati, proceeding towards the main gate of the Dakshineswar garden and disappearing behind the tree. He witnessed that, absorbed in the love of God, Gauranga, the moon of Navadwip, was proceeding with a slow gait in the centre with Nityananda and Advaita on either side, surrounded by a dense multitude. They were all in a state of spiritual inebriation produced by God-love, some expressing the bliss of their hearts by losing control over

themselves and others by wild ecstatic dances. The crowd was so
great that it looked as if there was no end to the number of people
there. A few faces in that wonderful *Sankirtan* got impressed on
the canvas of the Master's memory in bright colours. When he saw
them coming as his devotees shortly after he had had that vision,
the Master arrived at the certain conclusion that they had been the
companions of Chaitanya in their previous lives.[27]

Just as he has visions of events before they happen, he sees events
that are happening at a distance. It is 1885. The cancer in Sri
Ramakrishna's throat is advancing. He is quite ill. He has been
brought to a house in Shyampukur. He has great difficulty in talking,
and yet he continues to teach all who come, and as mention of the
Mother, of God and other deities comes up, he repeatedly goes into
ecstasy. A devotee, Surendranath Mitra, has arranged to conduct the
Durga puja at his home. Relatives oppose his plan. The puja had been
discontinued some years earlier because of a mishap. He persists in
the arrangements. Relatives fall ill. He is blamed for the illnesses. He
goes ahead with the puja. His regret is that, because of the cancer,
Sri Ramakrishna cannot be present. In faraway Shyampukur, Sri
Ramakrishna is conversing with the doctor and disciples. He goes
into samadhi. He regains consciousness half an hour or so later. He
tells the disciples, 'I saw that there opened a luminous path from
here to Surendra's house. I saw, further, that attracted by Surendra's
devotion, the Mother had appeared in the image and that a ray of
light was coming out from her third eye. I also saw that rows of
lamps were lighted in the front verandah and Surendra was sitting
and weeping piteously in the courtyard in front of the Mother. Go
you all together to his house now. He will feel much comforted to
see you.' They proceed to the house, and are astonished to see that
things are, and Surendra's condition is, exactly as the Master had
just described it.[28]

Ghosts Who Eat By Smelling

And the ghosts. Sri Ramakrishna has gone to the house of a devotee.
The devotee's mother has cooked for him and Rakhal (a young lad
whom Ramakrishna looks upon as his son). The old lady has made a

bed for them to rest after taking the meal. She has gone down to have her own meal. Rakhal has fallen asleep. Sri Ramakrishna is awake when he sees two ghosts. They implore him to go away because his presence is causing them great pain. Swami Saradananda's account of the incident tells many a tale:

> ... The Master saw a strange thing there at that time. We venture to state it here only because it was heard from the Master himself; otherwise we would have suppressed it. The Master used to have only a little sleep during the whole of day and night. He was, therefore, lying quiet. Rakhal fell asleep by his side. The Master said, 'A bad smell was felt. Then I saw two figures in a corner of the room. Their appearance was hideous. Out of their bellies, the entrails were hanging down and their faces, hands and feet were exactly like the human skeletons arranged in the Medical College, which I saw at some time. They said to me humbly, 'Why are you here? Please go away from this place; we feel much pained (perhaps to remember their own condition) to see you.' On the one hand they were thus supplicating and, on the other, Rakhal was sleeping. Seeing that they felt pained, I was going to get up and come away with my small bag and towel when Rakhal woke up and said, 'Where are you going?' Saying, 'I will tell you later on,' and catching hold of his hand, I came downstairs, and taking leave of the old woman (she had just finished taking her food), I went and got into the boat. I then said to Rakhal, 'There are two ghosts there. The Mill of Kamarhati is situated near the garden. They live in that room by smelling (for, with them smelling is eating) the bones etc., thrown away by the Europeans after they have taken their meal.' I said nothing of it to the old woman, lest she should get afraid for she has always to live alone in that house.[29]

The temper of the times, of course. But also the temper of the Master?

He takes to tantric worship under the guidance of Bhairavi Brahmani. During this sadhana, there is a rush of visions. He has learnt that sometimes the Mother assumes the shape of a jackal, that dogs are the carriers of Bhairava. 'I practised the discipline of the Tantra under the *bel*-tree,' he tells devotees. 'At that time I could see no distinction between the sacred *tulsi* and any other plant. In that state I sometimes ate the leavings from a jackal's meal, food that had been exposed the whole night, part of which might have been eaten by snakes or other creatures. Yes, I ate that stuff—as *prasada*.' 'Sometimes I rode on a dog and fed him with *luchi*, also eating part of the bread myself,' Sri Ramakrishna recounts. 'I realized that the whole world was filled with God alone. One cannot have spiritual realization without destroying ignorance; so I would assume the attitude of a tiger and devour ignorance...'[30]

A Few Preliminary Symptoms

Several features of these visions of Sri Ramakrishna will strike the reader:

- They are numerous; they are almost an everyday occurrence.
- They are vivid.
- They become a part of his memory—they are not just phantoms that flit by and vanish; instead, they leave a mark deep enough so that he recalls them vividly years later.
- Often they all too obviously reflect his apprehensions at the time—for instance, that he must not fall for temptations. Recall the two women decked in ornaments; recall 'Sin' as he appears in the form of an English soldier offering him 'wealth, honour, sex, pleasure, various occult powers, and such things'; recall the Mother herself with that basket of worldly honours.
- Often they reflect the needs of the moment on the spiritual path that he is treading. We will soon encounter a sanyasi with the trident in hand who emerges from his own body and threatens to plunge the weapon into his body should his mind stray from God; and a young man looking 'exactly like' Sri Ramakrishna who emerges out of his own body and guides him through rituals and meditative states.
- When the image itself is ambiguous, the interpretation that Sri Ramakrishna reads into it is what our religious teaching contains: recall the reservoir of water covered by scum, and the wind moving a little of the scum—maya—and the scum covering the clear water again...

- The forms and attributes of the deities, and what they do, and the counsel they give in the visions are exactly what are prefigured in our mythologies.

One can maintain that our mythologies ascribe those forms and attributes to the deities because those are what the forms and attributes are, and that is why Sri Ramakrishna divined those very forms and attributes. Or that he experienced them because those are the forms and attributes that, because of our mythologies, we have internalized with our mothers' milk. Was it not William James who said that visions reflect not just the temper of the one having them, but the temper of the times?

- Sri Ramakrishna was prone to trances from his childhood, as we have seen by the frequency with which they occurred and the sorts of things that triggered them.
- Sri Ramana, as he stated himself, used to have fits.

ENTERING SAMADHI, DURING IT, AND RETURNING TO NORMAL AWARENESS

As we have seen, Sri Ramakrishna used to go into samadhi time and again. Mahendranath Gupta and other disciples have left descriptions of the symptoms that would precede his ascending into samadhi as well as his outward appearance when he was in samadhi:

- He would be engaged in ordinary activities—talking to the devotees, walking, listening to songs; and he would become abstracted, 'absent-minded'; he would stop what he was doing—walking, talking, eating...
- Soon, his body would become completely motionless and rigid; his eyes would get transfixed, often at the tip of his nose; his breathing would become next to imperceptible; what he was doing till a moment ago—like reaching his hand out to pick up a morsel of food—would remain where it was; it would be as if he were an inert object, completely oblivious of anything happening around him: the singing would continue, people would put garlands on him. One day

to test him a doctor poked a finger in his eyeball, another day Keshab Chandra Sen arrived and raised his voice, 'I am here, Sir, I am here,' he took the Master's left hand and stroked it—Sri Ramakrishna would neither feel nor know anything...

- Sometimes the onset would be preceded by some ancillary symptoms. To cite just one instance, 'As Narendra sang the line, "And he who chants Thy name becomes immortal," the Master went into *samadhi*. At first his fingers, especially the thumbs, began to tremble...'[31]

- On occasion, he would be 'with his countenance beaming and his lips parted with a smile'.

- On occasion, tears of joy would flow down from the corner of his eyes.

- On occasion, his hair would stand on end.

- Often in that condition, he would talk to the Mother or some other deity.

- Often, he had visions during samadhi. By what we may think of as 'lucid envisioning', he described these in detail on several occasions—the beauty of Sita, Radha, of course of the Mother; the instructions that he had received from, the exchanges that he had had with the Mother...

- When recounting his first experience of samadhi—the one he had while seeing the swans fly across those dark clouds—he added, 'There are certain characteristics of God-vision. One sees light, feels joy, and experiences the upsurge of a great current in one's chest, like the bursting of a rocket.'[32]

- After varying lengths of time, he would 'return to the plane of relative consciousness'—generally, as he did so, he would draw a deep breath, and would be uttering 'Mother! Mother!' or some similar refrain.

- Often, he would have to be supported even as he came out of samadhi—devotees have left accounts of his 'reeling like a drunkard', and having to be helped down the stairs to the waiting carriage...

Sri Ramana discouraged all queries and speculation about and all discussion of that effulgent experience, telling the questioner to concentrate on the task at hand, and that when he had the peak experience she or he would need no confirmation from anyone else. Sri Ramakrishna tried to describe that experience from time to time but gave up, saying, for instance, that the Mother was preventing him from describing the experience one had as the Kundalini ascended beyond the throat, certainly beyond the penultimate chakra in the middle and at the back of one's eyebrows.[33] As he was fond of saying, a salt doll thought it would find out the depth of the ocean; it plunged into it and dissolved. Who could then describe how deep the ocean was?

SRI RAMANA MAHARSHI'S VISIONS

When he was young, even before he had left for Tiruvannamalai, Sri Ramana used to go into trances—he himself referred to these on occasion: for instance, talking about his second 'death experience' on the Tortoise Rock, which we will consider in some detail later, and how, among other things, it confirmed his belief about the location of the 'Heart', Sri Ramana began by saying, 'I had been saying all along that the Heart centre was on the right, notwithstanding the refutation by some learned men that physiology taught them otherwise. I speak from experience. *I knew it even in my home during my trances.* Again during the incident related in the book *Self-Realization* I had a very clear vision and experience...'[34]

January 1936: Paul Brunton asks Sri Ramana whether the Arunachala Hill is hollow. 'The *Puranas* say so,' the Maharshi replies. 'When it is said that the Heart is a cavity, penetration into it proves it to be an expanse of light. Similarly the Hill is one of light. The caves, etc., are covered up by the Light.' 'Are there caves inside?' Brunton continues. 'In visions I have seen caves, cities with streets, etc., and a whole world in it,' the Maharshi affirms. 'Are there *siddhas* too in it?' 'All the *siddhas* are reputed to be there,' Maharshi answers. 'Are there only *siddhas* or others also?' 'Just like this world...' says the Maharshi. The conversation drifts to Mount Kailash being the abode of Shiva and Arunachala being Shiva Himself...[35]

Here we have one of the few instances in which Sri Ramana talks of a specific vision that he has experienced. But it is by no means the only instance.

October 1946: Sri Ramana is talking with a few devotees. A devotee asks, 'It seems Bhagavan once had a dream and saw so many *siddhas* assembled before him, that they looked all familiar to him and that he sat there on a dais with *chinmudra*.' Sri Ramana replies, 'Is that the only thing? *I have seen several such visions.* What am I to say? Once I came across a *sunai* (a spring in a cave); I went towards it. As I approached, it was getting wider, and there were trees on either side. It became broader and broader. There was good light and the passage led to a big tank. In the middle of the tank was a temple.' Mudaliar asked, 'This was not a dream?' 'Whether it was a dream or *jagrat* (waking),' Sri Ramana replied, 'call it what you like.' Narrating another instance, Sri Ramana clearly alludes to it as a dream—in which he sees vast streets with imposing houses on either side leading to the Ashram, and from which he suddenly wakes up. From this, Mudaliar drew an inference: 'When Bhagavan distinctly calls this [the second instance] a dream and the previous experience he leaves to others to call, dream or waking, I am led to believe that the other vision of the tank and the temple was in the waking or some other stage, which was not dream.'[36]

15 January 1949: It is afternoon. Nagamma Suri reaches the hall. One of the devotees asks Sri Ramana about the high temples and gardens he had said he had seen on the Arunachala Hill.

> Yes. That was perhaps when I was in the Virupaksha Cave. I closed my eyes. I felt I was walking on the hill itself towards the northeast. I saw at one place a nice flower garden, a big temple, a fine compound wall and a big Nandi (a bull carved in stone). There was a strange light. It was extremely pleasant. As I was looking at all these, it was time for *puja*. The bell was rung and immediately after that I opened my eyes.

The devotee says, 'Bhagavan told us some time back that there was a big cave also.' Sri Ramana elaborates:

> Yes, yes. That also happened when I was living on the hill. I was wandering about aimlessly when I found at one place a big cave. When I entered the cave, I saw a number of waterfalls, beautiful gardens, tanks within those gardens, well laid paths, fine lighting; everything there was most pleasing. As I went farther

and farther I saw a Realized Person (*Siddha Purusha*) seated like Dakshinamurthy under a tree on the banks of a tank. Around him, a number of saints (*munis*) were seated. They were asking something and he was replying to them. That place appeared to me very familiar. That is all. I opened my eyes. Subsequently, after some time, when I saw *Arunachala Purana* in Sanskrit, I found the following slokas wherein Lord Siva says...

Sri Ramana recites the slokas, and continues:

In these two shlokas that cave and that *Siddha Purusha* have been described and so I was surprised that what appeared to me in a trance was to be found in that book. So I translated them into Tamil: '*Angiyuru vayumoli mangugiri yaga...*' Its meaning is: 'Though you are in the form of fire, you have kept away the fire and have taken the shape of a hill mainly to shower your blessings on the people. You are always living here in the form of a *Siddha*. The cave that appeared to me is in you with all the luxuries of the world.'

Recently when the temple in Adi Annamalai was renovated, it has been reported that in the *sanctum sanctorum* of the temple a large tunnel was found and when people tried to find out its extent they saw that it was extending to the very centre of the hill. As they could not go in very far, they came back. I therefore thought that which occurred to me and that which is in the *Purana* appears to be true and that the tunnel was the way to the place I had seen. It is reported that *Siddha Purushas* come from the cave inside to the temple through that tunnel night after night and go back after worshipping Ishwara. Why so far? Recently, something like that was seen even here. I was going on to the hill as usual when, as I was getting near the steps over there, a big city appeared before me. There were huge buildings of several varieties, well laid thoroughfares, good lighting; and it appeared to be a great city. At one place a meeting was being held. Chadwick was with me. He was even saying, 'Bhagavan, all this is so self-evident! Who will believe if we say this is all a dream!' Everything appeared as if it was actually happening. Meanwhile, I opened my eyes.

As is apparent, Sri Ramana takes the vision literally—he finds confirmation in verses written centuries earlier, as well as in the fact that more recently diggers have found a tunnel going down from the sanctum sanctorum. Second, the ending this time is more ambiguous than Devaraja Mudaliar had inferred.

'Is all this really a dream?' the devotee inquires.

Sri Ramana: 'I can't say whether it is a dream or not. What is real?'[37]

CONSIDERATIONS

Other instances can be cited. But four points stand out.

First, the atmosphere in which both our saints grew up was intensely religious. It is not necessary to hypothesize that their parents and families were extraordinarily religious from their childhood. It is just that they were *ordinarily* religious. The family and environs of Sri Ramakrishna were, of course, intensely and conventionally religious. Visions with religious overtones; festivals that were intertwined with religion; watching, staging, acting in plays around religious themes; singing devotional songs; narrating and listening to stories from the Puranas; shaping clay and stones into tiny deities; following sadhus around when they wandered through the village and listening to them ... religion was the warp and woof of life. The atmosphere in which Sri Ramana grew up was no different. A single fact will give us a glimpse of what those days were like. After observing that 'As for spirituality, philosophic culture, or religious devotion, Sundaram Ayyar'—the young Venkataraman's father—'could not boast of any marked trait'; that the usual pujas would be performed by a priest, food would be given to tiny images, there would be the occasional visits to the temple, Narasimha Swami adds, 'We note with interest, however, a peculiar feature of his family. One member of each generation gave up home and all comforts and turned ascetic.' Narasimha Swami lists the cases, as well as the legend that is 'narrated by the old folk about the origin of this family trait'. An ascetic had come to the family. He had not been shown the proper respect, nor been given a meal. Thereupon, he cursed the family that 'one member of the family should turn ascetic and wander about in quest of food'.[38]

Second, the temper of the times was intensely religious—people routinely believed our myths to be historical facts; they believed in goddesses and gods; they believed in the efficacy of rituals; they believed in ghosts, and in paranormal phenomena. To take an instance, both Sri Ramakrishna and Sri Ramana thought little of siddhis, of what would conventionally be regarded as supernatural powers—they were a diversion, if not a trap that would lead the aspirant astray; but both thought it perfectly feasible for sadhakas to acquire them if they were bent upon doing so.

Both the sages believed in anthropomorphic deities. For Sri Ramakrishna, the Devi could not just be seen in different female forms, she talked, she guided, she answered prayers, her moods changed, she, though all-knowing—'God can hear the anklets of an ant,' Sri Ramakrishna used to say—felt it necessary to test devotees. Sri Ramana, of course, was a non-dualist, and yet his veneration for the hill, Arunachala—his conviction that the hill was Shiva himself—was akin to our customary propensity to endow life into an inanimate entity.

In a word, though the sages were so far above anyone that we can even imagine, their conception of deities was as conventional and familiar as, say, the paintings that Raja Ravi Varma made are to us. They wore the kinds of dresses that were common in the days of these sages, they were often bedecked in ornaments that were equally familiar—recall the Sita and Radha that Sri Ramakrishna saw in his visions. Did our sages see these forms because that is how the gods and goddesses, in fact, are? Or did they see them thus because that is what they had grown up believing the gods and goddesses look like? The gods and goddesses were conventional in another sense, one that is vital for a devotee. Presumably, their bodies did not need what our bodies need—food, water, etc. But they thought and reacted like so many ordinary humans would, or, more accurately, they thought and reacted like the good and compassionate among us would do—except, we have to concede, in one respect: they put their devotees through trials that were far more severe than ordinarily compassionate and good persons would put anyone through.

Third, in the case of Sri Ramana, the instances of visions that have been recorded are far fewer than the ones we encounter in the case of Sri Ramakrishna—Sri Ramakrishna revelled in and seemed to live amidst visions.

Fourth, the visions that are reported in Sri Ramana's case and those in the case of Sri Ramakrishna differ in their content; and the differences correspond to the differences in the religio-cultural milieu in which the two grew up—the visions of Kali the Mother, of Krishna and Radha, of Sri Chaitanya in one case, and those of siddhas, of the cavity inside the Arunachala Hill in the other.

TRIGGERS

There is another, enormous, difference between the states of Sri Ramakrishna and of Sri Ramana. In the case of Sri Ramana, once he has been through those three-and-a-half years of superhuman austerities and absorption, he more or less stays in an even state. As he said little about the state in which he lived, we can only hypothesize about it: we can either assume that he was forever in an exalted state, 'one with the universe'; or that he lived in the state of ordinary consciousness, and talked, and triggered glimpses of the ultimate experience in devotees by his gaze, and walked around the hill, and ate, and studied, and composed poems and sutras in that state; and only on the special occasions, when he willed to do so, did he ascend into the exalted state.

Sri Ramakrishna, on the other hand, is forever moving from the ordinary to the extraordinary state. He said that the Mother had directed him to always remain between the relative and the absolute plain. He also preferred to do so, he said often: 'I do not want to *be* sugar'—that is, I do not want to lose myself in the Ultimate completely; 'I want to taste it.' Therefore, we always find him moving from one plane to the other. One moment, he is talking to his devotees, and suddenly—a mere word having been uttered, a sight coming into view—and he is lost to the world.

The incidents were a daily occurrence, and so it would take long to list them all. But to get a glimpse, let us list even a few of the triggers that propelled him to the exalted state, one in which he is lost to the world.

The sight of dark clouds, and a flock of swans flies across them ... He is acting the role of Shiva in a village play ... He is acting different roles in the drama troupe ... The priest initiating him into the duties of worshipping the Mother whispers a mantra into his ear ... Looking at the temple of Radhakanta ... As they approach

Benares ... At the various sights of Vrindavan connected with the life of Krishna ... At the sight of a disciple, Rakhal (often), at the sight of Narendra (often) ... On each and every one of these occasions, Sri Ramakrishna goes into samadhi, and just as often has a vision.

Sri Ramakrishna and his close disciples have sat down at lunch. A disciple sings a song in praise of the Mother. 'Hearing the song, Sri Ramakrishna went into Samadhi,' Mahendranath recorded, 'his whole body became still, and his hand remained touching the plate of food. He could eat no more. After a long time his mind came down partially to the plane of the sense world, and he said, "I want to go downstairs." A devotee led him down very carefully. Still in an abstracted mood, he sat near the singer. The song had ended. The Master said to him very humbly, "Sir, I want to hear the chanting of the Mother's name again."'[39]

Sri Ramakrishna is teaching devotees not to regard one path as superior to another: the mother prepares fish to suit the taste of each child—for the one who likes his dish spicy, she prepares a spicy fish; for another she make a soup of it ... The rishis followed the path of jnana, he tells them. When Rama entered the court, it is said he had the splendour of a thousand suns. Why did the rishis not get burned up? Because Rama's effulgence was like the warmth of the sun due to which lotuses bloom ... 'As the Master uttered these words, standing before the devotees, he suddenly fell into an ecstatic mood,' Mahendranath recorded. 'His mind was withdrawn from external objects. No sooner did he say, "the lotus of the heart burst into blossom", than he went into deep *samadhi*. He stood motionless, his countenance beaming and his lips parted in a smile. After a long time he returned to the normal consciousness of the world. He drew a long breath and repeatedly chanted the name of Rama, every word showering nectar into the hearts of the devotees. The Master sat down, the others seating themselves around him...'[40]

As he utters the words 'Eternal Consort of my soul' and 'Govinda', he again goes into samadhi ... As Rakhal repeats half-aloud the name of God ... At the mere mention of Krishna and Arjuna ... Standing before an image ... The moment he hears that Keshab Chandra Sen has talked to the Divine Mother and laughed and cried ... As he listens to the story of Prahlad's love for God ... As he looks at the sun ... As devotional songs are sung at a Hari Sabha—'That day they feared I might give up my body'...[41]

AT THE THEATRE

Accompanied by Mahendranath and a few other devotees, Sri
Ramakrishna goes to the Star Theatre. The *Chaitanyalila* is to be
performed. The play opens. The singer sings about the vidyadharis,
the munis and rishis having come down to earth to pay respects to
Sri Chaitanya who has just been born. 'Sri Ramakrishna watched
the scene and was overpowered with divine ecstasy. He said to "M":
"Look at it! Ah! Ah!"' '... The *vidyadharis* sing praises: the Master
went into deep *samadhi*. The orchestra played on, but he was not
aware of the outer world' ... Another scene: A guest has come to the
house of Nimai's parents; while departing, the guest sings a hymn
addressed to the parents ... 'Listening to the hymn, the Master
was thrilled with ecstasy' ... The next scene is on the banks of the
Ganga: 'M' was seated beside the Master. Sri Ramakrishna could not
control himself. He cried out, 'Ah!' and shed tears of love. He said to
Baburam and 'M': 'Don't make a fuss if I fall into an ecstatic mood
or go into *samadhi*. Then the worldly people will take me to be a
cheat' ... Nimai is invested with the sacred thread; the gods sing his
praises. 'Listening to the music, the Master went into *samadhi*. The
curtain fell and the orchestra played on...' The next scene: Nimai
has fallen at the feet of Srivas; Sri Ramakrishna looked at 'M'. He
was eager to say something but he could not. His voice was choked
with emotion; the tears ran down his cheeks; with unmoving eyes he
watched Nimai clinging to Srivas's feet and saying, 'Sir, I have not yet
attained devotion to Krishna' ... The play proceeds; Nimai sings. 'At
this song Sri Ramakrishna went into *samadhi*. He remained in that
state for a long time. The orchestra played on. Gradually his mind
came down to the relative plane...'[42]

He is in Vrindavan. He sees cowherds crossing the river. He
cries out, 'O Krishna, where are You?' and falls and becomes
unconscious...

He is taken to the Calcutta zoo. He sees a lion, and goes into
samadhi. He explains that 'the carrier of the Mother awakened in
my mind the consciousness of the Mother Herself'. He has to be
taken back without seeing the other animals...[43]

As he describes the nature of Ultimate Reality to his disciples
... As he begins to perform a little japa ... At the mere mention
of the Divine Wine ... As he scolds a Babaji ... On the way to the

Vishwanath Temple and inside it ... At Allahabad, at Vrindavan, at Mathura ... At the Govardhan Hill ... In Benares he wants to listen to the veena. An expert player is found. 'The first notes had scarcely fallen on his ears, when Sri Ramakrishna went into *samadhi*. Half regaining consciousness, he prayed to the Divine Mother, "Don't take away my consciousness, Mother, I wish to enjoy the veena." He listens to the recital for three hours...[44]

On ever so many occasions, those who were present recorded how, upon hearing a song, upon the mention of the Mother or Krishna or Radha or Gauranga ... Sri Ramakrishna would go into a trance.*

---

*Catholic readers will be reminded of the Blessed Giles of Assisi (d. 1262). As Butler narrates in his *Lives of the Saints*, 'Simple though he was and devoid of book learning, Brother Giles was endowed with an infused wisdom which caused him to be consulted by persons of all conditions. Experience soon taught those who sought his advice to avoid certain topics or words, the very mention of which sent the friar into an ecstasy, during which he appeared lost to the world. Even the street urchins knew this, and would shout "Paradise! Paradise!" when they saw him. He held learned men in veneration, and once asked St Bonaventure whether the love of ignorant folk for God could equal that of a scholar. "Yes, indeed," was the reply. "A poor illiterate old woman can love Him better than a learned doctor of the Church." Delighted at this response, Brother Giles rushed to the garden gate which overlooked the entrance to the city and shouted, "Listen, all you good old women! You can love God better than Brother Bonaventure!" He then was rapt in an ecstasy which lasted for three hours...' (Alban Butler, *Lives of the Saints*, Complete Edition, edited, revised and supplemented by Herbert J. Thurston and Donald Attwater, Christian Classics, Westminster, Maryland, 1990, pp. 1594-96, at p. 1595). There is another instance associated with Blessed Giles, which could as well relate to Sri Ramakrishna! The Pope had heard a great deal of the simplicity, poverty and piety of Blessed Giles, as also of the penetrating insights of his direct and heartfelt sermons. Passing near Perugia, he decided to visit Giles. The conversation turned to God and matters divine. Giles went into ecstasy ... Another incident puts one in mind of Sri Ramana: 'As far as possible he lived a retired life, in the company of one disciple who afterwards declared that, in all the twenty years they spent together, his master had never uttered a vain word. His love of silence was indeed remarkable. A beautiful story relates that St Louis of France on his way to the Holy Land secretly disembarked in Italy to visit its shrines. At Perugia he sought out Brother Giles, of whom he had heard much. Having clasped each other in loving embrace, they knelt side by side in prayer and then parted, without having outwardly exchanged a single word' (Alban Butler, op. cit., p. 1595). Except for the embrace and kneeling to pray together, a description of someone meeting Sri Ramana!

A few features would be apparent:

- Sri Ramakrishna has a very high sensitivity,
- A wide variety of stimuli propel him into an ecstatic state,
- These stimuli are both visual and auditory,
- They are triggered just as often and as readily by what he is doing or saying as by what someone else is doing or saying, and
- All of them have one thing in common: they relate to religion and to religious figures that he venerates—perhaps the veena too as it is the instrument Goddess Saraswati plays.

CONSEQUENCES

By the end of his sadhana, Sri Ramakrishna sees God in everything, in everybody. 'One day I was riding in a carriage. I saw two prostitutes standing on a verandah. They appeared to me to be embodiments of the Divine Mother Herself. I saluted them,' he tells his devotees. 'I cannot cut a lemon,' he tells them. 'The other day I managed to cut one only with great difficulty; I chanted the name of Kali and cut the fruit as they slaughter an animal before the Goddess. One day I was about to gather some flowers. They were everywhere on the trees. At once I had a vision of Virat; it appeared that His worship was just over. The flowers looked like a bouquet placed on the head of the Deity. I could not pluck them.' 'God sports through man as well,' he continues. 'I see man as the embodiment of Narayana. As fire is kindled when you rub two pieces of wood together, so God can be seen in man if you have intense devotion. If there is suitable bait, big fish like carp gulp it down at once. When one is intoxicated with *prema*, one sees God in all beings. The *gopis* saw Krishna in everything; to them the whole world was filled with Krishna. They said that they themselves were Krishna. They were then in a God-intoxicated state. Looking at the trees, they said, "These are hermits absorbed in meditation on Krishna." Looking at the grass they said, "The hair of the earth is standing on end at the touch of Krishna."

'Let me tell you a very secret experience,' Sri Ramakrishna confides in his devotees. 'Once I had entered the wood near the pine-grove, and was sitting there, when I had a vision of something like the hidden door of a chamber. I couldn't see the inside of the chamber. I tried to bore a hole in the door with a nail-knife, but did not succeed. As I bored, the earth fell back into the hole and filled it. Then suddenly I made a very big opening.' Uttering these words, the Master remained silent, Mahendranath Gupta recorded. After a time he said: 'These are very profound words. I feel as if someone were pressing my mouth. ... I have seen with my own eyes that God dwells even in the sexual organ. I saw Him once in the sexual intercourse of a dog and a bitch ... The universe is conscious on account of the Consciousness of God. Sometimes I find that this Consciousness wriggles about, as it were, even in small fish...'[45]

As Brahman had come to pervade everything and everybody, Sri Ramakrishna went into ecstasy at the mere mention of the word 'wine' or 'hemp', and 'obscene words'; or even the vagina—as that reminded him of the Brahmayoni from which all creation emanates. For the disciples, this was a bit strange at first sight, but soon they saw it as manifestation of the fact that the Master had transcended notions of good and bad, of decent and indecent. Here is how Swami Saradananda describes what used to happen:

Many thoughts are cropping in our minds in connection with the Master's inability to take wine. Many were the occasions on which we actually saw that mentioning the words 'hemp', 'wine', etc., in the course of conversation, he became filled with divine inebriation and even entered into *samadhi*. Many a time we saw the wonderful Master enter into *samadhi* uttering the name of that part of the female body, at the very name of which, our rougish minds, proud of culture, are filled with the idea of vile enjoyment; or, knowing that such ideas were sure to arise in their minds, those who consider themselves refined, call it obscene, shut their ears against it or protect themselves by flying to a distance. Again, as soon as he got down from the plane of *samadhi* and regained a little normal consciousness, we heard him saying in this connection, 'Mother, Thou hast indeed assumed the forms of the fifty letters. [Saradananda explains that the Sanskrit alphabet has fifty letters.] Those letters of Thine constitute also the obscene and indecent words. The *ka, kha,* of Thy Veda and Vedanta, and those of obscene and indecent words, surely are not different. The obscene and indecent words as well as the Veda and Vedanta are verily Thyself.' Saying so, he entered into *samadhi* once more. Alas, who will understand, far less explain, what an indescribable wonderful Light beyond the grasp of our minds and intellects there was in the eyes of that extra-ordinary god-man, that used to illumine all the things, good and bad, of the world!...[46]

Being driven in a carriage, he sees drunkards making merry in a grog shop—and that is enough to send him into samadhi.[47] He has a vision of Lord Jagannath. Trying to embrace him, he falls and breaks his arm. The temple music sends him into samadhi. He sees someone close an umbrella, and that sends him into samadhi—'It reminded him of withdrawing the mind from the world and giving it to God.'[48]

All-encompassing Sensitivity

In the same way, and for the same reason—that he saw Brahman pervading everyone and everything—Sri Ramakrishna's sensitivity came to encompass everything and everybody. Swami Saradananda describes how Sri Ramakrishna saw Rama in a butterfly with a tiny stick stuck in its tail. On another occasion, he was looking at new durva grass that had come up in a patch in the garden of the Kali temple. He had 'transcended the normal consciousness and was feeling identified with that spot when a man just happened to walk across that field at which he became very restless, feeling considerable pain in his chest. Mentioning that event he said, I then felt just that kind of pain which is felt when anybody tramples on one's chest. That state of *Bhavasamadhi* is very painful. Although I had it for six hours only, it was very painful.' And yet again, Swami Saradananda narrates:

One day the Master while in *Bhavasamadhi* was looking on the Ganga, standing at the spacious *Ghat* with the open portico. Two boats were anchored at the *Ghat* and the boatmen were quarrelling over some matter. The quarrel became gradually bitter and the stronger man gave a severe slap on the back of the weaker. At that, the Master cried out suddenly with pain. Hriday heard it from the Kali temple, went there quickly and saw that the Master's back had become red and swollen. Impatient with anger, Hriday said repeatedly, 'Uncle, show me the man who has beaten you; I'll tear off his head.' When afterwards the Master quietened down a little,

Hriday was astonished to hear of the event and thought, 'Is it ever possible?'

'Girish Chandra Ghosh heard the event from the Master's lips and narrated it to us,' Swami Saradananda added.[49]

HENCE, A PURPOSE IN EVERYTHING

As everything is Brahman, nothing happens but for a purpose. Sri Ramakrishna is in samadhi. He falls, and breaks his teeth. That has happened, he concludes, because the Mother had asked him to remain in bhava, and he has strayed. He breaks his arm trying to grasp Lord Jagannath in a vision. He concludes that this has happened to erase his ego further—excessive of the Mother, I would think, for Sri Ramakrishna is the embodiment of humility already. In the end, he is seized by the most excruciatingly painful cancer. He concludes that this illness has been sent down so as to sift the genuine devotees from the ones who have flocked for boons; on another occasion, he says that the illness has been sent upon him so that he may transit from the saguna to the nirguna.

Sri Ramana had the same conviction. He affirmed time and again that not a leaf moves but that it is foreordained to do so. Even so trivial a matter as to whether I will pick up a glass of water or not, whether I will move from this room to another one or not, whether the orange pickle Sri Ramana wants will be sent by some devotee or not, whether an aspirant will renounce the world or not, *everything*, he declared, has already been determined. And to everything there is a purpose: everything happens because of God's Will—which is inscrutable sometimes, or because our prarabdha karma is being fulfilled.[50]

A TRAIT

Were the persons not Sri Ramakrishna and Sri Ramana, we would be reminded of the psychologists' talk of a proclivity to detect a pattern in almost everything, even in random events, and to read significance into them: the person discerns faces in clouds, figures in the weave of a carpet, a random noise is taken to contain a message from on high, portents are read into coincidences, a divine purpose is read into an illness.

Ordinary persons also tend to see mere coincidences as miracles, to see faces in clouds, in weaves of carpets, in a word to detect patterns. Evolutionary psychologists tell us that this is a faculty that has evolved because it helps survival: the bush rustles because of the breeze, but our brain alerts us to danger—maybe there is a wild animal there; if there isn't, no harm is done; but if there is a tiger, and we did not apprehend it, we may end up as his lunch. Even in ordinary persons this built-in faculty eventually paves the way for our believing in the supernatural.[51]

COUNTERPARTS

We will learn more about the visions that the two saints saw, the conversations that Sri Ramakrishna had with the Mother, the conviction that they so often had of the deity being present— sometimes so very close to them—as we go along. In the next chapter, for instance, we will glimpse a particular feature of the visions that Sri Ramakrishna saw and that will contain a possible clue to the origin of the saints' visions in general. And soon we will turn to explorers and mountaineers, to sailors sailing across oceans by themselves, and to the certainty that so many of them have felt—that another person is present who is guiding them out of danger.

We will find it easier to approximate possible explanations if we distance ourselves from the fact that the narratives we have just read are accounts by and about two saints. Second, if we peel away symptoms from each other. And, third, if we use some word other than 'hallucinations'—for the word 'hallucinations' has got so intertwined with pathologies, even with some forms of mental illness. Perhaps 'imaginings'? With these steps taken, consider one symptom, and what physicians would say if they did not know that the person involved was Sri Ramakrishna.

A SYMPTOM THAT WAS CURED

One particular symptom tormented Sri Ramakrishna a great deal. It was cured by the Brahmani; it recurred, and was again cured, this time by a lawyer who was interested and well versed in spiritual matters—and there is a clue in each of the cures that neurologists and psychologists would pick out. From the beginning of his sadhana, Sri Ramakrishna began to have a severe burning sensation over his body. 'It increased by degrees and became unbearable,' Sri Ramakrishna recalled. 'Various kinds of oils prescribed by physicians were used; but it could by no means be alleviated. One day, while I was sitting under the Panchavati, I saw that a jet-black person with red eyes and a hideous appearance came reeling, as if drunk, out of this (showing his own body) and walked before me. I saw again another person of placid mien, in ochre-coloured dress with a trident in his hand, similarly come out from the body, vehemently attack the other and kill him. The burning sensation in the body decreased for a short time after I had that vision. I suffered from that sensation continually for six months before the *paap-purush* was burnt up.'

The sensation began to torment him again a short time after the paap-purush had been burnt up. Sri Ramakrishna was told that this sensation had arisen because he had gone beyond the limits of devotion enjoined by the scriptures. He persevered. The sensation became more and more unbearable. He said that he found no relief even when he put a wet towel on his head and kept his body immersed in the Ganga for three or four hours at a time; and even though, on coming out, he would 'roll on the marble floor of the proprietor's mansion carefully wetted with a damp cloth'. Later, when the Bhairavi Brahmani heard of it, she declared that it was not a disease but the result of his intense love of God. She prescribed a cure: adorn him with garlands of scented flowers, and smear his body with sandal paste. This cured the sensation.

The sensation returned when he started practising the Madhurabhava, the aspect of being the spouse of the Lord. Hriday described it as if 'a pot-full of live embers is placed within one's breast'. Eventually the sensation was cured by a lawyer who was a sadhaka: he advised that an amulet with a mantra enclosed in it be worn by Sri Ramakrishna. This cured him of the sensation.[52]

An ailment that comes on under extreme anxiety—the singular, exclusive intense, overpowering, all-consuming longing for realizing God, and the constant apprehension that one may not be able to attain that goal: recall Sri Ramakrishna's remarks to Totapuri when the latter was guiding him to the peak experience of non-duality. An ailment that comes on under extreme anxiety, an ailment that yields to garlands of scented flowers, sandal paste, and an amulet with a mantra enclosed in it.

What would the physician say if the bare ailment, the burning sensation alone, its recurrence when there was a new goal and the anxiety whether one would reach it, and the cures that worked, were narrated, and the physician was not told that the subject concerned was none other than Sri Ramakrishna? Assume as a thought experiment that the burning sensation occurred to an athlete before each great tournament. What would the physician diagnose the ailment to be? That it is almost a textbook case of a psychosomatic affliction?

Clues from Elsewhere

That whenever it is released a trigger may set off a cascade of events in the brain, of course, is a well-known phenomenon that occurs in several other conditions. Epileptic seizures are a ready example. And among triggers that have been well documented is music. There are fascinating parallels between cases of persons in whom the way seizures are triggered by music and the way ecstasy was triggered in Sri Ramakrishna by names, events, sights, and yes, music.[53] Going into the parallels, and the manifest differences will take us too far afield. One point described by Oliver Sacks in his *Musicophilia* though deserves mention as it contains a clue.

A patient, 'Mrs. C', Sacks tells us, had lost some of her hearing. She used to have musical hallucinations. Sacks told the concerned doctors that these hallucinations were not psychotic but neurological, 'so-called "release" hallucinations'. 'Given her deafness,' Sacks said, 'the auditory part of the brain, deprived of its usual input, had started to generate a spontaneous activity of its own, and this took the form of musical hallucinations, mostly musical memories from her earlier life. *The brain needed to stay incessantly active, and if it was not getting its usual stimulation, whether auditory or visual, it would create its own stimulation in the form of hallucinations.* Perhaps the prednisone or the sudden decline in hearing for which it was given had pushed her over some threshold, so that release hallucinations suddenly appeared.'[54]

Now, here is a clue: a sensory input diminishes, the brain keeps active, it creates its own stimulus in the form of a hallucination. During meditation, in particular in what the Buddhists term as 'immersion states', we abstract ourselves from sensory inputs. To put it in terms that would be closer to the way Sri Ramakrishna spoke, the more we lose ourselves in God, the more we cut out things of the world, and happenings in it, the less we hear and taste and see of the world.

Sacks recalled what a university dean who was also a professional clarinet player had written to him. He—the dean—'had spent a week at a monastery retreat deep in the woods, where he took part in a *sesshin*, an intense meditation practice of nine or more hours a day. After two or three days of this, he started to hear faint music, which he took to be people singing around a distant campfire. The following year he returned, and once again he heard the distant singing, but soon the music got louder and more specific.' 'At its height the music is quite loud,' he wrote. 'It is repetitive and orchestral in nature. It is all slow passages from Dvořák and Wagner...'[55] Sacks also wrote about one of his friends who had sailed the Atlantic by himself. '... there were calm days with nothing to do,' Sacks recalled the friend telling him. On such days, 'he sometimes "heard" classical music "stealing across the water"'. Another person, a botanist, wrote to Sacks about a sea voyage he had undertaken. 'We were at sea for a total of twenty-two days,' the botanist wrote. 'It was very boring. After the first three days, I had read every book that I brought with me. There was nothing to do for entertainment except to watch the clouds and take naps. For days and days, there was no wind, so we simply puttered along at a few knots by running the engine while the sails luffed. I would lie on my back on the deck or on a bench in a cabin and stare out through the Plexiglas window. It was during these long days of complete inactivity that I had several musical hallucinations...'[56]

Sensory deprivation, monotony ... the person starts hearing music...

Sacks saw great merit in the explanation that a Polish neurologist, Jerzy Konorski, had advanced for hallucinations. There are 'afferent connections' of course going from the sense organs to the brain, Sacks wrote, summarizing Konorski's hypothesis; but there are also in addition 'retro connections' going from the brain to the sense organs. In the normal course, the sensory input from our eyes, ears, nose and other sense organs inhibits the 'backflow of activity from the highest parts of the cortex to the periphery,' Konorski had said. *'But if there is a critical deficiency of input from the sense organs, this will facilitate a backflow, producing hallucinations physiologically and subjectively indistinguishable from perceptions...'* 'Konorski's theory provided a simple and beautiful explanation for what soon came to be called "release" hallucinations associated with "de-afferentation".'[57]

Sacks drew attention to the work of another neuroscientist, Rodolfo Llinas. Llinas, Sacks recalled, has written about the role of the nuclei of the basal ganglia, and how they 'seem to act as a continuous, random motor pattern noise generator'. 'When a pattern or fragment might escape now and then and thrust into consciousness a song or a few bars of music, Llinas felt this was purely abstract and "without its apparent emotional counterpart",' Sacks noted, summarizing Llinas's account. 'But something may start randomly—a tic, for example, bursting out of overexcited basal ganglia—and then acquire associations and meaning...' 'Fragmentary music patterns may be emitted or released from the basal ganglia as "raw" music,' Sacks continued, 'without any emotional coloring or associations—music which is, in this sense, meaningless. But these musical fragments make their way to the thalamocortical systems that underlie consciousness and self, and there they are elaborated and clothed with meaning and feeling and associations of all sorts. By the time such fragments reach consciousness, meaning and feeling have already been attached.'[58]

Sensory deprivation ... A random noise generator within the brain ... Some disjointed, meaningless strands break through to conscious awareness ... And the great 'interpreter' as Michael Gazzaniga has termed the left hemisphere, more accurately, a module in the left hemisphere, endows significance and emotional salience to those fragments. It 'discerns' a pattern. It weaves a story, a melody.

One further observation of Sacks, and the similarity will become even more visible. Sacks observed:

Musical hallucinations draw upon the musical experience and memories of a lifetime, and the importance that particular sorts of music have for the individual must surely play a major role. The sheer weight of exposure may also play a significant part, even overriding personal taste—the vast majority of musical hallucinations tend to take the form of popular songs or theme music (and, in an earlier generation, hymns and patriotic songs), even in professional musicians or very sophisticated listeners ... Musical hallucinations tend to reflect the tastes of the times more than the tastes of the individual.[59]

A clue to what our saints 'heard' and 'saw' during their trances? They had from the beginning an exceptional sensitivity, and had honed it into an even more delicate one. The practices they subjected themselves to reduced sensory inputs, in effect they made the saints deaf and blind to such inputs. Phenomena that are universal—because of the 'de-afferentation' that we just read about—occurred. The saints interpreted the phenomena in accordance with their experience and memories; in accordance with what they had so assiduously honed themselves to believe—about God, the Mother, about Krishna, Rama, Chaitanya Mahaprabhu; in accordance with 'the tastes of the times'.

In fact, so much had the saints attuned themselves to their single-minded goal, and, in the case of Sri Ramakrishna, to the celestial beings connected with that goal, that even that initial external trigger—the uttering of a name, the words of a song being sung by someone—would not be necessary. The great neurosurgeon Wilder Penfield, whom we will encounter soon, distinguished between 'sensory precipitation' of seizures—when a sight or sound may trigger one, for instance—and what he called 'psychical precipitation'. The mere effort to recall a name or trying merely to recollect whether the patient had seen a thing before—in some instances, that would be enough to trigger the seizure.[60] Could the same processes trigger a vision?

The intense longing that all our mystics teach is the sine qua non for the ecstatic experience as well as the practices that are to be done again and again and again—like prolonged exercises in visualization—would certainly qualify as the mental processes that could trigger the 'psychical precipitation' to which Penfield alluded.

Nor is this consequence of sensory deprivation and monotony limited to auditory hallucinations.

The Context

Consider the context in which the visions occurred:

- Every concern save one, every goal save one has been foregone: that singular, exclusive goal is to realize God in Sri Ramakrishna's case, and to realize the 'Self' in Sri Ramana's case.
- For this realization, unimaginable austerities have been undergone for years.
- These include complete immobility—'for weeks he sat there like a stone'; sleep deprivation; starvation.
- That shutting out of sensory inputs includes whatever is happening to and in even one's own body.
- During these years, the world and everything that is happening in it have been shut out completely: there may be the occasional lady who brings food, or onlookers, but the aspirant knows nothing of them, he is completely isolated, hermetically sealed.
- The mind is wholly inner-directed, it is turned wholly to what is happening in it: in effect, all sensory input is blocked out.
- As anyone who has entered the meditative stream knows, at first all sorts of thoughts and emotions arise in the mind and all sorts of experiences erupt. If one perseveres, and the saints certainly did—for years and years—a total calm comes to pervade: a vast, calm-to-the-point-of-unchanging ocean is all that remains.

If we could but abstract ourselves from the two saints we would see that this is another textbook case—the textbook circumstance for those imaginings to arise. Sensory input is shut out, and, just as important, whatever is there is unchanging—whether it is the vast expanse of the ocean, or the repetitive sound of a rivulet.

And the person begins to hear music. He gets convinced that there is another being near him, that the being is talking to him, and giving him directions. The music can be so elaborate, the conversations so detailed, and so cogent and clear that, as Oliver Sacks reminds us, the imaginings are known as 'the prisoner's theatre'. Moreover, the sounds are more vibrant, the colours more vivid than the person normally hears or sees, the scenery is more magnificent, the persons who appear are more beautiful than he has ever seen. That is why the person maintains that the sounds and sights are 'realer than real'.

Now, the visions, the sounds are all just firings inside the brain, but the person experiences them as coming from, as being outside. Moreover, to the person they are more real than real. And anyone who has had to attend on a person suffering from hallucinations will testify how difficult it is at that time to convince the person who is 'imagining' that the sounds and sights and persons she is hearing and seeing are not there at all, that they are all happening inside her brain, in the theatre of her own mind.[61]

6

'The collyrium of love'

Sri Ramakrishna develops an intense yearning to see the Mother in one form, and then in another, and then in yet another. Every time, he meditates on that particular form, and she reveals herself to him in that specific form. This is how Sri Ramakrishna explained this phenomenon to his disciples:

> Look here, just as one who always lives on the sea coast sometimes feels a desire to see what a variety and number of precious things lie hidden at the bottom of the ocean, which is said to be the mine of all gems, so also, although I realized Her and remained always beside Her, I felt a desire to enjoy the Mother, who is of innumerable forms and is the embodiment of endless relations, in as many forms and relations as She would be pleased to show me. Therefore, whenever I desired to see or enjoy Her in any particular form or relation, I persisted in praying importunately to Her to reveal Herself to me in that form or relation. The compassionate Mother on Her part made me personally do whatever was necessary and supplied me everything required and revealed Herself to me in that form and in that relation. It was thus that all the various disciplines were performed.[1]

In Various Bhavas

The same sequence follows when Jatadhari, a sadhu of considerable attainments, passes through Dakshineswar. The sadhu has an idol of the child Rama, Ramlalla. He is utterly devoted to it. He bathes it, offers it food ... Sri Ramakrishna observes the sadhu, and his devotion to the idol. Soon, Sri Ramakrishna begins to see the idol as a living, prancing child: '...by various sweet childish pranks, the Master said, the extraordinary effulgent Child made him forget everything else, tried to detain him daily near It, watched his path in expectation of his coming and accompanied him everywhere in spite of his requests not to do so.' The idol is cheerful only when Sri Ramakrishna is around, his biographer tells us; it dances, it jumps on Sri Ramakrishna's back, it sits in his lap, it runs off to the Ganga in spite of Sri Ramakrishna admonishing it not do so lest it burn its feet in the sun ... so much so that '... sometimes I lost my patience and slapped him. With tearful eyes and trembling lips he would look at me ... Oh what pain I would feel then for having punished him! I would take him in my lap and console him...' Days pass. Eventually, Jatadhari sees that Ramlalla would rather stay back at Dakshineswar than continue roaming with him ... 'This in short is the story of Sri Ramakrishna's *Vatsalya* form of devotion to Sri Rama,' writes Swami Nikhilananda—the form in which the devotee worships God as her or his own child.[2]

There are several bhavas of worship, Swami Nikhilananda reminds us—shanta, that of calm placidity in the Mother's presence; dasya, that of being the servant of the Lord; sakhya, that of being the friend and companion of the Lord; vatsalya, that of being the mother of the God-as-child; madhura, that of being the beloved of the Lord. Sri Ramakrishna practised each of the bhavas to perfection, and in each he lost himself completely.[3]

LORD HANUMAN

Soon after obtaining that vision of the Mother which we have noticed earlier, Sri Ramakrishna is attracted to Lord Rama. His family deity had been Raghuvir. He, therefore, began sadhana in the dasya bhava, believing himself to be Hanuman, the loyal servant of Sri Rama. He described to his devotees later what transpired:

> At that time, I had to walk, take my food and do all other actions like Mahavir. I did not do so on my own accord, but the actions

so happened of themselves. I tied my cloth around my waist so that it might look like a tail and walked, jumping; I ate nothing but fruits and roots, which again I did not feel inclined to eat when skinned. I spent much of my time on trees and always cried, 'Raghuvir, Raghuvir', with a deep voice. Both my eyes assumed a restless expression like those of the animals of that species, and it is marvellous that the lower end of the backbone (coccyx) lengthened at that time by nearly an inch.

Wonderstruck, the disciples, hearing this, asked whether that part of his body was as long still, Swami Saradananda reports. Sri Ramakrishna answered, 'No, in course of time it assumed slowly its previous normal size when the mastery of that mood over the mind had ceased.'

SITA BEQUEATHS HER SMILE

And then:

One day at that time I was sitting under the Panchavati—not meditating, merely sitting—when an incomparable, effulgent female figure appeared before me illuminating the whole place. It was not that figure alone that I saw then, but also the trees and plants of the Panchavati, the Ganga and all other objects. I saw that the figure was that of a woman; for, there were in her no signs of a goddess, such as the possession of three eyes, etc. But the extraordinary, spirited, and solemn expression of that face, manifesting love, sorrow, compassion, and endurance, was not generally seen even in the figures of goddesses. Looking graciously at me, that goddess-woman was advancing from north to south towards me with a slow, grave gait. I wondered who she might be, when a black-faced monkey came suddenly, nobody knew whence, and sat at her feet and someone within my mind exclaimed, 'Sita, Sita who was all sorrow all her life!' Saying, 'Mother' repeatedly, I was then going to fling myself at her feet, when she came quickly and entered this (showing his own body). Overwhelmed with joy and wonder, I lost all consciousness and fell down.

'Before that, I had no vision in that manner without meditating or thinking,' Sri Ramakrishna told his devotees later. 'That was the first vision of its kind. I have been suffering like her all my life perhaps because I saw first of all Sita, who was miserable from her birth.' Swami Saradananda narrated, including to the translator, Swami Jagadananda, that Sri Ramakrishna added that while merging into him Sita had gifted her smile to the Master: 'So,' Swami Jagadananda added, 'those who saw the Master smile, knew how she smiled.'[4]

He often commends the example of Sri Hanuman—as one who is so totally immersed in Lord Rama and in serving him that he knows not, and he cares not for what day of the month it is, of what hour it is. 'A man attains this state when his mind is one hundred per cent absorbed in God. When Hanuman returned from Ceylon, Rama said to him: "You have seen Sita. Tell me, how did you find her?" Hanuman said, "O Rama, I saw that only the body of Sita lay there; it held neither her mind nor her soul. She has indeed consecrated her mind and soul to Your Lotus Feet. Therefore I saw only her body in Ceylon. Further, I saw the King of Death prowling about. But what could he do? It was only a body; it had neither mind nor soul."' 'If you meditate on an ideal you will acquire its nature,' Sri Ramakrishna continues. 'If you think of God day and night, you will acquire the nature of God. A salt doll went into the ocean to measure its depth. It became one with the ocean...'[5]

LORD KRISHNA AND RADHA

Sri Ramakrishna is doing sadhana in madhur bhava—to be the consort of Sri Krishna, as his beloved Radha was. He begins to yearn to know Lord Krishna as his beloved Radha knew him. Dressed as a woman, he begins wearing ornaments of gold, even a head of artificial hair. Because of his devotion to Sri Ramakrishna, and because he understands the Master's goal so much better than others, Mathur arranges these appurtenances for him. Sri Ramakrishna's gestures, his mind become completely that of a woman. He begins to beseech the Mother 'to let him have Krishna for his husband'. 'That prayer became gradually converted into copious weeping and that longing into restlessness, an anxious pining away for the beloved and a sort of madness, making him give up food, sleep, etc.,' Swami Saradananda informs us. The 'burning pain and intense heat' return to torment him. Blood begins to ooze out of the pores of his body. 'All the joints of the body seemed slackened or almost dislocated, the senses completely desisted from functioning and the body lay motionless and unconscious sometimes like that of a dead man—all because of the extreme anguish of the heart.'[6] Sri Ramakrishna comes to realize that he cannot obtain the vision of Krishna without Radha's grace. Hence, he begins to yearn for a vision of Radha. Radha appears to him in a beautiful form and disappears into his own body. 'From now on, the Master began to realize himself as Srimati in ecstasy. He completely lost the consciousness of his separate existence, on account of his profound contemplation of the holy form and character of Radha through his ceaseless feeling of identification with her...' Shortly after the vision of Radha, he is blessed with the vision of Krishna himself. This form of the vision also unites with his body. He is now constantly immersed in thoughts of Krishna, he sees everything, including himself, as Krishna.[7]

ISLAM, JESUS

In 1866, a Sufi, Govinda Ray, visits him. Sri Ramakrishna decides to reach the heights scaled by Islamic mystics. He begins following the prescriptions of Islam. 'I then devotionally repeated the holy syllable "Allah", wore cloth like the Muslims, said *Namaz* thrice daily and felt disinclined even to see Hindu deities, not to speak of saluting them, inasmuch as the Hindu mode of thought vanished altogether from my mind,' Sri Ramakrishna recalled later. 'I spent three days in that mood, and had the full realization of the result of practices according to that faith.' At the time of practising Islam, Swami Saradananda adds, the Master at first had the vision of an effulgent, impressive personage with a long beard; afterwards he had the knowledge of the all-pervading Brahman with attributes and merged finally in the attributeless Brahman, the Absolute.[8]

Eight years later, he is 'seized with an irresistible desire to learn the truth of the Christian religion,' the chronicler records. To the south of the Kali temple, Jadunath Mallick has a garden house. Mallick and his wife are ardent devotees of Sri Ramakrishna. On occasion, he goes to their garden for a walk. In one of the rooms, there is a picture of Mary holding the infant Jesus. Looking at it one day, he sees it come alive, 'and effulgent rays of light, coming out of the bodies of the mother and the Child, entered into his heart and radically changed all the ideas in his mind'. '...the waves of those impressions completely submerged the Hindu ideas in his mind,' Swami Saradananda tells us. 'His love and devotion to the *Devas* and *Devis* vanished, and in their stead a great faith in and reverence for Jesus and his religion occupied his mind...'

The Master came back to Dakshineswar temple and remained constantly absorbed in the meditation of those inner happenings, Swami Saradananda tell us. He forgot altogether to go to the temple of the divine Mother and pay obeisance to her. The waves of those ideas had mastery over his mind in that manner for three days. At last, when the third day was about to close, the Master saw, while walking in the Panchavati, that a marvellous godman of very fair complexion was coming towards him, looking steadfastly at him. As soon as the Master saw that person, he knew that he was a foreigner. He saw that his long eyes had produced a wonderful beauty in his face, and the tip of his nose, though a little flat, did not at all impair that beauty. The Master was charmed to see the extraordinary divine expression of that handsome face, and wondered who he was. Very soon the person approached him and from the bottom of the Master's pure heart came, with a ringing sound, the words, 'Jesus! Jesus the Christ, the great Yogi, the loving Son of God, one with the Father, who gave his heart's blood and put up with endless torture in order to deliver men from sorrow and misery!' Jesus, the godman, then embraced the Master and disappeared into his body and the Master entered into ecstasy, lost normal consciousness and remained identified for some time with the omnipresent Brahman with attributes. Having attained the vision of Jesus thus, the Master became free from the slightest doubt about Christ having been an incarnation of God.[9]

Later, Sri Ramakrishna inquires of his disciples what the Bible says about Jesus' physical appearance. They tell him that it does not describe it. But that, as he had been born a Jew, he must have been fair, they say, but that, for the same reason, he would have had an aquiline nose. Still later, the disciples are surprised to learn that there are three different accounts of Jesus' appearance, and 'according to one of them the tip of his nose was a little flat'.[10]

At one stage—this is when he is practising the tantra mode of worship—Sri Ramakrishna sees the awakening of the Kundalini shakti, the 'Serpent power', Swami Saradananda tells us. Sri Ramakrishna sees it lying asleep at the bottom of the spine. As he meditates, it awakes, and rises through the sushumna nadi from chakra to chakra, and eventually reaches the Sahasrara, the thousand-petalled lotus at the top of the head. As it ascends, the lotus of each chakra blooms. And the ascent is accompanied by visions and trances, Swami Saradananda reports. Later, Sri Ramakrishna describes to his disciples and devotees the various movements of the Kundalini: like the movement of a fish, of a bird, of a monkey...

'AFFECTIVE MYSTICISM'?

Psychologists, of course, have a particular way of looking at what they term 'affective mysticism'—one in which the devotee yearns for the divinity as a person. In particular, when he yearns for the deity as one who is his mother; or whose mother he or she is; or, as in madhur bhava, when the devotee yearns for the divine as his bride or as her husband—as Radha for Krishna, to use Sri Ramakrishna's terms. They observe that such states are common across a wide range of religions, sects, cultures and periods. Recall the yearnings of St Teresa, of the Sufi mystics, of the way the same terms are used for Allah as for the beloved in so much of Urdu and Persian poetry. Recall the 'surrender' to the divine in all traditions, to being the 'bride' of Jesus in convents, to the 'spiritual marriage' in Christianity in general. Recall the deep pathos and longing in the compositions of our bhakti poets, say Meera. So many of the courses that Sri Ramakrishna pursued during his twelve-year sadhana, and through which he had visions of Krishna and others, are exact parallels.

Several analysts recognize that there must have been many factors that ignited such pursuits—the cultural and religious traditions of the people, for instance. A few have pointed to especial, entirely secular factors that seemed to have triggered the movements.[11]

Such special circumstances apart, the underlying explanation that strikes psychologists is that the longing for a mother, lover, husband, infant is the manifestation of, to continue with Herbert Moller, 'substitute gratifications in fantasies'. They would point to the particular bhavas through which Sri Ramakrishna put himself; to his sexual allusions and language and metaphors and similes, which, as we have seen Swami Vivekananda ruled must be sanitized out of the accounts; to his unrelenting warnings against 'kamini, kanchan'; to the extravagant beauty of the female figures—of Sita and Radha, for instance—who appeared in his visions; to his adorning himself in a woman's clothing and ornaments and his gait and demeanour at those times—the psychologists would point to each of these as strong evidence for their thesis. And they would say that as rationalism advanced, and as the 'fulfillment of fantasies was secularized', such 'affective mysticism' waned—it did so from the sixteenth and seventeenth centuries in Europe and it has in India during the last 100–150 years. Perhaps it is easier for us to read such constructions when they are made about persons other than the ones we revere, so here are a few sentences, some literal, some slightly paraphrased from Moller's paper:

> Regressive desires became manifest in preoccupation with the Savior's blood and, in the craving for eating Christ's body (frequent communion), in the contemplation of his sacred heart, and similar phenomena. The eroticized deity could reveal himself as a loving father as well as a helpless infant in a crèche or as a radiant youth. The divine object was experienced by some as a female figure, either as Sancta Sophia or as a feminized Christ with an open wound and helpless in his humiliation. On a still more regressive level, Christ as a mother figure whose breasts gave blissful satisfaction to the mystic ... The soul represented as the bride of God experiencing mystical union through a reflux into the divinity ... Jesus or God as the Divine Husband ... Bride mysticism of Western Europe ... In Judaism and Islam, the remoteness of God and His unconcern with human feelings did not set up an insurmountable dogmatic obstacle to emotional closeness ... In the Middle East too, enthusiastic women, of whom Rabia, a native of Basra, was the most prominent [d. 801 in Jerusalem] ... Her poetry was very similar to the ideas and feelings expressed by Western mystics of the affective type— Allah becomes a composite figure of father, lover, and bridegroom, and the mystic's yearning for union with her 'Divine Friend' ... Whereas among most populations of the world marriage is entered into at an early age the marriage pattern of western and central Europe has been less permissive but highly flexible. Varying with regional customs and economic conditions, the usual age at first

marriage was comparatively late. It appears that this late average age at first marriage and, furthermore, the existence in Western civilization of a relatively large number of persons who never married promoted in the population a psychic susceptibility to affective mysticism ... addressed himself to the Savior as his spouse and his child ... saw in the Holy Spirit or Wisdom (Sophia) a female personage, his 'marvellously beautiful bride' ... The fantasy productions of some male mystics had pronounced homosexual connotations. Participation in the broader movement of affective mysticism permitted these men to deal with their unconscious needs symbolically, through verbalization within an officially recognized thought system, and thus to find relief without arousing anxiety. Others found a chance to compensate their sense of alienation by philosophizing about reunion with 'the One', even though their audience of affective mystics had to assimilate this Neoplatonic symbolism to its specific emotional needs...[12]

Psychologists would see enough triggers in the complete suppression of all worldly desires and goals for such sublimation. In fact, they would conclude that the sublimations would be a natural and ineluctable consequence of such extreme suppression. Most among us would attribute Sri Ramakrishna's vocabulary and similes and his direct speech to the fact that that was the language, that was the manner of speaking and those were the similes and metaphors of the villages of nineteenth-century Bengal. While psychologists would see in the dread of, and in the incessant admonitions against kamini, kanchan almost a sufficient cause for madhur bhava, and vatsalya bhava, most of us would point to three factors:

- In his experience, the slightest trace of worldly desires will thwart the spiritual quest—even one hair sticking out will prevent us from putting the thread through the eye of the needle.
- Of worldly desires, lust and greed are the most potent, and, therefore, the most powerful obstacles that the aspirant must shun.
- His principal concerns centred around the young boys who he intended must devote themselves entirely to a goal far beyond themselves, through whom he aimed to revive our

religion and save our country; precisely because they were young boys, they would be most susceptible to the lures of lust and greed. For these reasons, most of us would think that his incessant warnings about kamini, kanchan were entirely natural.

In short, most persons brought up in the religions and cultures of India would regard the explanations of psychologists as overly reductionist. And in a sense, in the perspective of the psychologists, the emphasis on the 'explanation' drowns out the experience itself—in part because of the seductive powers of something scandalous, something salacious—'O, there is nothing to it. It is just the bursting forth of repressed sexual urges.' Look at Sri Ramana himself: almost none of the features from which psychologists come to conclusions about these phenomena being 'substitute gratifications in fantasies' is visible in Sri Ramana and yet he points in the same direction, his experiences are of the same nature as those of Sri Ramakrishna.

THE STRAIGHTFORWARD EXPLANATION

There is a more straightforward explanation. To discern that, let us read—a little slowly—descriptions of the states into which Sri Ramakrishna was plunged from time to time. Soon after his first trance, the lad Gadadhar, as he was known then, is permitted to worship the idol of Raghuvir, Swami Nikhilananda tells us. 'He so gave his heart and soul to the worship that the stone image very soon appeared to him as the living Lord of the Universe...' A while later, a play is to be staged in the village on Shivaratri. At the last moment, the lead actor who was to play the part of Lord Shiva falls ill. Gadadhar is chosen to play the part, and this is what ensues:

While friends were dressing him for the role of Shiva—smearing his body with ashes, matting his locks, placing a trident in his hand and a string of *rudraksha* beads around his neck—the boy appeared to become absent-minded. He approached the stage with slow and measured step, supported by his friends. He looked the living image of Shiva. The audience loudly applauded what it took to be his skill as an actor, but it was soon discovered that he was really lost in meditation. *His countenance was radiant and tears flowed from his eyes.* He was lost to the outer world. The effect of this scene on the audience was tremendous. The people felt blessed as by a vision of Shiva Himself. The performance had to be stopped, and the boy's mood lasted till the following morning.[13]

This total immersion, this experience—that every idol he worships, that every deity and form he contemplates becomes a reality—becomes the pattern. At Dakshineswar each idol—of the Mother, of Krishna, of Radha—is not an embodiment of some trait of Kali, or Krishna or Radha, it becomes the deity—*the living deity*—itself. He decorates the idol, he feeds it, he converses with it, he teases it, he dances with it...

He has begun assisting his elder brother at the Dakshineswar temple. As part of the preliminaries, a circle of fire and water is symbolically formed around the place of worship to keep evil spirits out. 'As he sat facing the image, a strange transformation came over his mind,' we learn. 'While going through the prescribed ceremonies, *he would actually find himself encircled by a wall of fire—with hundreds of tongues spread out*,' Swami Saradananda says—'protecting him and the place of worship from unspiritual vibrations, or he would feel the rising of the mystic *Kundalini* through the different centres of the body...' He sees the letters of the mantras that he is chanting 'set in his body' in bright colours. Soon, he is being initiated into the duties of priesthood. The officiating priest has but to whisper the Shakti mantra into his ear, and he is '*overwhelmed with emotion, utter[s] a loud cry and plunge[s] into deep concentration*'. He becomes '*still and insensitive and dead to all appearance*'.[14]

He is appointed priest. 'When he sat down to worship,' Swami Nikhilananda writes, '*a curtain of oblivion separated him from the outside world*: he was totally unconscious of the presence of those who usually gathered to attend the services. *Sometimes he would sit motionless for hours, being recalled with difficulty to ordinary consciousness...*' Not much later, 'He could no longer conduct the worship regularly. He would sit before the image like a stone. *At one moment he behaved like a demented person, at the next he would cry like a child*. While meditating in the course of worship, he would put a flower on his head and sit silent for a couple of hours; or while offering food, he would gaze at the Mother as if She were actually partaking of it...' Hriday, his nephew who looked after his needs during this period, reported, 'I noticed that my uncle, taking flowers and *bel* leaves in his hand, touched his own head, chest, in fact, the whole body, including the feet, with them and then offered them at the feet of Kali. At other times, with eyes and chest flushed, like a drunkard he would move with tottering steps from his seat to the throne of the goddess, touch her chin as a sign of endearment, and begin to sing, or talk, joke, laugh, or even dance, taking the image by the hand! Sometimes he would approach the throne with a morsel of food in his hand, and putting it to Her lips, entreat Her to eat...' He would start talking to her—would she eat first or did she want him to do so? ... When the evening services were over, he would ask whether she would like him to rest ... and he would lie down on the silver bedstead meant for her...[15]

We have seen the same sequence repeat itself in regard to the idol of the child Rama that the sadhu Jatadhari has come with to Dakshineswar.

Similarly, as we have seen, after Totapuri left, Sri Ramakrishna remained continuously in a state of nirvikalpa samadhi for six months. Swami Saradananda sets out the Master's own description of his condition and symptoms during this period.[16]

It is a state, Sri Ramakrishna explained to devotees, 'from which ordinary mortals never return'. Indeed, the body dies within twenty-one days. During this period, Sri Ramakrishna had no awareness at all. Flies flew into and out of his nostrils as they do into and out of those of a corpse. He did not even answer the calls of nature consciously. And the only reason he got fed was that a wandering yogi recognized the condition in which he was, and, after beating him into a semi-awake state, from time to time forcibly thrust some food into his mouth.[17] So absolute was his immersion in the state.

Indeed, biographers of Sri Ramakrishna mention several incidents in which his absorption in the role of being a woman was so complete that even those—like Hriday and Mathur—who had known him for years at the closest proximity were not able to recognize him among other women. The worship of the Divine Mother has been arranged. Men are standing on one side of the hall, and women on the other. Dressed in a woman's clothes and ornaments, Sri Ramakrishna is

among the latter. The aarti commences. Here is the sequel as Swami
Saradananda describes it:

> Surrounded by the ladies, the Master began to fan the image
> with a *Chamara*. The ladies stood on one side of the hall and
> the gentlemen including Mathur Babu on the other and were all
> witnessing the *Aarati* of the Divine Mother. As soon as Mathur
> Babu's eyes fell on the ladies, he saw that a lady stood near his wife
> and was fanning the Mother with a *Chamara*, radiating wonderful
> beauty from her person, dress, and ornaments. Although he looked
> again and again he could not know who she was. He thought at
> last that she might be a friend of Jagadamba [Mathur's wife], some
> rich man's wife who had perhaps come by invitation.
>
> The *Aarati* was over. The ladies saluted the divine Mother, went
> back to the inner apartments and were busy doing their duties. In
> that state of partial consciousness, the Master went into the inner
> apartment with Mathur Babu's wife and came gradually to normal
> consciousness. He then took off the dress and ornaments, came
> out and sat with the menfolk and raising various religious topics,
> charmed all by his lucid explanation and apt illustrations.
>
> A little afterwards, Mathur Babu went to the inner apartment on
> some business and asked his wife, in the course of the conversation,
> about the lady who had been standing near her and fanning the
> Mother with a *Chamara* at the time of the *Aarati*. Mathur Babu's
> wife smiled and said in reply, 'Could you not know who she was?
> "Father" in ecstasy was fanning the Divine Mother thus; that is
> quite possible, for one cannot know "Father" to be a man when
> he puts on dress and ornaments like a woman.' Saying so she told
> Mathur Babu everything from beginning to end...[17]

Often, as he sat down to meditate, his body would get locked, so to
say:

> I used to show my mind the image of Bhairava in meditation on
> the parapet of the roof of the music-hall and say to it, 'You must
> be firm and motionless like it and meditate on the Mother's Lotus
> Feet.' No sooner had I sat down for meditation than I heard
> clattering sounds produced in the joints of my body and limbs
> from the direction of the legs upwards; and they got locked one
> after another as if someone from within turned the keys. As long

as I meditated, I had no power to move my body and change my posture even slightly or give up meditation and go elsewhere or do anything else at will. I was, as it were, forcibly made to sit in the same posture, as long as the joints did not make clattering sounds as before and were unlocked, this time from the direction of the head to the legs. When I sat and meditated I had, in the beginning, vision of particles of light like groups of fire-flies; I saw sometimes all quarters covered with masses of mist-like light; and at other times I perceived that all things were pervaded by bright waves of light like molten silver. I saw these things sometimes with my eyes shut and sometimes with my eyes open. I did not understand what I saw nor did I know whether it was good or bad to have such visions. I therefore prayed to Mother with a troubled heart, 'I don't understand, Mother, what is happening to me; I don't know *mantras* etc., by which to call Thee; please teach me personally what may enable me to realize Thee. Mother, if Thou doest not teach me, who else will? For, there is no refuge for me except Thee.' I used to pray thus with a concentrated mind and weep piteously on account of the eagerness of my heart.[19]

The Collyrium of Love

What is common to each of these episodes? Total immersion, absolute absorption. And what is the sine qua non for this degree of absorption?

Longing, Sri Ramakrishna said again and again—profound, exclusive, desperate, superhuman longing. We have seen the frantic condition into which Sri Ramakrishna had fallen in moments before he had a vision of the Mother. That was his condition to which he was reduced, or elevated again and again—throughout the twelve years of sadhana. And by the end of it that longing had become an ever-present constituent, the overwhelming constituent of his being. 'Weeping bitterly during the moments of separation from Her, he would pass into a trance and then find Her standing before him, smiling, talking, consoling, bidding him be of good cheer, and instructing him...' we are told.[20]

'One cannot see God if one has even the slightest trace of worldliness,' Sri Ramakrishna tells his disciples. If there is even one fibre sticking out, the thread will not pass through the needle, he cautions devotees. 'Match-sticks, if damp, won't strike fire though you rub a thousand of them against the match-box. You only waste a heap of sticks. The mind soaked in worldliness is such a damp match-stick.' And, as is his wont, Sri Ramakrishna tells them a story: 'Once Sri Radha said to her friends that she saw Krishna everywhere—both within and without. The friends answered: "Why, we don't see Him at all. Are you delirious?" Radha said, "Friends, paint your eyes with the collyrium of divine love, and then you will see Him"...'[21] 'One should weep for God,' he instructs devotees. 'When the impurities of the mind are thus washed away, one realizes God. The mind is like a needle covered with mud, and God is like a magnet. The needle cannot be united with the magnet unless it is free from mud. Tears wash away the mud, which is nothing but lust, anger, greed, and other evil tendencies, and the inclination to worldly enjoyments as well. As soon as the mud is washed away, the magnet attracts the needle, that is to say, man realizes God. Only the pure in heart see God...'[22]

That love for God, that longing must eclipse all else, most certainly 'kamini, kanchan', 'lust and gold', Sri Ramakrishna's metaphors for worldliness. I can scarcely resist reproducing one incident, as it has a direct parallel with Gandhiji testing himself late in his life, when he decides to sleep with his niece in the same bed. Sarada Devi has come to Dakshineswar. She has fallen ill on the way—she and her father had trudged the distance. She has had a vision of a beautiful dark girl who blesses her. She recovers enough to complete the journey. But she is still ill and frail when she reaches Dakshineswar. Sri Ramakrishna is concerned. He has a cot put for her in his room. When she asks him how he looks upon her, he tells her that he looks upon her as an embodiment of the Holy Mother. One night, as she is asleep, he addresses his own mind:

'This is, O mind, a female body. People look upon it as an object of great enjoyment, a thing highly prized, and they die for enjoying it. But if one goes for it, one has to remain confined in the body and cannot realize God who is Existence-Knowledge-Bliss. Do not, O mind, harbour one thought within and a contrary attitude without. Say in truth whether you want to have it or God. If you want it, it is here before you, have it.' He discriminated thus; but scarcely had he entertained in his mind the idea of touching the person of the Holy Mother, when his mind shrank and at once lost itself so deeply in *samadhi* that it did not regain its normal consciousness that night. He had to be brought back with great effort to normal consciousness the next morning by the repeated utterance of the name of God in his ears.[23]

A Brahmo devotee asks him, 'What are the means by which one can see God?' 'Can you weep for Him with intense longing of heart?' Sri Ramakrishna asks him in return. 'Men shed a jugful of tears for the sake of their children, for their wives, or for money. But who weeps for God? So long as the child remains engrossed with its toys, the mother looks after her cooking and other household duties. But when the child no longer relishes the toys, it throws them aside and yells for its mother. Then the mother takes the rice-pot down from the hearth, runs in haste, and takes the child in her arms.'[24]

'Is it possible to understand God's action and His motive?' Sri Ramakrishna asks those assembled around him, among them some who have suffered blows of fate. 'He creates, He preserves, and He destroys. Can we ever understand why He destroys? I say to the Divine Mother: "O Mother, I do not need to understand. Please give me love for Thy Lotus Feet." The aim of human life is to attain *bhakti*. As for other things, the Mother knows best. I have come to the garden to eat mangoes. What is the use of my calculating the number of trees, branches, and leaves? I only eat the mangoes; I don't need to know the number of trees and leaves.'[25] This is a constant refrain of the Master: that all that happens is because of God's will, it is his lila, play; we must give our 'power of attorney' to God, and trust that whatever happens, happens for the good; further that neither can we nor do we need to understand why God does what He does.

It is eight in the morning. Sri Ramakrishna is talking to Mahendranath Gupta. A doctor arrives. The conversation continues. 'The whole thing in a nutshell is that one must develop ecstatic love for Satchidananda,' Sri Ramakrishna says. 'What kind of love? How should one love God? Gauri used to say that one must become like Sita to understand Rama; like Bhagavati, the Divine Mother, to understand Bhagavan, Siva. One must practise austerity, as Bhagavati did, in order to attain Siva. One must cultivate the attitude of Prakrati in order to realize Purusha—the attitude of a friend, a handmaid, or a mother. I saw Sita in a vision. I found that her entire mind was concentrated on Rama. She was totally indifferent to everything—her hands, her feet, her clothes, her jewels. It seemed that Rama had filled every bit of her life and she could not remain alive without Rama.' Mahendranath interjects, 'Yes, sir. She was mad with love for Rama.' '*Mad*!' exclaims Sri Ramakrishna. '*That's the word. One must become mad with love in order to realize God...*'[26]

Sri Ramakrishna is taken by Mathur on a pilgrimage to Benares, Mathura, Vrindavan, Allahabad. As they approach Benares, he has a vision of it as a city of gold ... At place after place, he is overwhelmed. The party of pilgrims has reached Vrindavan: 'I wanted to visit Shyamakunda and Radhakunda; so Mathur Babu sent me there in a palanquin. We had a long way to go. Food was put in the palanquin. While going over the meadow I was overpowered with emotion and wept: "O Krishna, I find everything the same; only You are not here. This is the very meadow where You tended the cows." Hriday followed me on foot. I was bathed in tears. I couldn't ask the bearers to stop the palanquin...' 'I used to cry for God all alone, with a longing heart,' Sri Ramakrishna recalls to the devotees. 'I used to weep, "O God, where art Thou?" Weeping thus, I would lose all consciousness of the world. My mind would merge in the *Mahavayu*...'[27]

'The Master was in *samadhi*,' Mahendranath Gupta writes. 'He began to come gradually down to the normal plane. His mind was still filled with the consciousness of the Divine Mother. In that state he was speaking to Her like a small child making importunate demands on his mother. He said in a piteous voice: "Mother, why haven't You revealed to me that form of Yours, the form that bewitches the world? I pleaded with You so much for it. But You wouldn't listen to me. You act as You please" ... The Master was weeping and praying to the Mother in a voice choked with emotion. He prayed to Her with tearful eyes for the welfare of the devotees...'[28]

'Ah, That Restlessness Is the Whole Thing'

The Master is talking with Bankim Chandra Chatterjee, in fact he is talking with him sharply, admonishing him about the futility of mere learning. It is yearning for God that one must develop, he tells the great writer. 'One must have for God the yearning of a child. The child sees nothing but confusion when his mother is away. You may try to cajole him by putting a sweetmeat in his hand; but he will not be fooled. He only says, "No, I want to go to my mother." One must feel such yearning for God. Ah, what yearning! How restless a child feels for his mother! Nothing can make him forget his mother. He to whom the enjoyment of worldly happiness appears tasteless, he who takes no delight in anything of the world—money, name, creature comforts, sense pleasure—becomes sincerely grief-stricken for the vision of the Mother. And to him alone the Mother comes running, leaving all Her other duties.' 'Ah, that restlessness is the whole thing,' he continues. 'Whatever path you follow—whether you are a Hindu, a Mussalman, a Christian, a Shakta, a Vaishnava, or a Brahmo—the vital point is restlessness. God is our Inner Guide. It doesn't matter if you take a wrong path—only you must be restless for Him. He Himself will put you on the right path...'[29]

And he narrates a parable: 'A disciple asked his teacher, "Sir, please tell me how I can see God." "Come with me," said the guru, "and I shall show you." He took the disciple to a lake, and both of them got into the water. Suddenly the teacher pressed the disciple's head under the water. After a few moments he released him and the disciple raised his head and stood up. The guru asked him, "How did you feel?" The disciple said, "Oh! I thought I should die; I was panting for breath." The teacher said, "When you feel like that for God, then you will know you haven't long to wait for His vision."'

The Master asks Bankim, 'Let me tell you something. What will you gain by floating on the surface? Dive a little under the water. The gems lie deep under the water; so what is the good of throwing your arms and legs about on the surface? A real gem is heavy. It doesn't float; it sinks to the bottom. To get the real gem you must dive deep.'[30]

Expecting Is Seeing

One feature stands out: Sri Ramakrishna longs for a vision of the Mother, of Sri Rama, of Sita, of Hanuman, of Sri Krishna and Radha, of the different forms of the Mother—and in each instance as the consummation of that phase, the vision he gets is the one for which he has been pining. Not just psychologists, would neuroscientists too not have much to say about this consistent coincidence? As long ago as 1890, William James advanced the concept of 'ideomotor action'—that merely thinking about behaving in a particular way increases the chances that we *will* in fact behave in that way. Surely, there must be a counterpart of that in the realm of imaginings and visions: pining for a vision of the Mother in a particular form multiplies the chances that one *will* envision Her in that form. In cultivating such intense longing, such intense and *exclusive* longing is one not, in a sense, inducing self-hypnosis, and thereby ensuring that the outcome will be what one yearns it be? Is the resulting state what Freud called an 'auto-hypnotic' state in his *Studies in Hysteria*?

That degree of longing, that blocking out everything else for twelve long years: what changes would it not bring about in the very structures in, and processes of the brain! After all, even momentary events lead us to view happenings one way rather than another. A person has been plunged deep in depression since he heard that someone dear to him might have cancer. He reads the morning paper. His mind latches on to reports of things going down the drain ... At last the biopsy report arrives. The initial diagnosis was wrong—she does *not* have cancer. Suddenly, the colour of the world changes. His mind now notices so many things that are going right—a bird he hasn't seen before; a mother smiling into the eyes of her child...

There is not the slightest suggestion of dishonesty in any of this. As it is, we do not see 'things as they are'. We do not hear 'sound'—what reach us are perturbations of air. What is spoken or played by someone is transformed in half a dozen ways before it reaches the threshold of our brain, and there the vibrations are transformed into electrical impulses. We do not see colours. What reach us are frequencies of light. Our auditory and visual systems receive and process them, and we hear 'sound', we see 'colours'— those with synaesthesia 'see' voices, they 'hear' colours. Growing up in a world in which religion is everywhere; shutting out all goals save one—spiritual realization; convincing oneself that the senses are not just misleading, they are enemies; that the mind itself is the enemy-in-chief; and then putting oneself through extreme austerities over extended periods—twelve years in the case of Sri Ramakrishna, three-and-a-half years in the case of Sri Ramana—would change the brain deeply and extensively. The person would 'see' the world and its events very differently. Nor would this be limited to just one event or two, occasionally. His inner 'spectacles' would have changed. He will henceforth see every object in a different light, he will read something very novel into every event, howsoever trivial it might be. And that would apply not just to objects out there in the world. He would infer something very consequential from any and every thought or emotion that arises spontaneously within his mind.

Moreover, he would now reckon on his yearnings coming true—Sri Ramakrishna vis-à-vis the Devi, the devotee vis-à-vis Sri Ramakrishna. When over years and years, we keep dinning the image and traits of the Devi in our mind; when we keep drilling into our mind for years on end that all that we see is unreal, that the only truth is Brahman, the Great Effulgence, we predispose ourselves to *interpret* the ambiguous experiences or visions that arise during meditation, during prolonged sensory deprivation as being flashes of the Devi or the Great Effulgence as the case may be. Meaningless sounds become words. Words become messages. These become Messages from on High. When we keep conditioning our mind into believing that 'no one goes empty-handed from the doors of the Mother,' that she never lets down a believer, that she *does* appear to the one who yearns for her with all his heart, we transform the wish into a longing, longing into anticipation, anticipation into expectation, expectation into confidence, and confidence into certainty. And that in turn conditions us into 'seeing' her come dancing into the temple, we predispose ourselves into 'hearing' her anklets.

In her evocative and empathetic account of the evangelicals in America, the anthropologist Tanya Luhrmann describes how evangelicals learn to feel the presence of God, how they learn to hear Him, how they learn to receive His decisions and guidance even in regard to their smallest day-to-day choices, how they learn to believe and to respond to what their senses deny. She says it is a 'skill' they

develop. The entire process of acquiring that skill she characterizes
as 'attentional learning'. A 'skill', 'attentional learning'—terms that
describe well at least some of the practices that our saints pursued
and the beliefs that they ultimately internalized, and, of course, a
description that will do just as well for the devotees.[31]

Auditory illusions that have been devised and discovered by Diana
Deutsch, professor of psychology at the University of California, San
Diego, and others show us what happens. Four words taken out of
a speech, played over and over again, begin to sound like a song. A
person is speaking; another coughs and blots out a word; our brain
fills in the gap. A singer's voice is removed from the sound track; yet
we hear it distinctly when the track is played. The sound of insects
turns into song. The words we hear alter depending on whether we
see or do not see the speaker's lips. We hear what sounds like an ever-
ascending scale. In fact, the notes are just going round and round like
Escher's staircase. Indeed, some hear the scale going on ascending,
others hear it descending forever. History comes in—in the form of
predispositions that it has created in the individual.

Context comes in. Meaningless sounds are played; but we start
detecting words. And it turns out that the words that we detect come
to be influenced by the language with which we grew up; they come
to depend on whether the person is male or female; they come to be
influenced by our current concerns.[32]

7

'A young sanyasin looking like me would emerge from my body and instruct me in all matters...'

'Almost from the commencement of his *sadhana*,' Swami Saradananda tells us, Sri Ramakrishna began to have the vision of a young sanyasi within his own body. *'The figure of a young sanyasin looking like me used to come out again and again from within me and instruct me in all matters*; when he emerged, sometimes I had a little consciousness and, at other times, lost it altogether and lay inert, only seeing and hearing his actions and words; when afterwards he entered the gross body, I regained full consciousness.'[1]

On another occasion, devotees are sitting around Sri Ramakrishna. At one stage, one of the painful ailments that tormented him was a burning sensation in his body, he tells the devotees. During worship, he would imagine that a 'sinner' was inside him, he says, and he meditated on killing him. One day as he was meditating, he tells them, '*...he saw come out of him a red-eyed man of black complexion, reeling like a drunkard*'. ... '*Soon there emerged from him another person*,' Sri Ramakrishna continued, '*of serene countenance, wearing the ochre cloth of a sanyasi and carrying in his hand a trident. The second person attacked the first and killed him with the trident.*' Sri Ramakrishna says that after that vision, he became free of the pain.

This sanyasi is a stern guide. Sri Ramakrishna tells devotees:

> As I sat down to meditate, *I would find a sanyasin emerging from my body with a trident in hand and directing me to concentrate my mind on God leaving aside all other thoughts.* He threatened to plunge his weapon into my body if I did not do so. When the *paap-purush* (the personification of sin) came out of my body, it was the same *sanyasin* who killed him. When I wished to see some deities in distant places or participate in religious chantings held far off, *I would see this shining figure step out of my body, go along a luminous path to those places, and re-enter my body after fulfilling the particular desires.*[2]

It is winter, Sri Ramakrishna is sitting in his room, wrapped in a shawl. He looks at the sun, and goes into samadhi. His eyes stop blinking, our chronicler tells us, and he loses all consciousness of the outer world. 'After a long time, he [comes] down to the plane of the sense world.' He turns to a devotee who used to live at the temple but caused him a world of trouble. 'The state of *samadhi* is certainly inspired by love,' Sri Ramakrishna tells him. He recalls how he had gone to another devotee's house, and a kirtan had been organized. 'There I had a vision of Krishna and the *gopis* of Vrindavan. *I felt that my subtle body was walking at Krishna's heels...*'

On another occasion, Sri Ramakrishna recounts to devotees another experience that he had during his sadhana. 'I distinctly perceived the communion of Atman,' he tells them. '*A person exactly resembling me*'—on another occasion, recalling the same experience, Sri Ramakrishna says that the boy was twenty-two or twenty-three years old—'*entered my body and began to commune with each one of the six lotuses.* The petals of these lotuses had been closed; but as each of them experienced the communion, the drooping flower bloomed and turned itself upward.'

Sri Ramakrishna recalls an incident involving a youth of twenty-four whose father used to visit him. The youth had lost his wife soon after their marriage. The young man was going to the temple, Sri Ramakrishna recalls. '*I clearly noticed that a flame-like thing came out of this* and followed him...*'

He continues recalling other instances when he distinctly saw someone emanating from him, or accompanying him. 'Another time,

---

*Meaning his own, Sri Ramakrishna's body.

in an ecstatic mood, *I saw that a sanyasi was leading me by the hand*,' he says. 'We entered a temple and I had a vision of Annapurna made of gold...' Another day, listening to devotional singing in his village, he says, he saw the Mother of the Universe. '*At that time a naked person, emerging from my body, used to go about with me. I used to joke with him*,' Sri Ramakrishna says. 'He looked like a boy and was a *paramahamsa*...'

Sri Ramakrishna is proceeding from his village, Kamarpukur, to Sihar, a village where Hriday has his house. The sky is deep blue. Fields are covered with paddy, and rows of fruit trees. Sri Ramakrishna is being taken in a palanquin. His heart is full of joy. '*Two beautiful boyish figures' emerge from his body; they dash off into the fields; they walk along the palanquin; they laugh, and joke, and converse. Eventually, they re-enter his body.* A year and a half later, when she is told of this vision, the Brahmani pronounces that they were Chaitanya and Nityananda, and that they had come to signal that they reside in Sri Ramakrishna's body. Told that this is what the Bhairavi had said, Sri Ramakrishna observes that, yes, she had said so, 'But how can I say what the real meaning of it is?' From this ambiguous answer, Swami Saradananda inferred that the incident had, indeed, given Sri Ramakrishna a clear indication that '...some ancient soul known to the world for very long ages was dwelling here* with a view to accomplishing some important purpose,' and that over time, this indication led him to realize and acknowledge, as he did much later, 'The One who became Rama and Krishna is now within this case (showing is body). But His advent this time is secret.'[3]

And the Devotees See Him

Several devotees had visions of Sri Ramakrishna, especially in the wake of his passing away. The instances are set out in several first-person accounts, beginning with that of Sri Sarada Devi herself. For ease of reference, I will reproduce a few instances that are culled from these primary accounts in two excellent anthologies edited by Swami Chetanananda.[4]

---

*That is, in Sri Ramakrishna's body.

Hriday has been attending on Sri Ramakrishna for long. His young wife dies. Naturally, he is disconsolate. After much travail, he decides to devote himself to earnestly worshipping the Mother. He importunes Sri Ramakrishna for spiritual experiences. The Master says that they will come when he—Hriday—is ready for them. Hriday has wonderful visions and experiences ecstasy with partial consciousness. Then one night,

...Hriday saw the Master going towards the Panchavati. Thinking that he might require his waterpot and towel, he took them and followed him. As he was going, Hriday had an extraordinary vision. He saw that the Master was not a human being, that he was not composed of flesh and blood, that the Panchavati was illumined by the light coming out of his body and that while the Master was walking, neither of his feet, which were also of light, did touch the ground but carried him through the air. Taking all this to be an optical illusion, Hriday rubbed his eyes again and again, observed all the surrounding things in their natural state and looked at the Master once more. But to no purpose. Although he saw all other things—trees, creepers, the Ganga, the hut, etc.—to be what they were, he repeatedly saw the Master in that luminous form. Extremely amazed at it, Hriday asked himself whether there was any change in his mind which made him have that experience. Thinking thus, he looked at his own body and saw that he too was an effulgent being, made of light, an attendant and companion of God Himself serving Him eternally, a part, so to say, of His person which was light embodied, and now having a separate existence for the sole purpose of serving Him. When he had this experience and came to know the mystery of his own life, his heart was flooded with a strong current of bliss. He forgot himself, forgot the world and forgot to consider whether the people of the world would speak well or ill of him. He was now in ecstasy with only partial normal consciousness and cried aloud repeatedly like one mad, 'O Ramakrishna, O Ramakrishna, we are not mortal beings. Why are we here? Come, let us go from country to country and set souls free from bondage! I am also what you are.'

The Master said to us, 'Hearing him crying out thus, I said, "Ah, stop, stop. What's the matter with us that you are doing all this? People will run up here thinking some evil has befallen us." But did he give ear to it at all? I then came hurriedly to him, touched his heart and said, "Make the fellow dull and drab again, O Mother."' Hriday came down to ordinary consciousness...[5]

Rani Rasmani, a wealthy widow, has had the Dakshineswar temple constructed. Sri Ramakrishna is the priest there. His practices, his mode of worship are of a kind—often, they lead people to conclude that he has gone insane. Mathur Nath Biswas is the Rani's son-in-law. He oversees the affairs of the temple, and is very solicitous of Sri Ramakrishna. He keeps people from impeding Sri Ramakrishna, whatever the latter does, howsoever strange, even offensive his way of worshipping the Holy Mother may seem to them. That he happened to view the Master with a benevolent, indeed reverential, eye, was the reason why the latter had not so far been driven away from the temple. One day, Sri Ramakrishna is pacing in the veranda adjoining his room. He is lost in his own world. Mathur watches him for a while. Mathur begins to weep. Suddenly, he runs up to Sri Ramakrishna and falls at his feet. Sri Ramakrishna is first taken aback, and then a bit alarmed. Recalling the incident, Sri Ramakrishna told devotees:

> I asked, 'What is this you are doing? You are a Babu, the son-in-law of the Rani, what will people think if they see you act like this? Be calm and get up.' But did he give ear to it? Afterwards when he became collected, he narrated everything without any reserve. He had had a strange vision. He said, 'Father, you were walking, and I saw distinctly that it was not you but my Mother in the temple over there as you were coming forward in this direction and that it was Mahadeva Himself immediately when you turned about. I thought at first that it was an optical illusion; I rubbed my eyes well and looked, but saw the same thing. This happened as often as I looked.' He repeatedly said this and wept. I said, 'Why, as a matter of fact, I know nothing.' But would he listen? I was afraid lest someone should come to know of it and tell the Rani of it. What would she think? She might perhaps say that I put a spell on him. He became calm when I consoled him in various ways.

Mathur's faith in Sri Ramakrishna becomes even stronger ... Soon, good fortune smiles on him...[6]

The Master is talking to his disciples. He becomes abstracted,

and remains in that state 'for ten or twenty minutes'. As he returns
to ordinary consciousness, he says, 'I have been with Suresh.' 'Suresh
himself told later that he was sitting before the newly set up image
of the Divine Mother [in his home], weeping because the Master had
not come to see it, for it was the first time that he had remained away
from Durga Puja,' we learn. 'Suddenly he saw the Master before
him, consoling him.'

The Master is in Dakshineswar. A devotee who is in Dhaka
suddenly sees him. To make sure that he is not having a hallucination,
the devotee touches the body of Sri Ramakrishna. When he gets
back, he narrates his experience to other devotees. Sri Ramakrishna
makes light of it: 'It must have been someone else,' he says. But
the young Narendra, who will be Swami Vivekananda, exclaims,
'I too have seen him many times. How can I say I do not believe
your words?' On another occasion, a devotee tells himself that
if the Master appears in his shrine during his meditation, he will
accept that Sri Ramakrishna actually is an avatar. Sri Ramakrishna
appears. The devotee had actually been an alcoholic and a debauch.
He decides to visit a prostitute. As he enters the lady's room, he finds
none other than Sri Ramakrishna standing there. The devotee flees.
A devotee is initiated by Sri Ramakrishna. From then on, he sees the
Master everywhere: walking on the street in front of him, sometimes
looking at him. As he stands, sits, or lies down, 'I saw the Master
accordingly.' One day as he bows down to the image of Goddess
Kali, he sees Sri Ramakrishna standing before him.

After Sri Ramakrishna Passes Away

The Master passes away. Sri Sarada Devi wants to leave her body.
Sri Ramakrishna appears before her and tells her, 'No, you must
remain here. There are many things to be done.' Sri Ramakrishna's
body has been cremated and the ashes are brought to the house in
which he had passed his last days. Sri Sarada Devi begins to remove
the few jewellery items she has been wearing. As she is about to take
off the bracelets, Sri Ramakrishna appears before her. 'Pressing her
hand, he said, "Am I dead that you are acting like a widow? I have
just moved from one room to another."' She continues to wear the
bracelets. Sri Ramakrishna had been given a golden amulet to abate

the burning sensation that used to grip his body when he practised spiritual disciplines at Dakshineswar. Later on, Sri Sarada Devi used to wear it on her arm. She is in a train on her way to Vrindavan. She lies down on the berth with her arm on the windowsill. The amulet is visible. Sri Ramakrishna appears, she is to recall later, and says, 'Why are you keeping the amulet that way? You may lose it.' After that vision, we are told, she took off the amulet and kept it in a box along with a photograph of the Master. At Vrindavan, Sri Ramakrishna again appears to her and instructs her to initiate Swami Yogananda. Back in their native village, Kamarpukur, her fears come true: people criticize her for wearing a sari with red border, and gold bracelets. She takes off the bracelets. Sri Ramakrishna appears: 'Do not discard your bracelets,' he tells her. 'Do you know the Vaishnava scriptures?' She doesn't. Sri Ramakrishna tells her that Gauri-maa will come and explain them that afternoon. Gauri-maa comes and explains that Sri Sarada Devi can never be a widow as the one to whom she had been married was God Himself. Sri Sarada Devi continues to wear the bracelets.

Others have similar experiences. It is nightfall. The youthful Narendra and others are standing near a little pond at the house where Sri Ramakrishna had spent his last days. They see a luminous form walking towards them. After some trepidation, and wondering whether it is Sri Ramakrishna, Narendra demands of the form, 'Who is there?' The form, which has reached within five yards of the young disciples, vanishes. 'This vision made a deep impression on Narendra's mind,' we are told, 'and he believed that the Master still existed in his subtle body.'

The young disciples—who are to later be known far and wide as Vivekananda, Shivananda, and others—often discuss and argue over spiritual and philosophical matters among themselves. Buddhist doctrines are often the subject of exchanges—what with their appeal to the rational minds of the young. 'This phase of ours lasted quite awhile,' Swami Shivananda is to write later. 'Even after the Master had passed away and we were living in the monastery at Baranagore, these ideas persisted. We were still atheistic.' 'One day,' Swami Shivananda wrote, 'the Master appeared to me and said, "The guru is all in all. There is no one higher than the guru." The moment I had that vision these ideas left me and did not return. Sri Ramakrishna was a divine incarnation, born to establish religion.'

A disciple is in Benares. He is collating teachings of the Master. The Master guides him to make corrections, telling the disciple what he had actually said.

Hari Prasanna Chattopadhyay has studied engineering. He is later to become a district engineer, give up his job, be initiated by Sri Ramakrishna, join the Ramakrishna Mission, establish the Mission's ashram in Allahabad, and become one of the prominent monks of the order, Swami Vijnanananda. But that is in the future. He has come to visit the Master. That is the moment when the Master complains of a sore throat—the soreness will turn out to be a symptom of the cancer that will eventually take his life. 'That was my last visit to the Master,' he is to write later. 'Afterwards I went to Bankipur (in Bihar) for my last two years of college. The house where I lived is now an *ashrama*. The day the Master passed away I saw him standing in front of me. I wondered, "How did the Master come here? What is the cause of this vision?" The next day I read of the Master's passing away in the *Basumati* newspaper.'

After the Master passes away, the young disciples are as orphans. A lay devotee is meditating in his shrine. The Master appears: 'What are you doing here?' he remonstrates. 'My boys are roaming about without a place to live. Attend to that before anything else.'

An accomplished yogin—Yogin-ma—who has known Sri Sarada Devi for long comes to doubt that the latter is divine. She is sitting by the Ganga, meditating. Sri Ramakrishna appears. He directs the yogin's gaze to the corpse of an infant that is being carried by the water, and to notice that simultaneously people are worshipping the river. 'Can anything make the Ganges impure?' he asks. 'Regard her [the Holy Mother] in the same way. Never doubt her. Remember she is not different from this [meaning himself].' Yogin-ma immediately rushes to Sri Sarada Devi, we are told, and after telling her what has transpired, apologizes. 'The Holy Mother smiled and consoled her.'

On still another occasion, Sri Ramakrishna leads a devotee to find Rs 76 that the devotee has misplaced...

As They Are Dying

Devotees see him as they are dying ... Rasik had been a sweeper at the Dakshineswar temple; Sri Ramakrishna had promised him that he would appear to him at the time of the latter's death. As Rasik lies dying, he begins to exclaim, 'Father, you have come. The Father has come.' Another devotee is dying of influenza. His wife and others who have known Sri Ramakrishna are sitting around him. Suddenly, they see a dark cloud. It takes the shape of a chariot. Sri Ramakrishna alights from the chariot, takes the devotee by the hand into the chariot, ascends and vanishes into the sky ... He appears to another long-term devotee who is dying, and guides him to various holy places ... A devotee has had some fever for three days. Nothing else is the matter with him. He tells his wife and others living in the village that he will be dying at 9 a.m. the next morning. No one takes him seriously. But when he insists again the next morning, a few of them gather around him. At 8.30 a.m. he begins his japa. 'People knew that it was his nature to do so. All of a sudden they noticed a change coming over Hazra's face, as if he were intently watching somebody. After a while he bursts forth with the words, "Welcome! Most welcome! Here comes the Master! Master, after such a long time you have remembered me."' He asks his wife to make a seat for Sri Ramakrishna to sit. The sequence is repeated for two others—a devotee of Sri Ramakrishna and Swami Yogananda, who also had been initiated at the Master's saying: Hazra welcomes them, has seats prepared for them. Hazra pleads with Sri Ramakrishna to stay till he dies. He then implores him to accompany him to the tulsi grove where, Hazra says, he wants to give up his body. They proceed to the sacred grove. He has the three seated on asanas. He continues his japa. And then pronounces, '*Hari! Hari! Hari!*' thrice, and dies ... A devotee comes to Dakshineswar from Calcutta by boat. Accompanied by the devotee, Sri Ramakrishna sets off for Calcutta in the boat. The devotee has the boat go to the middle of the river. There he implores Sri Ramakrishna to be with him at the time of death—to lead him by the right hand ... 'I shall always be with you then,' the devotee says. 'You will have to fulfil this prayer of mine.' Out of compassion, Sri Ramakrishna gives his word that, indeed, the devotee's prayer will be fulfilled: 'My goodness, you have brought me to the middle of the Ganges and have created such a scene.' Swami Adbhutananda is witness to Sri Ramakrishna making this promise thrice ... And as the devotee lay dying, we learn, 'Just as Kalipada breathed his last, he raised his right hand. Swami

Premananda was present there. Hearing the news of Kalipada's death from Swami Premananda, Swami Adbhutananda said to some devotees: "Look, the Master came to Kalipada at his last moment. Holding Kalipada's right hand, the Master guided him away. Brother Baburam saw it clearly. Whatever the Master said to anyone is bound to be fulfilled."'

A worshipper of Lord Rama walks all the way from Ayodhya to Dakshineswar to see Sri Ramakrishna. Upon reaching Dakshineswar, he learns that the Master has passed away. The monk is heartbroken. He retreats to the garden around the temple. He doesn't eat for two or three days. One night, Sri Ramakrishna appears before him: 'You have not eaten anything for several days. I have brought this pudding for you. Please eat it.' The monk eats. Sri Ramakrishna disappears. The monk is filled with joy. The next day, he tells others what has happened. He even shows them the earthen bowl in which the Master had brought the pudding.[7]

A Few Features

Each instance invites commentary. In most, to reach a conclusion we would need far more information than is available in the memoirs of the disciples and companions. And yet, a few things stand out even from the fleeting sketches that have come down to us:

- The accounts are by persons who were deeply devoted to Sri Ramakrishna.
- Several of them were under severe emotional strain at the time they had these visions—for instance, the young disciples and others whose world revolved around him would have felt orphaned at the passing away of the Master, and would therefore have been under a 'denial of death' compulsion.
- Several of them had been under physical stress—for instance, when, in addition to the emotional depression of having journeyed all the way to Dakshineswar only to learn that the Master had passed away, the mendicant had not eaten for several days.
- Several of them had visions of the Master when they were ardently longing that he be with them—for instance, that he

be present at the puja that the devotee is performing at his home.

- It was a firm article of belief that, once the Master has given his word, he *will* keep it; several of the appearances followed upon his having given his word—for instance, that he *would* appear at a devotee's deathbed, or that he *would* personally lead the devotee by the right hand upon the latter's passing away; now, it is obvious that more the longing for a promise to be fulfilled, the more intense the belief that the Master always fulfils his promise, the greater the *expectation* that the event longed for will transpire.

- Several of them had the visions at moments of the greatest emotional turmoil—the moments when they were themselves dying.

- Some of the accounts of such events manifestly involve a leap of inference: a disciple has thrice heard the Master promise a devotee that he *will* come and lead him by the right hand as he is dying; the right arm of the man rises as he is dying; the disciple infers that the arm has risen because the Master has come and is leading the man by the hand...

THE WAY WE REACT

None of this implies in the slightest that any of the devotees, and certainly not sacred persons like Sri Sarada Devi, were inventing things, that they were not telling the truth. We must start with the assumption that they really remembered having seen him when, in fact, he was somewhere else, or when he had, in fact, passed away.

The only assumption that we have to stick to is the one that underlies our consideration of other issues in this book: to understand an occurrence, let us first look for natural explanations before invoking the supernatural one.

What would we have thought of the accounts that we have just glimpsed if they had been about some run-of-the-mill godman of today? Our instinctive reaction would have been to doubt them. Now, reverse the exercise. Recall the instance in which we learnt that Sri Ramakrishna had become abstracted, and, when after fifteen to twenty minutes, he returned to normal consciousness, he remarked that he had been with Suresh—a devotee who was disconsolate at the fact that he had to perform the Durga puja at his home, away from the Master. Our natural inclination is to believe the account. How do we react when we click to Wikipedia, type 'Bilocation', and read, 'Several religious figures have historically claimed to have bilocated. In 1774, St. Alphonsus Liguori claimed to have gone into a trance while preparing for Mass. When he came out of the trance he said that he had visited the bedside of the dying Pope Clement XIV'? If we are devout Catholics, our natural inclination is to believe *this* account, even as it was to doubt the one relating to Sri Ramakrishna. And if we are devout Hindus?

In any case, what happens when in the same entry in Wikipedia, citing a source which cites a source, we learn that 'Vladimir Lenin was reportedly seen in his Moscow Kremlin office digging through papers in October 1923 while he was critically ill in Gorki'? Catholic or Hindu, we are not inclined to believe that of Lenin. Especially if we are good communists, and, thereby, unalloyed materialists!

There is an important lesson in the way our mind reacts, in the way our presumption somersaults when we encounter accounts of a particular phenomenon—in essence, the same phenomenon—given about persons we revere, about persons we do not think much of, and about persons we dislike. Unless we can consider all the three sets of accounts with the same, unruffled eyes, in particular until we shed the impulse that someone who asks questions about accounts of supernatural events involving persons we revere is guilty of blasphemy, we will just not be able to examine the accounts in any worthwhile way. There is also the other point: too sharp a reaction to such examination betrays an anxiety. Is it that we are overly defensive, that we react in anger so as to kill the inquiry at the very first pass because, deep down, we are apprehensive that the account may not withstand scrutiny? We would all hope the answer will be 'No', but the fact may be 'Yes'.

Once we put our minds at ease, that is, once we are more open and less defensive than we normally are, such accounts of sightings and of the devotee feeling that he is in the presence of the Master, as well as the circumstances in which several of the events occurred, will bring other events and circumstances to mind. For it turns out that the feeling that someone is present, even perceiving her or him with our senses—'seeing' him, 'hearing' her, feeling that she or he is touching us—are far more widespread than we may think.

'A Number of Full Moons Thrown Together'

Many became devotees because they had visions of Sri Ramana. Others had visions of him after they had become his devotees. And yet there was a difference—not in the ardour of the devotees, nor in the vividness of what they experienced, but, as we shall see, in what Sri Ramana himself made of those visions.

Raghavachari was an overseer at Tiruvannamalai. He used to visit Sri Ramana from time to time. But whenever he went to Sri Ramana's abode, several persons would be present around the Maharshi. He yearned to spend a few moments alone with the sage. Once, he framed three questions in his mind. As was to happen in many other cases, events so transpired that he felt the first two questions he had in mind were already anticipated by Sri Ramana, and answered in what happened and what the Maharshi said to others while he was just sitting in the hall, listening. The third question in Raghavachari's mind was, 'Will you please enable me to see your real form if I am eligible to see it?'

This is what followed:

My second question also being thus anticipated, I waited with an eager mind for the third answer. After half an hour I said, 'Just as Arjuna wished to see the form of Sri Krishna and asked for *darshan*, I wish to have a *darshan* of your real form, if I am eligible.' He was then seated on the *pial* with a picture of Dakshinamurthy painted on the wall next to him. He silently gazed on as usual and I gazed into his eyes. Then his body and also the picture of Dakshinamurthy disappeared from my view. There was only empty space without even a wall, before my eyes. Then a whitish cloud in the outline of the Maharshi and of Dakshinamurthy, formed before my eyes. Gradually the outline (with silvery lines) of these figures appeared. Then eyes, nose, etc., and other details were outlined in lightning-like lines. These gradually broadened till the whole figure of the Swami and Dakshinamurthy became ablaze with very strong and unendurable light. I closed my eyes in consequence. I waited a few minutes and then saw him and Dakshinamurthy in the usual form. I prostrated and came away. For a month thereafter I did not dare go near him, so great was the impression the above experience made on me. After a month, I went up and saw him in front of Skandasramam. I told him, 'I had put to you a question a month ago and I had this experience,' and narrated the above experience to him. I requested him to explain it. Then, after a pause he said, 'You wanted to see my form. You saw my disappearance. I am formless. So that experience might be the real truth. The further visions may be according to your own conceptions derived from the study of *Bhagavad Gita*. But Ganapati Sastry had a similar experience and you may consult him.' I did not in fact consult Sastri.[8]

The vision of another devotee, who gravitated to the Maharshi very early, M. Sivaprakasam Pillai, is mentioned as frequently in accounts of Sri Ramana's life. Pillai had graduated in philosophy. He had worked in the revenue department. He had first gone to Tiruvannamalai on official work. Having seen the young Swami, he visited the town from time to time. He lost his wife. And was soon plagued by questions: How should he escape the sorrows of the earth? Should he marry the girl he had in mind? If not, why not? If so, how was he to raise the funds for the marriage? He placed the questions before the young Swami. The Swami remained silent. But Pillai got his answers: by observing what life the Swami was leading, he realized that he too should lead a life devoted to the inner quest. What followed is recounted by Narasimha Swami as follows:

When he thought of going back to his village on 4th May 1913, something remarkable took place. There were many persons with the Swami; Pillai also was sitting nearby. He went on gazing at the Swami; and ere long, he had a strange vision. The Swami's face was no longer the ordinary human face. A dazzling aura was surrounding him. From his head, lo! a golden child gradually emerged and before long re-entered it. This strange phenomenon repeated itself twice or thrice. Sivaprakasam Pillai could hold out no more. He felt deeply agitated at this sudden proof of the existence of a higher benign power. His heart welled up with emotion; tears of ecstasy flowed from his eyes; and he sobbed, unable to express what he felt. Those present did not see any vision and wondered what the matter was with Pillai. When later he communicated his vision, they cracked jokes at his expense. He was in no joking mood however.

Next evening, that is, on the 5th May, he sat before the Swami. This day also he saw a vision. The Swami was suddenly seen surrounded by a halo which was as powerful as a number of full moons thrown together. The Swami's body was shining like the golden morning sun, and again his entire body smeared with holy ashes. His eyes beamed with mercy. There were others in the room at the time, but they did not see any such vision. Pillai did not ask the Swami about these matters, nor did the Swami say anything. Two days later when Pillai went and saw the Swami, the latter appeared like a mass of crystal to Pillai's eyes. Pillai's heart overflowed with joy and he had obtained the grace of the Swami. He resolved to lead a similar life of *tapas*, curbing all sex desires and observing *brahmacharya*.[9]

'While You Profess to Talk to Me Here...'

The vision that Echammal saw features just as often in accounts about Sri Ramana, in part because of the great affection in which she was held by Sri Ramana and is held to this day by his followers. This simple and pious lady had suffered blow after blow in her life. She had lost her husband, her son, her daughter. She had then adopted her brother's daughter as her own, and brought her up. True to the pattern of this good lady's life, soon after giving birth to a son, that young girl also died. A kind soul urged her to go to Sri Ramana for peace. She took to cooking food for the sage, and taking it up to him on Arunachala Hill—and she did so every single day from 1907 to 1945 when she died. Sri Ramana had great regard for her perseverance and devotion, and felt for the suffering that had afflicted so many dear to her—Nagamma Suri remarked that Echammal 'was like a mother to Bhagavan'.[10] Months after her passing away, when the talk turned to her, and the son who had been born to her adopted daughter, Sri Ramana remarked, 'On seeing the babe, I could not help thinking of his mother, and I wept for her.' Recording the conversation in 1946, Devaraja Mudaliar wrote, 'Bhagavan was moved even now after several years when recounting the event to me.'[11]

One day, Sri Ramana was engaged in discussion with a Sastri.

Echammal was making her way up the hill as usual. When she reached the Maharshi, 'Her face showed much agitation and she was trembling,' Narasimha Swami writes. What has happened? she was asked. While bringing the food, as she passed the Sadguruswami cave, she reported, '...she saw two persons standing near her path. One of them was Ramana Maharshi and the other a stranger.' As she continued her climb, Ramana Maharshi said to her, in Tamil, 'When one is (i.e., he is) here, why go further up?' Narasimha Swami's account continues:

> She turned to see the place where the figures had stood, but not a soul was there nor anywhere in the vicinity. This frightened her; and, shivering and perspiring, she climbed up to the Maharshi's *Asram*. When Echammal gave this explanation, the Sastri became envious of her. 'What, Swami!' said he, 'while you profess to talk to me here, you show your form to this lady on the way. To me you do not deign to show any similar mark of your grace.' When thus upbraided for partiality, the Maharshi had to defend himself and explain that Echammal's vision was due to her thinking of him constantly.[12]

DEVOTEES SEE HIM WHEN AWAKE, AND IN THEIR DREAMS

Incidents follow incidents. A Western visitor loses his way on the Hill. Sri Ramana appears and shows him how to get back to the Ashram. When he at last makes it to the Hall, and narrates what has happened, everyone is surprised—as Sri Ramana has not left the place at all. A principal from Kathmandu has been to the Ashram and had darshan of the Maharshi. Before boarding the train, he goes to the great temple in Tiruvannamalai. He is taken into the sanctum sanctorum. There, in the flickering light of a lamp, 'strange to say, instead of the *Lingam* I see the image of Maharshi Bhagavan Sri Ramana, his smiling countenance, his brilliant eyes looking at me. And what is more strange, it is not one Maharshi that I see, nor two, nor three—in hundreds I see the same smiling countenance, those lustrous eyes, I see them wherever I may look in that *sanctum sanctorum*. My eyes catch not the full figure of the Maharshi but only the smiling face, from the chin above. I am in raptures and beside myself with inexpressible joy—that bliss and calmness of mind I then felt, how can words describe? Tears of joy flowed down my cheeks...'[13]

In another category of visions, Sri Ramana appears to the devotees in their dreams. One evening he asks Palaniswami—the latter stays by the Maharshi's side at all times—whether he has any lime fruit. Palaniswami doesn't. The same night, a person living faraway dreams that Sri Ramana has asked him to bring some lime fruit. He takes them to the Maharshi ... Another time, he asks a devotee to fetch a notebook—the one that is long and has a black cover, as he wants to write a commentary on *Sri Ramana Gita*. The person forgets. But another person has a dream in which the Maharshi asks him to bring him that notebook. He does. The Maharshi composes his commentary ... The Maharshi's cousin—he and she had been suckled together by his mother—is dying, and is by now unconscious. He appears, touches her to bless her. She awakens, asks who has touched her, and relapses into unconsciousness ... She dies. Sri Ramana has never left his place...[14]

SRI RAMANA AFTER MAHASAMADHI

The biographies written after Sri Ramana passed away—I am talking of biographies written by persons like Arthur Osborne and Professor K. Swaminathan—do not mention instances of the sage appearing to or talking to devotees or others after passing away. They speak of a continuing presence, of the enduring instruction that his teaching continues to bestow, of facets of the Ashram and its environs which make one feel that he is still present, that things are as they were. Instead of accounts of actual appearances, these devotee biographers recall Sri Ramana's remarks as he lay ill: 'They take this body to be Bhagavan and attribute suffering to him. What a pity! They are despondent that Bhagavan is going to leave them and go away— where can he go, and how?' 'They say that I am dying but I am not going away. Where could I go? I am here'—'Not even "I shall be here" but "I am here",' Osborne noted...[15]

RECAPITULATION

Let us go back to some of the circumstances in which devotees either felt that the Master was present or actually 'saw' him:

- They were intensely devoted to the Master—so much so that several of them would neglect their worldly duties, and soon give them up entirely, they would spurn worldly concerns, they would even defy the admonitions of their elders, and spend long hours around him.
- In a sense, not just their hours, their thoughts and emotions, their very lives had come to revolve around him—talking about him, jousting over subjects that circled around his teachings, living as he would want them to live, embracing what he urged, shunning what he deplored ... all their waking hours were spent around him and immersed in him.
- Indeed, doing the spiritual work he urged them to do; performing the tiny errands that he asked them to carry out; in the final months, serving him, nursing him had become the very purpose of their lives.

When he lived, the Master was an ever-present presence: when they were not with him, they longed to be where he was, or to have him where they were. When he was gone, the very centre of their lives was gone. The very ground on which they stood was gone. They were literally orphaned.

Think of a mundane situation. A couple have been married for fifty to sixty years. They have had a happy marriage. They have shared joys; together they have been through and sustained each other through tragedies. Now they are old. The children have gone to live out their lives elsewhere. The infirmities of old age are upon both of them. Helping each other through the day fills the hours of each of them; it is, quite literally, the purpose of each of their lives. One of them dies. We say the other is 'widowed'. We might as well say, she or he is orphaned, and see how closely the circumstance enveloping Sri Ramakrishna's devotees and disciples or Sri Ramana's has been recreated.

SAVIOURS TO ORPHANS

A number of researchers, working in a number of varied countries and regions in which the standard beliefs—in religion in general, in afterlife in particular—vary over the widest possible range—countries as varied as Japan, UK, Sweden—have found that one of the principal aftermaths of bereavement is that very significant proportions among the surviving spouses see and hear the deceased, that ever so often they feel that the partner who has passed away is actually present. Ever so often, and even though many years have passed since their companion died, they feel that the deceased companion is guiding them out of difficulties, that at critical junctures she or he is showing them which path to take and which to shun. I well remember how struck I was when I first heard Fali S. Nariman, one of the most distinguished lawyers of our time, say that about his grandmother. He was addressing a large gathering in memory of my father. Nariman said that, based on his own experience, he firmly believed that those who have loved us and whom we have loved, continue to look over us, and, at crucial turns, show us the path to take. When I asked him later about this, he said that he had been very close to his grandmother, and that even years after she passed away, and when he was faced with a critical choice, she had guided him.

J. Yamamoto and his colleagues studied twenty widows in Tokyo in the 1960s. Eighteen of them, that is 90 per cent, said that they had felt the presence of their deceased husbands. They did not feel—and here we see the effect of the culture and religion in which they had grown up, and in which they had spent their entire lives—that this feeling was in any way unnatural, nor that it in any way suggested that they were losing their mind.[16]

In a study that has been much cited since it was published, W. Dewi Rees, a general practitioner in Wales, reported the results of interviews with 227 widows and sixty-six widowers. They formed over 80 per cent of all widowed people resident in a defined area in central Wales. And, excluding those whose condition disabled them from being interviewed, they constituted 94 per cent of those who could be interviewed.[17]

Almost half the people interviewed reported that they had hallucinations or illusions of the dead spouse. The hallucinations often occurred over many years but were most common during the first ten years of widowhood. Furthermore, and here we see indirectly the effect of the intensity of the relationship, the incidence of hallucination increased with the length of the marriage and was particularly associated with a happy marriage. Of those whose marriages had lasted nine years or less, 28 per cent said that they had seen, heard or felt the presence of their dead spouses. On the other hand, 57 per cent of those who had been married for fifty years or more had had these experiences. And the factor of happiness: eleven of 227 widows who had been interviewed said that they had had unhappy marriages; none of them had any of the kinds of experience that the others had.

Close to 40 per cent of the widowed felt the presence of the deceased; 14 per cent said that they saw the deceased; 13 per cent that they heard the deceased; close to 12 per cent said the deceased partner spoke to them; 3 per cent went so far as to have felt that the deceased actually touched them. A telling feature was that these feelings—of seeing, hearing, being in the presence of, etc., the deceased—diminished with the number of years that had passed since the person had died: while 52.6 per cent of those who had been widowed for ten years or less experienced these feelings, the percentage of those who had been widowed for forty years and had this experience was around 32. The type of experience—seeing or hearing, for instance—also varied with the time that had elapsed since the person had passed away.

Rees's findings also have a parallel of receiving directions from the Master after he has passed away: those among the widowed who had experienced the presence of their departed spouse, it turned out, were more likely to decline an opportunity to remarry than those who had not had that kind of an experience. Of those whom Rees studied, four rejected subsequent remarriage; all four had the experience, and they maintained that they did not want to remarry because their dead spouse was opposed to their doing so.

Most felt that they had been helped by the experiences: 78 per cent of those who had seen the dead spouse, 67 per cent of those who had heard him or her, 73 per cent of those who had felt the deceased's presence and 82 per cent of those who believed they had spoken to the dead person felt they had been helped.

The results of a study done around two decades later in Sweden differed in a few particulars—for instance, the number of years for which the marriage had lasted did not seem to be associated with either the intensity of grief or the hallucinated experiences—but by and large, the results were similar.[18] Grimby examined fifty persons who had recently lost their spouse: fourteen of them were men, thirty-six women. Of these, *82 per cent* experienced hallucinations or illusions in the first month after bereavement. The experience occurred more frequently among those who had been suffering most from loneliness, who, as a result, had been crying, or who had memory problems.

The most common experience? That the spouse was present: 52 per cent of the sample had this experience. Thirty per cent felt they heard the spouse, and that the spouse speaks to them. About a quarter felt that they had seen the spouse, 6 per cent that she or he had touched them. The incidence of each type of experience diminished over the years.

Except for one widow, for all subjects the presence of the deceased had been a pleasant experience. The number of pleasant experiences turned out to be directly correlated to the intensity of grief. That the marriage had been a happy one turned out to be correlated to both: the frequency as well as the pleasantness of the experience.

Several other researchers have examined the bereaved, and arrived at similar findings. Several of the respondents reported that their spouse had come to specifically warn them of some impending danger.

And the elderly or the recently bereaved are not the only ones who come to feel that the other is present or that they hear or see him. In an influential book, a scholar, P.C. Horton advanced the argument that 'soothers' are needed at all stages of life: children are known to develop imaginary companions, for instance, especially children who have to spend a lot of time alone, or who are either neglected or maltreated by their parents. Horton argued that there is a pattern to the way the 'soother' transforms over the years: from a blanket to a toy to an imaginary companion, to, on his telling, religion, and the mystical experience itself—each is a 'soother'; although each is so different from the other, each caters to the same need.[19]

From 'Soothers' to Saviours

Men had been trying to climb Nanga Parbat since 1895. By the early 1950s, the mountain had claimed the lives of thirty-one of the most intrepid of men. In July 1953, a new expedition consisting of Austrian and German mountaineers was on the mountain. Among them was a mountaineer, Hermann Buhl, who was to become a legend, and an inspiration to the generations that would take to the mountains later.

Buhl became the first man to set foot at the summit of this formidable mountain. He attained the summit without oxygen and without modern aids. It is impossible in a passing summary to convey the hazards and extreme travails that Buhl went through to complete the mission—there can be no substitute for reading his own, thrilling account, *Nanga Parbat Pilgrimage: The Lonely Challenge*.[20] The base camp at 13,000 feet; the violent storms on the way up; the fierce, frightening, raging gales and blizzards—the adjectives are all his; the thick mists that reduced visibility at times to almost nothing; the crippling cold; the avalanches, some a mile and a half wide and 600 or 700 feet high; the treacherous abysses ... An hour to cover just 40 or 50 feet ... Slopes of 45 degrees ... Suffocation, gasping for air, even while lying down in a tent ... Having to go down repeatedly only to trudge back up again ... To learn on one of these descents that the leader of the team had taken all helpers down ... The insistent orders of the leader that he and the two others who were left on the mountain should abandon their effort, and return forthwith ... The withdrawal in effect of all support...

Of the two who still remain with him, one decides that he can go no further ... On the final day when they are to begin the ultimate attempt, the last companion also can't get himself out of the tent ... Buhl sets off at around 1.30 a.m. ... Treacherous crevices ... A sheer wall, plunging 17,000 feet ... A single wrongly placed step would hurtle him down 6,000 feet ... Has to take five breaths at every step ... Completely exhausted: 'Now the slopes tilted more steeply to the Subsidiary Summit. It was ten o'clock. I lay in the snow face downwards on my rucksack, panting, panting, panting. This looked like the end...' By the time he reaches around 25,500 feet, he can no longer swallow the meagre rations he has brought ... He is unable to carry the rucksack—though it contains the minimal and absolute essentials, including his heavy pullover...

Yet he continues ... 'I was finding great difficulty now in keeping myself upright. I kept sitting down on the rocks, wanting to go to sleep, overcome by a terrible feeling of lassitude. But I had to push on ... I finally reached the Gap at two o'clock [he has been climbing now for twelve hours] and stood in that deep notch between the Subsidiary and main summits at 25,658 feet, completely exhausted. I fell down on the snow. Hunger racked me, thirst tortured me, but I knew I had to save the last drop as long as possible...'

Almost vertical rock walls block the way forward ... 'I simply slumped to the ground and lay there fighting a desperate battle for that essential commodity—air. All the old altitude symptoms were there again, only worse—or was it my raging thirst? I forced myself on again, struggling to gain every yard...'

He has to shed everything. It is already six in the evening by the time he reaches 26,000 feet: 'The realization of that gave me a horrid fright; I had thought it would take only an hour from the Bazhin Gap. I was finished. For my eyes the Summit was almost near enough over there for me to touch it; for my condition it was an eternity away. I took a last gulp from the flask ... Apparently the Cocatee had its effect. I felt a little fresher and after laying everything I could dispense with on a boulder, I staggered to my feet again. I took nothing but my ice axe, the flags and my camera. Indescribably wearily I dragged myself along a horizontal rock-ridge. I realized that I was only obeying the dictates of a subconscious which had only one idea—to get up higher; my body had long since given up. I moved forward in a kind of self-induced hypnosis...'

He keeps putting one painful step after another. All he can see is a projecting rock. The summit must be beyond it. 'But how far? And had I the strength to get there? That ghastly fear obsessed me. I could no longer stand upright; I was but the wreck of a human being. So I crawled slowly forward on all fours, drawing imperceptibly nearer to that rocky spur, towards which I was struggling with such grim doubts ... To my joy and relief, there was nothing but a little crest, a short snow-slope, only a few yards long, easier now, easier ... I was on the highest point of that mountain, the Summit of Nanga Parbat, 26,620 feet above sea-level...'

It is around 7 p.m. by now. He has been climbing for about eighteen-and-a-half hours...

The descent turns out to be equally trying, and brings Buhl closer to peril. The strap tying the crampon to his left shoe snaps and falls off. He has to put the crampon into the pocket of his anorak, and walk over ever-treacherous ground—with one foot only in a shoe, and other with a crampon. Suddenly, pitch darkness. Buhl gropes his way down as long as he can. At last, he finds a tiny spot on which he can place his two feet. It is too small for him to be able to sit down. And it is exposed on three sides—to his back is a rock face tilted at 50 to 60 degrees. He fights sleep—if he were to fall asleep, an abyss awaits him. And yet: 'Utter weariness came over me. I could hardly stay upright, and my head kept falling forwards, my eyelids pressed my eyes like lead, and I dozed off ... I woke with a start, and straightened my head up. Where was I? I realized with a pang of fright that I was on a steep rock slope, high up on Nanga Parbat, exposed to the cold and the night, with a black abyss yawning below me ... The cold grew more and more unbearable...'

At last the dawn. He commences his descent again...

Bear in mind the extreme weariness, the pangs of hunger, of thirst, the brushes with death, the unbearable circumstances as you read what follows.

'*During those hours of extreme tension,*' Buhl was to record later, '*I had an extraordinary feeling that I was not alone. I had a partner with me, looking after me, taking care of me, belaying me. I knew it was imagination, but the feeling persisted...*'

The path becomes fragile, everything he touches breaks away. He has to take off his gloves. He tries to get to a gully. 'It seemed too great a risk, for one small slide or fall would be the finish of me, and *I would certainly drag with me my companion and friend,* non-existent though he be ... I had to exert extreme care every foot of the way down...'

He can't find his gloves.

'*Horrified, I asked my mysterious companion, "Have you seen my gloves?"*'

'*I heard the answer quite clearly: "You have lost them." I turned around, and there was nobody there. Had I gone crazy?*'

'*Was I being mocked by some phantom? I recognized a familiar voice, but did not know to which of my friends it belonged. All I knew was that I knew it...'*

He continues to search frantically for his gloves. At last he finds the reserve pair ... Exhausted, he is able to trudge down to the gully and back up again.

'*The whole of this time my companion was with me,*' Buhl recorded, '*that staunch companion whom I never saw, and whose presence was more definite at danger spots. The feeling calmed me, lulled me into security: I knew that if I slipped or fell, this "other man" would hold me on the rope. But there was no rope; there was no other man. A moment or two later I would know that I was quite alone and dared not risk one moment's heedlessness.*'

Buhl continues to trudge and lurch down the perilous paths. He ties the crampon on to his shoe with the cord of his overall trousers. In little time, the crampon slips out and is at a right-angle to his shoe ... 'I had to repeat the dangerous game every ten or twenty yards. Bending down was a fearful exertion...' he wrote, adding, '*I raged at my partner behind me for giving me such a wretched crampon. (He was still following close behind me.)*'

Hunger and thirst plague Buhl. His reasoning deserts him. He hears voices. 'The snow robbed me of my last vestige of strength and my progress across the plateau became veritable torture ... I moved at a snail's pace, finding it necessary to take twenty breaths to a single stride. Every yard or two I fell down on the snow ... I suppose I fell down again and slept. When I woke my eyelids were like lead, and when I tried to get up I collapsed again, utterly exhausted. This was it, I thought—journey's end...'

Around 5.30 p.m., he sights the camps—remember he has been climbing since 1.30 a.m. the previous day. Around 7 p.m., he crosses a point he had passed forty-one hours earlier. At long last, frostbitten—two of his toes will have to be amputated—he reaches the camp. His fellow mountaineer is so thankful at seeing him that he does not even ask him whether he reached the summit. Both break down...[21]

Notice the unimaginable physical exhaustion, the mental state to which he is stretched. Notice how one colleague after the other falls away. Notice the utter loneliness. Notice the unseen companion. Notice the voices that are familiar but which he cannot place. Notice the reassurance that the companion imparts. Notice, in this case, the parallel to the lucid dream—the dream in which the dreamer knows he is dreaming: even as he draws reassurance from the sensed presence of the companion, even as he converses with him, even as he rages at him, Buhl remains convinced that there really is nobody there.

Offering Cake

Twenty years earlier, in June 1933, Frank Smythe, a member of a British expedition, had the same experience on the Everest. The expedition was large. However, one by one, all but Smythe had been unable to continue. Smythe was now above 26,000 feet, the altitude at which there isn't enough oxygen for one to breathe. At last, he was barely a thousand feet from the summit. But he just could not go on, and had to give up his great endeavour. Throughout the ultimate attempt, indeed from the time all others had fallen away, Smythe recalled that he had a companion who was accompanying him. So real was the presence of this other that Smythe did not feel alone at all. Indeed, he felt that he was tied to this person by a rope, and that, should Smythe stumble or fall, the companion would rescue him. At one point, he—Smythe—was so famished and exhausted that he took out the slice of mint cake that he still had. But instead of eating it, he broke it in half, and turned to give the half to the companion— so real was the feeling of presence, and so real his feeling that his companion also must be as famished and, therefore, as much in need of the cake. As he turned to hand the piece, he was shocked to find that there was no one to give it to. The feeling of presence continued till the moment he had descended enough so that he could see the camp from which he had begun his final climb.[22]

While reading such accounts, in particular about experiences on the Everest, I came across a communication to the *British Medical Journal* by Dr Charles Clarke—he had been the medical officer to the British Everest Expedition in September 1975.[23]

In the communication, Clarke had described the experience of two climbers—Doug Scott and Dougal Haston—who had made the first ascent of the south-west face of Everest. After a fourteen-hour climb, they had reached the summit at 6 p.m. Unlike Buhl, they had used an oxygen-on-demand system. They had commenced descent as the sun was setting, and had returned to the south summit. Here, Clarke wrote, they had dug for themselves a snow hole on the Tibetan side at about 28,600 feet. They were without food or oxygen after 8 p.m. The still-air temperature was probably about minus 35 degrees Celsius. They used a small propane gas stove—but this too did not last long. They had no extra clothing to meet this contingency ... After an indescribably cold night, they descended to Camp 6 (at 27,000 feet) and then gradually down during the day to Camp 2 (at 22,000 feet).

When they were examined at Camp 2, Dr Clarke found them very tired, they had sore throats, and minor frostbite on their fingertips, but otherwise completely lucid. They gave a clear-headed account of the climb, Dr Clarke wrote. *'They also told of a curious sensation that a third person had been sharing the snow hole during the night* ... These two experienced climbers owe their survival to their remarkable persistence in maintaining their body temperatures by warming each other's extremities throughout the night and remaining awake despite particularly strenuous prolonged work at high altitude on the preceding day...'

On reading the communication, I remembered that my brother-in-law, Suman Dubey, himself a keen mountaineer and trekker, knew Dr Clarke and many other famous climbers. I requested Suman to ask them about similar experiences. In his reply to Suman, Chris Bonington, who led that 1975 expedition, recalled three experiences, two involving himself, as follows:

> In Feb '72, Dougal Haston and I were in winter in the Mont Blanc Massif. Stopped the night in the empty Argentiere Hut, slept downstairs and *both of us heard what sounded like someone walking on the bare floors upstairs.* There was no wind and it definitely was not a mouse or a rat. We later learnt that the previous hut guardian had died in an avalanche (I think), the previous year.
>
> In 1975, Nick Estcourt was doing a carry from Camps 4 to 5 on the south-west face of Everest on a moonlit night. *He rested about halfway up and saw clearly a figure following up on the fixed ropes, but when he got back to the camp, learnt that no one had left camp after him.*
>
> In 1985, when I was climbing the Hillary Step on Everest, totally exhausted, *I became conscious of Doug Scott floating beside me and giving me quiet encouragement...*[24]

It turns out that this experience—that someone else is present—happens often at high altitudes, especially beyond 26,000 feet. Reinhold Messner is often written of as having been the greatest climber ever. He has been a purist—he has maintained that to carry oxygen and the kind of elaborate equipment that is commonplace today is to cheat the mountain. He has climbed the fourteen greatest peaks without any oxygen, and with the barest minimum aids. He has distinctly felt a presence several times, including on both Nanga Parbat and the Everest. Like several others, Reinhold has maintained that the felt presence is a working out of processes in our brains, and that it can be harnessed and used as an aide. Asked whether we can control the third-man presence, John Geiger, the author of the gripping book, *The Third Man Factor*, had this to say about Reinhold and Vincent Lam, the doctor who wrote the foreword to the book:

> I think we do have control, but because of the lack of recognition of the phenomenon, people are unaware and unable to access it and make use of it. But if you talk to someone like Reinhold Messner, the great climber who's had the third man experience a number of times, it's almost now expected in certain situations. He knows when it's likely to happen. So for people who have found themselves in these situations more than once, the third man is sort of always there and can be called upon when needed. Vincent Lam, a medical doctor and a guy who practices both emergency and expedition medicine, who wrote the foreword to my book, had this experience, and he feels like he can call upon it when he needs it. It's now fundamentally part of who he is.

Geiger—he had spent six years researching the phenomenon—further told the interviewer that the presence could be harnessed not just in extreme situations, but even in dealing with the vicissitudes of our day-to-day lives:

> Fundamentally, the most important thing is that people are aware of the phenomenon—that they realize that it is real and has been quantified and that there are scores of high-achieving people who have come forward and admitted to having had the experience. Once people recognize the phenomenon and realize that it's an

experience many have had, then the ability to utilize and harness it to good effect is tremendous. As much as anything in our ability to cope with severe stress, the third man factor is a fundamental tool in our arsenal for self-preservation. I'm talking not just physical situations like being trapped under a boulder in the wilderness, but in our everyday experiences...[25]

Are we getting a glimpse here of why and how devotees whose very lives have come to revolve around a Master may 'see' and 'hear' him or feel that he is present—in situations where they desperately want or need him, especially when he has passed away?

NOT JUST AT VERY HIGH ALTITUDES

The first thing to remember is that even as far as mountains are concerned, it is not only at very high altitudes that the presence of another has been felt. As Arzy and colleagues have noted, Moses saw the burning bush, and encountered God three more times, on Mount Sinai which is just about 2,600 metres. Jesus was transfigured 'up a high mountain apart'—identified as Mount Tabor in Israel, and this is just 588 metres, or Mount Hermon, on the borders of Lebanon and Syria, which has a height of 2841 metres. He appeared to Peter, John and James in a cloud of glory on the road to Damascus. The Prophet received the Quran from Gabriel on Mount Hira in Saudi Arabia, a height of around 2000 metres...[26] Not altitude, but several other factors were common among the three—and they paralleled the sorts of situations and persons we have encountered at extreme altitudes. For instance, like our single-minded Buhl or Smythe, they were intense seekers. They had shut off all other pursuits and concerns. Similarly, the revelations, the seeing of the burning bush, hearing the voice of Jehovah or Gabriel—all of these had been preceded by being cut off, by intensely felt loneliness.

'WE WERE FOUR, NOT THREE'

Perhaps the best-known and celebrated account of a felt presence is that by Sir Ernest Shackleton who had led an expedition to the Antarctica. He and his crew had watched in trepidation and helplessness as their ship, *Endurance*, was crushed by ice. They made their way to an ice floe in the hope that it would drift to an island. After two harrowing months, they transferred to a second floe. They had been on it for but five days, and it cracked in two. The largest of their lifeboats was a mere 20 feet ... There was no alternative but for Shackleton to trudge and see if he could get help. Two of his mates and Shackleton had then set out on a menacing mission to get help. They trudged through storms and blizzards, across hazardous, unchartered terrain, unnamed ice hills for thirty-six hours. Dread, utter exhaustion, hunger—the perils were as extreme as they are unimaginable by us. Shackleton was to write later:

> When I look back at those days I have no doubt that Providence guided us, not only across those snowfields, but across the storm-white sea that separated Elephant Island from our landing-place on South Georgia. *I know that during that long and racking march of thirty-six hours over the unnamed mountains and glaciers of South Georgia it seemed to me often that we were four, not three. I said nothing to my companions on the point, but afterwards Worsley said to me, 'Boss, I had a curious feeling on the march that there was another person with us.' Crean confessed to the same idea. One feels 'the dearth of human words, the roughness of mortal speech' in trying to describe things intangible, but a record of our journeys would be incomplete without a reference to a subject very near to our hearts.*[27]

Several others have had the same experience—that another whose presence they could feel was guiding and encouraging and protecting them: explorers—among them Sir Edmund Hillary's son, Peter; 'single-handers'—those who set out to sail around the world alone; a woman who dived deep into a cave well under the sea; survivors of a torpedoed submarine; a captured submarine commander who escaped from a Turkish POW camp ... Most recently, Ron DiFrancesco, the last man to have made it out of the South Tower on 9/11. Each of them had the distinct feeling that they were steered to safety by a person who they could feel was present throughout their travail. A few among them could recognize who it was: Peter Hillary felt it was his mother—she had died almost twenty years earlier; the lady who almost lost her life in that watery cave felt it was her late husband. In other instances, the person felt the person was familiar, but she or he could not quite place her or him. In still other cases, the person was convinced—as Shackleton had been—that the person was a divine angel.[28]

OTHER CIRCUMSTANCES

In addition, the presence of another has been felt in sleep paralysis—while falling into or coming out of sleep. It has been felt by patients suffering from a wide range of psychological and neurological ailments: for instance, studies of patients suffering from Parkinson's disease reveal that anywhere from 34 per cent to 40 per cent of them have felt the presence of another.[29]

We can see from the accounts of these great men, and from studies that have followed, that the feeling that someone is present near us occurs much oftener than we imagine. I well remember my mother's elder sister. She was quite the anchor of our extended family—the one who would make us laugh our heads off, the one who would have our horoscopes cast and read. Psychologically, she was tough and resilient as can be, and truthful to the core. This was soon after Partition. We had come over from Lahore, and were staying at my grandfather's house in Jalandhar. Her house was a few miles away. She used to walk over. One day, on the way back to her house, she had gone but a part of the way, and a furious rainstorm came down. She was not just soaked, she was at her wits' end as to how she would reach her house or turn back and reach where we were. She told us that just as she had almost given up, a kindly Sikh rickshaw driver appeared. '*Bibi, baith jaa. Main lai chaldaan.*' In spite of flooded streets and that torrential downpour, he brought her to the gate of her house. Drenched, but full of gratitude, she unwound the palla of her dhoti and turned to give the rickshaw man money. There was no one...

In a word, the experience occurs in a wide range of conditions. And it takes a wide range of forms and intensities: we may be able to identify the person or we may not, to the point that he or she may be just a shadow in the fog; she or he may address us or not; the feeling itself may be fleeting—lasting no more than a few seconds—or it may last for hours; while immersed in the experience, we may perceive the presence we feel to be real or, even as we are *in* the experience, we may retain insight—that is, as was the case with Buhl and Messner, we may know that the presence is a product *of* our mind, *in* our mind.

Given the variety of persons who come to feel the presence of another, and the diversity of circumstances in which they come to have this feeling, we should not expect to encounter one or two causes; neither should we expect to discover exact parallels with the sightings and the felt presence of the Master with which we started, nor with the occasions on which Sri Ramakrishna saw a person come out of his body and guide him. We should be content with cues.

THE PHYSICAL CIRCUMSTANCES

First and foremost, as we have seen in the case of Buhl, of Shackleton, and as is evident from the accounts of so many other explorers and mountaineers and sailors, extreme exhaustion—to the point, as Critchley had noted, of 'utter collapse'—starvation, thirst, dehydration, sleeplessness, lack of oxygen, bitter cold, all work to bring one to that state.

Second, mortal danger, with little hope of rescue.

Third, not just being alone, but feeling intense loneliness—the feeling that, faced with life-threatening odds, one has no one to turn to. Ever so often, recall Buhl again, the other has made his appearance when companions have left him or have fallen by the way.

For the mystic, attaining the vision—of the Mother in Sri Ramakrishna's case, of the Self in that of Sri Ramana—is literally a matter of life and death: recall the state of Sri Ramakrishna before the first vision of the Mother. And the quest is certainly a solitary one: almost the first precondition is that he turn his back on everyone, on every relationship, on every object of the world.

And then, as we learnt from Oliver Sack's books, sensory deprivation and monotony. The unending sea, the unrelieved harsh light of the sun, the howling wind. True, there is a lot of 'sensory input' from the buffeting of the sea, from the howling winds on an exposed mountain slope, but it is repetitive, monotonous. Think of the lamp flame on which you focus during meditation, or the mantra. The flame flickers, the mantra consists of many syllables, or different words. But the mind soon abstracts from them. The monotony entails that.

With sensory deprivation, psychologists point out, our minds become hyper-vigilant to any cue from the surroundings, as well as to the least flicker within the mind itself. Isolation and danger compound the effect: the 'hyper-vigilant system' within the brain becomes even more at an edge. Especially so to any cue that may either aid our survival or be a reason to hope. In an informative review paper, Peter Suedfeld and Jane S.P. Mocellin put the point about the effects of attenuated external inputs as follows (I will omit the references they give at each step; for these, please look up the original article):

Suedfeld [in an earlier paper] has suggested that restricted environmental stimulation (REST) presents an environmental anomaly. Individual and species history focus attention on external information, vital for survival. This limits the ability to attend to any but very intense internal stimuli ... In REST, information from the ambient world is greatly attenuated and attention is refocused to residual and endogenous stimuli. These newly attended internal stimuli could be the origin of the externalized sensed presence. Zusne and Jones ... refer to self-generated stimuli, hallucinations found in REST research. While in actuality hallucinations are seldom found in the laboratory ... there are indeed hypnogogic images, vivid dreams and daydreams, and complex elaborations of residual stimuli. The hypothesis is also related to the perceptual release theory of hallucinations, that a reduction in ambient information leads to the emergence and awareness of previously encountered and processed material...

These hypotheses related to our current topic in two ways. The monotonous environment common to sensations of presence may be similar to REST; and because of the nature of most presence-evoking environments, the individual becomes hyper-vigilant to any information that could be of help in survival. *Awareness and elaboration of residual or endogenous signals, combined with high motivation, produce perceived images, particularly those that have an impact on coping and the hope of success...*[30]

THE ONE THAT FILLS IN THE GAPS

To all these we must add the nature of the brain. To begin with, it actively fills in. To take an example that we can verify for ourselves, each of us has a blind spot—where the optic nerve is located; but we do not see an empty or blank hole in the spot: the brain fills in the hole with inputs derived from the surrounding area.[31]

But it doesn't just 'fill in' when something is missing. Neurologists teach us that even what we take to be simple, straightforward perception is an active, creative process. Even the eyes may not just be taking a photograph. What they see, and what they omit to see, will be greatly influenced by our concern at that moment; our history too would have predisposed us to notice some features and ignore others. This is all the more so when fragments are missing. As Michael Gazzaniga, one of the leading figures in neurobiology, has pointed out, the brain, in particular the left hemisphere, has a fertile 'interpreter': from fleeting flecks of cues, a module in the left hemisphere weaves stories, it discovers, and where necessary invents patterns and causes.

And the story it will spin, the pattern it will conjure up will in turn be influenced by the culture in which we have been brought up, by our personal history, by our circumstances at that moment, by our expectations, our longings and fears.

I have myself seen this happen. As my wife Anita's Parkinson's advanced, at one stage she started having both auditory and visual hallucinations. She would say that someone—in the next room, or in the neighbouring house—had left the record player on, that she could distinctly hear M.S. Subbulakshmi singing. At other times, she would see spiders having woven their webs—but with black thread—along the ceiling, and especially around our son Adit's eyes. The former would disturb her—she is very fond of and very sensitive to classical music, and when she wants to listen she wants to listen with all her being; she doesn't want the music to just go on, she doesn't want it as an intrusion. The latter—those webs the spider had woven around Adit's eyes—would naturally alarm her.

There must have been some random sounds. Her mind wove them into a familiar rendition. The light from the bulbs would be making subtle, alternating lines of light and shade on the wall, or across Adit's face as he slept, and her intense concern and fears for him would weave them into a spider's web around his eyes. Almost invariably, she would hear the song and see the spider's web as she awakened from sleep.

These processes were taking place within her brain, but she was exteriorizing them. Something she loved in one case. Something she dreaded in the other.

William James, in words that are often recalled, said that the sensed presence is an 'imperfectly developed hallucination'. Critchley referred to it as a 'rudimentary hallucination'.

There is in addition another layer: the sensed presence is what the evolutionists call an 'adaptive' phenomenon. The one we feel present is the sort of presence that our desperate condition requires.

To summarize, what seems to be happening is:

- The person has been reduced to a state of extreme physiological exhaustion, and has been driven to the edge of the psychological precipice.
- Random cues from the environment register in his mind's eye.
- Combining them with stored knowledge and experience, his brain constructs a presence out of them.

The presence gives him the reassurance he needs; it gives him instructions and guidance, it advises the caution that he needs—the instructions and cautions are born out of his accumulated experience, lessons that had receded into, had got buried into his unconscious. The instructions and guidance are arising from within his mind and brain, but he externalizes them as if they are coming from that being outside himself.[32]

While particulars naturally differ, and while we cannot expect all the features to be present in every case, the parallels with the situation of the aspirant undergoing sadhana for years on end, and later of the devotees in relation to the Master are striking. Longing to the point of despair. Beliefs that have been internalized because of the religious and cultural milieu in which the aspirant grew up, and those that the devotees have internalized in the vicinity of the Master—that, as he has promised he will come, he certainly will do so because he never breaks his word; if he doesn't, well that would mean that I am not as dear to him as that other devotee to whom he

did appear ... The shutting out of sensory inputs—during meditation
or prayer or focusing on the Master...

The parallels are almost literal. Here is what Suedfeld and
Mocellin observed in regard to the role of expectancy in generating
the feeling of a presence:[33]

> Among other contributory factors, expectancy is likely to be
> relevant. For spirit questers and other religious seekers, the mystical
> encounter with the sensed entity is the cultural norm; its lack would
> be considered a failure. By contrast, some cultures (including
> ours) have developed mechanisms that suppress the experience in
> objectively identical situations ... Individual expectations may also
> play a part: some single-hander sailors and climbers were known
> to be oriented toward events of a mystical or religious sort ... Reed
> ... noted the role of expectancy linked with specific locations,
> and there are Antarctic reports of presence experiences in shelters
> formerly occupied by Shackleton and Scott...[34]

Recall, first, the remark of Charles Clarke about that Alpine hut the
caretaker of which had died the previous year: he and his companion
had distinctly felt that someone was walking around in the room
above them; in Clarke's recollection it was *later* that they learnt of
the caretaker having died the previous year. Second, of course, not all
climbers have been religiously inclined: as we noted, both Buhl and
Messner looked upon the presence as an emanation of their minds.
But all devotees of spiritual masters can safely be assumed to be
religiously and spiritually inclined!

PROFANING A DIVINE EXPERIENCE?

In speculating thus, are we, as the senior monk at the Ramakrishna
Mission told me, profaning a divine experience?

Well, let us see what the first general secretary of the Ramakrishna
Mission himself said about the experiences of Sri Ramakrishna
that we have considered in this chapter.* After reproducing Sri

---

*Swami Saradananda was a direct disciple of Sri Ramakrishna. He was chosen
as the very first general secretary of the Ramakrishna Math and Mission; and
remained general secretary till he passed away in 1927.

Ramakrishna's descriptions of the young man who looked just like the Master and would come out of his body and guide him; after reproducing Sri Ramakrishna's descriptions of the sanyasi with a trident who threatened to pierce Sri Ramakrishna's heart if his mind strayed from God, who leapt out of Sri Ramakrishna's body and killed the paap-purush, who used to visit distant places on behalf of the Master and return and re-enter his gross body, Swami Saradananda reported what Sri Ramakrishna said about the gurus who had shown him the way.

'The Brahmani, Totapuri and others came and taught me afterwards what I had heard from him previously—they taught me what I had already known,' Sri Ramakrishna told Swami Saradananda and other disciples. 'It seems from this that they came as Gurus in my life in order that the authority of the scriptures, such as the Vedas, might be maintained by my honouring their injunctions. No other reason can be found for accepting the "naked one" and others as Gurus.' Based on what Sri Ramakrishna told him and other disciples, Swami Saradananda says that, once the aspirant reaches a certain level, it is his own mind that becomes his guide, and that this is what had happened in the case of Sri Ramakrishna, and that the sanyasi whom Sri Ramakrishna saw as emerging from and re-entering his body, and was guiding him and giving him instructions was Sri Ramakrishna's own mind.[35]

8

'I suddenly felt my body carried up higher and higher...'

A devotee decides that he will celebrate the coming puja at his own home. It will be performed over three days. He is eager that Sri Ramakrishna blesses the puja with his presence. Sri Ramakrishna is agreeable, but Rani Rasmani's son-in-law, Mathur, who handles the affairs of the temple, so to say, puts his foot down. The devotee is wounded, but can do little. To console him, Sri Ramakrishna tells the devotee, 'Why are you pained? In my subtle body I shall daily go to see your worship; nobody except you will see me!' And he gives him detailed instructions on how the devotee should prepare himself for the worship, and how to conduct it. He tells the devotee that if he follows these instructions and conducts the worship in accordance with them, 'God will certainly accept your worship.'

The devotee is delighted. He does as he has been instructed. And lo and behold! During the worship on each of the days, he finds Sri Ramakrishna in his resplendent body standing next to the idol.

He narrates this to Sri Ramakrishna. The Master is not surprised at the news: 'At the time of the *Aarati* and the "juncture worship",' said the Master to him, '*I felt indeed a great yearning to see your worship and I went into ecstasy, and felt that I went along a path of light and was present in your worship hall in a luminous body.*'

SRI RAMANA

Ganapati Sastri was an erudite scholar of Sanskrit, and an accomplished poet—he came to be known as Kavya Kanth because of the fluency and rapidity with which he would, as if spontaneously, compose verses. About the same age as Sri Ramana, he is the one who, through five verses he wrote during one of his first encounters with Sri Ramana, shortened his name from 'Venkataraman' to the name by which he came to be known, 'Ramana', and he is the one who declared that the sage must henceforth be referred to as 'Maharshi' because he had all the marks associated with that appellation. Ganapati Sastri is also the one who composed the *Ramana Gita*, a text of eighteen chapters in verse, setting out Sri Ramana's answers and doctrines. Sri Ramana regarded him highly, and on occasion gave his own compositions to Ganapati Sastri for improvement and correction.

Ganapati was prone to seeing visions. Once—in 1908—when he was staying with Sri Ramana, he saw a meteor-like object at dawn; the object came and touched Ramana's forehead six times, Ganapati saw in his vision. A while later, he—Ganapati Sastri—went away to Tiruvottiyur, a place near Madras for tapas. The course of pujas and austerities was to last eighteen days. On the eighteenth day, Narasimha Swami writes, '...when he was lying wide awake, he saw the figure of Maharshi coming in and sitting next to him. Sastri sat up in wonder. But Maharshi pressed him down holding him by the head. This gave him something like an electric shock, which he regarded as *hastadiksha*, i.e., grace of the Guru conferred by a touch of his hand.' But the Maharshi had not left Tiruvannamalai since he had first arrived there twelve years earlier and had never been to the place at which Sastri was doing his pujas and dhyana. When eleven years after this experience, Sastri happened to narrate the incident in the presence of the Maharshi, the latter observed:

> One day some years ago I lay down, but I was not in *samadhi. I suddenly felt my body carried up higher and higher till all objects disappeared and around me was one vast mass of white light.* Then suddenly the body descended and objects began to appear. I said to myself, 'Evidently this is how *Siddhas* appear and disappear.' The idea occurred to me that I was at Tiruvottiyur. I was on a high road

which went along. On one side and some distance removed from it was a Ganapati temple. I went in and talked, but what I said or did, I do not recollect. Suddenly I woke up and found myself lying in Virupaksha Cave. [One of the sites on the Arunachala Hill in which Sri Ramana stayed.] I mentioned this at once to Palaniswami who was always with me.[1]

A Pioneer's Explorations

As is the case with so many phenomena that have been studied later, the great neurosurgeon Wilder Penfield had observed them much earlier. He performed a legendary number of surgeries to treat epileptic patients who could not be helped by other treatments. The surgeries would be performed under local anaesthesia—it is possible to do this as there are no pain receptors inside the brain. The patients would be fully conscious during the operation—this was necessary for identifying the exact points along which surgical intervention was required. To pinpoint the areas of the brain that needed to be surgically excised or the connections that needed to be cut so as to prevent the epileptic seizures from spreading across the brain, Penfield, after he had opened the skull, would stimulate different spots.* This would be done by passing a weak electrical charge through an electrode to a designated spot.

As he did so, the patients reported a range of experiences—of hearing music, of remembering events of long ago, of things being far away, of everything including the patient's voice going away, of being in their house, of hearing music, of having a dream. In several instances, patients described sensations and experiences that we would today characterize as paranormal. In at least two instances, the patients had what we would today call out-of-body experiences.

---

*You would have recently read an account of an operation that was performed on a twenty-seven-year-old Jazz musician in Malaga, Spain. A tumour that was triggering involuntary tremors had to be removed. To pinpoint the exact source of the tremors, as the surgeons explored different points in the brain of the musician, he was asked to read some sheet music and play a tune on his alto saxophone. He did so with his skull open, and his brain being explored. The paper even published a photograph of his doing so on the operating table. Amy Ellis Nutt, 'Play "Misty" for me during brain surgery', *The Washington Post*, 22 December 2015.

G.A. had a very difficult birth. The mother went into labour. After thirty-six hours had passed in labour, the child was delivered through forceps. She had generalized convulsions two weeks after birth. The seizures recommenced when she was ten. They had continued for six years when, as a sixteen-year-old, she was referred to Penfield. A large part of her brain was exposed for surgery. When Penfield stimulated a point on the first temporal gyrus on the right side, G.A. said, 'I have a queer sensation as if I am not here.' A little later she added, 'As though I were half and half here.' She had never felt that way before. As the stimulus was continued, after a while she asked, 'Am I here?' She said that she felt she was 'floating away', and that her right arm was moving—she did move her right arm. When, a little later, Penfield stimulated the same point again, she said, 'I feel like I am going away again.' The sensation continued for a few seconds even after the stimulus was terminated. As the electrode was applied to another point farther to the rear and just below the posterior end of the Sylvian fissure, she said, 'I feel queer again.'

'This sense of unreality or remoteness had no particular relationship to visual or auditory impressions,' Penfield wrote. She seemed to have a sense of unreality, he observed, as though she were somewhere else and yet still in the environment in which she was—'half and half here,' as she said. Hughlings Jackson had termed such an experience 'mental diplopia', Penfield noted.

That expression—'mental diplopia', a double vision of the mind so to say; in the present instance, the feeling of being here as well as elsewhere—often seems so apt as we read accounts of our mystics.[2]

Penfield triggered the same experience when he stimulated an electrode placed deep in the patient's Sylvian fissure. He narrated the case in the Maudsley lecture he delivered in 1954. V.F. was a thirty-three-year-old patient. During the operation, the right temporal lobe was exposed, and a point 2 cm deep 'along the superior surface of the temporal lobe, within the fissure of Sylvius' was stimulated. 'The stimulating current was shut off,' Penfield said, 'and the electro-corticogram showed that a slow wave of 4 per second generalized rhythm had been set up as an after-discharge. While this was continuing, the patient exclaimed: "Oh God! I am leaving my body." Dr Karagulla, who was observing him, said he looked terrified at the time of the exclamation and made gestures as though he sought help...' Stimulation in the temporal lobe at another point nearby 'produced vestibular sensations. Once he said he was spinning around. Once he felt as though he were "standing up".' Summarizing the case, Penfield observed, 'This patient had, during minor seizures, a sensation of dizziness probably produced by discharge in or near the transverse gyrus of Heschl deep in the Sylvian fissure. This was followed by complicated psychical illusions, interpretive illusions, during which he felt unjustified fear, a sense of familiarity [a feeling that he had been through the experience earlier] and an altered relationship to his own person as though he were outside his body. The record at the time of stimulation fails to state whether he experienced the illusory feeling of false familiarity then, but stimulation did produce the illusion of fear and of leaving his own body.'[3]

RECENT CONFIRMATION

Sixty years after these operations were performed, Olaf Blanke and associates had to operate on a forty-three-year-old lady whose epileptic seizures were not responding to medication. As Penfield used to do, so as to locate the exact source of the trigger for the seizures, and so as not to impair any vital part of the brain unnecessarily, they positioned electrodes under the skin in the brain and studied what happened in the lady's brain as these were stimulated successively.

She was lying on the bed, the upper part of her body being supported at an angle of 45 degrees, her legs were stretched out. When they stimulated the electrode that had been placed at the right angular gyrus, the lady had the feeling that she was 'sinking into the bed' or 'falling from a height'. When the current amplitude was increased, she had an out-of-body experience—she felt she was floating above her body, and looking down on it. The stimulus was repeated, and each time she had an out-of-body experience.[4] 'Two further stimulations induced the same sensation,' Blanke and associates reported, 'which included an instantaneous feeling of "lightness" and "floating about two metres above the bed, close to the ceiling".'

She was then asked to watch her legs as the stimulus was applied. She reported that they seemed to have become shorter. When the legs were bent to a 90-degree angle, she felt they were rushing to her face, and she took evasive action, Blanke and his colleagues wrote. When she was asked to look at her arms, she said that her left arm seemed to have shrunk. During these tasks, she saw her body only hips downwards, and her shrunken arm. 'It is possible that the experience of dissociation of self from the body is a result of failure to integrate complex somatosensory and vestibular information,' Blanke and his co-authors concluded.[5]

Three years later, Blanke and Arzy reviewed studies of patients who had reported out-of-body-experiences (OBEs). The studies had specified the locations of lesions that had been discovered in the patients. Furthermore, three features of the OBEs stood out: the person saw his own body from a distance or at a distance; she or he saw it from a height, and, while seeing the real body from a height, it was as if she or he was in a horizontal position; third, he located his 'self' in that illusory body. Now, it is at the temporoparietal junction that inputs from several senses in regard to one's body and its location in space, as well as one's sense of 'self' and agency—the feeling that I am the one who, for instance, is typing these words—are integrated. And, secondly, as the illusory body is felt to be elevated and 'horizontal', there must also be an otholithic dysfunction. The clinical findings and these features led them to argue that OBEs arose from two dysfunctions, not one—the 'integration failure of proprioceptive, tactile, and visual information with respect to one's own body ... and by a vestibular dysfunction leading to an additional disintegration between personal (vestibular) space and extrapersonal (visual) space'. 'We argue that both disintegrations are necessary for the occurrence of OBE,' they concluded, 'and that they are due to a paroxysmal dysfunction of the TPJ [temporoparietal junction].'[6]

RELIGIOUS TYPE OF EXPERIENCES THROUGH ELECTRICAL STIMULATION

Seventy years after Penfield's pioneering explorations, A. Selimbeyoglu and J. Parvizi reviewed the findings of ninety-three studies of electrical stimulation of the brain. Their review was selected from 9,272 old and new reports. Two points in this review are of significance for us.

They list the brain areas that were stimulated, and the perceptual, motor and behavioural symptoms that the patients reported in consequence. Some of these bear directly on religious experiences:

- Symptoms when the *insula* was stimulated: The patient reported a feeling of going into a trance and could not get his thoughts straight. Another patient said he had a sensation of being out of this world. Patients reported a sensation of unreality.

- Symptoms when the *parietal lobe* was stimulated: Out-of-body experience; an illusory sensation that someone, a ghost shadow, was standing behind the patient. When the dorsomedial parietal and precuneus area was stimulated, the patient had the feeling of levitation. And when the stimulus was applied to the parietoccipital junction, the patient reported seeing phosphenes—particles of light.

- When the *temporal lobe* was stimulated: The patients reported a feeling of unreality, of being familiar with the sensation, of having an illusion of dream-like state; they also reported emotional feelings such as feeling of loneliness, fear, urge to cry, anger, anxiety, levitation, lightness; several recalled past experiences.

- When the site of stimulus was in the *orbitofrontal* and *ventromedial frontal cortex*: Patients went into memory recall.

- When in the *occipital lobe* a point in the *striate cortex* was stimulated: Visual sensations (e.g., seeing simple patterns, white or black spots, stars, stardust or a blob of flashing light, colour or phosphenes. When the stimulus was applied to the *temporo-occipital junction*, the patients saw things tremble.

- When in the *temporal lobe* points in the *inferior temporal gyrus* were stimulated, patients reported delusions of unreality and unusualness. When the points were in the *parahippocampal region*, they experienced feelings of unreality; and remembering experiences from the past.

The second point is a corrective. From the way I wrote up the findings of Penfield, we may have gathered the impression that the stimulation of a particular point in the cortex or the subcortical region resulted in sensations and delusions of specific kinds. As Selimbeyoglu and Parvizi reported, the consensus has shifted. As more has come to be known about the intricate and elaborate networking of neurons, what happens as a result of applying the stimulus to one point in the cortex, say, is not only because that particular point has been stimulated but because as a result of the stimulus having been applied to that point, a specific network of which this point is a part is stimulated. Furthermore, it is now realized that the resulting experiences may not be merely because the activity at that point or in the network has spiked or got excited, but because, as a result of the stimulus, it has been modulated—in varying ways and to varying degrees. As they note, citing earlier studies, this may happen either at the cellular level or in axons; the stimulus may alter the firing pattern of cortical neurons of the activity of glial cells in the surrounding area; the effects may extend to the subcortical region, and, therefore, the results may have triggers deeper in the brain than just the cortex.[7]

The results that Penfield observed, as well as the results that Selimbeyoglu and Parvizi reported from the studies they examined, were obtained by applying an electrical stimulus to points in the brain. The question these findings raise from the point of view of our inquiry is whether, as a result of their practices, our sages had learnt unwittingly to stimulate points or areas in the brain, or trigger other changes—for instance, in the flood of neurotransmitters—which led to the extraordinary experiences that they had. But it turns out that we need not go as far as intrusive explorations of the Penfield-kind to stumble upon at least some of the extraordinary experiences.

AM I THIS ONE? OR THAT ONE?

In 2009, through an ingenious experiment, Olaf Blanke and associates were able to elicit an illusionary experience—the same 'out-of-body' experience—by a completely non-intrusive method.[8] The subject came to feel himself to be out of his body, viewing it from a distance merely because of dissonant visual and tactile inputs. What happened is as follows.

A display monitor was secured across the forehead of a person so that he could see the image in it. It received signals from a camera and made a 3-D image visible to the person. A camera was placed behind the person. The person was now able to see the image of his body—in front of his actual body or behind his actual body.

The image of his body was projected on to the device. His actual back was stroked with a stick. Through his goggles, he saw the body in front of him being stroked. The surprising thing was that he came to feel that the body in front of him—the 'virtual' body projected on to his display—was being stroked. That is, he had come to identify his *self* with the *seen* body: he came to feel that the virtual body was his own body, and not the body, his real body, which was actually being stroked. This displacement is termed 'visual capture'—the person identifies with the body he *sees*, not with the body that is feeling the strokes. The visual information about stroking prevails over the tactile sensation, and this causes him to erroneously situate his 'self' where the touch is *seen* and not where it is felt.

In the next round, not his back, but his chest was stroked (the stroking was hidden from the camera). In this variant, when the stroking of the chest was synchronous, he identified himself with the point from which he was seeing—that is, his actual body; he identified himself less with the body he was seeing in the display, it was as if the body he was seeing belonged to someone else.

The third variant was even more akin to the 'out-of-body' experiences that we hear about so often. As in the first and second rounds, first his back was stroked and then, later, his chest. But in this round, the person was lying down. The result? He localized his self with the virtual body lower down in the former instance; and with the body floating above him in the latter. And the feeling that he was floating was stronger when his chest was being synchronously stroked than when his back was being stroked.*

Furthermore, the identification with the virtual body was stronger when the stroking was synchronous with the seeing.

---

*As to which 'body'—the one floating above or the one floating below his actual body—he was identifying himself with was itself discerned through an ingenious mode. The participant was made to hold a ball in his left hand, and a button in the right. He was then asked to *imagine* dropping the ball, and to press the button when he thought it would have hit the ground. He pressed the button in a shorter time span when his back was stroked and the virtual body was lower than the real body, closer to the ground, than when his chest was stroked, and the virtual body was floating higher up.

Finally, when the stroking was asynchronous, the perceptions were reversed! Now, he perceived himself to be where he felt the strokes (his actual body), not where he saw them to be administered (his virtual body). 'This suggests,' Blanke and associates hypothesized, 'that during asynchronous conditions the somatosensory body representation (or somatosensory capture) prevails.'

Blanke and associates observed as a result that 'global bodily self-consciousness can be systematically manipulated through conflicting multisensory inputs in healthy subjects'. They pinpointed three specific conclusions:

> First, confirming previous data, synchronous back stroking (compared to asynchronous stroking) led to increased self-identification and illusory touch on the seen body. Synchronous chest stroking led to opposite effects: decreased self-identification and illusory touch sensation on the seen body. Second, the present data show that synchrony between visual and tactile information about the stroking may systematically change bodily self-consciousness, leading in the prone body position to predictable and implicitly measurable upward and downward drifts in self-localization. Third, the present set-up rendered the induced illusory perceptions more comparable to related clinical conditions such as out-of-body experiences ... This seems especially relevant since the subjective elevated self-locations in the present study were combined with a floating sensation, suggesting a modulation of vestibular sensations.[9]

IMPLICATION

It is entirely possible that had he done even more than the 1,300-odd operations that he did, and had he, while operating, stimulated even more points with those electrodes, Penfield may have elicited an even wider range of experiences. That is why one of the far-reaching implications of Penfield's experiments was the premise that almost every emotion—affection, aversion, fear, longing, even pain—and memories, pleasant and unpleasant, could all be triggered artificially. The subject could be made to experience pain without actually hurting his body. The subject could be made to feel elated or depressed without anything actually having happened to her or around her. The subject could be made to remember something that happened to her long ago without her making any effort to recall it.

In several instances, patients described sensations and experiences that we would today characterize as paranormal. Among these were 'the illusion of fear' and that of things being larger—stimulation of the temporal lobe of the patient triggered one of the precursors of the full experience that would seize him during a seizure, a sensation in his left arm. Another patient had 'the illusion of remoteness', a feeling of being 'a stranger from earth'—in the case of this patient, the lesion or other disturbance could not be localized. A third patient reported hearing strange words—Penfield surmised that some speech areas were involved because of an epileptic discharge. A fourth patient reported a feeling of 'unreality', 'a not infrequent aura', Penfield observed. In many of the patients reporting this kind of a feeling of unreality, the problem could not be localized with definiteness. But one patient whom Penfield and Erickson mentioned—'M Bu'— 'described a "far away" sensation each time her right supramarginal gyrus was stimulated'.

BACK TO THE SENSED PRESENCE

Even a single experience requires that we recruit several constituents of the brain. The person hears voices—and that means that the auditory cortex, and probably the speech areas would have been stimulated. He reads meaning into them, or strings comprehensible sentences or words from random noises—and that means the superior auditory cortex would have been yoked in. He 'sees' the presence, often as a mere shadow, sometimes as someone he recognizes—and that would involve mobilizing the area in the right hemisphere that makes out shapes. For the presence to give counsel, assuming that this counsel consists of lessons that the person himself has learnt in his life and which had got buried deep in the recesses of his memory or even further down in his unconscious, areas of the brain in which these are stored would have been lit up—and this would mean a number of areas scattered all over the brain. Furthermore, we can be certain, the mind would be constantly testing the feeling of a presence as well as the sights and sounds and counsel against reality—that, as well as several other facets of the experience, would entail the temporal lobe. The person would be feverishly assessing what he is experiencing now with what he has experienced in the past—that would require summoning both episodic and autobiographical memory—that is, accessing the hippocampus and associated regions. And the experience is most likely to have pressing emotional dimensions to it—in the case of the beleaguered mountaineer, for instance, the relief that help has arrived, the gratitude for guidance and companionship that the presence is providing—and this would entail components of the limbic system, in particular the amygdala.

In short, when we look at the *totality* of the experience—of even just this one experience, that of a felt presence—we would not expect to find it to be originating in just one component or region of the brain. And there is the additional difficulty—one to which Critchley had drawn attention decades ago in his original paper: on the one hand, the same symptom can be caused by a variety of neurological causes or conditions; on the other, one neurological cause or condition can trigger a number of varied symptoms.

Even so, a number of neuroscientists have been pointing to the temporal lobe, in particular the junction of the temporal and parietal lobes as the locus for the felt presence experience—the junction is where information from several senses is organized, it is involved in processing information, concepts, relating to one's feeling of 'self', of the distinction between one's 'self' and other 'selves', of the position of one's body in relation to the rest of space.

'I See the People in This World and in That World Too'

Penfield and Perot wrote up 'a final summary' of the responses that a set of patients experienced when sites in their cortex were stimulated. These were patients whose response recalled an earlier experience.[10] While, as the title of their paper indicated, they were reporting only those instances in which the patient's response tallied with an experience she or he had had earlier—a song that she had heard, the house in which she lived as a child, her mother scolding her baby sister for something the latter had done, etc.—it is evident that at least some of the responses, even in that collection, could not have been the mere recollection of 'the brain's record' of past experiences.

Patient G. Le. was a twenty-nine-year-old woman. She had been having seizures for nine years. She was on the operation table. Her left temporal lobe had been exposed. Stimulation of specific points triggered a series of responses. A doctor was sitting beneath the drapes protecting the patient. He gestured to her. She remained silent. When the stimulation was stopped, and she was asked whether she had noticed what the doctor was doing, she answered, 'I don't know what he did, *I was trying to see what they were doing. The scenery seemed to be different from the one just before. I think there were people there, but I could not swear to it.* That is what I call an attack.' Asked again about the doctor's gestures, she said, 'Yes, I saw his hand. *I see the people in this world and in that world too, at the same time.*'[11]

Similarly, consider Case 25, of patient H.P. She was fifteen years of age. She had had seizures since she was eleven. She was on the operation table. Her right temporal lobe was being explored. As a particular point was stimulated by the electrode, she said she was feeling dizzy, and exclaimed, 'A dream is starting. *There are a lot of people.*' She was asked if they were speaking, she replied that she did not know. Where are they? she was asked. 'In the living room,' she replied. 'I think one of them is my mother.' As the electrode was shifted to an adjacent point, she said, 'I felt that feeling again. *Someone is in the room.*'[12]

Or Case 36: M.M. was a twenty-six-year-old woman. Her seizures commenced when she was just five. She used to have 'flashes', sudden recollections of events that had happened in the past. Hers was also the only case in which the doctors recorded an olfactory hallucination in a seizure. She was now on the operation table. The right temporal region was being explored. Upon a point being stimulated, she exclaimed, 'I heard something familiar, I do not know what it is.' The stimulus was repeated. She said, 'Yes, sir, I think I heard a mother calling her little boy somewhere. It seemed to be something that happened years ago.' Asked whether she knew who it was, she replied, 'Somebody in the neighbourhood where I live,' and that it was happening close enough for her to hear. Up till this point, all of this sounds as if a record in her brain of past events was being activated. The stimulus was repeated at the same point eighteen minutes later. M.M. said, 'Yes, I hear the same familiar sounds, it seems to be a woman calling. The same lady. That was not in the neighbourhood. It seemed to be at the lumber yard.' 'She added,' the doctors recorded, '"*I have never been around any lumber yard.*"'

In short, while most of the experiences that the patients reported could be taken to be recalls of ones that had happened earlier and whose record had surfaced upon the site being stimulated, the portions that I have italicized above—'*I see the people in this world and in that world too, at the same time*', '*Someone is in the room*', '*I have never been around any lumber yard*'—would suggest that not all of them were. And some of them indeed are akin to the felt presence that we discussed.

A Presence Sensed by 80 Per Cent?

For thirty-five to forty years now, in a book as well as over 300 scientific papers, the Canadian neuroscientist, Michael Persinger, has been advancing the thesis that religious, and even mystic experiences, are '*normal* consequences of spontaneous biogenic stimulation of temporal lobe structures'. He has backed this proposition with a series of experiments. Some of the results have been hotly contested. And yet, his thesis and the central experiment remain an important landmark on the way, and it will pay us to take note of them.[13]

While Persinger's work covers the entire range of religious and spiritual experiences, we can glimpse the central proposition as well as get to know the experiments and device by which he arrives at it by considering just the question at hand—that is, the sensed presence.

Persinger starts with the proposition that has been advanced by others also—that our principal sense of self is a verbal one: we are social animals, and so our sense of self, defined in relation to and for interacting with others, is a linguistic sense of self; as the speech areas—both for speaking, and for comprehending speech—are in the left hemisphere, this is where our principal sense of self is located, according to Persinger. But, he maintains, there is a corresponding 'maximally affective and minimally linguistic' homologous self that is located in the right hemisphere.

Normally—that is, in normally healthy individuals in normal

circumstances— the two senses of self are integrated seamlessly. But certain conditions of the brain—such, for instance, that result in schizophrenia; as well as certain circumstances—for instance, recent bereavement, or starvation, hypoxia, a sudden drop in sugar levels in the blood, life-threatening danger, etc.—can disrupt communication between the two hemispheres. At the moment of extreme danger, for instance, we do not need a verbal skill, but an assessment of the danger in a holistic, intuitive way. In such a sudden and extreme circumstance, the right hemisphere may come to dominate our awareness. The sense of self from the right hemisphere, in a manner of speaking, intrudes into the left hemisphere. The left hemisphere, with its verbal abilities, now interprets it as an *other*, as someone other than oneself, as someone outside the boundaries of our body. This is the presence we sense.

That sensed presence is a continuum. It may be a vague shadow or feeling of 'someone there' or be specific—say, the clear vision of a personal deity: Krishna or Jesus; we may sense sounds that range from the indistinct all the way to specific commands.

Religious and spiritual experiences have an evolutionary value, Persinger emphasizes, as do many others. With self-awareness comes awareness of the fact that our self will die, it will be extinguished. The God experience helps allay this anxiety of extinction.

Persinger adds three points about this sensed presence. First, whether we will experience God or a lesser presence, a sound or a vision, or a smell, will depend on which component of the brain has got stimulated. Second, the intensity with which we will feel the presence will be affected by our 'lability'—that is, our excitability, our sensitivity to fluctuations in electromagnetic fields, our receptivity; and this varies from person to person, as well as, for an individual, from time to time. Third, how the experience will be interpreted will be influenced by the person's life history—that means the culture and religion in which he grew up, the experiences he has had in his life, and, through these, the beliefs and presuppositions he has formed.

For long, temporal lobes have been the focus of those who have studied religious and spiritual experiences. One reason has been that patients of temporal lobe epilepsy were found to be deeply religious; they displayed great interest in and keenness to discuss religious, even philosophical issues. One incidental result has been that, from the scantiest of reports about what their condition was just before they broke into an ecstatic experience, or, as in the case of the Prophet, the revelation burst forth, it has been said of many figures—St. Teresa, Joan of Arc, the Prophet and several others—that they suffered from temporal lobe epilepsy.

In any event, the temporal lobes have been the focus of Persinger's work. In particular, temporal lobe transients—the fleeting micro-seizures within the temporal lobes. They can range from the extremely ephemeral and hardly noticeable increase in electrical activity to longer-lasting and more intense episodes. They are what are said to trigger spiritual experiences, ranging, for instance, from the vague feeling that someone else is present to a full-blown experience of being in the presence of 'God'. By occurring repeatedly, or by a few occurrences being very intense, the spiritual experiences that these transients cause can transform one's beliefs, one's very life.

The seizure, fleeting and mild though it may be, can affect components that lie deep within the temporal lobes: as the experience can be deeply emotional, the inference is that the amygdala would be implicated; as the experience, and in particular the interpretation that would be placed on it, will be affected by one's earlier experiences, one's accumulated memories, the surge in electrical activity would touch the hippocampus also.

In hypothesizing about these transients, Persinger has maintained that they can be set off by personal crisis—for instance, bereavement, or life-threatening danger—a bout of extreme anxiety, lack of oxygen, a fall of sugar levels in the blood, exhaustion. You will notice how this enumeration includes conditions we had encountered when we were recalling explanations of what happens to explorers, mountaineers, single-handers and others.

Some of us are genetically prone to these transients, Persinger notes, because their temporal lobes are electrically more unstable. Others, and this is a point crucial to our subject, can learn to trigger the transients through meditation, and routines that often accompany extended meditation—for instance, drastic reductions in food intake.

During Persinger's experiments, the subject is placed in a soundproof, dark room. The eyes are covered. His or her head is covered by a 'God Helmet' designed by Persinger's colleague, Stanley

Koren. The helmet has solenoids—coils that carry electrical current which acts as a magnet—that emit very weak electromagnetic fields, weaker 'than the hair-dryer that you use', we are told. The solenoids are positioned close to the head over the temporal lobes. During the experiment, the fields are varied continuously and very rapidly to disrupt communication between the two hemispheres and to reach into the subcortical structures in the temporal lobes. Doing so, we are told, has a range of effects: as the new, disruptive patterns reach the amygdala, for instance, they trigger emotionally significant sensations; as they penetrate the hippocampus, the new patterns make one feel drowsy; as communication between the two hemispheres is disrupted, the sense of self in the right hemisphere intrudes into the left hemisphere and that, as we just noted, generates the sense of presence.[14]

Persinger has claimed that 80 per cent of those who were targeted for sensing that someone else was present, in fact, came to have that feeling during the experiment.

Before we proceed, three points in brief from what Persinger has been maintaining, points that have significance when we contemplate the frequent states into which Sri Ramakrishna, say, used to be transported and his 'more real than real' conviction that the Devi was present, and his conversations with her:

- Those having temporal lobe transients may not even realize that they are having them—so subtle and fleeting they may be.
- Even though subtle and ephemeral, the transients can have profound effects on the individual and his attitudes and beliefs.

V.S. Ramachandran has suggested that these two features—that the person may be unaware of the transients and yet these transients may have profound effects—may be due to the fact that the occurrences are taking place at the neuronal level.

- Persons can learn to trigger these transients—for instance, they can learn to put themselves in circumstances that trigger these.

Experiences, but Not the Ones Intended

Susan Blackmore is well known for her work on consciousness. She is hard-headed as they come: her work that traced near-death experiences to the manner in which the brain unspools while we are dying is testimony to that. The BBC had commissioned her to do a programme on alien abductions. In search of material for the programme, she went to Persinger's laboratory and went through a session with the God Helmet. She has recorded the experiences that she had during the session.[15]

She has had many weird experiences, she says—from the out-of-body experience to those that followed in the wake of her ingesting drugs. But the weirdest experiences she has had, ones that were totally different from all that she had been familiar with, she says, are the ones she had during the Persinger session. At first nothing much happened. She felt relaxed, sort of drifting away. Then suddenly, as if her body was being stretched, as if her left leg was being pulled up the wall. Next, she felt someone had got hold of her shoulders and was pulling her up (she was reclining on the cushioned chair in the lab) ... She felt at one point that she was on the verge of having an out-of-body experience but it never really materialized. Instead, suddenly she felt angry, 'really angry ... so mad', and just as suddenly the feeling was gone. And then she felt frightened, really frightened, a 'creepy skin-crawling horrible fear' gripped her ... And then it was gone.

In retrospect she was struck by the fact that the experiences had been so powerful. She was aware that she had the God Helmet on. What if the experiences had happened when she did not have the helmet on, what if they had happened when she was drifting at the edge of sleep? What if in that state she had felt as strongly pulled by someone? Couldn't she have concluded that aliens were abducting her?

As she left the room, she was totally disoriented. She felt very odd, she says in the recording.

Would the experience count as one in which she sensed a presence?

Richard Dawkins, on the other hand, did not have experiences that were all that extraordinary. He certainly did not feel that he

was in the presence of 'God' or of anyone else. Nor did he have
anything resembling an out-of-body experience.[16] Dawkins's session
lasted forty minutes. At first you hear him saying that he is feeling
nothing unusual at all. Then that he is feeling slightly dizzy ...
that he is feeling strange ... that he is feeling a twitchiness in his
breathing ... the feeling that his left leg is moving ... that his right
leg is twitching...

As he recounts the experiences, still lying on the chair, Dawkins
says that he felt 'pleasantly relaxed' but that he did not have
the sensation of someone being present. He says that he is very
disappointed, that he would have liked to have the experience and
feel what religious people feel.

Persinger explains Dawkins's 'absence of experience' by the fact
that they had found Dawkins's temporal lobe sensitivity to be much,
much lower than that of the average person.

Because of his prominence, Richard Dawkins's account that he
did not have any religious experience during Persinger's experiment
caught a great deal of attention. Persinger responded with a new
explanation. He wrote in his blog that Dawkins had been drinking
wine just before going into the chamber; second, that the BBC crew
had taken a long time in setting their apparatus up when, in the
normal course, the subject enters and waits in a silent, dimly lit room
for the experiment to commence. Both these factors would have
interfered with the experience Dawkins had.[17]

Jack Hitt, an author well known for his writings in an array of
journals, also went through the experiment, and wrote about it in
the magazine, *Wired*.[18] His experiences fell between those of Susan
Blackmore and Richard Dawkins. His account is worth reading in
the original. He journeys to north Canada, at last he reaches the
handful of buildings that are the University of Laurentian, the place
where Persinger has worked for over thirty years. He is taken into
the darkened room. He is put through a questionnaire—the answers
presumably give an indication of his inclinations, maybe of his
'lability'. Persinger arrives. Exchanges. And the experiment is about
to begin:

> When the door closes and I feel nothing but the weight of the
> helmet on my head and the ping-pong balls on my eyes, I start

giving serious thought to what it might be like to 'see' God, artificially produced or not. Nietzsche's last sane moment occurred when he saw a carter beating a horse. He beat the carter, hugged the horse while sobbing uncontrollably, and was then carried away. I can imagine that. I see myself having a powerful vision of Jesus, and coming out of the booth wet with tears of humility, wailing for mercy from my personal savior.

Instead, after I adjust to the darkness and the cosmic susurrus of absolute silence, I drift almost at once into a warm bath of oblivion. Something is definitely happening. During the 35-minute experiment, I feel a distinct sense of being withdrawn from the envelope of my body and set adrift in an infinite existential emptiness, a deep sensation of waking slumber. The machines outside the chamber report an uninterrupted alertness on my part. (If the researchers see the easily recognized EEG pattern of sleep, they wake you over the speakers.) Occasionally, I surface to an alpha state where I sort of know where I am, but not quite. This feeling is cool—like being reinserted into my body. Then there's a separation again, of body and soul, and—almost by my will—I happily allow myself to drift back to the surprisingly bearable lightness of oblivion.

In this floating state, several ancient childhood memories are jarred loose. Suddenly, I am sitting with Scott Allen on the rug in his Colonial Street house in Charleston, South Carolina, circa 1965, singing along to 'Moon River' and clearly hearing, for the first time since then, Scott's infectiously frenzied laughter. I re-experience the time I spent the night with Doug Appleby and the discomfort I felt at being in a house that was so punctiliously clean. (Doug's dad was a doctor.) I also remember seeing Joanna Jacobs' small and perfect breasts, unholstered beneath the linen gauze of her hippie blouse, circa 1971.

Joanna was my girlfriend when I was 14. When I was sent off to boarding school, she and I recorded cassette tapes to one another. As a teenager, Joanna was a spiritual woman and talked a lot about transcendental meditation. Off at boarding school, I signed up and got my *mantra* from Maharishi Mahesh Yogi, right around the time Joanna dropped me to move on to a tougher crowd.

If I had to pin down when I felt this dreamy state before—of being in the presence of something divine—it would be back then,

in the euphoric, romantic hope that animated my adolescent efforts
at meditation. That soothing feeling of near-sleep has always been
associated with what I imagined should have happened between
Joanna Jacobs and me. Like the boy in James Joyce's *The Dead*,
Joanna was a perfect memory—all the potential of womanly love
distilled into the calming *mantra*-guided drone of fecund rest.

I'm not sure what it says about me that the neural sensation
designed to prompt visions of God set loose my ancient feelings
about girls. But then, I'm not the first person to conflate God with
late-night thoughts of getting laid—read more about it in Saint
Augustine, Saint John of the Cross, or Deepak Chopra.

So: Something took place. Still, when the helmet comes off
and they shove a questionnaire in my hand, I feel like a failure.
One question: Did the red bulb on the wall grow larger or smaller?
There was a red bulb on the wall? I hadn't noticed. Many other
questions suggest that there were other experiences I should have
had, but to be honest, I didn't.

In fact, as transcendental experiences go, on a scale of 1 to 10,
Persinger's helmet falls somewhere around, oh, 4. Even though I did
have a fairly convincing out-of-body experience, I'm disappointed
relative to the great expectations and anxieties I had going in.

Hitt wonders whether the priming before the experiment—that
he *would* experience God, etc.—had put his rational hackles up.
Persinger explains that it may have to do with Hitt's lability—
'Persinger jargon meaning sensitivity or vulnerability,' explains Hitt.

So, we have the figure from Persinger's group—that of the
thousand or so who have been put through the experiment, 80 per
cent have felt the presence of an *other*. And we have the differing
reports of Susan Blackmore, Richard Dawkins and Jack Hitt.

Further Doubts

In view of continuing controversies, and because of the deep
implications that Persinger's experiments had for religious and
spiritual disciplines, a Swedish group of researchers set out to
replicate the results that Persinger had attained in his laboratory.[19]
They got a portable device from Persinger and his colleague Stanley
Koren, the inventor of the device. They discussed with Persinger and

his associates the procedure to be followed. They took great care to ensure that the study was double blind—they made sure that neither participants in the control and the non-control group nor examiners knew who was being subjected to what.

Eighty-nine subjects were taken through the experiments. The results showed no significant correlation between experiences such as sensed presence, etc., and the weak complex magnetic fields that were generated. But they *did* show a correlation between such experiences and their scores on suggestibility indices that figure in psychological tests and neuroscience—the Tellegen Absorption Scale, the New Age Orientation Scale, and the Temporal Lobe Signs Inventory.

Granqvist and colleagues concluded that 'the assumption of temporo-limbic activation in religious experiences is overly simplistic', and, in experimental design even more damningly; that the differences between their findings and those that Persinger had reported may have been due to the fact that Persinger's experiments had not been blind.

The publication of their results in *Neuroscience Letters* created a stir. Persinger and colleagues re-examined the data that had been generated by their experiments.[20]

In this exercise, they re-examined data from nineteen experiments that had included 407 subjects and had been conducted over fifteen years. The results reconfirmed the conclusions that Persinger and his colleagues had been reporting, they said. While reanalysing the data, Persinger and his colleague maintained that they had controlled for both suggestibility as well as temporal lobe sensitivity. Both experimenters and subjects were blind to the experimental purpose, they said, about their falling in one group or another, and other details.

The presence was felt as predicted. When the field was stopped without the subject's knowledge, the feeling faded in about two to three seconds.

They attributed the results of Granqvist and colleagues to the computers that they had used, to the fact that the proper magnetic wave patterns had never been generated as the time for which this was done was fifteen minutes rather than twenty, and to differences in other aspects of the two labs.

Granqvist and his team remained unconvinced. They reiterated their findings, this time with emphasis.[21] Their expectation was that their experiment would confirm Persinger's findings, they wrote. Two of them had visited Persinger's lab for discussions about what was to be done, they reported. Persinger and Koren had given them the portable unit to be used. Both had confirmed that the software the Swedes had received could be used for the computers they were going to use provided that a calibration procedure was followed. This was done. Contrary to what was being said, the room they had used was only marginally smaller than that used by Persinger and his co-researchers. Persinger himself had suggested that '15-20' minutes would do, they wrote. They now showed that the studies that Persinger was citing—the data from which he and his colleague had reanalysed—were *not* double blind. The Swedish team noted that double-blind studies require that neither the experimental subject nor the experimenter knows which treatment the person is being administered. They maintained that this basic difference in design is what accounted for differences in results.

The stuff of contention in science. Soon, a group in Brazil was reporting that, contrary to the Swedish group, they *had* been able to replicate Persinger's results...

In the meantime, a much more definitive result has been obtained in a lab in Switzerland.

A Telltale Experiment

As we saw, when a disorder like epilepsy becomes very troublesome and when it does not yield to any medication, a brain operation becomes unavoidable. When the skull is opened, surgeons have to feel their way to the right spot that needs to be worked on. For instance, once the effects of Parkinson's disease—the tremors, the rigidity and postural problems, the garbling of speech—have become well-nigh unbearable, electrodes are implanted at specific spots deep inside the brain. They function like pacemakers do for heart patients, and help regulate motor and other functions. To locate the exact spots in which the electrodes will best help the particular patient, after openings have been drilled in the skull, the electrodes—they are on the end of leads—are moved around, and the patient is asked to report the effect on her or his condition. For him or her to be able to assess and respond accurately, the patient has to be conscious during this part of the procedure.

In 2005-06, Olaf Blanke and his team in Switzerland—we encountered them earlier in the chapter—were confronted with the case of a twenty-two-year-old lady. She had normal psychiatric history, but had been suffering from epilepsy.[22] By now, her condition required surgery—often connections between the part of the brain where the epileptic focus is located and other parts of the brain have to be severed to ensure that the seizure does not spread across the brain. The doctors were exploring locations in her brain to determine the precise areas that they should tackle. As part of this exploration, they applied electrical stimulation to the left temporoparietal junction.

The lady began to feel that another person—a man, to boot—was present, near her, but outside her. Each time the stimulus was applied, she felt the presence. Each time it was switched off, the feeling of presence vanished.

This presence closely mimicked the position and posture of the woman herself: when she was lying down on her back, she felt the person—'He'—lying down beneath her back—'He is behind me, almost at my body, but I do not feel it,' she said; when she sat, embracing her knees, she felt that the 'man' was also sitting behind her, and holding her in his arms—she felt uncomfortable at this; when she was asked to name a card that was being held in front of her, she felt that the 'man' was sitting along with her to her right, and was trying to interfere with her performing the task—'He wants to take the card. He doesn't want me to read.'

The researchers wrote that 'because the illusory person closely mimicked the patient's body posture and position, we conclude that the patient was experiencing a perception of her own body'.

Given the functions that are associated with this junction—'self-processing, self-other distinction, the integration of multisensory body-related information, and other illusory own-body perceptions'—the neuroscientists concluded that 'electrical stimulation of this area in our patient disturbed multisensory (proprioceptive and tactile) and sensorimotor integration of information with respect to her body, leading to the appearance of a first-rank schneiderian symptom of schizophrenia in a person with no psychiatric history. It is notable that hyperactivity in the temporoparietal cortex of patients with schizophrenia may lead to the misattribution of their own actions to other people.' Furthermore, they observed, 'Although our patient was aware of the similarity between her own postural and positional features and those of the illusory person, she did not recognize that that person was an illusion of her own body, like many deluded schizophrenic patients...'

Could it then be that the physiological and psychological conditions together—not all the conditions in each instance, obviously—that we have been observing—in explorers, mountaineers, single-handers, devotees, the Masters themselves—brought about such electrical discharges or chemical changes so as to stimulate the temporoparietal junction, and this is what in turn made them 'see', 'hear', or 'feel the presence' of another? Or that, given the plasticity of the very structure of the brain, those long periods of sadhana— *twelve years*—brought about such alterations at the temporoparietal junction and so rewired its connections with other regions that the experiences continued to occur repeatedly over the ensuing years?

9

Sangat and suggestibility

Transport yourself to the presence of one of our godmen—the kind to whom thousands flock today, the kind who presides over, who controls and is the chief marketing officer of a huge financial and real estate empire. You have gone there because of some severe problem affecting you or someone near you—a grave illness, perhaps. The doctors have been prescribing medicines for months. The illness has been getting worse. The prognosis is fearsome. Someone has told you that this godman has miraculous powers to heal, to save.

But, your friend tells you again and again, it all depends on your faith: *you* have to do *your* part, he emphasizes, *you* have to believe in the godman, you must *see* that the godman in fact is God, the incarnation of Shiva himself.

As things get worse, you agree to go to the godman with your friend. The sangat is all around him. Bhajans are being sung—addressed to the godman-as-God. He calls on a devotee to tell the sangat what her condition was, what the doctors had told her, what he, the godman, did, and what has been the result. The devotee narrates the miraculous way in which she recovered. A second devotee is called: he narrates how the doctors had insisted that he undergo the surgery at once, as his heart could give way at any moment. How he had been scared to death of the operation. How the godman told him to have the operation postponed for a week, and blessed him, put some leaves from the kitchen on his heart and asked him to keep them there all night. And how, at the next check-up, the two blocked arteries had cleared completely.

Your faith is being strengthened. So many of the devotees have told you of similar miracles that by now you believe that, if you are not getting better, it is because *you* do not have sufficient faith in the godman. The onus has shifted on to you.

Guilt enters. If, believing such miracles to be 'impossible', you entertain any doubt about what has happened, you are in a sense implying that your guru-bhai has fabricated the story. Worse, you are subliminally entertaining the doubt—that the godman does not have powers to heal, or transport himself to another place via his subtle body, or be at two places simultaneously, as the case may be. On the other hand, if you believe the account wholesale, and have not had any comparable experience, manifestly that devotee is in the better books of the godman than you are. So, a subtle competition is triggered. Others—and that includes you—feel compelled to remember, and sure enough the memory comes back to them that the godman has conferred comparable boons on them also.

Your desperation on one hand. The 'evidence' around you on the other. The opportunity of getting cured on one hand. The guilt of not believing and thereby of letting yourself and your relative down on the other ... And the undertow of competitive devoutness.

Over the coming months, this devotion—the word should actually be *dependence*—is deepened. By your being exposed every second day to those accounts of miraculous cures. By a subliminal obstacle course being drawn up: Did the godman look at you today? Were you able to get close to him or did you have to have the darshan from far away? Did he inquire after you? Did he let you touch his feet? Just fleetingly? Or did you get to massage them? Did he give you prasad? The prasad that was given to everyone? Or some morsel of what he was eating from his thali? Has he at last asked you to do something for *him*? To run some errand? To talk to some official so that the adjacent land can become available for parking cars of the devotees?

You begin 'connecting the dots'. Some days are good, some days are bad—just as they used to be. But you connect the good days to the fact that he gave you something from his thali. You connect the bad days to his not having looked at you the previous evening.

Indeed, you begin seeing the dots themselves in a selective way:

You remember the day he gave you the morsel with his own hand *if* something especially good happened the following day. Looking back from a day that did not go well, you remember that the previous day he had not looked at you.

With each session, you become and more and more anxious to 'get to the next stage'—not of spiritual attainment, but of marks that show he is concerned about you, that he is *especially* fond of you.

The word 'especially' is appropriate—for by now the competition vis-à-vis other devotees has set in true and proper.

The initial desperation and the initial accounts that you heard every time you went to the sangat had already put you in a suggestible frame of mind. That hardened into conviction. By now, pride itself has entered—that you *believe* in him even more than the others, and that *therefore* he is particularly fond of you.

This itself is sufficient to work the miracle, or at the least to convince you that a miracle has been worked. If no improvement has occurred, how do you know, the sangat asks, that you would not have been in a worse state but for his grace?

There are exceptions, of course: Sri Ramakrishna is without guile; Sri Ramana is transparent and straightforward as can be. But today so many, so very many are masters—not in matters spiritual but in putting us in a suggestible frame of mind, and then putting that suggestibility to work.

They are caricatures. But precisely for that reason, they may help us glimpse more readily how we come to detect miracles—even in the case of the great and manifestly pure masters like Sri Ramakrishna and Sri Ramana.

The Devotee Becomes an Accomplice

In the early 1960s, M.T. Orne wrote a paper that was to have significant effects on the way that experiments were designed in the ensuing decades, especially in psychology.[1] Orne pointed out that the subject taking part in an experiment is not a passive automaton. He is an *active* participant. As you read Orne's propositions, think of the sangat, the devotee and the godman: for instance, read the preceding two sentences as 'The devotee taking part in the sangat is not just a passive automaton. He is an *active* participant.' As much as the experimenter, Orne pointed out, *the subject develops an interest in the success of the experiment*—in proving what he takes to be the hypothesis that the experimenter is seeking to verify; in 'advancing the cause of science'. Most participants, even if they are not told the hypothesis or the purpose of the experiment, will guess what it is. This is what Orne characterized as the 'demand characteristics of the experimental situation'—what is expected of the subject by the experimenter in his experiment. And accordingly, even if he is not told anything directly, the subject forms an idea of what is expected of him, of what answers will and which will not advance the hypothesis or the cause of science, etc. As a result, the demand characteristics may account for some of the results that are attributed to variables—like magnetic fields ... Or, in our case, to the powers that are attributed to the man-who-is-God.

This effect is by now well documented in psychology and other disciplines, and its variants are known by many names—such as 'reactivity' and the 'Hawthorne effect'. Experiments in factories, in offices, in schools show that people behave in one way when they think they are being watched and in another when they think that no one is looking. They alter their conduct in accordance with what they think is expected of them—in a congregation, in an experimental study.

And there is the well-documented 'contagion effect'—our behaviour, our beliefs are influenced by what others around us are thinking and doing.

Finally, as we have noted earlier, people connect random dots and infer a pattern—they see 'faces in the clouds', to recall the well-known book. The brain does it on its own, unknown to us.

A Song

Two years after Orne's paper, T.X. Barber and D.S. Calverley did an experiment that became just as famous. The song, '*White Christmas*', sung by Bing Crosby was very popular in the 1960s.[2]

They recruited seventy-eight female volunteers. The volunteers were taken through two routines before the actual test. The experimenter told them '"to close your eyes and hear a phonograph record with words and music playing '*White Christmas*' until I tell you to stop". Mark whether you heard the record clearly and believed that the record was playing; whether you heard the song clearly but knew that there was no record actually playing; whether you had a vague impression of hearing the record playing "*White Christmas*"; whether you did not hear the record.'

Next, the volunteers were told: 'Look at your lap and see a cat sitting there. Keep looking at the cat till I tell you to stop.'

In each instance, the process was kept up for thirty seconds. That period over, the volunteers were asked to stop hearing or, in the second routine, looking.

The pretest routines over, the volunteers were primed—with one of two suggestions. One group was told that they were going to be hypnotized; the second group was given 'a motivational talk'. Barber and Calverley reproduce the talk that was given. Do read it—and as you do so notice how very closely, in fact literally, it corresponds to what the new devotee, desperate for a boon, hears in the sangat. Here is what the volunteers in the Barber–Calverley experiment were told after the first pretest round: 'You did not do as well on these tests as you really could. Some people think it is difficult to see an animal sitting on their lap or to hear a phonograph record playing and therefore do not really try hard.'

The corresponding sentences after the sangat will be: 'You have definitely improved, but, yes, it is apparent that you have not yet received the full benefit of being in the Master's presence, from his blessing. That is because you still have some residual doubts about him and his powers. You have not yet come to fully believe that he is the incarnation of Shiva himself. That is why you are not trying hard enough.'

Read each sentence of the Barber–Calverley 'motivational talk' in this way, that is, by transposing it to the sangat:

> However, everyone is able to do this if they really try. I myself can do it quite easily and all the previous subjects that participated in this experiment were able to do it when they realized that it was an easy thing to do and tried harder the second time. This is now a matter of your being able to do two things: first, to control your mind so that it will do what you want it to do; and, second, to take the attitude that these tests are easy to do and that you can do

much better than you did before. This time I want you to really try
to see and to hear the things that I ask you to. Don't assume that it
can't be done. It's really quite easy. Just let yourself really see and
really hear what I ask you to.

The suggestion to half of the volunteers that they will be hypnotized
and the motivational talk to the other half over, they were asked to
hear another popular song, '*Jingle Bells*', and to see a dog in their
lap—exactly as was the case in the first, pretest round.

In neither round was any song played, nor was there any animal
in the lap of the subject.

Even in the pretest round, 54 per cent said that they heard the
song clearly. Five per cent said that they heard the song and believed
that the song was being played on the phonograph. Forty-nine per
cent said that they heard the song even though they knew that it was
not being played.

There was an even greater surprise: there were startling jumps
after the hypnotic routine and the motivational talk. From among
those who had been subjected to the 'hypnotic routine', *73 per
cent* said that they heard the song. Of those who had been given
that 'motivational talk', an astonishing *81 per cent* said that they
had heard the song. Whereas in the pretest round, less than 4 per
cent thought that they had heard the song and believed that it was
actually being played, now 42 per cent and 27 per cent respectively
thought that they heard the song and knew that it was being played.
The figure for the control group went *down*—from 65 per cent to
42 per cent.

Recall that just as no song had in fact been played, there was
never a cat or a dog in the subject's lap. And yet the results jumped
in the same way! In the pretest situation, close to 35 per cent of the
control had said that they could see the animal clearly. Close to 4 per
cent had said in fact that they knew the animal was actually present
in their laps. In the second round, close to 46 per cent said that they
could see the animal clearly in their laps, though none of them felt
that the animal was actually in her lap. Among those who had been
taken through a standard hypnotic routine (in which the steps and
words of an actual hypnosis were mimicked), close to 38 per cent
maintained that they could see the animal clearly; an astonishing 27

per cent maintained that they had felt the animal in their lap. Of those who had been given the 'motivational talk', one half said that they could see the animal clearly; around 15 per cent said that they had felt it in their laps.

One conclusion, of course, was that while the hypnotic routine was effective, the motivational talk was even more so. But the even more telling point was that either routine could induce both auditory and visual hallucinations in such a large proportion of subjects.

Barber and Calverley wrote several papers on these themes— academic interest in hypnosis was very high at the time.*

Merckelbach and van de Ven felt that, as it was originally administered in the 1984 experiment, 'the *"White Christmas"* task more or less invited people to come up with hallucinatory reports', and that the recollection that was sought in that experiment was 'a short-term memory rather than an auditory perception task'. Accordingly, they redesigned the experiment into a more neutral form.

---

*To recall just one of their studies, they enlisted 136 female nursing and secretarial students. They compared the comparative effect of the five components that were routinely used in putting a person under hypnosis: telling the subject that she would be put under 'hypnosis'; asking her to close her eyes; suggesting to her that she was feeling relaxed, that she was feeling drowsy, that she was drifting into sleep; motivational instructions; giving the suggestion that it is easy to respond to further suggestions. Barber and Calverley found that being told that the subjects were being put under hypnosis had substantial effect as did being given a 'task motivating talk'. There was little difference in other variants that were standard to the hypnotic routine—whether eyes were kept open or were shut, or telling the subjects that the task was easy to do or difficult. But a motivational talk *coupled with* the suggestion confidently asserted that the task was easy had as much effect as telling them that they were going to be hypnotized and administering the suggestions of relaxation, drowsiness and sleep. [Cf. T.X. Barber and D.S. Calverley, 'Empirical evidence for a theory of hypnotic behavior: effects on suggestibility of five variables typically included in hypnotic induction procedures', *Journal of Consulting Psychology*, Volume 20, Number 2, 1965, pp. 98-107.] The matter was, of course, not settled, and isn't as yet, as we shall see by glancing at a more recent study—except that that study shows up even more parallels with what happens in congregations around godmen. [Cf. H. Merckelbach and Vincent van de Ven, 'Another White Christmas: fantasy proneness and reports of "hallucinatory experiences" in undergraduate students', *Journal of Behavior Therapy and Experimental Psychiatry*, Volume 32, 2001, pp. 137-44.]

They recruited forty-eight normal, healthy undergraduate students. Participants were brought to a soundproof room. While they were entering the room, Bing Crosby's '*White Christmas*' was playing. The participants were asked whether they were familiar with the song. All participants indicated that they were. Next, they were told that they would hear over headphones a tape for three minutes with white noise. They were also told:

The '*White Christmas*' song you just heard might be embedded in the white-noise below the auditory threshold. If you think or believe that you hear the song clearly, please press the button in front of you. Of course, you may press the button several times if you think that you heard several fragments of the song.

Of course, the song was not embedded at all in the white noise. Nonetheless, *one-third* of the students pressed the button at least once. The groups did not differ on imagery vividness measures. Nor on measures of sensitivity to social demands—of what they might have thought was expected of them. What they did differ to a statistically significant extent was on measures of 'fantasy proneness', a general tendency to endorse odd items, 'a deep and profound involvement in fantasy and imagination'.

That is a result of some significance in the context of the original experiment. But from our point of view, the four variables on which Merckelbach and van de Ven focused—to assess which of them would go farther in explaining the differences between the 34 per cent who pressed the button to indicate that they heard the song, and the rest—are themselves of interest.

These were: imagery vividness, social desirability (that is, what we think the company in which we are would want to hear), hallucinatory predisposition, and fantasy proneness. Each of these is heightened by the godman; by his aura; by what we have heard of him—his miraculous powers; by that which has led us to go to him in the first place—for instance, our desperation; and by the sangat. Each of these leads us to read deep significance in events that may be ordinary happenings; each of them leads us to see patterns in events that may be random; each of them leads us to interpret the Delphic ambiguities of the godman in ways that confirm our belief in him and his powers, in his ability 'to see the future'.

For an excellent demonstration of how very suggestible we can become even without the nudge of factors that permeate the sangat, of how easily we can be 'primed' to perceive what someone wants us to perceive, of how apt we are to 'hear' what we think we should be hearing, please switch on the Internet and go to: https://www.ted.com/playlists/74/our_brains_predictably_irrati

Here, Michael Shermer, the editor of the *Skeptic* magazine, plays a song. Next, he plays it in reverse, and asks you to detect the message 'hidden' in the words played backwards. You can't discern any message. He then has the song replayed in reverse again; but this time, as the song is replayed in reverse, a text is displayed on the screen, and, sure enough, as you read it, you hear the words that aren't there! And all this happens in a secular, non-charged environment. When we are in the presence of the godman, when we are enveloped by the sangat, to this natural 'suggestibility' are added the godman's aura; what we have led ourselves to expect of him and in his presence; the surround sound, so to say, from the sangat; and, most of all, our desperation to believe that the godman really has the powers that all say he has—for only if he has them can he rid us of our troubles.

ANOTHER SET OF CLUES?

Ambiguous cues—fleeting shadows; muffled, unclear sounds; a wafting feather that brushes against us as we make our way home in the dark; retention in our memories of only those occurrences that confirm the beliefs that we have held, etc.—all these come together in another sphere: what we experience in, and what we remember of our visits to places that we have heard are haunted. Over the years, there have been a large number of studies of persons who have visited or were visiting such places. Some of these link back to Persinger's experiments of inducing paranormal and spiritual experiences in the laboratory; some link back to his hypotheses as well as those of others that such experiences are caused by electromagnetic currents on the earth's surface; still others take us even closer to our encounters with godmen, to what we read into what happens in their presence, and, even more so, to what we remember of those encounters in retrospect. Let us race through a few of the studies.

Some places acquire the reputation of being haunted. The feeling that people get in them, that there are ghosts and the like there have been attributed to a host of factors—for instance, to the fact that someone was killed there or had died in exceptional circumstances; to electrical and magnetic fields there, etc. R. Lange, J. Houran and associates studied 924 experiences that had been reported in 127 cases.[3] In earlier papers, they had suggested that the experience occurred because of ambiguous cues in the experiencer's environment or circumstances. A round object may be interpreted as an orange, they wrote, if the person is hungry, or a cup of water if he is thirsty. What we make of something ambiguous that we see or hear or something that brushes against our arm as we are walking down a thicket is also liable to be affected by the culture in which we have been brought up: if we have grown up in a culture in which belief in ghosts is widespread, we are liable to feel that a ghost has caressed our arm even if it was just a bough; or if we are in a place in which, we have heard, a man was strangled to death because of his love for the landlord's daughter, and that his restless spirit still haunts the place, we are liable to take the rustle of leaves to be his spirit wafting by.

There is in addition another set of variables that influences what we read into the ambiguous cue as also how we remember or report it, Lange, Houran and their associates pointed out. These are the objects that were in the line of sight at that time even though we were not consciously looking at them, and ambient sounds even though we were not consciously hearing them. Among these, they wrote, would be an object placed in the subject's line of sight but never mentioned, or a slightly emphasized word or phrase, or a word or phrase that evokes a particular penumbra of associations: the name of a site such as 'Dead Man's Curve', they write, or a specific time of day—for example, '12.00 midnight'. These become prisms through which we see or filters through which we hear what we are focusing on, and thus influence our perception of them.

Their study showed that in approximately two-thirds of experiences, demand characteristics—that is, what the subject thought of the setting or experiment, or the group expected to hear—played a part; in one-third of the instances, prior belief in the paranormal, and in one-fourth cues embedded in the environment—

that object in the line of sight which the subject did not look at consciously, that sound he did not focus on—influenced the outcome. *An astonishing 70 per cent of experiences were 'congruent with cues in the environment'*—that is, if the embedded cue had been 'a lady who died here after being tortured for days', they point out, the subject was liable to perceive a ghost in human form rather than, say, in the form of a hyena.

Two further inferences of the authors and a conclusion have a bearing on our subject. From the statistically significant correlation between belief and alertness to the experience, the authors inferred that believers notice conditions that confirm their expectations. Second, they found that visual cues had a greater impact than auditory ones: as visual stimuli are less ambiguous than auditory ones, they inferred that groups of percipients are susceptible to contagion effects in the detection, interpretation and report of ambiguous stimuli. As for the conclusion that bears on our concerns, it was that contextual variables alone are sufficient to account for many hallucinatory experiences, and magnetic fields, etc., may not be necessary for understanding them.

One of the factors that seemed to lead one to experience paranormal phenomena was one's past or immediate experience: if a person had just seen a phenomenon that seemed to be out of the normal, his mind was liable to be on the alert for similar occurrences, and, therefore, more likely to 'detect' them, or read paranormality into mundane happenings. On one hand, even events that were only vaguely or peripherally like the one he had noticed are now more likely to catch his attention; on the other, each subsequent event or cue, having been interpreted through the prism of the original 'paranormal' event, is now going to reinforce the person's belief in that kind of paranormal occurrence. You just have to transpose a few words and see how exactly they fit what we experience around godmen: if one 'miraculous' recovery has caught our attention, our mind will be alert to other reports of the same kind; each new report is liable to be interpreted through the prism of the first report; and each new report, having been interpreted in the light of the original account, will deepen our belief in his powers.

Houran and Lange devised a small but instructive experiment to assess this hypothesis. They asked a married couple to be on the lookout for extraordinary events that might be occurring in their home. The home was, as they wrote, 'a thoroughly unhaunted house'! It was an apartment in a college complex; no unusual occurrences had ever been reported in regard to the apartment.[4] They started with two assumptions: (1) the environment provides a stable supply of events that can be interpreted as paranormal—just as, we may add, the random firing of neurons in our brains that can be woven into a story; and (2) the probability of noticing an additional anomaly is directly proportional to the number of anomalies that have already been noticed as well as the remaining potential anomalies—just as, we may add, the probability of detecting another miracle is directly proportional to the number of miracles we have already convinced ourselves about.

Though the house was 'thoroughly unhaunted', once the couple had been primed to look for such events, sure enough twenty-two 'unusual' events occurred. One of them was an auditory sensation; in sixteen instances, the equipment behaved in an erratic way; five objects moved—over an average distance of 1.96 metres. Furthermore, if one particular piece of equipment, say, had malfunctioned or moved, it is the one that was more liable to malfunction or move from then on. The authors termed this as the 'Focusing effect'. It turned out that three of the five objects that had moved were the same. All the events involving malfunctioning equipment involved the same apparatus. The same effect showed itself in regard to individuals also. The one who has noticed the paranormal phenomenon is liable to notice it more often in the next round: in this experiment, the lady experienced abnormal events sixteen times when alone; the husband, only twice. And, finally, there was our familiar friend, an attentional contagion: there was a gradual increase in extraordinary events that came to the couple's attention between days one and four; there was a flurry of them between days five to fifteen; after the fifteenth day, the reports gradually died out. The sudden shower of the Master's blessings…

In yet another experiment, Lange and Houran recruited twenty-two persons to roam an abandoned theatre.[5] Orne[6] had demonstrated that a mere suggestion that a particular environment is associated with unusual experiences can induce physical complaints, physiological alterations and hallucinations. Eleven of the twenty-two were told that the theatre was reputed to be haunted—they were instructed to look out for unusual experiences and report them. The other half were told that the theatre was under renovation—they were told that the research that was being conducted concerned people's reactions to such environments. The subjects were randomly assigned. They visited the same five areas of the theatre. The reports of the two groups differed both in terms of the nature of what the persons perceived as well as in terms of the contents of these sensations. Thus, the instructions had not just stimulated vague experiences, they had also induced specific forms that the experiences took. The data strongly support the hypothesis, Lange and Houran concluded, that the 'context effects' alone could be sufficiently powerful to stimulate the temporal lobe in a manner similar to stimulation by electromagnetic fields.

A related study showed another feature that we encounter repeatedly in the company of godmen: the expectation that something extraordinary is certain to occur and the 'experience' that it has occurred come to form a mutually reinforcing feedback loop. Lange and Houran examined the role of fear in forming a confirmatory loop of this sort.[7] Something occurs, some ambiguous cue in the environment entails fear: we enter a park at night for an after-dinner walk; shadows, rustling sounds, a waft of breeze ... If we have been brought up in a culture in which belief in the paranormal is normal, our mind jumps to inferring paranormal phenomena. That genre of explanations having been strengthened, the next ambiguous cue, and we jump to that sort of an explanation even more swiftly, indeed instinctively. Lange and Houran got together fifty-eight students from different countries. Statistical analysis provided clear evidence of a positive feedback loop between belief, experience and fear of the paranormal in those with a high level of fear. Fear interferes with people's attempts at understanding their environments by inducing circular patterns of reasoning from which it may be extremely difficult to escape, they concluded. To 'fear', we can readily add the frame of mind in which we are when we turn to the godman, namely expectation born of desperation.

A glance at two more papers, and the point will be manifest. Richard Wiseman is professor of public understanding of psychology at the University of Hertfordshire, in the UK. He is justly famous for his instructive and arresting work in the service of rationality.[8]

'The Woman in White'

Hampton Court Palace in Surrey, England, has long had the reputation of being a notoriously haunted site. Henry VIII had his fifth wife executed after the unusually long marriage of fifteen months: he had her charged with adultery; she protested her innocence; she begged for mercy; but he had her dragged to what came to be known as 'The Haunted Gallery', and killed. People began to have unusual experiences in this Gallery: they saw a 'woman in white', they felt the presence of someone, they felt dizzy, etc. Nor were such experiences confined to only the Gallery; they struck people in other parts of the Hampton Court Palace also. Richard Wiseman and associates set out to discern explanations for these experiences.[9]

Earlier studies—by Lange and others—had indicated that participants' belief in the paranormal strongly affected the allegedly paranormal experiences they had. For instance, studies of persons who were put through a fake seance, and asked two weeks later whether the table had risen, had indicated a significant correlation between those who believed in the reality of seances and the recollection that the table had indeed risen. Accordingly, Wiseman and associates made it a point to ascertain whether the person believed or did not believe in the paranormal. Second, the studies of Lange and others, as we have seen, had shown that the slightest suggestion that the place was one or the time or occasion was one in which they could expect to experience the unusual, greatly increased the likelihood of persons having such an experience. These subliminal suggestions could have originated from a variety of sources: rumours, advertising, or prior knowledge of previous experiences reported in the location; in one study, Lange and others had reported that almost 60 per cent of 900 reports of seeing ghosts, etc., had mentioned some form of prior suggestion that the location was haunted. Accordingly, Wiseman and his co-researchers tested this 'suggestion hypothesis' by systematically varying the suggestions they gave to participants about which part of the location had been associated with recent reports of unusual experiences. Third, apart from reporting experiments that showed that stimulation of temporal lobes triggered experiences that someone was present, etc., Persinger had been maintaining that there is a significant relationship between the time of onset of unusual phenomena and sudden increases in global geomagnetic activity; as well as with local magnetic activity.

In 2000, in three rounds every day over a week, Wiseman and his colleagues enlisted volunteers from among those who had come to visit Hampton Court Palace—678 of them. There were two locations which were said to be haunted—the Haunted Gallery and the Georgian Rooms. The two are roughly of the same size. Wiseman addressed each batch of participants for fifteen minutes. Half of the participants were told that the Gallery had been associated with several recent reports of unusual experiences, but few had experienced anything unusual in the Georgian Rooms. To the other half, he reversed the suggestions.

The participants were asked to answer two sets of questions— questions that assessed their prior beliefs in the paranormal, and what they experienced during their tour of these two sites. In addition, the magnetic fields were mapped.

Believers reported experiencing all eight of the unusual phenomena—emotional feelings, sense of presence, sounds, changes in temperatures, dizziness, smells, sights and tastes—significantly more frequently than disbelievers. Their answers showed that the believers had more prior knowledge about the areas associated with past unusual experiences than disbelievers. And they were also more likely to interpret their experiences as being due to a ghost.

The variation in suggestions did *not* significantly affect the experiences of participants. This unexpected result could be interpreted in different ways, Wiseman and colleagues noted: 'For instance, the Haunted Gallery has a considerable reputation for ghostly phenomena, and participants may simply not have believed the suggestion that the Gallery was not associated with recent reports of unusual experiences. Also, the suggestion itself was quite subtle and only made once during part of a 15-minute talk about the experiment.' The expectation that there would be significant interaction between participants' belief in ghosts and suggestion manipulation was also not confirmed.

Persinger's theses were surprisingly confirmed in one sense: there turned out to be a significant overall relationship between the location of experiences and variance of local magnetic fields—there was significant positive relationship between mean field strength and location in the Haunted Gallery, and a significant positive relationship between variance and location of paranormal experience in the Georgian Rooms. Again, Wiseman and colleagues noted, these findings could be interpreted in various ways: it could be that magnetic measurements co-varied with some other variables—for instance, visual features of the area or prior knowledge among participants about the area. Moreover, the data did not support the hypothesis that the correlations for believers would be significantly higher than those for disbelievers; and thus the data did not support the notion that belief in ghosts is related to sensitivity for geomagnetic activity, mediated by temporal lobe lability.

One fact stood out: the occurrence of unusual experiences was clearly non-random; the events were clustered in certain areas of the palace. This could be the result of several alternative factors, Wiseman and colleagues noted, of prior knowledge; or of some form of environmental signal—certain chemicals, subtle draughts, odours, electromagnetic fields, and light levels; or they could be the result of features of the rooms (corners, staircases, or doorways that conform to popular conceptions of haunted locations)—in short, the type of embedded cues that Lange and his associates had emphasized in earlier studies.

One related study,[10] and we can move on to list the similarities between these situations and those in which we would be induced to believe extraordinary events emanating in one set from the environment—recall the phenomena we encountered among mountaineers and explorers—and in the other set from the godmen to whom we have turned.

Conjuring 'Clues' from Normal Happenings

In addition to Hampton Court Palace, there is another site—this time in Edinburgh, Scotland—which has a strong reputation of being haunted, the South Bridge Vaults. These 'Vaults' were built in the late eighteenth century, Wiseman and his co-researchers inform us. They consist of rooms, chambers and corridors built under the arches of a bridge. They were used to house workshops, storage areas and accommodation for the poor. Because of ineffective waterproofing and overcrowding, we are told, they degenerated into a disease-ridden slum. They were abandoned in the late nineteenth century. In 1996, they were reopened for tourists. During some of these tours, several visitors reported unusual experiences—among these were the strong sense of presence, seeing several apparitions and hearing 'ghostly' footsteps. As a result, the reputation of the vaults being one of the most haunted places in Edinburgh was fortified.

This experiment built on the experience that had been gained in the Hampton Court Palace experiment. The areas were ranked more minutely: from the 'most' to the 'least' haunted. The participants were now to walk around not in groups but alone—so that noise would not decrease the probability of their sensing unusual occurrences.

Ten vaults were selected. The tour company had maintained records of reports of unusual experiences. Using this data, vaults were ranked between one and ten.

Participants were asked to spend ten minutes in the vaults on their own. They were asked to record all unusual experiences. The hypothesis was that earlier occurrences would predict the frequency of those occurring now as between vaults. The participants were also tested for prior knowledge: they were asked whether they had heard of the location at which people had earlier reported the unusual occurrences to have taken place. The hypothesis was that the correlations between the 'haunted order' and the mean number of experiences reported in each vault would be significant among participants who indicated no prior knowledge of the vaults. Finally, the study examined a wider range of environmental variables: the mean strength and variance of the local magnetic field, air temperature, air movement, lighting levels, lighting levels directly outside the entrances to the vaults, floor space and height of vaults. The hypothesis was that there would be significant correlations between these variables and both the 'haunted order' and the mean number of reported experiences in each vault.

The participants consisted of persons who came to visit the vaults. There were 218 of them. Six daily sessions were held each day over four days. Each session involved a maximum of ten persons. They were requested to fill in two questionnaires relating to prior knowledge; and the unusual experiences they had during the period they roamed around the vaults on this occasion.

The participants reported 172 unusual experiences. Were these due to a ghost? they were asked. 'Definitely yes,' said 0.67 per cent; 'probably yes,' said 2.67 per cent; 38.7 per cent responded 'uncertain'; 43.3 per cent said 'probably no'; 14.7 per cent were unequivocal, 'definitely no'.

There turned out to be a significant correlation between the 'haunted order' that had been prepared on the basis of data maintained by the tour agency and the mean number of unusual occurrences in each vault.

Those who acknowledged prior knowledge were then excluded. The correlation between the 'haunted order' and the mean number of unusual experiences reported by the remaining participants now turned out to be highly significant.

As for environmental variables, for those with no prior knowledge, there turned out to be significant correlations between the number of unusual experiences and exterior light levels, floor space and the height of the vault. Visual cues had the greater effect, and among these, lighting. It could either be that these features created the environment that is stereotypically related to hauntings, Wiseman and colleagues inferred, or that such circumstances directly cause unusual physical and psychological experiences. Going from a well-lit corridor to a dark vault; or an unusually high vault may trigger such experiences.

The frequency of unusual experiences in the two experiments turned out to be similar. It could be that group contagion counterbalanced the noisiness factor in the Hampton Court Palace experiment, the researchers concluded.

As had happened at Hampton Court Palace so also in the vaults, the locations of unusual experiences were clustered, not random. The locations remained consistent over time: the number of occurrences correlated with the 'haunted order'.

Surprisingly, prior knowledge did *not* account for frequency of locations in which the unusual experiences occurred.

In the Hampton Court Palace experiment, variance in magnetic fields in the haunted areas was much higher than in the control areas. And the number of unusual experiences was significantly correlated with magnetic variance. In the vaults experiment, on the other hand, the correlations were not replicated. Nor were they correlated between magnetic variance and haunted order. It may be that local magnetic fields subtly affect certain psychological, psychophysiological and health variables of individuals, Wiseman and colleagues noted, and thus lead them to interpret ambiguous stimuli as paranormal factors.

Together, the two experiments showed that the reputation for being haunted was not caused by questionable eyewitness accounts, nor by prior knowledge, but by environmental factors—including variance in magnetic fields, size of location and lighting levels. The alleged hauntings are not due to ghostly activity, the researchers concluded, but to people responding, perhaps unwittingly, to 'normal' factors in their surroundings.

PARALLELS

The legendary mountaineers and explorers we talked about were very tough individuals—physically, of course, but even more so psychologically. They were certainly not the run-of-the-mill 'suggestible' types. But the situations in which they found themselves—the sensory deprivation, the extreme hunger and thirst, the searing cold, the unimaginable danger—Buhl standing through the night on that tiny, exposed ledge—these too were not run-of-the-mill situations. The question, therefore, is legitimate: could it be that the life-threatening situations in which they found themselves, the extreme privation that was wracking their bodies and minds put them in a suggestible frame of mind?

In any event, the parallels with the godman–devotee situation stand out by a mile, all the more so, when the devotee, desperate for alleviating a problem, for attaining a boon, is in the presence of the godman, and is carrying out his directions. Moreover, the goings-on in the sangat, the spiritual practices and religious rituals are all aimed at putting one in a suggestible frame of mind.

In this situation, the devotee has a tremendous self-interest in both: doing as the godman says; and in experiencing and reporting success.

He has tremendous self-interest in being the 'true devotee', and therefore, in carrying out the instructions of the godman with absolute fidelity, with complete, unvarying diligence: as doing so is a mark of devotion to the godman, and is the sine qua non of getting the boon.

He has tremendous self-interest in obtaining the boon. For, apart from the direct benefit that this will confer—the alleviation of his problem—it is what will establish among other devotees the reputation that he is especially favoured by the godman. Obtaining the boon is just as essential for establishing in his own mind that the godman he has chosen is 'more powerful' and deserving of greater devotion than other godmen.

The first and foremost instruction, reinforced no end by peers, is: 'For the godman's blessing to work, you must have *complete* faith.' So, if it doesn't work, the devotee has lacked complete faith, or was not favoured by the godman—both outcomes that equally put one down among peers.

And then, as we have noticed in the case of hauntings, there is the trait that we all share: attributing significance both to random events; and to how one carries out the instructions. Orne had shown how, even in simple experiments, subjects will go on doing boring, repetitive, meaningless tasks for hours together. And here in the presence of the godman, there is the incomparably higher demand of the godman's personal command, and the need for his approval. The believer endows meaningless tasks with profound, indecipherable significance, he endows Delphic sayings with deep, unambiguous meaning.

The more onerous, the more meaningless the tasks that the godman asks him to perform, the more meaningful they become; the more they demand that we 'penetrate to the inner significance', the more they become a test of one's faith in the godman.

So internalized are these notions of fidelity that the devotee does not have to make a conscious effort to comply, or to report success. He does so unconsciously—insisting that what he is doing is what deserves to be done.

If the boon materializes, and even if the godman were to say, truthfully, 'No, no. I have done nothing. It is all the result of your hard work and chance,' he will *not* be believed by the devotee or the congregation. On the contrary, this will be taken to be but further evidence of the godman's endearing humility.

And if it be the case that even the godman—directly or through subtle hints—suggests that he looks upon complete compliance as the symptom of faith, the devotee will feign, in fact he will convince himself that the godman's blessings have indeed worked. The godman and the devotee thus enter into an unspoken agreement to 'see' success, and broadcast it.

If everything fails, the congregation, indeed the tradition itself, has developed deep formulae, deep convictions to ensure that the blame comes to lie with the devotee, and is not taken to be any evidence of an absence or dilution of powers of the godman.

Not accepting the blame becomes *proof of* less-than-perfect devotion, and more—that one's devotion falls short of perfection; that one did not perform the prescribed duties to perfection; that indeed one's motives were not pure.

The circle is completed. And all is set for us to experience the miracle.

Colour Me in Your Colour...

Think of the cousin who went to the US or UK to study when both of you were in your teens. This is the first time he has come back 'home'. You are struck by how American he has become, how British his mannerisms—including that stutter—have become. Psychologists call this the 'chameleon effect'—we mimic those we are with, we take on the colours of our environment. The mimicry may be purposive—as the chameleon's often is: by taking on the colours of the surrounding foliage, the chameleon becomes less visible to predators as well as prey. But so deep is the instinct that, ever so often, we mimic without even being aware that we are doing so. Experiments have long shown how we mimic strangers as much as those we know, that we mimic those we do not particularly like as those whom we like.[11] Even more telling for our current interest is the fact that people can be primed by the most indirect of suggestions to mimic some category of persons. Tanya Chartrand and John Bargh cite several studies which show that when, during what was supposed to be a language test, words related to rudeness ('rude', 'impolite', 'obnoxious' and the like) were spoken, the subjects were so much more likely to act offensively as against those to whom during the same test words associated with politeness ('respect', 'considerate', 'polite') were spoken—67 per cent of the former interrupted an ongoing conversation as against 16 per cent of the latter. When words associated with being aged and slow and weak were read out, on leaving the room the participants walked more slowly down the hallway. When participants were subliminally primed with stereotypes, they reacted as their stereotyped image of that category would react—they reacted more aggressively to a provocation when they were subliminally primed with faces of 'young male African Americans'. Another experiment showed that participants who were exposed to words associated with positive stereotypes ('professor') did markedly better in subsequent tasks than those who had been primed by words associated with negative stereotypes ('stupid'). Still other studies have shown that asking blacks to list their race before the commencement of a test adversely affects their performance compared to situations in which they are not asked about their race.

Transpose all this to the sangat, to what is talked of in the circle around the godman. Here the priming is not subliminal—it is overt, it is insistent. It is not just for a few fleeting minutes—it is unremitting. And the stakes are so much higher than merely participating in an academic experiment—getting over a tragedy, attaining a coveted goal … right up to salvation. Moreover, the persons around one are not unknowns—they are ones whose company we value, who have in fact become our points of reference. And to top it all, there is the godman's charisma, at the least, the aura that we perceive around him.

How much more likely are we to believe what others around us believe! How much more likely are we to 'see' and to 'experience' what those around us 'see' and 'experience'!

There is another, even more powerful impulse, and it will pay us to go through a classic, and typical study about it. At every step, transpose the experiment, the findings, the remarks of the participants to the situation around a godman.

Wages of Falling Out of Line

As is well known, the horrors of Nazism and Stalinist communism were terrible enough by themselves. But soon it became evident that [1] vast numbers had participated in what had been perpetrated; and that [2] the overwhelming proportion of the populations of the countries had internalized the notions by which the regimes had been functioning. When the Second World War ended, and there was time to reflect on the facts that had become known, there was intense concern. How did so many go along? How did so many actually participate in the atrocities? Recall, for instance, how very many layers of German society had participated in identifying Jews— not just immediate neighbours but those far away who manned land registers, birth and death registers. In the 1950s and 1960s, therefore, there were a series of studies on submission to authority; on the proclivity to rationalize what one does; on internalization of premises that are given to one, howsoever outlandish and extreme they might be.

One of the classic experiments was conducted by Solomon Asch.[12] Asch set out to assess the effect that an unanimous majority would have on a minority of one. The question he chose involved a very simple fact—one that in the normal course required almost no judgement, so manifestly evident was it. And the judgement that the majority was to declare regarding it was manifestly wrong. How would the individual react to that declaration? Would he go along and adopt the manifestly wrong judgement? What would he feel when he was confronted by the unanimity of the rest and his own judgement was to the contrary? Would it make any difference if he were not required to announce his judgement in front of the others, and were instead to just write it down?

Each of us is pulled by conflicting urges: to submit to social pressure versus the urge to stick to what one saw to be right, and be independent of the group. Some are impelled even to defy the group precisely because it is unanimous: would this last impulse be greatly diluted if the majority were not unanimous? What if the dissenter knew that, right or wrong, the majority or some agency on its behalf—some organization with cudgels, or the state itself, or a social group that had become significant in one's life—was liable to punish independence or what it saw as deviance?

The task was simple. One line on the paper was, say, 3 inches. There were three other lines: of 3¾ inches, 3 inches and 4¼ inches. The participant was to decide which of the latter three was of the same length as the first one? Two additional sets were readied: 5 inches vs 5 inches, 4 inches and 6½ inches; and 8 inches vs 6¼ inches, 8 inches and 6¾ inches. You would have noticed, that in each of the three sets the differences of the 'wrong' lines from the standard one were considerable, and would be obvious to anyone.

Seven to nine students were recruited as confederates—as partners in the experiment. They were told the trials in which they had to give, unanimously, the correct answer (the 'neutral' trials), and the ones in which they were to give, unanimously, the wrong answer (the 'critical trials'). Each of them would announce his answer when called upon to do so. A subject was led in. He was seated next to the last of the confederates. There were 123 such subjects—the 'critical subjects'.

There were six 'neutral trials'—in which the confederates gave the correct answer. And nine 'critical trials'—in which they gave the manifestly wrong answer. Among the latter, in some, by prearrangement, they gave the 'moderately' wrong answer: saying, for instance, that the line measuring 3¾ inches was the one that matched the 3 inches line. In others, by prearrangement, they gave the 'extreme' wrong answer—saying, for instance, that the line measuring 4¼ inches was of the same length as the 3 inches line.

When subjects judged the lines by themselves, they judged them correctly 99 per cent of the time. But when they were subjected to the announced opinions of the majority, *three quarters* gave erroneous answers.

The announced estimates of the majority distorted one-third of the reported estimates compared to less than 1 per cent errors when subjects were not exposed to the majority opinion.

In 'neutral trials', that is when the majority gave out the correct answer, there were only three errors in 738 judgements.

Even when the majority announced an erroneous judgement that was 'extreme', Asch found that '(a) most errors are extreme or in accord with the majority, and that (b) a significant proportion of the errors is moderate. Four-fifths of the errors were identical with the majority, while one-fifth were errors intermediate in size between the majority position and the true value.'

And the irony was that the subjects were uniformly of the view that one should be independent, and that going along with a majority when it was in the wrong was wrong!

That what the majority would think of one if one stuck to what was manifestly right had a major influence became even more evident in the next step. When subjects were told that they need not speak out their judgement, that instead they could write it down, the errors fell dramatically—the mean number of errors fell to one-third of the mean that had been registered when the subjects had to state their judgement publicly.

Even at this stage, we can discern several reasons on account of which the pressure of the sangat will be greater than of the majority in such a simple situation.

- The questions at hand—the extent of the powers of the godman; the veracity of his accounts of the visions that he has seen; whether his teaching about the soul, God, the world, maya, karma, is valid or not—would be much, much more complex than the simple one of comparing three lines drawn on a paper with one. As the questions are that much more complex, the participant is more liable to think that the majority may well be right and he wrong.

- Furthermore, the sangat is numerically much, much larger than just seven or nine persons: 'How can so many thousand, how can lakhs be wrong?' the doubting devotee will wonder.

- And as the pressure of numbers, of a mere 'group' is now mingled with devotion, fidelity, the prospect of the boon or relief for which one has been pining, it will be much more intense.

- Compared to a participant in a mere experiment, the participant in the sangat will be desperate to believe, to be part of the sangat.

During the interviews that followed the experiment, those who had yielded to the erroneous view of the majority underestimated the extent to which they had gone along, the extent to which they had yielded to the group—just as the devotee is liable to underestimate the extent to which he has abandoned his discretion and reasoning and just swallowed what the sangat has been telling him.

And then there was the telltale, vital finding of Asch's experiment: when the judgement of the individuals differed from that of the majority, the individuals began to doubt their own judgement, they began to find reasons on account of which they may be wrong and the majority right: my eyesight or my glasses may be misleading me; maybe I got the wrong instructions; 'something must be the matter with me'; 'there must be an optical illusion which the others have figured out and I have not'; they would think me to be 'a silly fool', 'a misfit', 'queer', 'stubborn', 'a wet blanket', 'a sore thumb', 'crazy', a person wanting to draw attention to himself by being contrary ... I will be left alone ... they told themselves. As we read the rationalizations for going along, we are struck by the exact correspondence they have to what will be going through the mind of the person who is assailed by doubts about what the sangat is telling him in regard to the godman, his uniqueness, his divinity, his experiences, his powers, the miracles he has wrought, his teaching.

Endowing Authority

It is not that the sangat or the godman is consciously trying to deceive us—though, of course, there is no shortage of conmen and frauds today. But we are talking about saintly figures like Sri Ramakrishna and Sri Ramana Maharshi: they were not into amassing followers, they were not building empires of men and assets, they were not maximizing TRP ratings. They were certainly not working to acquire dominance over others.

And yet even such saintly figures, such persons who have completely erased their egos, and completely quelled desires, persons who are pursuing no mundane objective at all—even they are in a sense 'authority figures'. There is first of all, the entire mythology, 'The guru is God.' Internalizing that notion, serving the guru in every way, following the advice, even the whims of the guru are essential instruments for erasing one's own ego, for subjugating one's desires, for drawing oneself back from pursuing any goal other than spiritual enlightenment.

Second, and this is just as powerful a factor that leads us to convert a guru into an authority figure, there are the circumstances that have brought one to the guru in the first place. One may have come out of a genuine and deep yearning for spiritual enlightenment, a longing for a vision of God, or for the 'peak experience': in that case, one would have already internalized the desiderata that are in the very air of our culture and heritage—of complete faith in the guru, of complete subordination and submission to him. Or one may have come for relief and help in the face of some blow, or some impending disaster—in this case also, we would have been convinced, by our conditioning or now by the sangat, 'The guru's blessing is always available, but you have to be ready to receive it; and that means that you must have complete faith in him, you must believe—that he *has* the powers to help you, and that he *will* help you...'

In either event we would have sculpted the godman into an 'authority figure'. The devotional counterpart of the effect brought about by the second experiment is the ineluctable consequence.

Stanley Milgram was a psychologist at Yale University. The shadow of Nazi horrors lay over every academic community: how could so many have participated in exterminating six million human beings? Eichmann had been captured, and his trial showed, as Hannah Arendt observed, that he was not particularly evil, he was just a mediocre, run-of-the-mill bureaucrat, and yet had played such an instrumental role in designing and running the extermination camps. Milgram designed an elaborate 'shock generator'. It had thirty switches ranging from 15 volts to 450 volts. Each successive switch would increase the shock by 15 volts. The switches from 75 to 120 volts were marked as delivering shocks of 'moderate' intensity; from 135 to 180 volts as delivering 'strong' shocks; from 375 to 420 volts as delivering 'severe shocks' and were marked as being in the 'danger' zone; those from 435 to 450 were marked an ominous 'XXX'.

Volunteers were recruited. They were told that the experiment was designed to test the relationship of learning and punishment. They were shown the machine, and were administered a shock to acquaint them with what they would be inflicting. They were introduced to another simple, affable person—who, unknown to them, was a confederate. A 'lottery' was gone through with each volunteer to determine who would be the 'teacher'—that is, who would be the one administering the shocks—and who would be the 'student'—and would therefore be receiving the shocks. The volunteer, having got a glimpse of what receiving a shock entails, accordingly understood that he could either be administering the shocks or just as likely be at the receiving end.

In fact, the outcome was rigged—the volunteer would always be the 'teacher' and the confederate the 'student'. The two were placed in different rooms—wires from the 'shock generator' led to electrodes that were pasted on to the 'student'. The experimenter was seated in the same room as the 'teacher'. The 'teacher' was to test the 'student' on word pairs. If the 'student' gave the right answer, the 'teacher' was to proceed to the next word. If he made an error, the 'teacher' was to administer a shock. Every time the error occurred, the intensity of the shock was to be increased by 15 volts. The 'teacher's' room was fitted with pre-recorded audiotapes of the reactions of the 'student' upon receiving the shock—these began from expression of mild pain to the 'student' pleading that the 'teacher' stop the experiment, to shouting that he had a heart condition, to banging the wall and screaming to be let out, to falling completely silent as if he had passed out.

Of course, no shock was being administered. The object was to find out how far the 'teachers' would go—in the face of more and more alarming reactions from the other room. As the voltage mounted, the 'teachers' administering the shocks became more and more uncertain about continuing—as Milgram reported, they began sweating profusely, trembling, stuttering, laughing nervously, some developed 'uncontrollable seizures'. Again and again they would turn to the experimenter and ask if they could stop. The experimenter—the 'authority figure' in this instance—would give one of the following standard replies: 'Please continue', 'The experiment requires that you continue', 'It is absolutely essential that you continue', 'You have no other choice; you must go on'.

And they went on giving worse and worse shocks. When the 'teachers' got frightened that they may well cause grave harm, even death of the 'student', and became worried about the consequences for themselves, the experimenter assured them, 'I am responsible.' That proved enough.

In a poll taken before the experiment began, *those polled had felt that just about 3 per cent would persevere to the end and go up to delivering the shock of 450 volts. Everyone was startled when it turned out that, in spite of their own misgivings, nay, in spite of their own revulsion, 65 per cent went all the way.*

The presence of an authority figure; the fact that the 'teachers' thought that they were subserving a higher cause—that of the experiment, of science itself; the presumption that as the experimenter knew what he was doing, and that he was at a prestigious university, and that, therefore, while the shocks hurt, they must be safe; that as there was someone to take responsibility for the consequences ... such considerations turned out to be enough.[13]

Reflecting on how two-thirds of the subjects were prepared to deliver shocks up to a voltage that they knew would be inflicting terrible pain, that may even be killing another person, and yet had gone on increasing the voltage even when they were themselves distressed, indeed revolted at doing so, Milgram had written in his classic, *Obedience to Authority*:

> This is, perhaps, the most fundamental lesson of our study: Ordinary people, simply doing their jobs, and without any particular hostility on their part, can become agents in a terrible destructive process. Moreover, even when the destructive effects of their work become patently clear, and they are asked to carry out actions incompatible with fundamental standards of morality, relatively few people have the resources needed to resist authority. A variety of inhibitions against disobeying authority come into play and successfully keep the person in place.[14]

Transpose the text to our current context: Ordinary people, simply trying to cope with the latest blow, and without any particular gullibility on their part, can become captives in a whirl of make-believe. Moreover, even when the baneful effects of their new notions, of their unquestioning faith, become patently clear, and they are asked to believe happenings incompatible with mere common sense, relatively few people have the resources needed to resist authority. A variety of inhibitions against being a host to doubts come into play and successfully keep the person in place.

Not the saint, but our circumstances make Oscar Wildes of us all: 'I can believe anything, provided that it is quite incredible.'[15]

Indeed, the more fantastical the happening associated with the Master is, the more we feel compelled to believe it. If it were within the realm of the possible, if anyone and everyone can be at two places at once, where is the question of faith? Where is the question of being true to the Master? We *believe* in the godman only when we *know* that he can do the impossible.

To Round Off

There can be no doubt about the sincerity of the devotees. We may well believe that they actually had those visions. Does juxtaposing their visions with what neuroscientists trigger by stimulating points on or in the cortex in any way call into question the truthfulness of the devotees? Before concluding anything of the sort, we should note that there was a difference of emphasis even among the sages; and in particular we should remember what Sri Ramana himself took the visions or visitations-in-dreams to signify.

Both Sri Ramakrishna and Sri Ramana, like sages before them, emphasized that seekers should not actively seek visions, that they should not get lost in them. They said that such visions, if they were experienced, were just stopping points that one naturally encounters on the path.

On occasion, Sri Ramakrishna himself made light of the visions others had of him. We saw, for instance, Sri Ramakrishna's reaction when a devotee reported seeing him in Dacca—'must have been someone else', Sri Ramakrishna exclaimed. But in general, Sri Ramakrishna took the accounts at face value, at least by implication.

While Sri Ramana did not always brush the visions away— recall, for instance, his narrating his own vision of what is inside the Arunachala Hill to Paul Brunton, or his account of his seeing siddhas to Mudaliar and others—more often he related the experiences to the mental processes of the person experiencing the vision. When the devoted Echammal arrived, agitated and sweating, and narrated how she had just seen Sri Ramana on her way up and he had told her that there was no need to trudge higher up, that she might as well give him the food there, as he was there, Sri Ramana remarked that the vision was due to the fact that she was constantly thinking of him. Similarly, when the Swiss lady described the vision in which she saw him and how his face had become like that of a child, Sri Ramana's immediate response was, 'The vision is in your mind. Your love is the cause.' As the exchange continued, he told the lady that she must have been thinking of a child at the time for that to have happened. To sum up, that such visions were not something happening externally, they were occurrences in the mind itself; and that they were triggered by the practices, and the yearnings of the person.

'Visions are better than no visions,' Sri Ramana remarked when devotees asked him about the depth of interest of foreign visitors in him and their ability to follow and practise his teaching. 'They get interested in that way. They do not take to foreign ideas; when once they do it, they stick on. So much for their merits.' He went on to remark on the vision that one of his earliest disciples Sivaprakasam Pillai had reported, a vision that figures in almost every book on the life of Sri Ramana. Sri Ramana said, 'Visions are not external. They appear only internally. If external, they must assert themselves without there being a seer. In that case what is the warranty for their existence? The seer only.'[16]

A few days later, a visitor to the Maharshi lamented the fact that, though he was of the lineage of the sage Vasishtha, he had not received visions of or 'thought-currents' from the Maharshi, and sought to know what penance he should do for this lamentable failing on his part. The Maharshi's answer indicates what he thought of the nature of visions, as well as his advice that one should not hanker after them—that what one has to seek is something different: 'Visions and thought-currents are had according to the state of mind,' Sri Ramana explained. 'It depends on the individuals and not upon the Universal Presence. Moreover, they are immaterial. What matters is Peace of Mind...'[17]

Visitors and devotees engaged the Maharshi in similar discussions about visions on other occasions. On each of these, the Maharshi taught them that the visions were taking place in the mind of the person concerned, and that they were influenced by the practices and beliefs of the person. Does God become manifest if one is pure and has strength of mind? a devotee asked—the two traits that the Maharshi had just mentioned as necessary. The Maharshi explained:

Such manifestations are as real as your own reality. In other words, when you identify yourself with the body as in *jagrat* you see gross objects; when in subtle body or in mental plane as in *svapna*, you see objects equally subtle; in the absence of identification as in *sushupti* you see nothing. The objects seen bear a relation to the state of the seer. The same applies to visions of God.

By long practice the figure of God, as meditated upon, appears
in dream and may later appear in *jagrat* also.

The Maharshi proceeded to recount the story of Namdev who
remonstrated with an ascetic as the latter was lying down with his
feet on the linga, personifying Shiva. The ascetic asked Namdev to
move his feet to where he felt Shiva was not. Wherever Namdev
shifted the ascetic's feet, right there the linga appeared. 'The moral of
the story is clear,' Sri Ramana remarked. 'Visions of God have their
place below the plane of Self-Realisation.'[18]

'Photisms'—sensations or visions of light—'add zest to
meditation and nothing more,' Sri Ramana observed during another
conversation. He elaborated on this in answers to a Polish lady.
She had visions of Shiva, and was greatly devoted to him. But the
visions are momentary, she told Maharshi. As the visions were full
of bliss, she sought to know how they could be made permanent.
The Maharshi told her that the vision was different from Shiva.
The vision could never be permanent, but Shiva is. So, she should
seek that which is permanent. As the exchange continued, the
Maharshi pressed the distinction further—even if the visions could
be permanent, they could not be ultimately satisfying:

> These questions arise because you have limited the Self to the body,
> only then the ideas of within and without, of the subject and the
> object, arise. The objective visions have no intrinsic value. Even if
> they are everlasting they cannot satisfy the person. Uma has Siva
> always with Her. Both together form *Ardhanariswara*. Yet she
> wanted to know Siva in His true nature. She made *tapas*. In her
> *dhyana* she saw a bright light. She thought: 'This cannot be Siva
> for it is within the compass of my vision. I am greater than this
> light.' So she resumed her *tapas*. Thoughts disappeared. Stillness
> prevailed. She then realized that BE-ing is Siva in His true nature.[19]

In the same way, as we have seen, while devotees put great store by
the fact that 'Bhagavan appeared to them in a dream', and told them
to bring a lime fruit in one case, a notebook in another, Sri Ramana,
when asked whether he had visited the devotees in their respective
dreams, said, 'I don't know. Who knows? He said so. That is all,'

in one case; and 'What do I know? They said so. That is all,' in the other.[20]

When he was directly asked, 'What is the difference between imagination and vision?' Sri Ramana answered, 'One is voluntary and the other is not'—that is, in the former case we deliberately set out to imagine; a vision, on the other hand, arises spontaneously. However, he adds, 'But in the ultimate analysis, though not in the immediate present, even vision must have its origin in the voluntary sphere'—that is, it too must originate in imagination. 'As dreams have their origin there?' the devotee inquired. 'Yes,' said the Maharshi categorically.[21]

Nor is this a surprise. Sri Ramana's conception of the mind might as well be that of a modern-day neuroscientist. 'The mind is what the brain does,' says the latter. The mind is just the bundle of thoughts, explained Sri Ramana.

We should also bear two subsidiary points in mind. First, as we have noted earlier, the *content* of the visions of Sri Ramakrishna and of Sri Ramana differed. And the content in each case had direct antecedents in the religious and cultural milieu in which the sage grew up and came of spiritual age. The point is even more striking when we consider the visions of the devotees. Devotees of Sri Ramana have visions only of Sri Ramana—whether while they are awake as in Echammal's case; or when they are asleep as in the case of devotees who concluded that Sri Ramana had visited them in their dreams. They never have a vision of another sage, say Sri Ramakrishna.

Finally, even in the case of such sincere and truthful devotees, we must bear in mind the confirmatory bias. The devotees would have had so many dreams. In many of them, the sage would have figured. The ones that happen to get recorded and become part of personal history, so to say, are the ones in which what they took to the sage—that lime fruit, that notebook—happened to correspond to what the sage had asked for.

10

Mind>Brain>Body>Mind>Brain>...

Sleep deprivation is just one of the elements that marks the period of sadhana. Starvation; blocking out all sensory inputs; blocking out thoughts and concerns and relationships of the world; singular, unremitting concentration; longing ... And each carried to an extreme that ordinary persons like us cannot even imagine.

The consequences will register not just on the body. The mind—for the moment, let us just take the mind to be 'what the brain does'—and the brain itself will be drastically altered. These changes in turn will set off another round of changes in the body. And those...

PLASTICITY AND ITS IMPLICATIONS

Even as everyone saw infants learn and the elderly forget, and some recover after strokes and others not, for centuries people believed that, once it has reached maturity, the brain is set for life. By now, almost everyone who reads would have heard about the plasticity of the brain.[1]

The number of neurons changes. The number of other neurons to which one neuron is connected changes. The strength of the connections between neurons changes. And then there is the feature that is crucial for our current subject—for recall that we are thinking of what effects twelve and three-and-a-half years of penitential sadhana would have had on the brains and minds of the saints. Sixty-five years ago, in his path-breaking work,[2] Donald Hebb taught the world, 'Neurons that fire together wire together': that is, the more frequently we perform a task, the more frequently a set of neurons gets mobilized as an assembly for performing that task, and as a consequence the stronger the connections in this assembly of neurons become. When a set of neurons is not used for the task for which they had specialized—for hearing, for instance—the connections within the assembly weaken and the neurons get assigned to assist in the execution of other functions—seeing, for instance. This is seen most dramatically in persons—especially children—who have had an entire hemisphere removed through surgery. As the need or cycle for performing a task changes, the brain adjusts the cubic space that it has set aside for the task. Begley tells us that male canaries learn new melodies every spring, and that during spring the regions of their brains that generate new melodies are 99 per cent larger than in autumn.[3] The area in the brain that processes inputs from the finger which a Braille reader uses for reading, to recall another example from Begley, is much larger than the area devoted to processing information from the finger that he does not use for reading.[4] On the other side, if a function is not performed, that part of the brain that had formed for that special task either gets reassigned or atrophies: if for some reason the eye of an infant has to be covered for long at a critical period of development, the child loses the capacity to see from that eye.

Just as changes come about as a result of things that may 'happen on their own'—like a stroke—they can also be brought about by voluntary effort. The ways in which the brains of meditation masters alter have been documented often. Of course, activity within the brain—the different kinds of electrical waves, for instance—changes. But that is not all. In various ways, the structure of and relationships within the brain change, and these changes persist beyond the periods during which the master is meditating. A change can be even more extensive, and can be brought about in even shorter time if we consciously aim at bringing it about and if, along the way, we learn how far we have got in bringing about the change. To take just one example, straightforward biofeedback has been successfully used for this purpose. The effectiveness of the feedback can be enhanced by using devices that give one more precise information about the impact that one's mental effort is having on some specific network or component of the brain. Reference to two related studies that sought to assess the efficacy of a particular type of feedback will suffice. Overt actions—say, moving my right arm—activate the somatomotor cortex. In one experiment, volunteers were asked to merely imagine moving the arm, and were given real-time feedback using functional MRI about the extent to which their somatomotor cortex, the target area, had got activated. The control group received the same sort of training but were not shown any rtfMRI (real-time functional MRI) results. '... the activation that subjects were able to produce due to the imagined movement had more than doubled, and had nearly reached the activation seen for overt movement,' the research team noted. The activation that the control group was able to achieve was much lower. Furthermore, the group that had been able to double the degree of activation in the somatomotor cortex while viewing an rtfMRI had, as a result of the experiment, learnt to activate the area even without rtfMRI information.[5] The second study by DeCharms and colleagues focused on the rostral Anterior Cingulate Cortex (rACC). The rACC is known to play a significant role in our perception of pain as well as its regulation. Twelve patients who had been suffering from chronic pain—pain that had not yielded to a host of therapies—were taught to influence their rACC by viewing in real time the results of their efforts using rtfMRI of the relevant region, the rACC. Compared to the control groups, they were able to alleviate the administered pain significantly better: they fared better than those who had not been taught how to direct their minds to control the rACC; they also fared better than those who adopted general efforts directed at the brain at large; and to those who were shown dummy rtfMRI images, or rtfMRIs of others.[6]

Furthermore, the changes of course come about by our performing or ceasing to perform a particular task. But changes also come about if we just *imagine* that we are performing the task. Athletes know that going over their moves when they are idling, or even dreaming, actually improves their performance.

Pause for a moment and recall that during those prolonged periods of extreme sadhana, inputs from the senses were shut out; every concern, every relationship that was 'worldly' was shut out; an incredibly strong longing was developed for one, exclusive object:

for seeing the Mother, or for realizing the 'Self'. Of one thing we can be certain: the brain would have been altered to a substantial extent. For, another fact that neuroscientists have established is that the brain can be altered and rearranged in very brief periods. In just weeks, the number of neurons, the number of other neurons to which one neuron is connected, the strength of the connections, the size of the ensembles that attend to one function, can all get drastically changed. In their influential book, *A Universe of Consciousness*, Gerald Edelman[7] and Giulio Tononi observe in passing that through biofeedback training, '*often in less than an hour*', we can learn to control the activity of a single, specific neuron in our brain.[8] 'Often in less than an hour'—and here we are talking of *twelve years*, of *three-and-a-half years* of intense activity consciously directed towards a goal. And during these extended periods, they were engaged in not casual, occasional activity, but unremitting activity of an intensity that we cannot imagine.*

MIND TO MIND

That we can influence what goes on in our mind by using our mind, or by putting it in a particular state—the object of rituals, of meditation techniques—can be illustrated in a hundred ways. We will confine ourselves to two: hypnosis and the placebo. Both have direct relevance to our subject: the intense focus on one goal, the induced and exclusive longing for it has an element of self-hypnosis; and the placebo effect is evident in the way persons who deeply believe that visiting a particular shrine or being blessed by a particular person will cure them of a malady.

---

*Of course, plasticity has its limits. If every neuron and every neuronal assembly could be just as easily tasked to perform any task, if they all had 'equipotentiality' as the neurologists say, all stroke patients, all children with cerebral palsy would recover fully, there would be no one with brain-related handicaps. Michael Gazzaniga, who has done exceptional work with split-brain patients, draws attention to the limits with emphasis: Michael S. Gazzaniga, *Who's In Charge? Free Will and the Science of the Brain*, Ecco, HarperCollins, New York, 2011.

Hypnosis

For us, the word 'hypnosis' is associated with trickery—'By his
eloquence, the speaker hypnotized his audience into believing that
he meant what he was saying'—or the show put up by a magician—
often associated with some confederate in the audience who acts
out the sequence. What would we think when we read in *The Wall
Street Journal* that hypnosis was certified as a legitimate method
of treatment in 1958 by the American Medical Association; that,
in 1996, the National Institutes of Health panel ruled it to be an
effective device for alleviating pain from cancer and other chronic
conditions? That it is used as a supplementary aid in several leading
hospitals? For curing a psychological condition—like a phobia, a fear,
or intense and long-lasting anxieties? For altering behaviour? For
overcoming addictions? For overcoming insomnia? For overcoming
conditions ranging from stress to depression to disorders such as
bulimia nervosa? For treating migraine headaches? For treating
irritable bowel syndrome? To relieve pain and anxiety during labour?
For getting wounds, burns, fractures to heal faster? For treating skin
conditions such as psoriasis and urticaria?[9] For preparing for and
recovering after surgery? For relieving severe or chronic pain—
even in a condition so severe as bone cancer? That reviews by the
American Medical Association and the National Institutes of Health
of the US, taking into consideration a large range of evidence, have
concluded that, indeed, hypnotism is a legitimate and potentially
effective supplementary therapy? And that among the organizations
using it are the Harvard Medical School, the Cleveland Clinic, the
Stanford Hospital in the Stanford University campus, the hospital
at the University of North Carolina, the University of Washington's
regional burn centre in Seattle, the Mount Sinai Medical Center, the
Beth Israel Medical Center, both in New York City.

In their book, *Irreducible Mind*, that we encountered earlier,
Michael Grosso and his co-authors advance another consideration
that shows the effect of the mind on the body. It isn't just that
hypnosis helps persons to get through surgeries without having to
be put under general anaesthesia. It isn't just that hypnosis helps
alleviate conditions like debilitating pain. They point out that by
hypnotic suggestion, conditions get created that just did not exist. A

man develops various symptoms of a false pregnancy: an enlarged abdomen, morning nausea, nipple secretion, and 'noticeable' enlargement of one breast. Women are able to increase their breast dimensions. Subjects looking at the same light source are able to dilate one pupil and contract the other. Warts occurring on both sides of the body are not cured as would happen in a general remission; warts on one side of the body or at the location that has been the target in hypnotic therapy disappear and not the others. Stigmata develop; subjects shed tears of blood; they develop burns without having been exposed to a heat source ... Furthermore, the authors give instances of changes not just at particular locations but of changes from and to specific shapes...[10]*

---

*In a volume devoted in part to reawakening the scientific world to the work of the long-neglected pioneer of psychology and psychical research, Fredric W.H. Myers, a friend of William James, the authors recount, among a host of other instances, the remarkable surgeries under hypnosis that were performed in Bengal by James Esdaile between 1845 and 1851. They recall, 'These surgeries included amputations of breasts, limbs, and penises, as well as less severe operations, but the largest number (161) were for removal of often enormous (up to 80 pounds) scrotal tumors, a condition distressingly common in those days in Bengal.' A single case will give a glimpse of what could be and was accomplished under hypnosis alone before modern-day anaesthetics came on the scene: 'One of Esdaile's nearly 300 surgeries illustrates in particularly vivid detail that we are not here talking about the "pinpricks" of most contemporary experimental studies. The case was that of a man who for two years had suffered from "a tumour in the antrum maxillare; the tumour has pushed up the orbit of the eye, filled up the nose, passed into the throat, and caused an enlargement of the neck" ... Although the patient proved difficult to mesmerize, Esdaile finally succeeded in doing so. Then, he reports, "I performed one of the most severe and protracted operations in surgery ... I put a long knife in at the corner of his mouth, and brought the point out over the cheek-bone, dividing the parts between; from this, I pushed it through the skin at the inner corner of the eye, and dissected the cheek back to the nose. The pressure of the tumour had caused the absorption of the anterior wall of the antrum, and on pressing my fingers between it and the bones, it burst, and a shocking gush of blood, and brain-like matter, followed. The tumour extended as far my fingers could reach under the orbit and cheek-bone, and passed into the gullet—having destroyed the bones and partition of the nose ... The man never moved, nor showed any signs of life, except an occasional indistinct moan..."

For the foregoing, see, Michael Grosso, et. al., *Irreducible Mind: Toward a Psychology for the 21st Century*, Kindle Edition, locations 4468 and 4547 respectively.

The leaders in this field, of course, are hospitals in Belgium—the Saint-Luc University Hospital in Brussels and the University Hospital of Liege. They have been doing surgeries for twenty years and more, using hypnosis with a local anaesthetic to desensitize the zone to be operated instead of general anaesthesia. At the University Hospital of Liege, they have been doing almost two operations a day in this way, and have done over 8,000 surgeries by now using hypnosis instead of general anaesthesia. In January 2009, the then eighty-year-old Queen Fabiola of Belgium underwent an operation to correct a thyroid condition: she chose to have it done under hypnosis instead of general anaesthesia. (As news got out, it was described as 'a minor procedure'.) Marie-Elisabeth Faymonville, an anaesthetist at the University Hospital of Liege, who popularized the practice with first aesthetic, then endocrine surgery, told research.eu in 2010, 'Today, it is also being used in breast, vascular, ophthalmic and ear, nose and throat surgery. You can also use it for removing peripheral tumours or operating hernias.' And in addition for thyroid operations of various degrees, for prosthesis to help with breathing, for skin grafting, for reconstruction of the jaws and face, and so on. The case that was the news peg for the article itself related to carotid artery surgery.[11]

The point of relevance for us is manifest: hypnosis shows the extent to which the mind can affect the mind—the perception of pain, for instance—and through it the body itself. And the mind that does this is not that of the hypnotist—he is just the facilitator. The mind that brings about the change is our own.[12]

PLACEBO SURGERY

The same goes for 'placebo'. We think of the placebo effect as something that isn't 'real'. 'That was just the placebo effect,' we say of a doubtful pill or a godman. But in fact the placebo effect shows what our minds can do on their own—to our minds and, through them, to our body. The improvement that comes about is brought about not by the pill but by what the person has come to believe the pill will do. Yes, it is evidence against the exaggerated claims of many a pill. Just as much, it is evidence *for* the power of the mind.

The placebo effect is so marked in several ailments that it sets the basic bar that new medicines must vault over to be accepted as effective medicines.

But what about surgery? Can persons whose condition has deteriorated to such an extent or is so recalcitrant that they need to be operated upon get better *when they merely believe that they have had an operation*?

An Ailment of the Heart

Angina pectoris can intensify to such an extent as to disable a person from doing most of the things that we do without a thought, such as walking for ten to fifteen minutes. In the late 1930s, a procedure that came to be known as internal mammary ligation was introduced in the belief that it increased blood flow to the heart through collateral channels in the vicinity of the ligation. By the 1950s and early 1960s, the procedure had become quite popular. Surgeons and professors at the University of Washington School of Medicine and the National Institutes of Health set out to examine the efficacy of the operation.[13]

They invited seventeen patients who suffered from angina pains that were attributed to coronary artery disease. The internal mammary arteries of eight of them were tied up. In the case of nine of them, only skin incisions were made—that is, while superficial cuts were made, the actual procedure was not carried out. While meeting the patients, the physicians maintained 'a reasonably optimistic attitude', even though they told the patients that the efficacy of the procedure had not yet been established fully. Many of the patients, the doctors reported, had seen 'the enthusiastic report [about the procedure] in the *Reader's Digest*'.

It is only as he commenced the operation that the surgeon would be handed a randomly selected envelope instructing him whether or not he was to actually bind the internal mammary arteries once he had isolated them. The patients were monitored for three to fifteen months: the number of anginal episodes, the number of nitroglycerin tablets they had to take, standardized exercise tests, respiratory efficiency, blood pressure, etc., were recorded, ECGs were taken regularly. The monitoring staff and doctors did not know whether, in the individual case they were examining, the operation had really been performed or not.

Two important results flowed from the study. First, there was no significant difference between those who had actually had the ligations, and those who had merely had the incisions and no ligation. 'From the results of this rather small group of patients,' the doctors concluded, '*bilateral skin incisions in the second intercostal space seem to be at least as effective as internal-mammary-artery ligation in the therapy of angina pectoris.*' In fact, the doctors reported, in the case of only two patients did endurance while walking improve significantly after the procedure: while before the operation, a typical patient could walk without pain for four to five minutes, these two were able to walk for ten minutes without the angina developing. 'It is noteworthy,' the doctors write, 'that both were in the nonligated group.'

Second, in the six months following the surgeries, five of the eight patients whose arteries had been tied reported 'significant' improvement. *But so did five of the nine who had been through merely the sham procedure.* The question certainly arose: Is it that the improvement that the patients in the ligated group had felt was also due, not to the ligation, but to the placebo effect of having had surgery?

At about the same time, another team, working at the University of Kansas medical facilities, carried out a similar study.[14] Eighteen patients with a history of angina pectoris were selected. Each had 'a distinctly abnormal electrocardiogram'. Of the eighteen, five were taken through a sham procedure. Neither the patients nor the evaluating doctors knew which patients had been put through a sham operation and in which the internal mammary arteries were in fact tied. As in the case of the University of Washington study, a number of variables were monitored in the case of each patient: anginal episodes, number of nitroglycerin tablets, exercise tolerance, etc. Each patient was asked to maintain a log.

It turned out that the two principal variables—'the patient's appraisal of his work capacity' and the changes in his ECG—were unrelated. All eighteen of the patients reported a 'materially lessened' angina pain immediately following the operation. This improvement was retained by fifteen of the patients: the remaining three felt the improvement for two days, two weeks and one month after the operation. And yet in the case of thirteen of the fifteen patients who continued to feel much better, 'a distinctly abnormal or "positive" electrocardiographic response to exercise could be provoked ... The degree of exercise necessary to produce a significant change was similar to that required before operation.'

The results led the authors to conclude that among those who had undergone the full operation and those who had been put through only a sham procedure, '*Patient improvement was identical. The exercise electrocardiogram was not altered by either procedure.*' They noted:

> Of the five patients subjected to the sham procedure, all improved subjectively in terms of tolerance to exercise, lessened need for nitro-glycerin and sense of well-being, and constitute, although a very small group, an important and unique group. Any proponent of either medical or surgical therapy for angina who cites as a criterion an improvement in the patient's work capacity, will need to remember and explain away the marked response in the five patients who underwent the sham operation.

They, therefore, concluded with an admonition: 'The benefits described by the five patients who underwent a sham operation should be remembered by all proponents of therapy for angina, either medical or surgical, who cite as their index of proof that the patient was relieved or had a decreased need for nitro-glycerin.'

That is as far as the question of whether tying up an artery is helpful or not is concerned. But the subjective appraisals by the patients hold another lesson. Spare a moment and read what the doctors reported had been recorded by the patients or physicians who talked to the five who had undergone the sham procedure:

> The five patients who had sham operations maintained the following records (or were directly quoted in the physician's records):
>
> Sham No. 12 (total follow-up eight months).
>
> *Questionnaire:* 'Have you noticed any change following surgery? If so, how soon did it occur? In what exact way are you better? Worse? Are you 100 per cent, 75 per cent, etc. better? Same?'
>
> *Answer:* 'Yes, practically immediately I felt better. I felt I could take a deep breath and I have taken about ten nitroglycerines since

surgery. These pains were light and brought on by walking. I figure I'm about 95 per cent better. I was taking five nitros a day before surgery. In the first five weeks following, I have taken a total of twelve.'

*

Sham No. 13 (total follow-up six weeks).

Office Note (two weeks post-operative): 'Has no angina pains since leaving the hospital and has felt well.'

Office Note (four weeks post-operative): Feels much better. Much calmer today. No anginal pain other pain since last visit.'

Office Note (six weeks post-operative): 'Had brief, slight episode of burning-type pain in the area of the incision yesterday while walking. Did not stop walking and pain disappeared within a few minutes. Has had no other pain. The patient is optimistic and says he feels much better.'

Office Note (next day): 'Patient dropped dead today following moderate exertion.'

*

Sham No. 14 (total follow-up three months).

Same questionnaire as Sham No. 12.

Answer: 'I can do anything except real hard lifting. I am running farm equipment and using maybe one nitro a week. I used to need fifteen a day. Believe I'm cured.'

*

Sham No. 3 (total follow-up seven months).

Doctor's Note: 'Internal mammary procedure this a.m. Is feeling well and happy with results. States he has lost the heavy feeling in "pit of stomach" and could feel the difference the moment the arteries were tied off.'

Doctor's Note (five days later): 'No chest trouble even with exercise.'

Doctor's Note (five weeks later): 'Since surgery has been feeling very well and is operating heavy machinery. Could not work before. Believes he has improved very much after surgery.'

Doctor's Note (twelve weeks later): 'Working every day, needs about two nitro a day, but can do about anything.'

*

Sham No. 9 (follow-up six months).

Same questionnaire as Sham No. 12 and 14.

Answer: 'The pressure has come off my chest. I still have angina if I push myself (yesterday, raking). Hiking over your wooden steps doesn't bother me now.'

Now, here were five persons who, at the time of selection for the study, had 'either at rest or on exercise, a distinctly abnormal electrocardiogram', to whom nothing material had been done, and yet who, as these jottings showed, felt so much better. What accounted for the change? The doctors had their hypothesis:

> The traditional relationship of angina and emotion is well accepted. A thoughtful appraisal of this group of patients makes one conclude that true angina was present in the entire group and that *under the strong psychotherapy of surgery* there occurred a rearrangement of the provoking myocardial metabolites, or a lessened sensory pathway or a lessened cerebral awareness.

Changes in perception alone? Or 'real' changes in the body leading to changes in perception? In either case, how? The mind working on the mind? The mind working on the body? The mind working on the brain and, through that, on the body?

THE KNEE

Osteoarthritis afflicts a large number of persons—close to 45 million in the USA alone. The affected joints become less flexible. Moving them triggers pain. The cartilage between the bones loses its smoothness and elasticity. Various consequences follow. Among these, the ends of the bones, no longer cushioned by the cartilage, develop spurs, and the bones on either side of the joint start rubbing against each other. Often the pain is excruciating. In extreme cases, the joint has to be operated upon—sometimes the joint has to be replaced with artificial constructs made of plastic or metal.

In 2002, J.B. Moseley and his colleagues published the results of a telling study about the efficacy of a widely used operation involving 'debridement' (in which the spurs that have grown on the bones are smoothened out) and 'lavage' (in which loose pieces of cartilage and bone and calcium crystals are 'washed out'). About half the patients had reported relief from pain from the procedures. Several studies had reported 'substantial pain relief'.[15] At the time, as they reported, in the USA alone, around 650,000 arthroscopic operations of this kind were being performed. Each cost around $5,000. Thus, even fifteen years ago, around $3.2 billion were being spent on this kind of operation alone.

Between 1995 and 1998, 180 patients were recruited from the Houston Veterans Center. They were randomly assigned to undergo arthroscopic debridement (fifty-nine patients), or arthroscopic lavage (sixty-one patients), or just a 'simulated debridement' (sixty patients) in which 1-cm incisions were made. The surgeon went through all the motions of affecting a debridement—asking for the instruments, etc.—but no instrument was inserted to actually smoothen the spurs. All operations were performed by one surgeon. Post-operative care and monitoring were identical for the three groups. Neither the patients nor those who assessed their condition after the operations knew which patient had come out of which group. The groups were monitored for two years after the operation (164 stayed through the study).

Moseley and colleagues found that *neither in regard to relief from pain in the knee nor in regard to its functioning was there any significant difference between those who had undergone the 'real' procedure and those that had been put through the sham procedure.* 'Indeed, at some points during the follow-up,' they reported, 'objective function was significantly worse in the debridement group than in the placebo group.'

'This lack of difference,' Moseley and colleagues said, 'suggests that the improvement is not due to any intrinsic efficacy of the procedures.' They took pains to refrain from attributing all of the perceived improvement in the third group merely to the mind-altering perception, observing, 'Although patients in the placebo groups of randomized trials frequently have improvements, it may be attributable to either the natural history of the condition or some independent effect of the placebo.' Concluding their review of the results, they cautioned that 'the billions of dollars spent on such procedures annually might be put to better use', and that 'health care researchers should not underestimate the placebo effect, regardless of its mechanism'.

The operations continued nonetheless! Questions were raised about the methodology that had been followed in the study. The overall conclusion that the surgeries were not effective as a treatment was disregarded. In 2008, Alexandra Kirkley and colleagues published results of a new study.[16] Between 1999 and 2007, out of 277 patients, 188 were selected through rigorous eligibility criteria. Eventually, eighty-six underwent surgery, and eighty-six did not. Both sets received optimized physical and medical therapy. The conclusion after two years of follow-up? *'Arthroscopic surgery for osteoarthritis of the knee provides no additional benefit to optimized physical and medical therapy.'* Patients who had been assigned for surgery did show greater improvement on one of the standard measures[17] within the first three months, Kirkley and associates noted, adding, '...however, this transient benefit was anticipated, since sham surgery is associated with a large, short-term placebo effect'. 'WOMAC scores at all other points did not significantly differ between the groups,' they reported. 'In addition to WOMAC scores, a broad range of validated patient-reported outcomes was assessed at multiple time points. None of these instruments identified a benefit of arthroscopic treatment.'

Because of these two studies, we learn, the surgeries have decreased dramatically in the USA. The wear and degeneration of the cartilage, and the consequential pain and loss of function remain as problems, of course. Arthroscopic partial meniscectomies have since taken over as the surgeries of choice for dealing with a tear in the cartilage between the thigh and the lower leg. We are told that around 700,000 of these operations are performed in the USA every year, and they entail a direct cost of four billion dollars.[18]

Between 2007 and 2013, Sihvonen and colleagues selected 205 patients from five orthopaedic clinics in Finland. To study the effect of the surgery for meniscus tear alone, the patients were selected so that each had a degenerative medial tear in the meniscus, but did not have osteoarthritis. Through further criteria, 160 were assigned for diagnostic knee arthroscopy. Eventually, 146 were selected for randomization: seventy were to undergo arthroscopic meniscectomy and seventy-six were to undergo a sham procedure mimicking the 'real' operation. All of them were monitored two, six and twelve months after the operation on three standard measures used for the knee.

The first finding was that *there was no significant difference on any of the measures between the two groups—between those who had undergone the meniscectomy and those that had been put through the sham procedure,* and so, the authors concluded, 'These results argue against the current practice of performing arthroscopic partial meniscectomy in patients with a degenerative meniscal tear.' They also recalled that by the time this study was done, this had become the most common orthopaedic procedure among those performed in the United States.

But the second finding was just as important: Both groups showed a 'marked improvement' on each of the three primary indices, including pain after exercise. That is, *the seventy-six who had undergone merely the sham procedure also improved to a marked extent.* What the authors had noted in the context of validating the aptness of a surgical procedure by comparing it with the results of sham surgery had a resonance beyond that particular context; they had alluded to the fact that '… *the act of performing surgery itself has a profound placebo effect…*' The seventy-six patients who had been put through a sham procedure without knowing that 'real' surgery had not been performed in their case had registered marked improvements on the principal criteria, solely by the impression they had formed that they had in fact had the surgery.

A CRUEL AILMENT

As is well known, Parkinson's disease is a cruel ailment: for reasons that are still unknown, the production of dopamine in the brain diminishes; as the deficiency spreads and affects different parts of the brain, the patient develops several heart-rending symptoms—his movements become slow; he loses balance and, therefore, is less and less able to walk by himself; his limbs begin to flail in uncontrollable ways; as his hands tremble, he begins to need help in eating; soon, he has difficulty swallowing; he comes to need help in performing even elementary functions—he is unable to hold a book, soon he reads less and less; he loses interest, more and more he thinks that the effort to keep up—through exercise, through speech therapy, through solving puzzles, through memorizing poems—is just not worth the effort; his autonomic systems go haywire so that he may, for instance, begin to sweat uncontrollably; his speech gets slurred and indistinct; he begins to hear voices and see visions; he is not able to sleep soundly or for long; his cognition gets impaired, and so his responses to even elementary questions become slow ... As the ailment advances, and for other reasons also, the medication has dwindling effect. The periods when the person can function moderately—the 'on' periods—become shorter. The 'off' periods—when the effectiveness of the drug is at an ebb—stretch longer and longer ... The dosage of the medicines has to be increased. And that intensifies the side effects, especially during the 'on' periods.

In short, cruelty is the principal fact about this disease. The other fact about the disease is that since Levodopa was discovered in the 1960s, there really has been no real breakthrough in drugs to deal with the disease. Supplementary drugs have been developed. Some drugs to supplement Levodopa have been developed—for instance, ones that would improve the absorption of the main drug. Others have been developed to counter the side effects of Levodopa—because the effectiveness of Levodopa decreases as the years go by, the patient has to go on taking more and more of the dopamine supplement; and that triggers several disabling side effects: for instance, freezing and uncontrollable flailing of the legs. But, while a very large number of leading scientists and companies have been working on the matter, no new drug has come up as yet that would have as dramatic an effect on the symptoms that afflict and disable patients as the initial discovery of Levodopa. Surgery has been the other option—from cutting off connections between some regions of the brain to implanting fetal cells to implanting pacemaker-like electrodes in the brain. Hundreds of thousands, among them our family, hope that a breakthrough will come before it is too late for them.

By the late 1980s, experiments had established that dopamine cells extracted from fetuses could survive when implanted in the brains of rats, and that they altered the behaviour of the rats. Fetal cells have the property that as they have not specialized, they have the potential to take on functions that their neighbourhood requires of them. So, the idea was that, if these could be implanted in areas of the brain where dopamine cells had died, and if they survived, they might start producing dopamine.

In 1992, Curt Freed and a number of other doctors published results of implanting fetal cells in the brains of seven patients.[19] The patients had suffered from Parkinson's disease for seven to twenty years. In two of the patients, the cells were implanted in the caudate and the putamen on the side of the brain that was the opposite of the one that displayed the worst symptoms. In the remaining five, the implants were made bilaterally in the putamen alone. The patients were monitored daily during their 'on' state for twelve to forty-six months after the surgery, and were assessed on standard scales that have been developed for the disease.

The first major finding of the experiments was that the dopamine cells were observed to have survived even forty-six months after surgery. Second, five of the seven patients showed significant improvement on all the standard measurements six months after surgery. These improvements included a reduction in the swings between the 'on' and 'off' periods, ability to carry out daily activities, etc. As a result of these improvements, the patients were able to reduce medication by almost 40 per cent. The authors' summary of the results would have warmed many a heart:

> All seven patients reported improvement according to the Activities of Daily Living Scale while in the on-state. Five of the seven patients had better scores on neurologic examination when in this state. Four patients and their examining physicians considered their improvement to have made an important difference in their daily lives. At best, fetal-tissue implants led to improvements in the patient's gait, speech, and speed of movement. Autonomic signs of Parkinson's disease such as constipation and urinary urgency appeared to have moderated in two patients. The dose of carbidopa-levodopa had to be reduced because of increased involuntary movements after surgery. Freezing spells persisted but were said to be shorter. The quality of on-time improved, with normal motor control in some patients and smoother control in others. Most patients were better able to sleep.

The passing remark—'The dose of carbidopa-levodopa had to be reduced because of increased involuntary movements after surgery'—

presaged a problem that would assume unanticipated magnitude, but, going by the overall report, almost every patient would have been willing to take the risk, especially because the doctors' text indicated that this side effect could be countered by reducing the dosage of the medicines.

In 2001, *The New England Journal of Medicine* carried the report of a second study by Curt Freed and colleagues.[20] This time, they studied forty patients who had suffered Parkinson's disease for an average of fourteen years. And a major dimension was added: in twenty of them, embryonic dopamine neurons were implanted; in the case of the remaining twenty, holes were drilled in the skull but the needles through which the cells were implanted did not penetrate into the brain and contained no cells—in other words, they were taken through the motions of the operation but the cells were not implanted. Patients were followed from one to three years. Neither the patients nor physicians who monitored them knew which of them had and which had not received the cells.

The results turned out to differ dramatically from the earlier study. One outcome was confirmed: The neurons had survived in the putamen of seventeen of the twenty in the transplantation group, and they had grown fibres that are needed for them to connect to other neurons.

Twelve months after the surgeries, there were significant improvements in one group: those who were younger—sixty years or younger—and that too only before they took the morning dose. All others reported that they felt worse. Overall, during their off-periods, patients who had received transplants scored better in regard to motor movements, but the improvement was not better to any statistically significant extent from those who had not received the cells. And the tremors were no less. During the on-periods, the best scores for the two groups were not significantly different. During the off-periods, the younger patients who had received the cells were able to perform their daily activities better than those who had been through the sham procedure. During the on-period, there were no significant differences.

But a year after they had received the cells, an entirely unexpected thing happened, though one that had been presaged by that passing remark in the 1992 paper. Five patients—and they were precisely the younger ones in whom at least during one period, the off-period before they had taken the morning dose, there had been significant improvement—developed aggravated dystonia, that is, rigidity, and dyskinesia, that is, uncontrollable movements. The patients had been told that those who, it turned out, had been put through the sham procedure would have the option of getting the cells subsequently. The procedure needed 'further refinement', the doctors acknowledged. Should fewer cells have been implanted? Should they have been implanted in a different region of the brain and in a different way? In any event, because of what happened to the five, the remaining patients were advised against having the implants.

'Catastrophic', 'A Nightmare'

The clinical prose of the doctors naturally did not quite convey what had happened. 'Parkinson's research is set back by failure of fetal cell implants,' reported the *New York Times*. The side effects were 'disastrous', the paper reported. They were 'absolutely devastating', it quoted a neurologist at Columbia University saying. 'They chew constantly, their fingers go up and down, their wrists flex and distend,' he told the correspondent. They writhe and twist, jerk their heads, fling their arms about. 'It was tragic, catastrophic. It's a real nightmare. And we can't selectively turn it off.'[21]

If one is on medication alone, it is often possible to alleviate the rigidity and the uncontrolled movements by reducing the dosage. But one could not switch off the cells from producing dopamine inside the brain.

Another study reinforced doubts about the efficacy of the transplants. Olanow and colleagues reported on a twenty-four-month study of thirty-four patients who had advanced Parkinson's disease.[22]

Of the thirty-four, thirty-one completed the study. The patients were enrolled and evaluated at Mount Sinai in New York and Rush in Chicago. Surgeries were done in Tampa, Florida. PET studies were done in Vancouver, Canada. Some patients received cells from one donor; some from four—the cells were from embryos aged six to nine weeks after conception; and some were subjected to a sham procedure in which the patients were treated exactly as patients in the other two groups except that after the burr holes had been made, needles were not inserted into the brain and no cells were implanted. No one other than the surgeon knew who had received the transplants, and who had been put through the sham procedure alone. Assessments were made at intervals over two years during the off-period—about twelve hours after the last evening dose—and the best on-period.

The results?

- The transplants did not improve the motor functions significantly.
- In particular, improvements were not any more marked in the younger patients as had been reported by Freed and colleagues.
- And this in spite of the fact that evidence indicated that the implanted cells had survived in high numbers.
- There were differences in the outcomes: [i] patients with transplanted cells were better off than those who had been put through the sham procedure after six and nine months of the surgery, but deteriorated after that; [ii] those who had received cells from four donors fared better than the ones who had received cells from a single donor—but they deteriorated after nine months: this was the interval after which the immunosuppressant drug, cyclosporine, had been withdrawn so that it could be that the grafts were partially rejected once the drug was withdrawn; [iii] patients who had the disease in its more severe form showed no significant change; [iv] those who had less severe disease fared better than ones who had it in a more severe form—'although this reflects failure of transplanted patients to deteriorate rather than improvement in Parkinsonian features'.
- Fifty-six per cent of the patients who had received transplants developed 'potentially disabling' dyskinesia during their off-periods, something they had not had before the transplants, and something that did not develop in patients who had undergone the sham procedure.

The conclusion? 'We cannot therefore recommend fetal nigral transplantation as a therapy for PD [Parkinson's disease] at this time.'

A TELLING PAPER

In a study that would turn out to exercise considerable influence
in the following years, Cynthia McRae and colleagues revisited
the analysis that Freed and his co-authors had published in 2001.
McRae's analysis showed that [i] there was a strong placebo effect of
the surgeries; and that [ii] the effect itself depended not on whether
the patients were young or old; nor on whether cells had actually
been transplanted in them or they had been put through just the
sham procedure, but on whether the patients *thought* they had
received the transplants or they *thought* that they had been merely
put through the sham procedure.[23]

Patients were grouped into eight categories: by whether or not
they had received the transplants; by whether they thought they had
received the transplants or not; and by their subjective assessment of
their ability to function and that of the medical staff. Each patient
had to report on and be assessed on a number of variables relating
to physical, emotional and social functioning. Three different scales
were used to measure functioning: an overall rating scale measuring
the subjective assessment of the severity of the disease; a scale that
measures the patient's ability to perform the tasks of daily living; and
a scale that indicates the degree to which the disease has advanced—
whether the person is able to walk, to walk with assistance, to move
around only on a wheelchair, etc.

The data showed that *both groups*—that is, those who had
received the transplants and those that had not—were significantly
better in regard to physical functioning, and that this improvement
was maintained over twelve months. There was a notable difference
between the two groups: the improvement in physical functioning
was steady in the case of the sham group; patients who had received
the transplants improved at a much faster pace in the first four
months, however some of the improvement was lost in the ensuing
eight months. *But the difference between the two groups—as
categorized by whether or not they had received the transplants—
was not statistically significant. Except in regard to one variable—
and that was social contact. And, in what must be a surprise, the
group that had been put through the sham procedure scored higher
on this criterion.*

The really significant differences, however, occurred between patients who *perceived* that they had received the transplants and those who *perceived* that they had not. There was no statistically significant correlation between patients who had received transplants and those who thought they had received transplants. But there was one significant trend as the months went by: a week after the surgeries, three quarters felt that they had actually received the transplants; a year later, this proportion had fallen to a third. In all probability, the improvements had not been as much as the patients had expected, and so more and more had come to believe that they had been subjected to just the sham procedure—as one can guess, this change itself has important consequences for the person's ability to function.

At every interval—four months, eight months, twelve months after surgery—on every variable, both the patients themselves as well as the medical staff rated those patients higher who *thought* they had received the transplants than those who *thought* that they had not. Reporting the figures, the authors observed, 'Thus, it seems that the placebo effect was very strong' and that 'These results suggest that *expectancy regarding which type of treatment patients received had a statistically significant effect not only on subjective parameters (Emotional functioning and Social Support) but also on motor symptoms (Physical functioning).* The effects on motor functioning were also recognized by the medical staff, as shown in the clinical ratings...'

And the effect was apparent over time also: those who continued to believe that they had received transplants continued to improve; those who came to believe that they had not received transplants— irrespective of whether they had or not—became worse.

That points to a cruel lemma: As cognition is impaired with the advance of Parkinson's or with the onset of dementia or Alzheimer's, one's ability to expect, to hope, to believe that one has received the genuine stuff—in this case, those implanted cells—will dwindle. And that will lessen the effect of the mind over the body.[24]

Thinking *does* seem to make many a thing so.

Indeed, the placebo effect is so marked, especially in some diseases—and Parkinson's is one of them—and it occurs in so many cases that some are concerned whether it is not impeding the search for improved drugs or surgical procedures. 'Researchers use placebo controls to weed out false positives,' a writer explains. 'But for patients, the real ogre is the false negatives—which can sink a therapy before it has been optimized. The better a trial is at stamping out the former, the higher the rate of the latter—which means at best delays, and at worst dead ends.'[25] Accordingly, one line of investigation has been to try and reduce the sample size that is required for testing a surgical procedure or implant by pre-identifying subjects who are unusually susceptible to placebo effects and to thereby exclude them from the sample.[26]

The point certainly is not that surgery is useless. Nor that the quest ended with the discovery that what the patients *thought* had happened is what was the significant determinant of the outcome. On the contrary, and to our good fortune, the search has continued—in regard to the effect of patients' perception as well as even in regard to embryonic cell transplants. Dopamine neurons have been harvested from stem cells grown in laboratories. The dopamine neurons that were implanted in brains have been observed to have been fully functional and healthy up to fourteen years after the implants, unlike the dopamine neurons that were native to the patients; as the disease advanced these did *not* get infected with the ailments that neutralized and eventually killed off the native ones.[27]

What Knowing Does

To continue with our narrative. The experiment of Ji Hyun Ko and colleagues had another outcome also. As we just noted, the investigation had been aimed at identifying the network that is different in the case of persons who are particularly susceptible to the placebo effect. The network was pinpointed. Activity in it was markedly low in some of the patients. The network became particularly active upon surgery in these patients. These turned out to be the ones who were especially susceptible to the placebo effect. And then came another outcome. At the end of the year, the patients were 'unblended'—that is, those who had been put through the sham procedure were told that they had, in fact, not received the cells. *They had but to be told that they had been put through only a sham procedure and the activity in the identified network subsided to its original levels. The motor disabilities returned.*[28]

From the point of view of the investigation of Ko and colleagues, the significance of this reversion was that it confirmed the original finding—namely, that the network that they had identified was indeed the one that was associated with the placebo effect. From the point of view of our present concern, it is yet another dramatic confirmation of the effect of the mind on the brain and, through that, on the body: when the patients thought that they had received the dopamine neurons, activity in the identified brain networks shot up, and their motor functions improved; when they got to know that they had not received the neurons, the brain networks subsided, and their disabilities came back.

A Dramatic and Famous Case

The literature throws up such instances again and again—and not just in Parkinson's disease. There is the oft-cited case of 'Mr. Wright'.[29] Klopfer, a pioneer in establishing diagnosis and therapies based on Rorschach methods, devoted his presidential address to the Society for Projective Techniques to what he called 'the symbiosis between the cancer patient and his cancer'. In this context, and to illustrate one type of personality—that with the 'floating ego'—he recalled the case of a patient who had been treated by a physician at the Veterans Hospital in Long Beach, California, Dr Philip West. As the account has got both pared and embroidered, having been retold many times,[30] it is best to recall it in Dr West's own words.

Wright had a generalized and far advanced cancer involving the lymph nodes, Dr West wrote in his account to Klopfer. He had developed resistance to all known palliative treatments. 'Huge tumor masses, the size of oranges, were in the neck, axillas, groins, chest and abdomen,' West reported. 'The spleen and liver were enormous. The thoracic duct was obstructed, and between 1 and 2 liters of milky fluid had to be drawn from his chest every other day.' He had difficulty breathing, and had to be supplied oxygen through a mask frequently.

'In spite of all this, Mr. Wright was not without hope.' He had put his faith in a new medicine that was expected to come along soon: Krebiozen. The medicine was still to be tried. There was no evidence till then that it would be able to arrest or reverse a condition

as severe as that of Wright. The American Medical Association
decided to send limited supplies to a hundred institutions. West's
hospital was one of those chosen, and it was sent supplies to treat
twelve patients. Poor Wright did not qualify on the criteria that had
been specified. Apart from everything else, only those whose life
expectancy was at least three months, preferably six months, could
be enrolled for the trial; Wright was not expected to last two weeks.
But seeing his strong will to live, and his entreaties, West decided to
enrol him for the trial nonetheless.

West recalled that he administered the first injection to Wright
on a Friday. 'I didn't see him again until Monday,' West told Klopfer,
'and thought as I came to the hospital he might be moribund or dead
by that time, and his supply of the drug could then be transferred to
another case.'

'What a surprise was in store for me!' he continued. 'I had left
him febrile, gasping for air, completely bedridden. Now, here he
was, walking around the ward, chatting happily with the nurses, and
spreading his message of good cheer, to any who would listen.' Other
patients registered no change or a change for the worse. 'Only in
Mr. Wright was there brilliant improvement. The tumor masses had
melted like snow balls on a hot stove, and only in these few days,
they were half their original size.'

Because of this dramatic turn, the injections were given thrice a
week 'much to the joy of the patient, but much to our bewilderment'.
Within ten days, he was discharged from the hospital, 'practically all
signs of his disease having vanished in this short time. Incredible as it
sounds, this patient, gasping his last breath through an oxygen mask,
was now not only breathing normally, and fully active, he took off in
his plane and flew at 12,000 feet, with no discomfort.'

Conflicting reports began to appear in the papers about the
effectiveness of Krebiozen, the drug in which Wright had placed his
hopes. His hopes waned, Dr West recalled, and after two months of
'practically perfect health', Wright became 'gloomy and miserable'.
The disease flared up again.

Dr West decided to lie to the patient, 'and play the quack'. He
told him that the reason for the relapse was that actually the drug
was indeed most promising, but what had happened was that the
lot from which Wright's injections were taken had deteriorated

while standing. 'A new, super-refined, double-strength' product was due to arrive the next day. Wright regained his optimism and was enthusiastic to start again.

'With much fanfare and putting on an act,' Dr West wrote, he administered an injection of 'the doubly potent fresh preparation'—this was '*fresh water* and nothing else'. 'The results of this experiment were unbelievable to us at the time, although we must have had some suspicion to have even attempted it at all.'

'Recovery from his second near-terminal state was even more dramatic than the first. Tumor masses melted, chest fluid vanished, he became ambulatory and even went back to flying again.' The water injections were continued. Wright remained symptom-free for over two months.

And then came the announcement from the American Medical Association: Krebiozen was worthless in treating cancer.

'Within a few days of this report, Mr. Wright was re-admitted to the hospital *in extremis*,' Dr West wrote. 'His faith was now gone, his last hope vanished, and he succumbed in less than two days.'[31]

Confirmatory Evidence

Three points are worthy of note. First, by now there have been a large number of studies that point to a strong placebo effect in a disease such as Parkinson's. These investigations have been carried out with utmost rigour: extreme care has been taken to ensure that neither the patients nor the evaluators knew which patients in a group had been given the 'real' medicine and which had been given a placebo, or which had been subjected to the 'real' surgical treatment—implants, deep brain stimulus, etc.—and which had been put through merely the sham procedure.

Second, confirmation that at least in part 'thinking makes it so' comes from several other kinds of studies also. Consider just one of these—the contrasting results when medication is administered 'openly' as against results when the medication is administered surreptitiously. The advantage is that in these trials the patient is not being deprived of the advantage that may accrue from the 'real' treatment and yet the analysts are in a position to assess the effect of the mind on the body. In one set, a patient is operated upon.

When he regains consciousness, a doctor or nurse comes and gives him an injection telling him that he is being given a strong analgesic, and that his pain will subside soon. In the other case, no doctor or nurse comes; the same analgesic in the same dose is administered intravenously through computer controls located in another room. Both sets are given the same painkiller in the same dosage. The only difference is that in the first set, patients know that the painkiller has been given; in the second set, they do not. The effects are dramatically different. The same difference is seen when an ongoing treatment is interrupted within the knowledge of the patient, and when it is interrupted unknown to him. As we have noticed earlier, electrodes are inserted for deep brain stimulation in patients. In one round, the patients were told that the stimulus was being stopped for a while. The stimulus was stopped in the same way for the same duration on another occasion, without the knowledge of the patients. Thirty minutes after the stimulus was stopped, the contrast was significant: when the stimulus was stopped with the knowledge of the patient, the pace at which the patient could do things was significantly less than when the stimulus was stopped without his knowledge. The results when the stimulus was revived conformed to the pattern: when it was revived with the knowledge of the patient, he recovered the improvement in his motor functions better than he did when the stimulus was revived without his knowing it. The difference in the response between the two ways of administering the treatment is a measure of the placebo effect—that measure having been obtained without administering the sterile 'medication' (the equivalent of a saline solution or distilled water) or putting the patient through a sham surgery.[32]

The third point to note is that the effect no longer comes out of a 'black box'. It is not 'just in the imagination'. It is real, and the placebo—for instance, the sham procedures recounted above—have real consequences inside the brain: at the synapses, the gaps between neurons, in the chemicals and neurotransmitters that pass across these synapses and flood the brain. In short, the procedures though sham, the medications though make-believe, have real, physiological consequences. And the consequences can occur within very brief intervals of time—within minutes, as some of the studies have shown.

Nor is the effect just something in the air, so to say. Sham surgery and placebo 'medication' work their effects through real, palpable, measurable modulations of activity within the brain. By now a good bit has been learnt about the neural mechanisms through which the placebo works its magic.[33]

Body to Mind

We have seen how the mind can be made to work on the mind. We have seen how the mind can alter the brain. We have seen how doing things with and to our body can alter our brain: how the cubic space devoted to the fingers is larger in the case of expert pianists than it is in our brains. When doctors tell us to exercise, they are getting us not just to tone up our muscles and keep our frame flexible. The exercise alters the structure and connections of our brain also, and it's working. Books are full of instances in which physical activity so altered the functioning of the brain that the malady was cured. To recall just one instance, in *The Brain's Way of Healing*, Norman Doidge[34] writes of a man who, as he puts it, walked off his Parkinson's symptoms. John Pepper was seventy-seven when Doidge wrote about him. He had begun having Parkinson's symptoms fifty years earlier. He had been diagnosed as having the disease twenty years earlier. But by walking five miles a day thrice a week, doing various exercise routines, and by mindfulness—by concentrating on every component of every movement—he had been able to give up medication completely, and had alleviated his motor symptoms to such an extent that Doidge had difficulty keeping up with him as they walked over rough terrain. Because of what he had achieved for himself and because of the help he rendered to other patients, Pepper had been elected the head of a Parkinson's organization. Alleging that he was advocating that patients give up medication all together—which he had never done—and was thereby putting patients at risk, doctors and others had him removed from the posts in the organization. One of the charges against him was that he seemed to have no symptom of the disease!

The walking and exercises and the mindfulness with which Pepper did these, Doidge tells us, must have had real effects in the brain to bring about the results. They would have triggered the higher generation of GDNF, the 'glial derived neurotrophic factor', a brain growth factor that restores damaged cells and protects dopamine-producing cells; as well as BDNF, the 'brain derived neurotrophic factor', which helps form new connections between neurons and protects neurons from degenerating.

WHAT WAS AT WORK?

In the light of these facts about the placebo effect, consider what we so readily believe in regard to cures brought about by blessings and pilgrimages.

As we have seen, Rani Rasmani was the one who built the temple at Dakshineswar. Sri Ramakrishna was employed as the priest. Mathur was the Rani's son-in-law, and the one who managed all her affairs, including those related to the temple. He was the one who shielded Sri Ramakrishna, and served him devotedly for over fourteen years.

We are told that he was very good-looking, and for this, among other reasons, Rani Rasmani had her daughter, Karunamayi, married to him. The daughter had died. The Rani had then got her younger daughter, Jagadamba Dasi, married to Mathur. After the Rani's passing away, the authority over her estate devolved on Mathur. It is because he was now the sole controller of the temple and other assets that Mathur could look after the needs of Sri Ramakrishna, and enable him to function as he willed.

Jagadamba Dasi got virulent dysentery. Every cure was tried. The doctors gave up hope. Mathur was heartbroken. Doubly so. As Swami Saradananda narrates, it wasn't just that Mathur was going to lose his wife so dear to him, he was going to lose control over all assets of the Rani, and thereby he would be left unable to serve the Master.

In the grip of intense anguish, Mathur went to Sri Ramakrishna. Noticing how distressed Mathur was, the Master inquired about what had happened. In 'a choked voice', Swami Saradananda writes, Mathur narrated what pass things had reached, saying, 'The worst is about to happen but, that apart, what grieves me most, father, is that I am going to be deprived of the privilege of serving you.' Taking pity on his condition, Sri Ramakrishna told him, 'Don't be afraid, your wife is going to come round.' Mathur left full of joy and hope.

And lo and behold, when he reached his house he saw that his wife had turned the corner suddenly. Sri Ramakrishna narrated the incident himself to his devotees later. 'Jagadamba Dasi was gradually coming round from that day,' Sri Ramakrishna said, 'and her sufferings from that disease had to be borne by this body (showing his own). As the consequence of bringing round Jagadamba Dasi, I had to suffer from dysentery and other diseases for six months.' Referring to this event later one day, Swami Saradananda reports, Sri Ramakrishna said to Saradananda and other devotees, 'Was it for nothing that Mathur served me for fourteen years? The divine Mother showed him various wonderful powers through (showing his own body) this. That is why he served so devotedly.'[35]

Pause for a moment. When a person seeks a Master's intervention, and is cured, we say, 'The Master has cured him.' When—either because the Master did nothing in response to the sufferer's pleas or in spite of what the Master did—the person dies, we say, 'But that was his (the patient's) karma. Nobody can deflect the prarabdha karma, the karma that has begun to bear fruit. It is certainly not the Master's job to deflect it.'

And how do we know that the patient has died because of his prarabdha karma? Precisely from the fact that he has died!

But no one can think of any ill that the poor fellow had done—no one can say what ill my son had done to be struck by cerebral palsy at birth. 'O, he must have done something in his previous birth.'

And how do we know that—to say nothing of our knowing that there are previous births? Simple: from the fact that he is suffering now! Or, in the case of persons who die in spite of the Master blessing them, from the fact that the Master's blessing did not save them.

Similarly, was the fact that Sri Ramakrishna suffered from dysentery and other illnesses in the ensuing six months just a coincidence—he was ill on several occasions? Or did he get dysentery and other ailments in the ensuing months because he had taken on the illness of Jagadamba Dasi?

Or because of the strong belief in our tradition that in relieving others of their suffering, a Master takes on their karma? That Sri Ramakrishna and others around him certainly held this belief is evident from the way that he as much as Sri Sarada Devi and others accounted for the horribly painful cancer in his throat that he suffered from in the end, and which eventually took his life: they attributed it to the fact that he had been taking on the ill karma of those who used to come to him. To confine ourselves to just one instance, Swami Saradananda reports that when Sri Ramakrishna was lying ill of the cancer at the Shyampukur house in Calcutta where he had been brought so that the doctors could be nearby, Sri Ramakrishna had a vision—he saw that his subtle body had come out of his gross one and was walking up and down. The Master said,

> I saw that it had sores all over its back. I was wondering why they were there and Mother showed that it was because people came and touched my body after committing all kinds of sins; and because out of compassion for their sufferings, I had to take upon myself the results of their evil actions, I had all these sores. That is why this (showing his throat) is there. Why otherwise should there be so much suffering, though this body never did any wrong?[36]

In another instance, also narrated by Swami Saradananda, a man who had developed leucoderma came to Sri Ramakrishna, and implored him to pass his hand over it. If he would only do that much, the disease would be cured, he begged. Sri Ramakrishna said, 'Well, I know nothing, but as you desire, I shall pass my hand. It will be cured if Mother wills.'

'For the whole of that day,' Swami Saradananda reports, 'the Master felt so much pain in his hand that he became restless and said to the Mother of the Universe, "I will never do such a thing again, Mother." The Master used to say later,' Saradananda continues, 'he [the patient] was cured of the disease but the suffering was experienced (showing his body) here.'[37]

Was the leucoderma taking its own course? Was the blessing—equivocal though it was: 'It will be cured if Mother wills'—and the subsequent cure just coincidence? Did the fact that the Master passed his hand over it cure the disease? Or the fact that the patient strongly believed that were the Master to pass his hand over him, the leucoderma would disappear? Similarly, was the Master struck by pain because he had taken on the suffering of another or because he firmly believed that, when he relieved another of the consequences of the latter's evil karma, he himself had to bear the consequences of that evil karma?

Hence, Three Questions

In bringing about the cures, was the power of the saint at work, or plain placebo? In bringing those diseases down on the saint, was a cosmic law at work? Or plain nocebo?* That is one question that arises from what we have considered in this chapter. There are two more that are even more central to our present concerns.

First, given how working on and with the body affects the brain— recall that exercise is what may have stimulated the production of GDNF, a neurotrophic factor whose signalling helps dopaminergic neurons to survive, and BDNF, a neurotrophic growth factor, which in turn led to the alleviation of Parkinson's symptoms—how very significant must have been the changes in the brain that those prolonged periods of extreme mortification of the body would have caused.

But mortification of the body was not the only practice that our saints undertook in those years. Even more intense was the conscious direction of the mind: they pulled it away from all sensory inputs; they pulled it away from all worldly concerns; they filled it with extreme longing for one single, exclusive goal. Given what we have learnt about the effect that the mind has on the mind—in curing diseases, in alleviating pain—how far-reaching must changes in the mind have been, caused by those prolonged periods of such severe disciplining of the mind, and through that of the brain.

---

*'Placebo: 'I shall please'; 'Nocebo: 'I shall harm.'

11

'A God-realised man behaves sometimes like a madman...'

On an occasion that we have come across earlier, Sri Ramakrishna and his close disciples have sat down at lunch. A disciple sings a song in praise of the Mother. 'Hearing the song, Sri Ramakrishna went into Samadhi,' Mahendranath recorded, 'his whole body became still, and his hand remained touching the plate of food. He could eat no more. After a long time his mind came down partially to the plane of the sense world, and he said, "I want to go downstairs." A devotee led him down very carefully. Still in an abstracted mood, he sat near the singer. The song had ended. The Master said to him very humbly, "Sir, I want to hear the chanting of the Mother's name again."'[1]

A few months later,

> It was a winter morning, and the Master was sitting near the east door of his room, wrapped in his moleskin shawl. He looked at the sun and suddenly went into *samadhi*. His eyes stopped blinking and he lost all consciousness of the outer world. After a long time he came down to the plane of the sense world. Rakhal, Hazra, M., and other devotees were seated near him.[2]

And now read the definition of 'Absence Seizures' formulated by the Commission on Definitions and Classification of the International League Against Epilepsy:

The hallmark of the absence attack is a sudden onset, interruption of ongoing activities, a blank stare, possibly a brief upward rotation of the eyes. If the patient is speaking, speech is slowed or interrupted; if walking, he stands transfixed; if eating, the food will stop on the way to the mouth. Usually the patient will be unresponsive when spoken to. In some, attacks are aborted when the patient is spoken to. The attack lasts for a few seconds to half a minute and evaporates as rapidly as it commenced.[3]

Or recall what happened when Sri Ramakrishna's dear mother, Chandramani, died. Here is how Swami Saradananda describes the incident:

Paying regard to the prestige and honour of *Sanyasa* and to the scriptural injunctions connected with it, the Master did not observe *Asaucha* or perform any other rites at the death of his mother. Feeling that he had not performed any action proper for a son, one day he was about to offer *Tarpana*. But no sooner did he take up an *Anjali* of water than a state of spiritual inspiration came to him; his fingers became insensible and separated from one another and all the water fell between his fingers, in spite of his repeated efforts to perform the rite. Then with a heart laden with sorrow he sorely pleaded to his deceased mother his utter incapacity to do it. He was told afterwards by a Pandit that this state comes to a man who has reached the state when actions drop off. With his progress in spirituality he reaches a state when performance of Vedic actions is naturally rendered impossible and he incurs no sin on that account.[4]

And here is how the classification of seizures by the Commission on Definitions and Classification of the International League Against Epilepsy continues as it describes an absence seizure in which, in addition to a lapse in awareness, there are some tonic components:

2. *Absence with mild clonic components.* Here the onset of the attack is indistinguishable from the above, but clonic movements may occur in the eyelids, at the corner of the mouth, or in other muscle groups which may vary in severity from almost imperceptible movements to generalized myoclonic jerks. Objects held in the hand may be dropped.

Typically, absence seizures occur in children and adolescents, but they do occur, less often, in adults also, and in them they are more pronounced and they last longer. The principal manifestation is the same—withdrawing from the world, so to say. The episode starts suddenly, and it ends just as suddenly. Unlike other types of seizures—at an extreme, the grand mal seizures of the type that gripped our Adit, with convulsions and the rest—absence seizures leave no after effects in the form of lassitude or confusion. Quite literally, a person is present one moment fully aware of and reacting to what is going on around him; the next moment, he becomes absent and unresponsive to the environment; and returns after a varying interval. Now he is wide awake. He thinks as clearly and talks as fluently as he was doing before the seizure.

The proximate cause for the seizure is abnormal electrical discharge that diminishes blood flow in the brain. Chemical imbalances also occur. But what triggers them in a specific case at a particular moment is not known, or, more accurately, may be so disparate that even qualified neurologists would have a difficult time pinpointing a specific trigger for a specific episode.

But two factors in general are known to trigger the episodes, and they would be instantly recognizable to a reader of accounts about our mystics: one is rapid breathing—hyperventilation—and the other is flashing lights. Hyperventilation is seen so often to trigger absence seizures—one study records that 90 per cent of the persons prone to absence seizures developed them when asked to breathe rapidly for three minutes—that it is often used as an aide in diagnosing the ailment: the patient is asked to inhale and exhale rapidly for three minutes, and the neurologist observes whether doing so has triggered the seizure.[5] Although hyperventilation is a standard component of standard pranayama regimens, and may well be a routine constituent of practices of our mystics during their years of sadhana, in regard to the subsequent period for which those absences were reported, I have not come across any reference to Sri Ramakrishna breathing rapidly and heavily before he withdrew into his own world, so to say.

SRI RAMANA AT THE TORTOISE ROCK

In the case of Sri Ramana, as we have seen, we have it on his own statement that he used to get fits. Let us go back and reread his account of the incident at the Tortoise Rock on the Arunachala Hill. He and two companions have gone down to a tank. They have had an oil bath, and then a bath. It is around 10 a.m. The day has turned quite hot. They are climbing back to the cave in which Sri Ramana lives. And this is what happens:

'I went to the tank in front of Pachiamman Koil with Vasu and others for a bath,' Sri Ramana was to recall later, 'and we were returning by a short cut, when, as we approached the Tortoise Rock, I felt tired and giddy and so sat down on the rock.' And then,

'Suddenly the view of natural scenery in front of me disappeared and a bright white curtain was drawn across the line of my vision and shut out the view of nature. I could distinctly see the gradual process. At one stage I could see a part of nature clear, and the rest was being covered by the advancing curtain. It was just like drawing a slide across one's view in the stereoscope. On experiencing this I stopped walking lest I should fall. When it cleared, I walked on. When darkness and a fainting feeling overtook me a second time, I leaned against a rock until it cleared. And again for the third time I felt it safer to sit, so I sat near the rock. Then the bright white curtain had completely shut out my vision, my head was swimming, and my blood circulation and breathing stopped. The skin turned a livid blue. It was the regular death-like hue and it got darker and darker. Vasudeva Sastri took me in fact to be dead, held me in his embrace and began to weep aloud and lament my death. His body was shivering. I could at that time distinctly feel his clasp and his shivering, hear his lamentation and understand the meaning. I also saw the discolouration of my skin and I felt the stoppage of my heartbeat and respiration, and the increased chilliness of the extremities of my body. Yet my usual current of "Self-effulgence" (*Atma-sphurana*, Self-awareness) was continuing as usual in that state also. I was not afraid in the least, nor felt any sadness at the condition of my body. I had closed my eyes as soon as I sat near the rock in my usual *padmasana* posture but was not leaning against it. The body which had no circulation nor respiration maintained that position. This state continued for some ten or fifteen minutes. Then I felt a shock passing suddenly through the body, circulation revived with enormous force, as also respiration; and there was profuse perspiration all over the body from every pore. The colour of life reappeared on the skin. I then opened my eyes, got up casually and said, "Let us go." We reached Virupaksha Cave without further trouble. That was the only occasion on which both my blood circulation and respiration stopped.'

Walking uphill in the heat, Sri Ramana

- Feels giddy;
- The view disappears, as if a white curtain is being drawn in front of the scenery in front of him;
- He feels, a second time, a darkness surrounding him and that he might faint;
- And then a third time;
- He feels that his blood circulation and breathing have stopped;
- His skin turns blue, and gets darker and darker;
- He feels increased chilliness in his extremities;
- He has no fear;
- A great surge brings him back to life, so to say;
- There is profuse perspiration 'all over the body from every pore';
- He remains fully conscious through the episode;
- Later on he is able to recognize the march of events in detail;
- He says later that it was the sort of fit that he used to have except that this time it took a very serious form, that it lasted longer, and that both his heart and respiration stopped.

This is manifestly distinct from an absence seizure:

- The onset of an absence seizure, as we have seen, is sudden. By contrast, Sri Ramana's episode is preceded by clear indications—he feels tired, giddy; the view becomes obscured by a white curtain. Neurologists have a word for such precursors: 'aura'. In common usage, an 'aura' is contemporaneous—when we talk of an aura surrounding a person, we think of the here and now, like a halo. Neurologists use the word 'aura' to describe the events that precede the actual seizure.

- It lasted longer than absence seizures do.
- The patient is not conscious of his surroundings during an absence seizure, and he is not aware that anything unusual is happening to him; by contrast, Sri Ramana was fully conscious through the episode
- The patient cannot recall what happened during an absence seizure; Sri Ramana could—in detail, and step by step.

The account would seem to come closer to accounts of a 'partial seizure'—although there is one manifest difference. Sri Ramana's account ends with the words, '...The colour of life reappeared on the skin. I then opened my eyes, got up casually and said, "Let us go." We reached Virupaksha Cave without further trouble...' Generally speaking, the immediate aftermath of a partial seizure—as distinct from, say, an absence seizure—would entail a degree of disorientation and of languor. Partial seizures affect either hemisphere of the brain. The symptoms can vary over a considerable range—depending on which part or region of the brain the focus is in. They may be ones affecting emotions—fear, anger, happiness—or motor functions—the limbs may get stiffened, and extended to an unusual, even awkward position. Often the neck will stiffen, and the head turn to one side— usually the side opposite to the hemisphere in which the focus of the discharge is located.

Partial seizures are classified into 'simple partial seizures' and 'complex partial seizures' depending primarily on whether the person retains or loses awareness during the seizure. Seizures are classified along several other axes, but the symptoms that are of interest for our current concern centre around partial seizures. In particular, along with motor symptoms, or independently of them, the person may have what are called 'somatosensory symptoms' and 'psychic symptoms'. So that their description does not seem to be tailored for the kinds of incidents that are the subject matter of this book, let us recall verbatim the description of these that was given by the Commission on Definitions and Classification of Seizures that we encountered earlier.

3. [Seizures] With somatosensory or special sensory symptoms.
Somatosensory seizures arise from those areas of cortex subserving sensory function, and they are usually described as pins-and-needles or a feeling of numbness. Occasionally a disorder of proprioception or spatial perception occurs.

That is, the person may develop a distorted perception of space or of the position that his body occupies in relation to that space.

...Special sensory seizures include visual seizures varying in elaborateness and depending on whether the primary or association areas are involved, from flashing lights to structured visual hallucinatory phenomena, including persons, scenes, etc. ... Like visual seizures, auditory seizures may also run the gamut from crude auditory sensations to such highly integrated functions as music ... Olfactory sensations, usually in the form of unpleasant odors, may occur.

Gustatory sensations may be pleasant or odious taste hallucinations. They vary in elaboration from crude (salty, sour, sweet, bitter) to sophisticated. They are frequently described as 'metallic'.

Vertiginous symptoms include sensations of falling in space, floating, as well as rotatory vertigo in a horizontal or vertical plane.

And then we have a description of seizures with psychic symptoms. These also fall into several categories. Among these are three that we encounter often in the sorts of descriptions that we have been considering.

First, there are seizures that are accompanied by distortion of memory:

Dysmnesic symptoms. A distorted memory experience such as distortion of the time sense, a dreamy state, a flashback, or a sensation as if a naive experience had been experienced before, known as *déjà-vu*, or as if a previously experienced sensation had not been experienced, known as *jamais-vu*, may occur. When this refers to auditory experiences these are known as *déjà-entendu* or *jamais-entendu*. Occasionally as a form of forced thinking, the patient may experience a rapid recollection of episodes from his past life, known as panoramic vision.

c. Cognitive disturbances may be experienced. These include dreamy states; distortions of the time sense; sensations of unreality, detachment, or depersonalization.[6]

The 'sensations of unreality' refer to a feeling that the environment surrounding one—'the world'—is unreal. 'Detachment' refers to a feeling of being distanced from what surrounds the person or from what is happening around him. 'Depersonalization' is the feeling of being apart from one's body, and feeling that the self we know is not real.

Furthermore, one may form illusions—perceiving a thing to be different from what it is: perceiving it to be larger or smaller, or nearer or farther from, or being of a different shape from what it is. Or one may develop full-scale hallucinations—imagining things to be that are not there at all.

A Classic Account

The character we all remember from *The Idiot*, Prince Myshkin, was diagnosed with epilepsy—in those days it was known, among other things, as 'the idiot disease', hence the title of Dostoyevsky's famous novel. At one stage, Myshkin had to be sent for a cure. The full attack used to so distort his countenance, and the wail he would let out was of such an unearthly nature that he was once saved by these—an acquaintance who had hidden to assault him was so startled by the wail and what he saw happen to the prince as the seizure took hold of him that he fled. But often, these full attacks were preceded by a blissful aura. So vivid were Dostoyevsky's descriptions of these auras that the condition is sometimes referred to as 'the Dostoyevsky epilepsy'.

In the novel, Dostoyevsky describes Myshkin having that ecstatic seizure, and the reconciliation that he arrives at in the end. The passage is oft-recalled. Myshkin is about to board a train. Some indefinable force or feeling suddenly makes him stop. He throws away the ticket. He is somewhat confused. He remembers two incidents but is suddenly uncertain whether they had happened at all or were just hallucinations. In one of these, he has seen an object with a price tag of '50 kopeck' in a cutler's shop window. He sets out to look for the shop: if the shop is there, and if the object is in the

window with that price tag, the incident had actually occurred, he
tells himself, and he has not hallucinated it. 'He felt in a very curious
condition today, a condition similar to that which had preceded his
fits in bygone years,' Dostoyevsky wrote. 'He remembered that at
such times he had been particularly absent-minded, and could not
discriminate between objects and persons unless he concentrated
special attention upon them' ... At last, he comes upon the shop. The
object is there, and it has that price tag. So that incident had actually
happened. But there was an important sequel. He remembers that
the moment he had seen the object, he had turned around and seen
Rogojin, the character who is to later plan to do him harm. And
then,

> ...Convinced, therefore, that in this respect at all events he had
> been under no delusion, he left the shop and went on.
>   This must be thought out; it was clear that there had been no
> hallucination at the station then, either; something had actually
> happened to him, on both occasions; there was no doubt of it.
> But again a loathing for all mental exertion overmastered him;
> he would not think it out now, he would put it off and think of
> something else. He remembered that during his epileptic fits, or
> rather immediately preceding them, he had always experienced a
> moment or two when his whole heart, and mind, and body seemed
> to wake up to vigour and light; when he became filled with joy
> and hope, and all his anxieties seemed to be swept away for ever;
> these moments were but presentiments, as it were, of the one final
> second (it was never more than a second) in which the fit came
> upon him. That second, of course, was inexpressible. When his
> attack was over, and the Prince reflected on his symptoms, he used
> to say to himself: 'These moments, short as they are, when I feel
> such extreme consciousness of myself, and consequently more of
> life than at other times, are due only to the disease—to the sudden
> rupture of normal conditions. Therefore they are not really a
> higher kind of life, but a lower.' This reasoning, however, seemed
> to end in a paradox, and lead to the further consideration: 'What
> matter though it be only disease, an abnormal tension of the brain,
> if when I recall and analyze the moment, it seems to have been one
> of harmony and beauty in the highest degree—an instant of deepest
> sensation, overflowing with unbounded joy and rapture, ecstatic
> devotion, and completest life?' Vague though this sounds, it was

perfectly comprehensible to Myshkin, though he knew that it was but a feeble expression of his sensations.

That there was, indeed, beauty and harmony in those abnormal moments, that they really contained the highest synthesis of life, he could not doubt, nor even admit the possibility of doubt. He felt that they were not analogous to the fantastic and unreal dreams due to intoxication by hashish, opium or wine. Of that he could judge, when the attack was over. These instants were characterized—to define it in a word—by an intense quickening of the sense of personality. Since, in the last conscious moment preceding the attack, he could say to himself, with full understanding of his words: 'I would give my whole life for this one instant,' then doubtless to him it really was worth a lifetime. For the rest, he thought the dialectical part of his argument of little worth; he saw only too clearly that the result of these ecstatic moments was stupefaction, mental darkness, idiocy. No argument was possible on that point. His conclusion, his estimate of the 'moment', doubtless contained some error, yet the reality of the sensation troubled him. What's more unanswerable than a fact? And this fact had occurred. The Prince had confessed unreservedly to himself that the feeling of intense beatitude in that crowded moment made the moment worth a lifetime. 'I feel then,' he said one day to Rogojin in Moscow, 'I feel then as if I understood those amazing words—"There shall be no more time."' And he added with a smile: 'No doubt the epileptic Mahomet refers to that same moment when he says that he visited all the dwellings of Allah, in less time than was needed to empty his pitcher of water.'[7]

Pause a moment; notice, first, that Myshkin remains conscious through the episodes, he is able to recall what he felt while they lasted—and not just in a general way, he is able to describe the elements of the experience. That situates the seizures close to the 'simple partial seizures' we encountered earlier, rather than the 'complex partial seizures' one of the characteristic features of which is that the person loses awareness. Second, recall the elements of the experience that Dostoyevsky sets out:

- ...when his whole heart, and mind, and body seemed to wake up to vigour and light; when he became filled with joy and hope, and all his anxieties seemed to be swept away for ever...;

- I feel such extreme consciousness of myself, and consequently more of life than at other times;
- [A moment] of harmony and beauty in the highest degree—an instant of deepest sensation, overflowing with unbounded joy and rapture, ecstatic devotion, and completest life;
- ...they really contained the highest synthesis of life;
- These instants were characterized—to define it in a word—by an intense quickening of the sense of personality;
- 'I feel then as if I understood those amazing words—"There shall be no more time."'

So full of bliss were the moments that the character in the novel says, '*I would give my whole life for this one instant, ... that the feeling of intense beatitude in that crowded moment made the moment worth a lifetime...*' Dostoyevsky puts these words in the mouth of Myshkin. In fact, he himself used these exact same words on more than one occasion while describing the seizures to his friends—that he would give ten years of his life for the bliss of one of those moments; that indeed, why just ten years, he would give his entire life for the bliss of that one moment.

Notice also the elements that Dostoyevsky lists in addition to bliss—the fact that all anxieties evaporate; that there is a heightened awareness of oneself, as well as of the world around one; that one is in complete harmony with oneself as well as everything around one; that one is in a timeless state.

Ecstatic Seizures

Dostoyevsky's descriptions of ecstatic seizures have proved truly prescient. A recent review reports that by now fifty-two cases have been described and analysed in neurological literature. The accounts of the experience that the patients have given tally almost literally with the accounts set out by Dostoyevsky.[8]

Let us start by reading two of five cases that Picard and Craig described in their 2009 paper:[9]

Case 1: A fifty-three-year-old right-handed female teacher described focal epileptic seizures that began in 2001 as a sensation of warmth filling up her body from her feet to her head. Asked to provide a more precise description of an episode, she explained, 'It was something that I have never felt before. It felt as though my body was filling up with a sensation which was quite surreal. The feeling was almost out of this world. This led to a feeling of complete serenity, total peace, no worries; it felt beautiful, everything was great.' She added: 'During the seizure it is as if I were very, very conscious, more aware, and the sensations, everything, seems bigger, overwhelming me.' When asked if it was like an orgasm, she answered, 'Maybe the closest sensation that I know would be an orgasm, but what I felt was not at all sexual. I have no religious feeling, but it was almost religious.' These episodes influenced her life. 'It is a big happening in your life to have these seizures. Thanks to these experiences, I do not fear death anymore. I see the world differently, every sensation is stronger; for instance I see more colours than before, and I have more detailed perceptions, particularly when listening to music.'[10]

And here is their description of the account given by Case 5:

A sixty-four-year-old right-handed woman who has had epileptic seizures with an ecstatic aura described her experiences as a 'well-being of almost spiritual consonance' and then a decreased consciousness with jargon aphasia. 'The immense joy that fills me is above physical sensations. It is a feeling of total presence, an absolute integration of myself, a feeling of unbelievable harmony of my whole body and myself with life, with the world, with the "All". I feel very, very, very present at that time; the consciousness of myself is very increased, rather on a psychic point of view. I am one hundred per cent concentrated on myself. Entirely wrapped up in the bliss, I am in a radiant sphere without any notion of time or space. My relatives tell me that it lasts two to three minutes, but for me these moments are without beginning and without end. These experiences brought me confidence. They confirm that there is something that surpasses us.'[11]

The resemblance of these to the reports of our mystics strikes us at once. Look at what Hansen and Brodtkorb report about the eleven patients they analysed:

Five of our subjects reported spiritual or religious experiential phenomena. Two felt contact with 'an undescribable phenomenon' (patient 1) or a 'divine power' (patient 6). One interpreted her ictal hallucinations to represent 'the voice of God' (patient 4). Three subjects described a sensation of receiving deeper messages during the seizures. Two felt that these experiences influenced their lives interictally; one interpreted the ictal experience as a prophecy with an objective of giving her life another dimension (patient 9).[12]

These reports were recorded by neuroscientists who were not looking out for any concordance between peak spiritual experiences and seizures; and they are accounts given by patients who were not particularly religious, to say nothing about being engaged in deep spiritual pursuits.

In their open-source review of thirty-eight patients including the two we have just read about, Gschwind and Picard group the observations of the patients into seven categories. It will pay us to glance through their table before we note three general points that have a special bearing on our subject. Here is the grouping provided by Gschwind and Picard:

1. *Intense serenity and bliss*

– 'This led to a feeling of complete serenity, total peace, no worries; it felt beautiful, everything was great.'
– 'The immense joy that fills me is above physical sensations.'
– 'It is a feeling of total presence, an absolute integration of myself, a feeling of unbelievable harmony of my whole body and myself with life, with the world, with the "All".'

2. *Enhanced physical well-being*

– 'It was something that I have never felt before. It felt as though my body was filling up with a sensation which was quite surreal. The feeling was almost out of this world.'
– '[...] a halo, something pleasant which fills my inner body, wrapping me, with a rapid crescendo. It is a well-being inside, a sensation of velvet, as if I were sheltered from anything negative. I feel light inside, but far from being empty, I feel really present. Something has taken possession of my body, to feel really good...'

3. *Heightened self-awareness and/or perception of external world*

– 'During the seizure it is as if I were very, very conscious, more aware, and the sensations, everything, seems bigger, overwhelming me.'

– 'I feel rooted to the spot with a more developed consciousness. I feel a stronger consciousness of the body and the mind, but I do not forget what is around me.'

– 'It affects both the cerebral thought, which is very intense and concentrated on itself, and the physique.'

– 'Being very conscious of myself, I feel discharged from anything else, although I do not lose consciousness.'

– 'I feel very, very, very present at that time; the consciousness of myself is very increased, rather on a psychic point of view. I am one hundred per cent concentrated on myself.'

4. *Feeling of dilated time*

– 'I escape into the time space of my body. It is a moment of fullness in the loophole of time, a return to myself.'

– 'Entirely wrapped up in the bliss, I am in a radiant sphere without any notion of time or space. My relatives tell me that it lasts two to three minutes, but for me these moments are without beginning and without end.'

5. *Feeling of overload*

– 'It is a physical state, an overload. The feeling is intense, with a sensation of fullness.'

– 'The sensation is certainly more intense than could be achieved with any drug.'

– 'This feeling became stronger and stronger, until it became so strong that it was unbearable and led to a loss of consciousness.'

6. *Mystic/religious experience*

– 'Maybe the closest sensation that I know would be an orgasm, but what I felt was not at all sexual. I have no religious feeling, but it was almost religious.'

– 'These experiences brought me confidence. They confirm that there is something that surpasses us.'

– 'It is a big happening in your life to have these seizures. Thanks to these experiences, I do not fear death anymore. I see the world differently.'

7. *Anxiety*

– '...soon after the very first seizures, an anxiety intermingled very rapidly with the bliss sensation.'

– A patient described anxiety because of the anticipated fear of how he would appear to other people during his complex focal seizures. However, as the bliss increased, it overcame the associated anxiety.[13]

Apart from the resemblance that they bear to what our mystics experience, in the accounts given by patients, three features are of great significance for our study.

The first, of course, is the immensity of bliss that they report. Dostoyevsky himself had told his friends that normal people just could not imagine the bliss that he felt during those episodes. Their patients too told neuroscientists that the bliss was total, indescribable. Of the eleven patients that Hansen and Brodtkorb examined, as many as *eight* wanted to experience the seizures, so full of joy were they. Two of the patients surreptitiously reduced the doses of the medicines that their doctors had prescribed—so that they may experience the seizures time and again. One patient said that he had become addicted to the auras.[14]

The second feature is the variety of triggers that set off the seizures: some particular piece of music; remembrance of an earlier episode; visiting a specific place; 'a joy or a sense of relief...'; 'a tractor with the harvest, a nice photo, a nice colour, a flower, a nice landscape, a bird singing, grazing animals, branches that move with the wind, a beautiful woman'; 'or on the occasion of a kiss, a caress, a nice thought about someone, a hope.'[15] In their 2016 review, Gschwind and Picard cite studies that extend this list: specific memories, a pleasant emotional context—'This supports the idea that epilepsies have a certain reflex component whereby a minimal level of functional activation of the epileptogenic (hyperexcitable) zone can trigger the epileptic discharge,' they note citing earlier studies; noises, 'the strong sensory input of a hot bath'.[16]

These two features—intense joy, and the variety of triggers— almost forecast the third. And that is that several patients had learnt to bring on the seizures themselves—by concentrating on former fits, by putting on that particular piece of music, in one case 'by trying to recall the smell of sawdust', 'by partial eye closure with upward deviation in front of a bright light, or a flickering television screen of former times (50 Hz)' ... As the patients came to find bliss in the seizures, and as they came to discover what, in each patient's case, triggered the seizure, they actively brought them on. 'The tendency to seizure self-induction and treatment non-compliance were striking features in several of these patients,' Hansen and Brodtkorb remarked.[17]

As an aside, recall the range of sounds and sights and thoughts and reveries that used to suddenly send Sri Ramakrishna into ecstasy.

WHERE IN THE BRAIN?

The earlier studies tracked ecstatic seizures also to the temporal lobe. In more recent studies, they have been tracked to a structure—the anterior insulae—that lies folded deep in the brain, more accurately in the Sylvian fissure that separates the temporal, parietal and frontal lobes. Gschwind, Picard, Craig and other researchers have suggested possible explanations for why the role of the insulae may have been missed: as EEG recordings are taken from the scalp, they may not have fully registered what was going on deeper in the brain—it is only after advances in technology enabled electrodes to be placed at depth that one could get an accurate record of what was going on in the insulae; the intricate and dense connections between the insulae and, among other sites, the temporal lobe, meant that a seizure originating in or implicating it could almost instantly—within a second—propagate to the temporal lobe and thereby mask the role of the insulae, etc.

These neuroscientists advanced a series of reasons to suggest that the temporal lobe was unlikely to be the site for ecstatic seizures. The seizures continued when removal of sites in the temporal lobe should have ensured that they stopped. On the other hand, seizures ceased when the insulae were tackled. The temporal lobe is not implicated in emotional bursts and yet these are characteristic of ecstatic seizures, they point out. On the other hand, one of the principal functions of the insulae is to assess and direct inputs as they bear on our emotions and feelings—so much so that some group the insulae in the limbic system. Moreover, imaging studies of patients with ecstatic seizures showed maximum activity, including increased blood flow in the insula. Furthermore, MRI studies of meditators showed that the anterior insula—in particular, the right insula—is significantly thicker. Craig and Picard also drew attention to the fact that a type of neurons specific to hominid primates—the von Economo neurons—are found in the anterior insular cortex and the anterior cingulate with which it is densely connected, and that the degeneration of this neuron type is what is associated in dementia with the loss of self-awareness, one of the principal functions in the execution of which the insular cortex is implicated. Of course, the seizure is not ascribed to the insulae in isolation: the insulae and an entire network of connections are activated during the seizure.

Soon, direct and telling evidence emerged. The neurosurgeons were dealing with the case of a twenty-three-year-old lady whose epileptic seizures originating in the right temporal lobe were not yielding to medication. During pre-surgical evaluation, electrodes were placed to cover the right temporal lobe as well as the insular cortex. Stimulation of electrodes placed over the right temporal lobe did *not* trigger seizures. But stimulation of a single electrode placed at the anterior-dorsal insula suddenly provoked the aura—the ecstatic prelude—that she used to experience before the onset of a full seizure. Gschwind and Picard narrate what this result revealed:

> The case of our patient demonstrates several highly interesting facts which complete our understanding of the function of the insula and of brain mechanisms leading to ecstatic seizures. First, the intense feelings of bliss with interoceptive and emotional components can be induced by the stimulation of a relatively small area within the right anterior-dorsal insula. Second, the stimulation was low in intensity, and there was no after-discharge effect, which further confirms the very localized region for this blissful feeling. Moreover and very importantly, this region did not correspond to the initial seizure generator zone, but was the symptomatic zone of seizure propagation, meaning that functional or plastic tissue alteration is not necessarily to be expected in this region. And finally, the fact that the patient reported such ecstatic symptoms since the very beginning of her epilepsy suggests that this anterior-dorsal insular region likely fulfilled a similar function originally, before any seizure related brain tissue destruction occurred in this place.[18]

In papers cited above, the neuroscientists advance persuasive reasons to relate each of the functions that the insulae perform to the different elements that have been reported by persons having ecstatic seizures—from feelings of bliss, to their being mixed with anxieties regarding what is to follow, to heightened self-awareness, to time dilation, and so on.

For the moment we have to bear a question in mind. As we have seen, many of the ascents of our mystics into ecstasy were indeed brief, almost fleeting. But on so many occasions, reports had them staying in that condition much, much longer. On the other hand, even though the person herself is often uncertain how long the seizure lasted—recall a typical narration that we encountered earlier: 'Entirely wrapped up in the bliss, I am in a radiant sphere without any notion of time or space. My relatives tell me that it lasts two to three minutes, but for me these moments are without beginning and without end'—in general, ecstatic seizures are said to be fleeting, lasting just a few seconds or minutes. Could the same insular cortex and its extensive and dense network of connections be the locus of blissful seizures lasting that much longer?

ALL THE GREATER

As is well known, the symptoms that attended the ecstatic states of many a mystic have led analysts to conclude that the mystic in question had temporal lobe epilepsy.

Sri Ramakrishna's behaviour was at times so wayward, his trances so beyond the comprehension of ordinary folk that, even though the people had grown up soaked in stories of saints and their God-inebriated states, they often thought of him as having been touched by madness. Once, when he returned to his village, even his mother thought him to be possessed and called an exorcist to free him from the grip of evil spirits.

That the experiences he had may have been triggered by an ailment was an anxiety that troubled many devotees also. Sri Ramakrishna himself was less concerned about what others said. But some of the experiences were so unexpected and so unusual that his own opinion about his condition swung between confidence and apprehension. As we have seen, he would often say that a God-realized man behaves sometimes like a madman—'he laughs, weeps, dances, and sings', 'Now he dresses himself up like a dandy and the next moment he goes entirely naked and roams about with his cloth under his arm'; sometimes like a five-year-old child—'guileless, generous, without vanity, unattached to anything, not under the control of any *gunas,* always blissful'; sometimes like a ghoul—'he doesn't differentiate between things pure and impure; he sees no difference between things clean and unclean'; and sometimes like an inert thing—'staring vacantly, he cannot do any work, he cannot strive for anything'.[19]

But sometimes during the twelve years of his sadhana, he himself became worried—'Am I going mad?' he wondered.

His disciples, of course, were touched to the quick by such murmurs. A single representative passage from Swami Saradananda's *Sri Ramakrishna: The Great Master* will illustrate the anxiety of the disciples to refute any notion linking Sri Ramakrishna's states and behaviour to any ailment. Here—and the passage is a typical one—is what he wrote:

> There is widespread talk nowadays that the Master learnt the methods of *Sadhana* leading to God-realization from those monks,* engaged himself in too severe austerities and went mad at one time, that his brain became deranged and there came on him a permanent physical disease of losing normal consciousness under the influence of excessive emotion of any kind. My God! We are such a herd of learned fools! The race of the *Rishis* of India showed in their own lives and explained to us through the Vedas and the Puranas, that the normal consciousness vanished, as one ascended to the plane of *samadhi* through the complete concentration of mind ... But, in spite of all this, if we still speak or listen to and believe those hollow words, God help us! O, reader, if you think it is desirable, you may hear those meaningless words credulously; may you and those who say so prosper! But kindly allow us the liberty of lying at the feet of this wonderful, God-intoxicated man. And try once more to understand it well, before you decide it one way or the other. See that the state described by the ancient author of the Upanishad does not come on you:
>
> 'Just as, one blind man guided by another, meets with disaster, so, people, devoid of discrimination, who consider themselves to be intelligent and well versed in the scriptures, live in ignorance and pass through various transmigrations.'
>
> It is not a new thing that the Master's *Bhavasamadhi* is called a disease. Many persons educated in the Western way said so, even while the Master was living. But as time passed on, the 'insane'

---

*Who used to visit him for their own spiritual advancement.

talks and predictions of that divinely inebriated man came true more and more; and the more his extraordinary ideas were eagerly sought and accepted by the people all over the world, the more did their statement lose its force. It met with the same fate as a handful of dust thrown at the moon...

Swami Saradananda went on to describe the statements of Sivanath Sastri, a teacher of the Sadharan Brahmo Samaj, to him and others even as Sri Ramakrishna was living that 'the Master's *Bhavasamadhi* was a disease (hysteria or epileptic fits) produced by nervous disorder and simultaneously expressed the opinion that he became unconscious at the time like ordinary people suffering from that disease'. The remarks had reached the Master, Saradananda noted. 'One day when he [Sivanath] came to Dakshineswar, the Master raised that topic and said to him, "Look here, Sivanath, is it true that you call these a disease and say that I become unconscious at that time? Ah, you people remain all right, although you apply your minds night and day to insentient things like brick, wood, earth, money, etc., and I, who think night and day of Him whose consciousness makes the whole universe conscious, become unconscious! Where have you borrowed your intellect from?"'

'The Master used the words "divine madness", "madness of knowledge", etc., to us every day,' Swami Saradananda continued, 'and freely said to all that a powerful storm of divine love raged in his life for twelve years. He used to say, "Ah, just as, when dust is raised by a storm, all things look alike and trees like mango, jackfruit, etc., cannot be seen, far less distinguished from one another, even so a state came on me which did not allow me to know good from bad, praise from blame, cleanliness from uncleanliness! There was one thought, one idea only, viz., how to realize Him. This was what occupied the mind every moment. People said, 'He has become mad.'"'[20]

To me such anxiety seems misplaced. So what if the symptoms indicate that Sri Ramakrishna used to have 'absence seizures' from time to time, or that the fits that Sri Ramana said he had were 'partial seizures'? That they attained such heights of ecstatic states, that they gleaned such deep insights, that they retained such overflowing compassion *in spite of a problem state* makes them all the greater, and their attainments even more worthy of veneration.

12

The self in the heart

A Swiss lady is complaining about the headaches that she gets if she meditates for long.* 'If the meditator and meditation be understood to be the same, there will be no headache or similar complaints,' Sri Ramana replies. The conversation moves to how notions like heaven arise. They arise, the Maharshi explains, because one is accustomed to relative knowledge, they arise because one's outlook is directed outwards ... The Maharshi explains how the Self which was undifferentiated in deep sleep is differentiated in the waking state, and sees the diversity of things around, and how one must bring about the state of deep, dreamless sleep even when one is awake. This is what jagrat sushupti is, this is mukti, he says.

---

*Most of the passages in this chapter are from *Talks With Sri Ramana Maharshi*, the most authentic of records of the answers that the Maharshi gave to devotees over four years, 1935 to 1939: 'The four years that are covered here,' we are told by Sadhu Arunachala (Major A.W. Chadwick, a long-standing devotee of Sri Ramana) in his Introduction to the volume, 'were the days when the *Asramam* reached the summit of its glory. Maharshi's health was on the whole good and the Hall, where he sat, was open day and night to welcome one and all. Visitors flocked there from every corner of the world, there was hardly a country that was not represented at one time or another...' Even more important, 'The completed notes were often shown the questioners for verification, but the whole had the seal of Sri Bhagavan himself, as the records were always shown him for his approval or the necessary alteration after they had been entered in the notebook.' See *Talks With Sri Ramana Maharshi*, Sri Ramanasramam, Tiruvannamalai, 1955/1984, pp. vii-viii.

The devotee remarks, 'The ego is the one which reincarnates.'
Maharshi: 'Yes.'
The answer continues, and we will take it up in a moment.
But pause for a moment, and note two points. In the course of the
answer, the Maharshi has said, 'The Self who was undifferentiated
in sleep is differentiated in the present state, and sees the diversity.'
Here and in his response, 'Yes', to the lady's observation, 'The ego is
the one which reincarnates,' and also in the expression, 'and *sees* the
diversity', he is using the word 'Self' as a synonym for 'ego'—that is
contrary to his general position which is that the Self is, and always
remains undifferentiated, that it never changes, and, as we shall soon
see, that it is not the seer.

As for the Self-reincarnating, the answer proceeds:

> Yes. But what is reincarnation? The ego remains the same. New
> bodies appear and hold it. The ego does not change. It does not
> leave one body, seek and find another. Just see what happens even
> to your gross body. Suppose you go to London. How do you do
> it? You take a conveyance, go to the docks, board the steamer and
> reach London in a few days. What has happened? The conveyances
> had moved, but not your body. Still you say that you travelled
> from one part of the globe to the other part. The movements of
> the conveyances have been superimposed on your body. Similarly
> also with your ego. The reincarnations are superimpositions. For
> example, what happens in a dream? Do you go to the dream
> world or does it occur in you? Surely the latter. Just the same with
> reincarnations. The ego remains changeless all along.[1]

The point about using 'ego' and 'Self' as synonyms apart, consider
reincarnation itself. The exchange above took place on 2 January
1937. Just a few months earlier, on 8 September 1936, a devotee
asked the Maharshi, 'What is the state just before death?' The
Maharshi explained:

> When a person gasps for breath it indicates that the person is
> unconscious of this body; another body has been held and the
> person swings to and fro. While gasping there is a more violent
> gasp at intervals and that indicates the oscillation between the
> two bodies due to the present attachment not having completely
> snapped. I noticed it in the case of my mother and of Palaniswami.

'Does the new body involved in that state represent the next reincarnation of the person?' the devotee asks.

'Yes,' Sri Ramana responds. 'While gasping, the person is in something like a dream, not aware of the present environment.'

Munagala S. Venkataramiah—later Swami Ramananda Saraswati, who recorded the exchanges—elaborates on the sentence in Sri Ramana's answer about the passing away of his mother and his close companion, Palaniswami:

> It must be remembered that Sri Bhagavan had been with His mother from 8 a.m. to 8 p.m. until she passed away. He was all along holding her head with one hand, the other hand placed on her bosom. What does it signify? He Himself said later that there was a struggle between Himself and His mother until her spirit reached the Heart.
>
> Evidently the soul passes through a series of subtle experiences, and Sri Bhagavan's touch generates a current which turns the soul back from its wandering into the Heart.
>
> The *samskaras*, however, persist and a struggle is kept up between the spiritual force set up by His touch and the innate *samskaras*, until the latter are entirely destroyed and the soul is led into the Heart to rest in eternal Peace, which is the same as Liberation.
>
> Its entry into the Heart is signified by a peculiar sensation perceptible to the Mahatma—similar to the tinkling of a bell.
>
> When Maharshi attended on Palaniswami on his death-bed, He took away His hand after the above signal. But Palaniswami's eyes opened immediately, signifying that the spirit had escaped through them, thereby indicating a higher rebirth, but not Liberation. Having once noticed it with Palaniswami, Maharshi continued touching His mother for a few minutes longer—even after the signal of the soul passing into the Heart—and thus ensured her Liberation. This was confirmed by the look of perfect peace and composure on her features.[2]

That 'Self', 'ego', 'soul' get used as synonyms in these accounts apart, in this account of what happens as a person is dying, is the soul just waiting for another body to come and envelope it? Or is it, to use the recorder's word, actively escaping through the eyes, say, to a higher birth in one case or to Liberation in the other?

THE SELF IN THE HEART

SEEING, DOING, KNOWING, WANDERING, ACTING— WITHOUT VOLITION, WITHOUT CHANGING

Or consider the basic tenet: that the Self is eternal, ever-present, all-pervasive and changeless. We are told again and again, as we shall soon see, that it is *not* the doer, it is *not* the seer, it is *not* the knower. It just is. But consider two typical passages.

The Maharshi is explaining that when one transcends the body, all forms and shapes disappear. The devotee asks whether that also happens in regard to plants, trees, etc.: Do they disappear also?

Yes, affirms the Maharshi. They do not exist apart from the Self. 'You think you see them. The thought is projected from your Self. Find out wherefrom it rises. Thoughts will cease and the Self alone will remain.'

The devotee says that he understands theoretically. 'But they are still there.'

The Maharshi answers using an analogy he gives often. Please go through the response with some care:

> Yes. It is like a cinema show. There is the light on the screen and the shadows flitting across impress the audience as the enactment of some piece. Similarly, also will it be, if in the same play an audience is shown. The seer, the seen, will then only be the screen. Apply it to yourself. You are the screen, *the Self has created the ego*, the ego has accretions of thoughts which are displayed as the world, the trees, plants, etc., of which you are asking. In reality, all these are nothing but the Self. If you see the Self, the same will be found to be all, everywhere and always. Nothing but the Self exists.[3]

'... *the Self has created the ego*...' Here the Self is not 'just Being'—it is acting, creating.

On another occasion, a devotee asks, 'What is the non-Self?' 'There is no non-Self in fact,' the Maharshi says. 'The non-Self also exists in the Self. *It is the Self which speaks of the non-Self because it has forgotten itself. Having lost hold of itself, it conceives something as non-Self, which is after all nothing but itself.*'[4]

Here again the Self is active: it '*speaks of*' ...; it has '*forgotten itself*'...; it has '*lost hold of itself*' ...; it '*conceives something as*'...

Indeed, the Self—the never-changing Self—is explicitly ascribed an active role in reincarnation. At the core of assertions about reincarnation has always been a conundrum: How is the Karmic dust, so to say, ferried from one birth to another? How are our predispositions carried from one birth to another, from the body that has died to the body that takes birth? Surely, not by the body. Surely, not by the mind. Sri Ramana discerns that it is the Self which carries these, predispositions in the present case, to the next body. The Maharshi is explaining the differences between the brain and an entity that he frequently cites, the heart, to which we shall soon turn. For the moment, it will suffice to think of it as the Self itself. The Maharshi says,

> The Heart is the most important centre from which vitality and light radiate to the brain, thus enabling it to function. The *vasanas* are enclosed in the Heart in their subtlest form, later flowing to the brain which reflects them highly magnified corresponding to a cinema-show at every stage. That is how the world is said to be nothing more than a cinema-show.
>
> Were the *vasanas* in the brain instead of in the Heart they must be extinguished if the head is cut off so that reincarnations will be at an end. But it is not so. *The Self obviously safeguards the vasanas in its closest proximity, i.e., within itself in the Heart, just as a miser keeps his most valued possessions (treasure) with himself and never out of contact.* Hence the place where the *vasanas* are, is the Self, i.e., the Heart, and not the brain (which is only the theatre for the play of the *vasanas* from the greenhouse of the Heart.)[5]

What an active role has been here ascribed to the Self: '*The Self obviously safeguards the vasanas in its closest proximity, i.e., within itself in the Heart, just as a miser keeps his most valued possessions (treasure) with himself and never out of contact...*'—it clutches on to the vasanas so as to ferry them across to the next body that it shall come to occupy.

Towards the end of this record of talks and exchanges—we are now in January 1939—Sri Ramana is recorded as giving an unusually detailed and long discourse on nadis, centres, and the like. Having described the sequences through which predispositions travel, through which creation takes place, he ascribes activity, literally, to the Self. Concluding the discourse, Sri Ramana says:

... The Self is bound to the Heart, like a cow tethered to a peg. The movements are controlled by the length of the rope. *All its wanderings centre around the peg.*

A caterpillar crawls on a blade of grass and when it has come to the end, it seeks another support. While doing so it holds on with its hind-legs to the blade of grass, lifts the body and sways to and fro before it can hold another. Similarly it is with the Self. *It stays in the Heart and holds other centres also according to circumstances. But its activities always centre around the Heart.*[6]

'Its *wanderings*', 'its *activities*'—each of these must involve volition, each must entail change. But the 'Self' was supposed to just *be*. It was supposed to be unchanging.

REASONS FOR WORDS

Such instances abound. And the reasons are not far to guess. The notes were transcribed by persons who, though they would have heard the Maharshi over years and years, would, like you and me, not have had the first-hand experience of the Self that always formed the backdrop of whatever the Maharshi said. Moreover, the Maharshi was not setting out a theoretical system in these *Talks*, nor indeed in the few booklets and poems that he composed. He was answering questions put by devotees, each of whom was at a different state in his quest. The Maharshi would naturally tailor his answer to lead the particular devotee to the next step that was appropriate for *that* devotee. Often he would seize upon what the devotee had just said, and draw him back to what the devotee had to do here and now. But just as often, the Maharshi would couch his response in words that the devotee had just used, or, more accurately, in words with which, the Maharshi discerned, the devotee was familiar. Accordingly, not just the emphasis, but words, and, in a sense, the content would differ. Furthermore, while everyone who flocked to him wanted to learn about the ultimate experience, and about the 'soul', etc., it may well be, as all mystics declare, that these—for instance, the ultimate experience as well as what seems to them to be the ultimate entity—are beyond description. For this reason, the Maharshi would often use similes and metaphors, and these, naturally, can only approximate what is sought to be conveyed.

But there is another reason which is of even greater consequence. The Maharshi was not concerned about teaching. He did crystallize his experience, and his method in a few booklets, stanzas and aphorisms. But he did not consider it any part of his function that he must lift others to enlightenment. An exchange in the *Talks* itself brings this into bold relief.

We are in June 1938. The Maharshi has been explaining satva, rajas, tamas, samadhi, the 'mind-ether' as reflected in the 'element-ether', the presence of the Self in both activity and peace ... He then turns to what people expect of the one who has attained enlightenment or liberation. He says:

> People often say that a *mukta purusha* should go out and preach his message to the people. They argue, how can anyone be a *mukta* so long as there is misery by his side? True. But who is a *mukta*? Does he see misery beside him? They want to determine the state of a *mukta* without themselves realizing the state. From the standpoint of the *mukta*, their contention amounts to this: a man dreams a dream in which he finds several persons. On waking up, he asks, 'Have the dream individuals also wakened?' It is ridiculous.
>
> Again, a good man says, 'It does not matter even if I do not get *mukti*. Or let me be the last man to get it so that I shall help all others to be *muktas* before I am one.' It is all very good. Imagine a dreamer saying, 'May all these wake up before I do.' The dreamer is no more absurd than the amiable philosopher aforesaid.[7]

'*Ridiculous*', '*absurd*'—harsh words, coming as they do from the Maharshi who instructed mainly through silence.

The moral for us is complex. On the one hand, we must stay close to the main propositions, and not get lost in parsing words. On the other, even as we make allowances for the fact that Sri Ramana often tailored his words to the level of understanding of the listener, even as he tailored them to swiftly bring the listener to what he should be doing here and now, the words are important. All the more so because Sri Ramana was as careful as he was economical in the words he used.

THE CENTRAL NOTIONS

Let us first list the central notions, get to know them a bit better by recalling what Sri Ramana said to explain them to devotees, and eventually parse two or three notions about which psychologists and neuroscientists have something to say. Here are the central notions:

- There is the Self. Rather, the Self *IS*—it just *IS*.
- It is 'just Being'. It is 'absolute Consciousness, devoid of objective knowledge'; it is 'perfect awareness, perfect stillness'.
- As such, it is not the doer; it is not the knower; it is not the seer.
- It is eternal, it does not change, it is all there is.
- Only that is real which is present always, and which does not change.
- As the Self alone is always present, as it alone does not change, it alone is real.
- It gives rise to, or from it springs the 'I'-thought.
- In a sequence, this 'I'-thought gives rise to other thoughts— trees, plants, the world, in a word everything other than the Self.
- Our task is to pierce this thicket of mere thoughts.
- The way to do so is to track each thought to its source, the 'I'-thought, and hold on to it.
- While one may get past the 'I'-thought by many methods, this is best done by a direct method, by pursuing one inquiry, 'Who am "I"?' If a dear one dies, and we are stricken by sorrow, we are instructed to ask, '*To whom* does the sorrow occur?' If we are worried on account of the slaughter in wars, we are instructed to ask, '*Who* is worried?' If pain seizes us, we are instructed to ask, '*Who* is in pain?' If we are at peace in the presence of the Maharshi, but when away from him are plunged into the same whirl, we are instructed to ask, '*Who* was at peace? *Who* is in turmoil?' If an 'involuntary fear' seizes us during meditation, we are instructed to ask, '*To whom* is the fright?' If we are concerned that our time and energy are all taken up by our work and, therefore, we are not able to do atma-chintan, we are instructed to ask,

'*Who* works?' If we long for liberation, we are instructed to
ask, '*Who* longs for liberation?'*

• The inquiry must be pursued to the 'root-thought'. It is not
enough to say, '*I* am seized by sorrow/*I* am worried/*I* long for
liberation...' That answer must be examined, 'Who am I?'
In a typical discourse—this was in response to a question by
B.V. Narasimha Swami, the author of Sri Ramana's biography
which we have encountered many times earlier—Sri Ramana
explained the steps that must be traversed: Narasimha Swami
asked how is the 'I' to be found. Sri Ramana explained:

Ask yourself the question. The body (*annamaya kosa*) and its
functions are not 'I'.

Going deeper, the mind (*manomaya kosa*) and its functions
are not 'I'.

The next step takes on to the question: 'Wherefrom do
these thoughts arise?' The thoughts are spontaneous, superficial
or analytical. They operate in intellect. Then, who is aware of
them? The existence of thoughts, their clear conceptions and
their operations become evident to the individual. The analysis
leads to the conclusion that the individuality of the person is
operative as the perceiver of the existence of thoughts and of
their sequence. This individuality is the ego, or as people say
'I'. *Vijnanamaya kosa* (intellect) is only the sheath of 'I' and
not the 'I' itself.

Enquiring further, the questions arise, 'Who is this
"I"? Wherefrom does it come?' 'I' was not aware in sleep.
Simultaneously with its rise sleep changes to dream or
wakefulness. But I am not concerned with dream just now.
Who am I now, in the wakeful state? If I originated from sleep,
then the 'I' was covered up with ignorance. Such an ignorant
'I' cannot be what the scriptures say or the wise ones affirm.
'I' am beyond even 'Sleep'; 'I' must be now and here and what
I was all along in sleep and dreams also, without the qualities

---

*These are the actual queries that Sri Ramana urged devotees to pursue,
devotees who had been struck by the blows of fate, who were worried about
the Second World War, who were at peace in his presence but concerned that,
while the peace lasted a few days after they returned to their usual environment,
soon enough they were back in the state in which they had been.

of such states. 'I' must therefore be the unqualified substratum underlying these three states (*anandamaya kosa* transcended).

'I' is, in brief, beyond the five sheaths. Next, the residuum left over after discarding all that is not-self is the Self, *Sat-Chit-Ananda*.

The devotee wanted to know, 'How is that Self to be known or realised?'

Sri Ramana explained, 'Transcend the present plane of relativity. A separate being (Self) appears to know something apart from itself (non-Self). That is, the subject is aware of the object. The seer is *drik*; the seen is *drisya*.'[8]

- When all else is seen through in this way, when all non-Self is seen through, the Self alone remains.
- The 'uninterrupted experience' of that state, or, more accurately, being in that state uninterruptedly is realization/liberation/mukti.

The Heart: What and Where It Is

Sri Ramana was specific. He was emphatic. He even specified a location within the body for the Self. He often said that this Self is in 'the Heart on the right side', in a cavity, alternatively in 'a pinhole on the right side of the chest'.

What is the 'Heart' of which he spoke? What is its relation to the Self? 'The Heart is the seat of the Self (if such could be said of it),' the Maharshi affirmed, 'wherefrom "I"-"I" arises'[9] —at first glance, the statements may appear to be affirming the same things, but please spare a moment to reflect on the expressions as they contain differences not just of emphasis but also of substance. The 'Heart' is 'the seat of spiritual experience'.[10] 'The tiny hole in the Heart remains always closed, but it is opened by *vichara* with the result that "I"-"I" consciousness shines forth.'[11] 'The mind now sees itself diversified as the universe,' Sri Ramana taught. 'If the diversity is not manifest it remains in its own essence, that is the Heart. Entering the Heart means remaining without distractions. The Heart is the only Reality. The mind is only a transient phase. To remain as one's Self is to enter the Heart.'[12] Or recall the passage that we encountered

just a while ago. In it, Sri Ramana speaks of the Heart as a place
or vessel in which the Self safeguards the vasanas: 'The Heart is
the most important centre from which vitality and light radiate to
the brain, thus enabling it to function. The *vasanas* are enclosed in
the Heart in their subtlest form, later flowing to the brain which
reflects them highly magnified corresponding to a cinema-show at
every stage. That is how the world is said to be nothing more than
a cinema-show ... The Self obviously safeguards the *vasanas* in its
closest proximity, i.e., within itself in the Heart.'[13] The Heart is
where the Self 'abides'.[14] The Heart is what the Self is 'bound to, like
a cow tethered to a peg'.[15]

At other times, Sri Ramana was even more specific: he recalled
sacred texts that described the physical shape of the 'Heart' and its
location. In *Who Am I?*, asked about the Heart, Sri Ramana said:*

> The sacred texts describing it say: Between the two breasts, below
> the chest and above the abdomen, there are six organs of different
> colours. One of them resembling the bud of a water lily and
> situated two digits to the right is the Heart. It is inverted and
> within it is a tiny orifice which is the seat of dense darkness
> (ignorance) full of desires. All the psychic nerves (*nadis*) depend
> upon it. It is the abode of the vital forces, the mind and the light
> (of consciousness).[16]

In expressions such as these, the Self is one entity, and the Heart
another—the Heart is the seat of the Self; it is a place in which the
Self 'abides'; the Self clutches the vasanas as it abides inside the
Heart; the Heart is a place that is entered by remaining in the Self; it
is a peg to which the Self is bound.

The general proposition that Sri Ramana taught, however, was
that the Self and the Heart are one. In that early text we just
quoted, Sri Ramana qualified the description given in the texts,
adding, 'But, although it is described thus, the meaning of the
word Heart (*hridayam*) is the Self (*Atman*). As it is denoted by the
terms existence, consciousness, bliss, eternal and plenum (*sat, chit,
anandam, nityam, purnam*) it has no differences such as exterior and
interior or up and down. That tranquil state in which all thoughts

---

*Who Am I? is a central text composed very early on. It was written up in
response to questions asked by one of Sri Ramana's closest and early disciples,
Sivaprakasam Pillai.

come to an end is called the state of the Self. When it is realized as it is, there is no scope for discussions about its location inside the body or outside.'[17] 'The Atman is in the Heart,' he said, 'and *is* the Heart itself. The manifestation is in the brain. The passage from the Heart to the brain might be considered to be through *sushumna* or a nerve with any other name.'[18] 'The Heart,' he said, 'is that from which thoughts arise, in which they subsist and where they are resolved ... Brahman is the Heart.'[19] The Self is the Heart, he affirmed. It is from where light rises and reaches the brain. That creates the mind. Which in turn creates awareness of the world.[20] 'Sri Bhagavan says that the Heart is the Self,' a Muslim professor remarks. 'Psychology has it that malice, envy, jealousy and all passions have their seat in the heart. How are these two statements to be reconciled?' 'The whole cosmos is contained in one pinhole in the Heart. These passions are part of the cosmos...'[21] A little later, the identity is affirmed with a twist: 'The centre of the ego is the Heart, the same as the Self.'[22] In the *Supplement to Reality in Forty Verses*, Sri Ramana invokes *Yoga Vasishtha* to affirm that the Heart is 'Pure Awareness', and it is this Heart which should be embraced, and the mere physical organ disregarded.[23]

Sri Ramana was equally emphatic about the location of this Heart. Almost at the very opening of the *Talks*, we have 'an educated young man' ask the Maharshi, 'How do you say that the Heart is on the right, whereas the biologists have found it to be on the left?' The young man is so bold as to ask the Maharshi for the authority on the basis of which he, Sri Ramana, maintains this to be the case. Sri Ramana replies:

> Quite so. The physical organ is on the left; that is not denied. But the Heart of which I speak is non-physical and is only on the right side. It is my experience, no authority is required by me. Still you can find confirmation in a Malayalam Ayurvedic book and in 'Sita Upanishad'.

'And', Venkataramiah added, 'he produced the quotation (*mantra*) from the latter and repeated the text (*sloka*) from the former.'[24]

Two years later, while recounting his 'near-death' experience, an episode that we have encountered earlier, the Maharshi elaborated on how his affirmation of the Heart being on the right side of the chest was borne out by his own experience. He told the devotees:

> I had been saying all along that the Heart centre was on the right, notwithstanding the refutation by some learned men that physiology taught them otherwise. I speak from experience. I knew it even in my home during my trances. Again during the incident related in the book *Self-Realization*.[25] I had a very clear vision and experience. All of a sudden a light came from one side erasing the world vision in its course until it spread all round when the vision of the world was completely cut out. I felt the muscular organ on the left had stopped work, I could understand that the body was like a corpse, that the circulation of blood had stopped and the body became blue and motionless. Vasudeva Sastri embraced the body, wept over my death, but I could not speak. *All the time I was feeling that the Heart centre on the right was working as well as ever. This state continued 15 or 20 minutes. Then suddenly something shot out from the right to the left, resembling a rocket bursting in air. The blood circulation was resumed and normal condition restored.* I then asked Vasudeva Sastri to move along with me and we reached our residence.
>
> The Upanishads say that 101 *nadis* terminate in the Heart and 72,000 originate from them and traverse the body. The Heart is thus the centre of the body. It can be a centre because we have been accustomed to think that we remain in the body. In fact, the body and all else are in that centre only.[26]

ON THE RIGHT SIDE?

He supplemented what he had learnt from his own experience with some homely evidence. 'When asked who you are, you place your hand on the right side of the breast and say "I am",' he told the devotees. 'There you involuntarily point out the Self. The Self is thus known...'[27] How is one to know that the Heart—which, when asked by the devotee, the Maharshi acknowledges is 'the psychic Heart'—is on the right? asks a devotee. 'By experience,' the Maharshi responds. 'Is there any indication to that effect?' the devotee persists. 'Point out to yourself and see,' says Sri Ramana.[28] 'Is there any stage when one might feel the Heart?' a devotee inquires later. 'It is within the experience of everyone. Everyone touches the right side of his chest when he says "I".'[29]

'Do left-handed persons also touch the right side?' I wondered when I first came across these statements. What about our son, Adit, who just cannot use his right hand? What about what Terzani says of the Chinese? In his alternately scintillating and searing book, he says, 'The Chinese say "I" by placing the index finger of their right hand on the tip of their nose,' and asks, 'But can a self live in the nose?'[30] What about persons who have lost their faculties to dementia or Alzheimer's? Will they point to the right side of the chest when asked about their 'Heart'? And yet, on Sri Ramana's doctrine, they do have a 'Self', and it must be residing in that 'Heart', presumably. And what about birds and animals and fish? According to what we have been taught, they too have a 'Self' which also, presumably, must be residing in the 'Heart'. But, as they do not or cannot point to the right side of their chests, where would it be located in their case?

Sri Ramana reiterated this location several times. And yet his remarks on other occasions would suggest that he talked of the Self being located in the Heart on the right side of the chest *only to help seekers*. Here is an exchange in which he states the purpose explicitly:

Devotee: There are six centres mentioned in the Yoga books; but the *jiva* is said to reside in the Heart. Is it not so?

Sri Ramana: Yes. The *jiva* is said to remain in the Heart in deep sleep; and in the brain in the waking state. The Heart need not be taken to be the muscular cavity with four chambers which propels blood. There are indeed passages which support the view. There are others who take it to mean a set of ganglia or nerve centres about that region. Whichever view is correct does not matter to us. We are not concerned with anything less than ourselves. That we certainly have within ourselves. There could be no doubts or discussions about that.

The Heart is used in the Vedas and the scriptures to denote the place whence the notion 'I' springs. Does it spring from only the fleshy ball? It springs within us somewhere right in the middle of our being. The 'I' has no location. Everything is the Self. There is nothing but that. So the Heart must be said to be the entire body

of ourselves and of the entire universe, conceived as 'I'. *But to help
the practiser (abhyasi) we have to indicate a definite part of the
Universe, or of the Body.* So this Heart is pointed out as the seat
of the Self. But in truth we are everywhere, we are all that is, and
there is nothing else.[31]

Later also, when a devotee says that he has read that the Heart is on
the right side, Sri Ramana says, '*It is all meant to help the bhavana*
(imagery). There are books dealing with six centres (*shadchakra*) and
many other *lakshyas* (centres), internal and external. The description
of the Heart is one among so many *lakshyas*. But it is not necessary.
It is only the source of the "I"-thought. That is the ultimate truth.'[32]
And later still, when he is expounding on the Heart mentioned in
the Vedas and the Upanishads, the Maharshi says, '...it is where the
mind rises and subsides. That is the seat of Realisation. When I say
that it is the Self the people imagine that it is within the body. When
I ask where the Self remains in one's sleep they seem to think that
it is within the body, but unaware of the body and its surroundings
like a man confined in a dark room. *To such people it is necessary to
say that the seat of Realisation is somewhere within the body.* The
name of the centre is the Heart; but it is confounded with the heart
organ.'[33]

A while later, an American visitor has the privilege of engaging
Sri Ramana in an extended exchange on several aspects of spiritual
practice. As the exchanges draw to a close, a question is asked about
the Heart. Sri Ramana remarks, 'Leave alone the idea of *right* and
left. They pertain to the body. The Heart is the Self. Realise it and
then you will see for yourself.'[34]

The moral for us is twofold. First, while the affirmation about
the Heart being on the right side of the chest has been of much
significance among Maharshi's devotees, and while in his own case
Sri Ramana spoke of the location as being on the right because that is
where he had experienced it himself, we would do well to remember
his avowal that he used to say this to help the practitioner direct his
mind. Second, while several statements would seem to suggest that
the Self is different from the Heart—that the former abides in the
latter, etc.—they are in fact one.

We, therefore, have just the Self.

WHAT REMAINS

At our level, the proposition that 'the Self alone is real' is a circularity:

- That alone is real which always is, which never changes;
- The Self alone always is, and never changes;
- Therefore, it alone is real.

But for the sage, the proposition is experiential.

And it has an ineluctable consequence: one thing after the other becomes unreal—sometimes because it changes and only that is real which does not change; sometimes because it is present in one circumstance—for instance, the waking state—and not present in another—for instance, deep sleep.

Birth and death are unreal;[35] as are the three states—deep sleep, sleep with dreams, waking—as none of them is permanent, each replaces the others;[36] above/below (as in 'heaven is above and hell below'), up/down, in/out as each of the poles is relative and, therefore, liable to be overturned as our vantage point shifts;[37] bondage itself—for we do not think of or experience it in deep sleep;[38] jnana and ajnana—they appear and disappear on the screen, the Self[39] forms—as we do not experience even our own form in deep sleep;[40] soul and God. As the last two may surprise some of us, perhaps we should read the actual exchange between the devotee and Sri Ramana, all the more so as it will acquaint us with the Maharshi's didactic way of teaching:

D.: There are pleasure and pain in ordinary life. Should we not remain with only pleasure?

M.: Pleasure consists in turning and keeping the mind within; pain in sending it outward. There is only pleasure. Absence of pleasure is called pain. One's nature is pleasure—Bliss (*Ananda*).

D.: Is it the soul?

M.: Soul and God are only mental conceptions.

D.: Is God only a mental conception?

M.: Yes. Do you think of God in sleep?

D.: But sleep is a state of dullness.

M.: If God be real He must remain always. You remain in sleep and in wakefulness—just the same. If God be as true as your Self, God must be in sleep as well as the Self. This thought of God arises only in the wakeful state. Who thinks now?

D.: I think.

M.: Who is this 'I'? Who says it? Is it the body?

D.: The body speaks.

M.: The body does not speak. If so, did it speak in sleep? Who is this I?

D.: I within the body.

M.: Are you within the body or without?

D.: I am certainly within the body.

M.: Do you know it to be so in your sleep?

D.: I remain in my body in sleep also.

M.: Are you aware of being within the body in sleep?...[41]

On the same reasoning, time and space, the entire world turn out to be unreal—they are not present in our sleep.[42]

But there is an important distinction, which we will take up when we consider the sense in which the world is 'unreal'. To anticipate, the Maharshi's position is not as absolute as such declarations may lead one to believe. After all, if the world, indeed everything other than the Self—the unchanging, formless, eternal, all-pervading Self—alone were real, why would even sages eat? And teach? And compose paeans to the hill, Arunachala, which too, after all, is unreal? In a word, Sri Ramana's position, as of Adi Shankaracharya, was that when the world and everything in it are seen as apart from Brahman, they are unreal; but when they are seen as Brahman, they are real. An exchange, a typical one on the question will help us reflect on what the Maharshi is emphasizing. Devotees are asking questions about being Brahman, about meditation. Sri Ramana has been answering them. A question comes up about thoughts that arise during meditation:

M.: Yes, all kinds of thoughts arise in meditation. It is but right. What lies hidden in you is brought out. Unless they rise up how can they be destroyed? They therefore rise up spontaneously in order to be extinguished in due course, thus to strengthen the mind.

A visitor: All are said to be Brahman.

M.: Yes, they are. But so long as you think that they are apart they are to be avoided. If on the other hand they are found to be Self there is no need to say 'all'. For all that exists is only Brahman. There is nothing besides Brahman.

D.: *Ribhu Gita* speaks of so many objects as unreal, adding at the end that they are all Brahman and thus real.

M.: Yes. When you see them as so many they are *asat*, i.e., unreal. Whereas when you see them as Brahman they are real, deriving their reality from their substratum, Brahman.

D.: Why then does *Upadesa Sara* speak of the body, etc., as *jada* i.e., insentient?

M.: Inasmuch as you say that they are body, etc., apart from the Self. But when the Self is found, this body, etc., are also found to be in it. Afterwards no one will ask the question and no one will say that they are insentient...[43]

We get a hint here. We are told that the body, thoughts, the world cannot be the Self as they change, and because they are present to us when we are awake but not when we are asleep. Next, what does 'not seeing them apart from Brahman' entail? They can't be *parts of* Brahman—for, in that case, Brahman would not be the undifferentiated Self it is; and, as the parts change, Brahman too would be subject to change—which can't, almost by definition, be the case. Is it that they are not to be seen apart from Brahman because Brahman/Self inheres in them all? But that is no different from the conventional saying that God is in every particle, or the Self is in every particle—the new affirmation is no more informative. In the passage quoted above, Sri Ramana says something different: thoughts, the world, etc., '(derive) their reality from their substratum, Brahman'. So, they *are* real—it is just that they are not real *suo motu*, so to say.

We thus have three proximate conclusions: first, the Self underlies all; second, the location of the Heart has been indicated to help the practitioner direct his mind inward; and, third, things other than the Self *are* real except that they derive their reality from the substratum, Brahman/Self.

But then how and why do these relatively unreal entities come about? Neither the deus ex machina nor the purpose is disclosed. But we *are* told about the sequence in which these unrealities come to be.

A Procession of Phantoms

Answering questions of a devotee, Sri Ramana is saying that the Self transcends the intellect, that the intellect must 'vanish' to reach the Self. The devotee asks whether his realization—the devotee's—will help others. 'Yes, certainly,' Sri Ramana says. 'It is the best possible help. But there are no others to be helped. For a realized being sees the Self, just like a goldsmith estimating the gold in various jewels. When you identify yourself with the body then only the forms and shapes are there. But when you transcend your body the others disappear along with your body-consciousness.'

As you will recall, when the devotee asks whether the plants and trees that we see around us are also phantoms of the mind, Sri Ramana is emphatic: '... You are the screen, the Self has created the ego, the ego has its accretions of thoughts which are displayed in the world, the trees, plants, etc., of which you are asking. In reality, all these are nothing but the Self. If you see the Self, the same will be found to be all, everywhere and always. Nothing but the Self exists.'[44]

To summarize, the Self creates the ego, the 'I'-thought. This in turn creates the world and everything in it, or, to put it more accurately, 'has its accretions of thoughts which are displayed as the world, the trees, the plants, etc.'

Why does the Self set off this cycle? We do not know.

How does the Self—formless, never-changing—transform itself not just into the ego, but also into material substances like trees and plants, and yet remain unchanging? We do not know.

As an aside: when we say, ever so glibly, 'Science does not answer all questions,' we should remember that neither does religion nor, indeed, spiritual discourse.

A few days after this conversation, talk turns to the souls of those who have passed away: Do prayers, etc., benefit them, the devotees want to know. So long as one identifies with the gross body, the Maharshi explains, 'the thought materialized as gross manifestations must be real to him [the devotee]'. 'Because his [the devotee's] body is imagined to have originated from another physical being,' the Maharshi continues, 'the other [the deceased parent] exists as truly as his own body. Having existed here once it certainly survives death, because the offspring is still here and feels he has been born of the other. Under these circumstances the other world is true; and the departed souls are benefited by prayers offered for them.'

Pause for a moment, and notice what the Maharshi is saying. The thought has materialized as a gross manifestation—his own body and the body of his parent. Now, this 'must be real *for him*'— for the offspring; the implication is that neither the son's body nor that of the parent is real *in fact*. Next, 'Because his body is *imagined* to have originated from another physical being...' The unreality is squared. And the body of the parent in some form 'certainly survives death' 'because the offspring is still here and *feels he has been born of the other*'.

Set aside the 'Why?' and 'How?' for a minute, and glance through the Maharshi's explanation of the way things evolve:

> ...On the other hand, considered in a different way, the One Reality is the Self from whom has sprung the ego which contains within itself the seeds of predispositions acquired in previous births. The Self illumines the ego, the predispositions and also the gross senses, whereupon the predispositions appear to the senses to materialize as the universe, and become perceptible to the ego, the reflection of the Self. The ego identifies itself with the body, and so loses sight of the Self and the result of this inadvertence is dark ignorance and the misery of the present life. The fact of the ego rising from the Self and forgetting it, is birth. So, it may be said that the birth of the individual has killed the mother. The present desire to regain one's mother is in reality the desire to regain the Self, which is the same as realizing one-self, or the death of the ego; this is surrender unto the mother, so she may live eternally.[45]

The sequence thus is: (i) the Self creates the ego; (ii) the ego proceeds in accordance with the predispositions it has acquired in and stored from earlier births; (iii) the Self illumines, among others, the ego and its senses; (iv) the senses now perceive the predispositions to have materialized as the Universe; (v) the Universe is perceived by the ego; (vi) and, inadvertently, the ego identifies itself not with the Self from which it sprang but with this Universe which has sprung from it.

Hence, the Self creates a false ego—this is often identified as the mind; the false ego/mind creates other thoughts; these thoughts create false phenomena; we thus have the false thoughts materializing as the body, trees, plants ... the Universe ... A procession of phantoms ... All of whom dissolve once we retrace our thoughts to the original 'I'-thought.

EVIDENCE

But how do we know there is an original Self at all?

For Sri Ramana, the Self is manifest: he speaks of it from his own direct experience of it. To make the notions and the sequence intelligible to people like us, Sri Ramana repeatedly points to sleep, and what we perceive and do not perceive when we are asleep.

Asleep, you are not aware of your body, of the world, of heaven and hell, of time and space, he points out repeatedly. But when you wake up, you say, 'I slept well.' There is continuity. 'That continuity is Pure Being.'

'But I am not aware when I am asleep,' the devotee demurs. 'True,' the Maharshi replies, 'there is no awareness of the body or the world. But you must exist in your sleep in order to say now, "I was not aware in my sleep." Who says so now? It is the wakeful person. The sleeper cannot say so. That is to say, the individual who is now identifying the Self with the body says that such awareness did not exist in sleep.'

Notice that the objects you now perceive—from your body to the rest of the world—were not present in sleep. Hence, 'There is continuity of Being in the three states [sleep, dream, waking] but no continuity of the individual and the objects ... That which is continuous is also enduring, i.e., permanent. That which is discontinuous is transitory ... Therefore, the state of Being is permanent and the body and the world are not. They are fleeting phenomena passing on the screen of Being-Consciousness which is eternal and stationary.'

Pause for a moment and return to the first sentence of the preceding paragraph—what Sri Ramana says is predicated on what it says: 'Notice that the objects you now perceive—from your body to the rest of the world—were not present in sleep.' Suppose the sentence had read 'Notice that the objects you now perceive—from your body to the rest of the world—were not present *in your awareness* during sleep.' Wouldn't that be a more accurate way to describe the facts? And would any of what is inferred follow—about our body and the world being present in some states and not in others, and, therefore, not being real?

The discourse continues—that while we are, in a sense, nearer pure consciousness when we are asleep, that does not mean that we should just keep sleeping. What we have to strive and attain is that state when we are awake: we have to still the thoughts so that the peace of sleep is gained—'That is the state of the *jnani*. It is neither sleep nor waking but intermediate between the two. It is called *jagrat-sushupti*...' 'It is not the same as sleep or waking separately. It is *atijagrat* (beyond wakefulness) or *atisushupti* (beyond sleep). It is the state of perfect awareness and of perfect stillness combined. It lies between sleep and waking; it is also the interval between two successive thoughts. It is the source from which thoughts spring; we see that when we wake up from sleep. In other words, thoughts have their origin in the stillness of sleep. The thoughts make all the difference between the stillness of sleep and the turmoil of waking. Go to the root of the thoughts and you reach the stillness of sleep. But you reach it in the full vigour of search, that is, with perfect awareness ... What are all our experiences but thoughts? Pleasure and pain are mere thoughts. They are within ourselves. If you are free from thoughts and yet aware, you are That Perfect Being...'[46]

Hence,

- We have the Self.
- We have the Self alone—as it alone is present in all the three states.
- The evidence of this is what we ourselves affirm when we get up from sleep.
- It is the interval between two thoughts. It is what we experience in the instant when we have awakened, that

moment when the 'I'-thought has arisen but has not got
identified with the body, etc.:

> The Self is pure consciousness in sleep; it evolves as *aham*
> ('I') without the *idam* ('this') in the transition stage; and
> manifests as *aham* ('I') and *idam* ('this') in the waking state.
> The individual's experience is by means of *aham* ('I') only. So
> he must aim at realization in the way indicated (i.e., by means
> of the transitional 'I'). Otherwise the sleep-experience does not
> matter to him. If the transitional 'I' be realized the substratum
> is found and that leads to the goal.[47]

And the intrinsic nature of this Self is bliss, indeed the Self *is* bliss,
Sri Ramana teaches. And for that proposition also the evidence is of
the kind that we have encountered above in regard to the heart. As
we have seen, ever so often, Sri Ramana would point to the three
states—of waking, dreaming and dreamless, deep sleep. Some entity
persists in each of the states, he would point out. How else would
one say, 'I slept well. I was happy in sleep?' Sri Ramana drew two
inferences from these spontaneous exclamations of people.

One, from the latter—'I was happy in sleep'—Sri Ramana
concluded that our intrinsic nature is bliss. That doesn't quite stand
to reason. After all, surely people just as often exclaim, 'I had a
very disturbed night. I was jolted out of my sleep by a nightmare in
which...' Would the latter imply that being agitated and disturbed is
our intrinsic nature?

As for the Self being the unchanging, constant witness, again,
another inference is possible. Neuroscientists working on vision
and those working with the visually impaired report that persons
who are blind from birth do not form visual images either in the
waking or dream states. By contrast, persons who lose sight later
in life because of damage to, say, the primary visual area, have little
difficulty in forming visual images both in the waking and dream
states. Finally, those who suffer damage to the 'higher' areas in
which visual inputs are processed—in particular the junction of the
occipital, parietal and temporal lobes—can see as they did before,
but they are unable to form visual images in their dream state. If the
Self were an unchanging witness, would these three different types

of injuries result in these different types of 'dreams'—some in which visual images occur and some in which they do not?[48]

Where does the lower case 'self' that neurologists and psychologists talk about, the 'self' that we ordinary folk know fit in?

THE 'SELF' WITH THE SMALL 'S'

We thus have the Self.

From it springs the 'I'-thought.

This 'I' identifies itself with the body.

And from that all our problems commence.

Why the Self gives rise to the 'I'-thought is not evident. After all, it is unalloyed, eternal, all-pervading, self-contained bliss. Why does it need to give rise to such a petty entity as the 'I', an entity that is by definition bound to mislead? There is also the other problem. The Self is an integral, non-differentiated whole. It is changeless. But the act of '*giving rise to*' the 'I'-thought will entail change. It will necessarily involve volition, purpose, a goal—all of which are by definition ruled out in the case of the Self.

Nor is it evident why, upon entering a body, this spark of all-knowing should do the ignorant thing and identify itself with the body and its ancillaries.

We thus have a supernatural explanation for the origin of the 'I'-thought, and two unexplained steps.

By contrast, evolutionary psychologists and neurologists give a natural explanation for the 'I'-thought and what comes in its wake, that is, the ego.

But first a few facts about the brain that will help us get a glimpse of what neurologists and psychologists posit in regard to the self—with the lower-case 's'.

The first is the devilish complexity of the brain, and therefore its unimaginable capacities. It is said to be the most complex organism in the known universe. Even the numbers are mind-boggling. Can we imagine an organism one cubic millimetre of which has a *billion* neurons—hold your thumb and forefinger a millimetre apart and imagine a billion entities coiled like spaghetti in that tiny space. Each neuron can have up to *ten thousand* connections to other neurons. In his book *The Self Illusion*, Bruce Hood gives an example that will help us imagine what the numbers mean, rather it will help us realize how far beyond our imagination the brain is. He points out that if we have just 500 neurons all connected together, and each neuron could either be 'on' or 'off', the total number of patterns would be 2^{500}—and that number would exceed the total number of atoms in the observable universe. But the brain has not 500 but billions of neurons. Of course, not all of them are connected to all others but still, for all practical purposes, the combinatorial possibilities are endless. Hence, it has an almost infinite capacity to register, retain and retrieve inputs. That goes for processing them also. After all, at the deepest level all that is going on in your laptop is multiplication and addition, and yet all sorts of operations are performed and data are processed in all sorts of ways by switches that are in just one of two states—'on' or 'off'.[49] The second point we have to bear in mind when we recall conversations of our saints about the mind, 'self', etc., is that the brain is a representational entity. When we look at a scene, for instance, it is not a picture that gets in and is then processed. A *representation* of that scene, and of the many associations connected with it, is what lights up in the brain. That representation consists of the pattern in which the neurons fire. I see green paint. The result is not that some part of the brain inside my head gets coloured green. A set of neurons lights up, the firing of which together represents to me the sensation of seeing green. And from that many, many other ensembles may light up: the one that represents the greenery I saw the last time I was at a hill station; the green of the leaves in our garden; the green in our national flag; the green flag of Islam. And not just that, it may trigger a set of neurons to light up the firing together of which represents something more abstract: the person who had become 'green with envy' on hearing of the success of another. Another set of neurons will 'look at' the context, and thereby, from among these possibilities, the ensemble most relevant to *that* context will win out. And thence, the set of neurons that is associated with the penumbra of emotions, memories that are woven with the experience we have had of that entity in that context. The neurons that fire in response to an input—say, from the eyes—may be near each other or they may be spread out in different regions of the brain, some quite far apart from each other. In fact, a visual input alone is processed in thirty-odd different locations.

Next, the reason the brain is able to process so many things at lightning speed is not because some super-brilliant Shakuntala Devi is sitting in it, but because it processes inputs and concepts in parallel.

The fourth feature is very important for our current concern. A number of regions are involved at each step—in processing an input, in reflecting on a proposition, in deciding what to do in response, in actually carrying out an act to execute the decision—and injury in any one of the regions can disrupt several aspects of that sequence. So, interconnections mean the closest possible interdependence. But while many regions are involved in accomplishing one task, the task is principally handled by one or a few entities within the brain, or one set of interconnections. In that sense, the brain is modular. One area—known as Broca's area—is responsible for our being able to speak. But another area—known as Wernicke's area—is the one that enables us to comprehend the words we speak or hear. If the former is injured, I will not be able to speak. If the latter is injured, I will be able to speak out the words but not string them into a meaningful sentence.

This modular character of the brain has several consequences. One of them is that the mind—for the moment, the thoughts that rush through the brain at this moment—can view itself. We observe this every time we sit down to meditate. We are asked to focus on sensations on or in our body—the cool of the breeze as it brushes past our skin ... the numbness that is creeping up the left leg ... We then turn to observing the thoughts that arise in our mind ... The thought of the conference I attended yesterday surfaces. I notice it. That noticing of the thought *bhasma karo*-s the thought. I have always thought of this noticing as being the 'third eye of Shiva': the moment you turn its gaze on the thought that has come up, this 'third eye' burns the thought away. Soon, if my noticing the thoughts strays, I notice that too. So, unlike the eyes which, we are reminded repeatedly, cannot see themselves without a mirror, the brain can loop back and observe itself. During meditation, we consciously direct the mind to observe itself. But, in fact, the brain is doing this all the time without any effort on our part, indeed without our even knowing that parts of the brain are observing what other parts are doing. Consider the state of 'lucid dreaming'—when we are dreaming, and are aware that what we are experiencing is a dream. Similarly, when we execute a movement, for instance, our brain, without our being aware of it, makes a representation of the action—an 'efferent copy', and uses it to compare the resulting sensory input with what was expected. This enables us to modulate our actions, and it also makes us realize that *we* have carried out that act, and not the external world.

Thus, no viewer is required to be sitting inside. Elements of the brain can themselves view what is happening in the brain— this ability is a result of evolution and adaptation of the brain over millennia. That is, of course, the crucial difference between what our saints have taught and what neurologists and modern-day philosophers contend. In the view of the neuroscientists and modern-day philosophers, the hypothesis of a 'Self'—with the capital 'S'— that witnesses, much less directs, is not necessary. All that happens in the body, brain and mind can be explained by much more proximate notions and much more accessible phenomena. Recall the notions that we encounter elsewhere—that operations of the brain are a self-organizing system; that consciousness is an emergent property; that, instead of a system emerging from the efforts and decisions of a designer, what we have is a Hayekian 'spontaneous order'—as in the emergence of language, of the market. In combination, these are sufficient to explain what happens in the brain and mind. Apart from the fact that no evidence has surfaced that leads us to locate or discern a 'witness', a decider, a homunculus, to use the word current in these circles, the argument goes that if one posits such an entity witnessing, deciding, directing, one has to posit another entity sitting within *that* witness, decider, director ... and that leads to an infinite regress.

In his scintillating book, *I Am a Strange Loop*,[50] Douglas Hofstadter builds in, and builds on two other, and it turns out, all-important features—the feedback loop, when the value of a variable at a particular time comes to be influenced by what its value was in a preceding point in time; and categorization as a device to deal with the myriad entities and phenomena that we encounter. As he shows through riveting illustrations, the simplest feedback rules which are mechanical and deterministic in themselves, lead to complex, unexpected and unpredictable, and in so many cases aesthetically delightful patterns. Moreover, to deal with our environment, the mind categorizes objects, events, stimuli. It represents them as symbols, each a pattern in which the neurons fire. Among humans, this category system is 'arbitrarily extendable' and flexible, Hofstadter points out. Not only can an almost endless series of categories be formed, categories come to nest within categories—so that we do not get stuck at just the colour category; we can proceed to a specific colour within that category—green; and within that to the green of leaves; and within that to the green leaves of the peepal; and within that to the green leaves of the peepal in my house making that rustling sound as the breeze rushes through them ... To deploy the categories efficiently, we develop the skill to think in abstractions and analogies, and to reason inductively.

The feedback loop does not just go round and round at the same level. Occasionally, it leaps to another level of abstraction, from raw stimuli to symbols. That is when it becomes, in Hofstadter's terminology, a 'strange loop'. And all sorts of consequences follow. An illustration from his book will drive the point home. Recall Escher's famous '*Drawing hands*'. One hand is drawing the other which is drawing the first. The abstract level shifts from the *drawn* to the *drawer*, who turns out to be the *drawn*, Hofstadter points out ... The leap has an upward feel to it, he writes, as [i] the drawer is always a sentient, mobile being while the drawn is inanimate, motionless; [ii] the drawer is three-dimensional, the drawn is two-dimensional; [iii] the drawer *chooses* what to draw, the drawn has no say in the matter.[51]

That is the sort of leap that happened, and resulted in the 'self', Hofstadter argues. To contend with the environment, our ancestors became more and more proficient in observing, classifying, categorizing objects, phenomena, experiences. At some stage of complexity, s/he started to apply the same system of categorization to itself. S/he started to build mental structures to represent itself in relation to the world. Every object, every phenomenon, every place and direction in space, every moment of time was now seen and its significance assessed in relation to this singular construct. Categories that are triggered more often, Hofstadter reminds us, become more real to us, and the one that is most often triggered is 'I' and its cousins—'me', 'my'. This then becomes the 'realest thing in the universe'.

As in Escher's drawing, the 'drawn' becomes the 'drawer'. The construct, our 'self' comes to exert 'an upside-down causality' on the world, Hofstadter points out. Our mind no longer looks at the myriad neurons and their firing patterns that made this mental construct, nor the myriad molecules it will set in motion—just as we look only at the 'table' and not at the myriad molecules of which it is made. A mental construct has become a 'solid' entity, an entity in its own right. But for all that, it is not fixed in stone. On the contrary, just as the environment hones us and every action of ours affects the environment, every action of a 'self' triggers reactions from others, and this mutual causation constantly, relentlessly hones and refines the 'self'.*

An Illusion, but a Useful Illusion

If we descend a bit from the notion of the 'Self' with the capital 'S', we come across some common affirmations between mystics like Sri Ramana Maharshi and our neuroscientists.

The mind is just the stream of thoughts, Sri Ramana says. 'Apart from thoughts, there is no such thing as the mind,' Sri Ramana says in *Nan Yar, Who Am I?*, the first recorded instruction by him. Neuroscientists seem to say the same thing—Steven Pinker, an influential thinker in the field, says, 'The mind is what the brain does.' But they have a wider concept in mind, so to say. For the brain does many a thing without a thought. Think of the vast array of functions it executes and regulates in the unconscious; think, for instance, of the vast array of self-regulating systems that keep various substances in our body and blood—sodium, potassium, white and red cells, temperature, blood pressure—within strict limits.

The 'I-thought' is the one that arises first, Sri Ramana teaches— as soon as we awaken, for instance; and in the wake of that follow all other thoughts. But that 'I-thought' is an illusion. Hence, in his teaching

- Mind is the stream of thoughts.
- Thoughts are 'the enemy'.

---

*The foregoing is scarcely even the barest summary of Hofstadter's thesis. I have just strung together some of his propositions and words to give an idea of the way he says the 'self' comes to be. There are several other sparkling points in his book—we will return to one or two of them in a moment.

- They arise as a consequence of, at least in the wake of the 'I-thought'.
- 'The enemy'—thoughts—is to be quelled by going behind the illusion, the 'I-thought'.

Neuroscientists also say that the 'I-thought', this sense of self, is an illusion—there is no elemental, undivided, integrated, unchanging 'self'. But that is where the agreement ends. They do not think there is anything behind it that is to be accessed by seeing the 'I-thought' for what it is: a construct, an illusion. Moreover, they feel that this illusion, the 'I-thought', this sense of 'self', is a *useful* illusion, and not the great obstacle Sri Ramana teaches it to be, and it arises precisely because it is so useful, indeed indispensable. And, finally, that it is itself the witness, it is itself the experiencer, not some other unchanging, deathless entity behind it.

Here in shorthand is how they come to these conclusions.

The sense that there is a 'me' to whom various things are happening is necessary in the first instance to make sense of them. Without it, they would be discrete, unconnected objects hitting our unconnected senses—some mere particles, some meteors, but each an isolated chunk. The sense of being a self enables us to string the particles together, to weave them into a narrative. The self, in the words of one of the influential philosophers on these matters, Daniel Dennett, is 'a kind of center of narrative gravity'. Having strung them into a narrative, we are positioned to react to them. The sense that I am a unified self, in other words, does not help me churn up a narrative alone; it is necessary for me to act in response to the knowledge that such-and-such has struck. So necessary is this sense of self for our survival that it is present in every living entity—from the tiniest thing that shrinks to the touch in the fear that the touch signals an intent to smother it. As the sense of self must, therefore, have been present as long as entities have had the instinct to survive, it must by now be embedded in genes.

This instinctive sense is reinforced from our infancy: from our very conception, everyone treats us as a distinct entity. Being held, and cuddled and loved, playing with others, learning to do things and speak a language by copying others—each of these involves others, and each of these has vital implications for the growth of our brains. Each has the farthest consequences for the connections that will be formed, discarded, strengthened in our brains. And, therefore, for the sort of person we will turn out to be. Diane Ackerman cites a telling statistic that gives us an inkling of how much greater the influence of others and of the environment is on humans than on their evolutionary cousins. She points out that as humans began to walk upright, hips became thicker to support the heavier head and torso. That shrank the birth canal. 'The solution humans found was to give birth earlier to a baby with an unfinished brain only about 25 per cent of its adult weight,' she writes. 'A new baboon's brain is almost 70 per cent of its adult weight.' As a result, as the human infant develops, a much greater proportion of its eventual personality is forged by interactions with those around him and his environment.[52]

Language develops. The child learns first by copying others. The constant use of language—in which the child is addressed as a distinct entity, and through which she addresses others as being distinct from herself—reinforces that sense of self.

The passage of life, the passing of days and nights, the cycle of seasons—all instil in us the concept of time. Language enables us to think in terms of past and future. The past extends to the obscure distance, the future extends into indefiniteness. But for each of us, both converge on the here and now—on the moment in which 'I' am at the moment. As does space, as do the directions—east and west, north and south; all of them converge on 'me'. Each of these features further reinforces that 'self'.

Moreover, as we grow up we do so not just in an inanimate environment. We grow up amidst others of our kind, in groups. And this has twofold consequences. First, living and moving in a group affects both the size and complexity of our brains. In his lively and instructive book, *The Self Illusion: Who Do You Think You Are?* Bruce Hood points out that birds of species that flock together have comparatively larger brains than those that live isolated lives. Locusts have tiny, rudimentary brains, he writes. But as they swarm together, and rub against each other, this tactile stimulation sets off a trigger in their brain to start paying attention to each other. Areas associated with learning and memory quickly *enlarge by as much as one-third* as they begin to swarm and become more tuned in to other locusts and soon become a devastating collective mass.[53]

There is the other aspect. To survive amidst others, it is necessary that we know what others are thinking—about what we are doing, as well as about the objectives that *they* are pursuing. Then alone can we pursue actions that would preserve and advance our interests in the face of what others are doing or planning to do. To use the expression that psychologists and others use, to deal with others we must have a 'theory of mind'. We acquire this by putting ourselves in the shoes of others, by mimicking their reactions to circumstances—of which we are a part. And we can do this only when we have a sense of ourselves being a distinct, integrated 'self', separate from the others. Others too develop a 'theory of mind' to anticipate *our* actions.

Once an individual comes to identify himself with his 'self', he is better impelled to excel, to establish himself in the eyes of others. Of course, this increasingly solidified 'self' doesn't goad us to do only those things which advance our interests and those of others. All too often it pushes us into doing things that we would not do if we had a more diffuse and weaker sense of self. Just as often, that 'self' filters the information we receive, it influences the way we process it, how and what we store and retrieve to justify and fortify itself. That creates problems of its own—for the person concerned as much as for others.

As interactions with others and with the environment, and what goes on inside our own heads as a result, have such far-reaching implications for our sense of 'self', we need hardly be reminded that what we conceive our 'self' to be is ever-changing. The conception we have of ourselves as a child, as an adolescent ... to the time our senses wane, naturally that conception differs. Moreover, a vital component of who we are, or, more accurately, of who we think we are, is shaped by our accumulated experiences, our memories. But we know that memories change: how we can remember an event in minute detail one day, and how, sometime later, we can recall just the salient features of what transpired. Hood gives an arresting simile: 'Memory is like garden refuse being fermented into compost: like garden refuse, experiences are laid down with the most recent still retaining much detail and structure but, with time, they eventually break down and become mixed in and integrated with the rest of our experiences. Some experiences stand out and take a long time to decompose but they are rare instances. The remainder becomes a mush...'[54] And so unreliable is what we remember even of events that have happened 'right before our eyes', and that too recently, that, as we saw earlier, eyewitness accounts are little relied upon in courts in some of the states of the United States. The tendency apart of our senses and our brain to make errors spontaneously, there is a veritable industry among some professions—lawyers arguing to get their client off, psychiatrists helping their patients shift blame—of 'creating' 'memories' of events that never happened. Just as what happened in the past, and after repeated revisions what we think happened in the past, what we think of the future and how we imagine our place to be in that future, and of course our present circumstances—these also influence our sense of self. Not just that each of these affects our perceptions about ourselves, each of the determinants change over time.

And that 'self' can be so easily influenced by others. Indeed, we see it being manipulated every day by godmen, demagogues and other illusionists, peers, persons wearing the emblems of authority—the doctor in his gown, the man in a police uniform—by advertising experts, by the crowd as it becomes a mob and sweeps us up to commit crimes we would never do on our own. Experiment after experiment has shown how merely being told that we, along with some others, are in 'Group A' and the rest are in 'Group B' leads us to change our behaviour: we tend to favour or be more lenient towards or report favourably about those *who we think are in 'our' group* as against those *we think are in the 'other' group*—when actually no groups have been formed at all. As this is what happens when there are no groups, when we do not know who is in 'our' group and who is in the 'other' group, how will people behave when in fact some of them are 'Hindus' and some are 'Muslims'? How will they behave when these differences are stoked by demagogues, and tensions mount? ... Which of these is our *real* self?

To paraphrase the Buddha, just as you cannot step into the 'same' river *once*, you cannot encounter the same self *once*—'same self' is a contradiction in terms.

Just as our 'self' is not an 'unchanging' self, it is not an integrated, undivided self. This is seen most dramatically in persons who suffer from brain disorders. When there is no other way to prevent epileptic convulsions from spreading from one hemisphere to the other, the connections between the two hemispheres through the corpus callosum are sundered. As Michael Gazzaniga has documented so acutely, each hemisphere receives information without the other knowing about it, even though the person does things that she or he would be doing had both hemispheres received, and therefore processed, the input in the normal way. Aren't there two selves in such split-brain patients? In others, a limb—say, the left hand— begins acting completely on its own: the person buttons his shirt with his right hand, and the left unbuttons it ... One, integrated 'self'? Or the most obvious case: of persons having multiple personalities embodied in them—one 'self' or many?

The location of the 'self' that we sense can be made to shift. In an out-of-body experience, as in a near-death experience, we perceive our 'self' to have shifted to some vantage point outside our body. Recall the experiments of the Swiss neuroscientist, Olaf Blanke, and his colleagues that we have encountered earlier. In those experiments, the sense of 'self' was artificially shifted to a vantage point outside the body. In one set of experiments, they induced the shift by stimulating the right temporo-parietal junction. In another set of experiments, they shifted the sense of 'self' to a virtual body imaged in front of or beneath the person. Olaf Blanke and his colleagues have recreated the experience of looking down on one's body—a familiar component of near-death experiences—by having the person lie prone facing down and the same sequence of his back being scratched as he watches it being scratched in a mirror beneath him. In each of these situations, the 'self' has shifted into the virtual body in front of or above the real body of the person. And they have even identified the part of the brain the dysfunctions of which lead to these illusionary experiences.

In a TED talk that you can see on YouTube, Blanke draws parallels with the rubber hand and phantom limb illusions that we in India have become familiar with through the work of V.S. Ramachandran. A man is seated. His hands are spread out on the table. In between them is a cardboard partition. Along the right hand, a rubber hand is placed. This rubber hand and the left hand are stroked simultaneously. Suddenly, a person plunges a fork into the rubber hand. Shocked, the subject immediately and swiftly pulls back his left hand. A bit of his 'self' had shifted into the rubber hand![55] Where then is the 'real self'?

But then how do we get the sense of being a stable, unified, continuing 'self'? Gazzaniga has the answer: A module or a constellation of modules in our left hemisphere is the great 'interpreter'. It generates the illusion of a unified self—because the illusion is so useful, indeed because it is indispensable for dealing with others around us and with our environment.[56]

A Reconciliation?

Each of us strives to retain solace even though the 'self' turns out to be a figment of our imagination.

I will live on through genes, we console ourselves.

Even though I may die, the causes for which I have fought, the values by which I have lived, the groups and culture and religion in which I have immersed myself will live on, we console ourselves.

Thinkers come up with more complex grounds for hope. Deeply distressed at the passing away of his wife, Hofstadter finds reason in his thesis of 'strange loops'. As we deal with each other, each internalizes the other. Thus, while one's 'principal domicile' is one's body, it is not the only place where one is present. We exist inside the brains and minds of those who know us. Hence, even when this 'principal domicile'—this body—is gone, the person continues to live in the brains and minds of those who knew her, and especially in the brains and minds of those who loved her, as in their minds her 'self'—in the sense of that 'strange loop'—would have been most deeply engraved, so to say.

Mark Johnston, a philosopher at Princeton, advances an approach that comes closest to the remarks of Sri Ramana that we have been reading.[57]

Over aeons, man's sense of 'self' developed for the sorts of reasons that we have glanced through in the foregoing. But the more deeply the sense of 'self' got ingrained in him, the more he came to fear death. For it would entail the extinction of that 'self'. Moreover, the world would continue on its course without him, as it had before he came to be. But the one who has come to identify himself with others, Johnston tells us, who has undergone 'a kind of death of the self ... lives a transformed life driven by entering imaginatively into the lives of others, anticipating their needs and true interests, and responding to these as far as is reasonable ... He thereby sheds a certain kind of self-delusion, as it were the practical counterpart of an enduring superlative self, and so finds that the death of a particular human being is so much less important to him than the onward rush of humankind that continues after his death. He is more identified with that and with its rich magnificence, so much so that he can find the end of his own individual personality to be a final release from the centripetal force that continued through his life to pull him back into his smaller self. Such a person's pattern of identification has given him a new identity, one that is not obliterated by the death of his body and the consequent end of his individual personality ... So, those who see through the self and adopt the outlook of *agape* will literally survive death. Of course, their individual personalities will not; but to them, lacking as they do any pure *de se* preference for their *own* individual personalities, this will be no great loss...'[58]

How then is one to obliterate the 'self'? Johnston argues that we do this by internalizing the third-person perspective, that we come to see ourselves as just an 'abstract other'. The mystic experience rearranges our brain and its functioning so that for the mystic this perspective becomes the new normal.

What understanding will take us towards this third-person perspective? The sense of self is reinforced by the way we perceive the world, Johnston says. Perceptions are '*perspectival*', 'that is, they present items to a particular viewing position, or more generally to a particular point from which someone might sense the surrounding environment'. We hear sounds coming to the point at which we are, we see sights from the point at which we are. That is, all our senses put us at the centre of the world. This way of experiencing the universe establishes and continually reinforces the sense of self. We see the past and future also from the point in time at which we are: the past and future converge in us. Johnston calls this 'an arena of presence and action'.[59] And at the centre of this 'arena of presence' is the 'self', the 'I'-thought.

But, in fact, there never was, and there isn't a centre from the point of view of the world, Johnston argues. Or, to put it another way, there are as many centres as there are living beings—each centre as 'real' or as much of an illusion as any other. Any particular centre and its boundaries are just virtual. The mystic sees this. He sees that he is just an 'arbitrary other'. And so he identifies with all others. And does good not because 'we are all the same under the skin', but because in doing good he is doing it literally to himself, to the himself-who-is-all-others. Hence the moral for us: the more an individual conditions himself to adopting the point of view of others—of the world, of the universe—to his self, the less consequential his death will seem to him. When all come to adopt that perspective, all strive to do good. And we have the Kingdom of Heaven on Earth.*

True, if we internalize the notion that we will live on through our genes; if we so erase our separateness and thereby completely identify ourselves with our culture, our religion, our country, or whatever will outlast us; or if we internalize the notion that we are truly just an 'arbitrary other' and come to identify ourselves with humankind—the fear of our particular death will surely abate. The Buddhists are counselled that to diminish the dread of death they should internalize the notion that absolutely nothing lasts, that everything is changing every moment. Hindus are counselled to lessen that dread by internalizing the notion that that which is the essence of each of us is indestructible, that it is unchanging, that it always was, and will always be.

The varied propositions themselves raise the question: Has the dread of death lessened because that particular notion—any one of the kinds of notions we have just glanced through—embodies the truth or because we have internalized it?

And does it really answer Woody Allen's riposte that we encountered earlier—of wanting to achieve immortality, not through his works being remembered forever but through not dying; of wanting to live on, not in the hearts of his countrymen, but in his apartment! To the extent that any of the soporifics we are fed succeeds in reconciling us to death, is it not that to that extent self-hypnosis has succeeded?

You decide!

Where in the Brain Is the Sense of Self Integrated?

We do not, of course, know exactly where in the brain the notion of the 'self' is integrated. It would be a safe bet nonetheless to assume

---

*As in Hofstadter's case, I have just strung a few sentences and propositions from Johnston's much-acclaimed book to give an idea of his thesis, and for us to see how close he comes to the sorts of things that our mystics say.

that the simultaneous activation of several components of the brain integrates inputs from an array of sources to generate this sense of being one 'self'. In an important paper, A.D. Craig drew attention to the anterior insular cortex, especially in its joint operation with the anterior cingulate cortex, as the site where inputs from many parts were integrated to yield this sense of 'self'.[60]

The insula lies deep in the lateral groove of the brain where the frontal, parietal and temporal lobes meet. It has dense connections with several components of the brain that are primarily associated with processing sensory inputs, with those ascribing emotional value to each sensation or input, including internally generated thoughts and feelings, as well as to components that are implicated in our motor functions. The rear, middle and frontal portions of the insula connect to different parts of the brain, and thereby play discrete roles in processing inputs and sending signals.

Craig recalled a number of studies that had shown that the insulae were involved in a very wide array of functions. Studies have shown how the anterior insula is activated in processing of vestibular sensations; awareness of one's body, maintaining the body in equilibrium, as well as the conviction that that this particular body is mine, a conviction that is lost when there is a lesion in the insula; awareness that I am the one who is doing a particular act, the sense of 'agency'; recognition of oneself; listening to music; perception of time; the joint activation of the anterior insular cortex and the anterior cingulate cortex, 'experiencing emotional feelings, including maternal and romantic love, anger, fear, sadness, happiness, sexual arousal, disgust, aversion, unfairness, inequity, indignation, uncertainty, disbelief, social exclusion, trust, empathy, sculptural beauty, a "state of union with God", and a hallucinogenic state (induced by ayahuasca)'. 'Thus,' Craig noted, 'the AIC is activated not just in association with subjective feelings from the body, but apparently with all subjective feelings.'

He noted that one attribute alone was common to this vast variety of functions, and that was awareness, and, therefore, he concluded, the insula, in particular the anterior insula, was implicated in generating awareness:

This brief review reveals that an astonishing number of recent studies from a broad range of fields reported activation of the AIC

[Anterior Insular Cortex]. These studies associate the AIC not just with all subjective feelings but also with attention, cognitive choices and intentions, music, time perception and, unmistakably, awareness of sensations and movements ... of visual and auditory percepts ... of the visual image of the self ... of the reliability of sensory images and subjective expectations ... and of the trustworthiness of other individuals ... In several key experiments, the AIC was activated without apparent activation in the ACC ... No other region of the brain is activated in all of these tasks, and the only feature that is common to all of these tasks is that they engage the awareness of the subjects. Thus, in my opinion, the accumulated evidence compels the hypothesis that the AIC engenders human awareness.[61]

But the awareness of an object or a sensation requires, to continue with Craig, that I first be aware of my *self*—that I be aware that 'I am'. This commences from perceptions about one's body—the insula plays a major part in this; proceeds to subjective feelings arising from and around the body, and then encompasses all subjective feelings, relating them to and modulating them in accordance with the environment. This sequence commences from the neural representation in the posterior insula of each feeling arising from the body. The mid-insula re-represents them, integrating them with inputs arising from maintaining the body in the environment in which the person finds himself. This higher representation, so to say, is re-represented in the anterior insula, combined this time with the significance which is attached to the feelings as well as the features of the environment and interpersonal and social circumstances in which the person is. The feelings, the others, the environment are all referenced back to the 'self'. What had begun as a merely physical 'self' has by now become a feeling, knowing 'self'. And thus we get not just the 'self' as it is at the present moment, but as it has been in the past and may be at future moments.

But, Craig reasoned, as the insula can store, even momentarily, and process only a finite number of moments, it must ascribe value—'salience'—to each condition at each moment, depending on its significance for one's body and feelings in the context of the social conditions and environment in which one is at that moment. This 'integration of salience across all these factors,' he concluded, 'culminates in a unified final meta-representation of the "global emotional moment" near the junction of the anterior insula and the frontal operculum'—'operculum', a sort of 'lid' as its name implies that covers the insula:

> This processing stage is key, because it generates an image of 'the material me' (or the sentient self) at one moment in time—'now'. An anatomical repetition of this fundamental unit, indexed by an endogenous timebase, is all that is required to generate a set of repeated metarepresentations of global emotional moments that extends across a finite period of time, and this anatomical structure (a 'metamemory') provides the basis for the continuity of subjective emotional awareness in a finite present.[62]

As one 'global emotional moment' follows another, we get successive images of 'self' at successive moments. And this is how we get to perceive time, Craig surmised. Now comes a vital step—it yields an experience that is often associated with the mystic trance. When a person is in an emotionally charged situation or condition, the number of 'global emotional moments' catapults, they succeed each other at lightning speed. So much more happens in a fixed moment of 'objective' time. Subjectively, the person feels that time has come to a standstill—in a word, as the 'global emotional moments' multiply and get more and more compressed, subjective time dilates. 'A similar process for the recruitment of global emotional moments could provide the basis for "heightened awareness" of the immediate moment and for the enhanced activation of the AIC that is associated with such moments,' Craig observed.[63]

There is one more function of the insula, or, more precisely of its dysfunction, which may be implicated in generating the certainty that mystics experience. Building on a host of brain-imaging studies, Fabienne Picard has advanced the thesis that the feeling of complete certainty that seizes many persons during ecstatic seizures may arise from the fact that during such seizures, the insula is blocked from one of its functions.[64]

She reproduces the written reports of two patients about what they felt during the seizures. Do read them to see how closely they resemble the feelings of absolute clarity and complete certainty that mystics report.

Patient number one was a seventeen-year-old Swiss apprentice
farmer. He had been having seizures for two years. All sorts of things
triggered seizures in him: 'an interesting discussion with several
people with whom he liked to talk … a tractor with the harvest,
nice photos, a nice color, a flower, a nice landscape, a bird singing,
grazing animals, branches that move with the wind, a beautiful
woman, or on the occasion of a kiss, a caress, a nice thought about
someone, a hope…' Picard summarized the patient's account of his
feelings during the seizures as follows:

> He experienced an extremely pleasurable state of consciousness
> during his seizures. He felt a deepening awareness of the situation
> or conversation going on around him, a sudden clarity. It was as
> if he clearly understood everything, especially if he happened to
> be in the midst of a discussion with several people. He grasped it
> all simultaneously. Things suddenly seemed self-evident, almost
> predictable (yet without the feeling of knowing the future).
>
> While he knew where he was and what he was doing, he did
> not want to interrupt the experience by talking. At the same time,
> very often he felt a taste, pleasant but nothing more (gustatory
> hallucinations). He could not compare this taste with any taste he
> knew. During the seizure, he could not 'be located in time'. It was
> as if time stopped. For him, these seizures lasted at least 40 sec
> while his family members could say it lasted 1 to 3 sec.[65]

The second patient was a thirty-nine-year-old American philosopher,
and, therefore, Picard wrote, with 'high introspective capacities'.
He had suffered from epilepsy since he was eighteen. The seizures
ended abruptly when he was twenty-one. By the time he was twenty-
three, he had been able to give up all medication. Initially, he
had seizures that were extremely unpleasant. These ceased, and he
began to have ecstatic seizures. His description of his experience
during the seizures—unpleasant and pleasant—was detailed, and
most informative. This is how he described what he felt during the
pleasant seizures:

> Every detail of my perceptions was every bit as accurate as they
> ever are.
>
> In dramatic contrast to the ordinary way of experiencing one's
> surroundings, during my seizures, all of these boundaries would

suddenly be erased. Although all my judgments of shape, size, color, texture, and so on would remain totally unchanged, the evaluation of my environment would undergo a sudden transformation. Everything would be joined together into one whole, as if every single thing in my surroundings were deliberately placed by an artist with the goal of composing a photograph. This would result in a sense of vividness which derived, not from any dramatic hallucination or visual 'trick', but from the fact that each object in my visual field was emphasized, so to speak, by everything else. When these boundaries are erased, a second phenomenon begins— all the ordinary facts about the environment seem suddenly to become infused with certainty and a sense of inevitability.

One often has (what is sometimes called) an 'aha!' moment when we can suddenly explain several puzzling facts simultaneously with the same answer. The sense that I had when I was experiencing some of these seizures was not unlike a continuous series of profound 'aha!' moments. Although nothing around me seemed to have changed in any concrete way, every observation of my surrounding environment seemed to 'make sense' in this way. It is the sense, as I mentioned before, that one might have when admiring an expertly composed painting or photograph—each detail seems to be the way it is for a reason, even if that reason is difficult to articulate or seems only to float at the very edge of one's consciousness.

The great consilience, coherence, and vividness of everything in the world seemed to demand an explanation of its organization. And the explanation was immediate and completely convincing— some mind or purposive agency was at the root of the world's organization. This was a conviction that was both incredibly vague and totally compelling. Speaking as someone who is not normally given over to such beliefs—I am an atheist who happens also to be a professor specializing in logic—these beliefs are wildly out of character for me. But, looking back on these experiences, I am struck by two features of these beliefs, which I now believe may be related. First, they were absolutely immune to any rational doubt; indeed, they seemed not even to be possible candidates for any such doubt. Second, they seemed—perhaps ironically, given my earlier statement—to have many of the same features as the most justified, and rationally derived beliefs that a person could possibly hold. For instead of merely being justified by one or several other considerations or observations, these seemed to be irrefutably supported by literally everything in the world. Literally everything that I could experience seemed to cohere with, and lend support to, the belief that there was some sort of agency behind it all. The level of apparent organization possessed by everything in the world simply demanded such an explanation.[66]

The peace. The clarity. The certainty. The feeling that everything was in harmony, that everything had been designed by an overarching, expert hand ... How literally the account accords with what a mystic might say about how he feels during his peak experiences.

Building on several earlier studies, Picard reasoned that we are averse to uncertainty; that the insula strives to minimize uncertainty by continually comparing what the brain had predicted with what environmental and other inputs indicate the situation or event actually is. The insula helps to continually update the predictions, successively narrowing the gap between predictions and outcomes. During a seizure, while the prediction and the latest inputs about the actual situation are preserved in the brain, a dysfunction of the insula disables it from carrying out the comparison between the two. The person, therefore, remains in a state of certainty, and the peace arising from it.[67]

13

But what about consciousness?

Even the few extracts from his conversations that we have glanced through are enough to suggest that Sri Ramana used 'consciousness' in several different senses: as a sort of ether that pervaded the universe; as some separate entity that resides in us also, and is the perennial, unmoved witness; as awareness. And the last, awareness, sometimes referred to the state in which a person was—as in, 'The child that the distraught mother wanted him to resurrect was dead, and, therefore, not conscious'; by contrast, 'As the surgeries to excise the tumour from his arm were carried out under local anesthesia, Sri Ramana was conscious throughout the operations.' Sometimes it referred to being conscious or aware of objects, including other persons or events. Often it referred to being conscious or aware of oneself.

Like our mystics, some neuroscientists and thinkers believe that consciousness is indeed a fundamental property of the universe and that just as physicists accept some entities as given—space, time, charge—we should take consciousness to be a given, and proceed with more mundane investigations. Wilder Penfield, whose pioneering explorations we have noted earlier, focused on a region encompassing the thalamus, basal ganglia and the upper brainstem. He concluded that this is the region that is responsible for consciousness. In the final scientific book that he wrote, summarizing his experiments and reflections, he looked beyond this region. 'Mind comes into action and goes out of action with the highest brain-mechanism, it is true,' he wrote. 'But the mind has energy. The form of that energy is different from that of neuronal potentials that travel the axon pathways.' His explorations had not revealed anything in the brain which could account for the non-reflexive functions that the mind performs, he wrote. And so, the mind must be taken to be a separate, 'basic element in itself. One might then call it a *medium,* an *essence,* a *soma.* That is to say, it has a *continuing existence...*' And it must have access to some other form of energy, he went on to say. From these propositions, he speculated about direct communication between one mind and another, between the mind of man and God. But these were speculations, he emphasized. 'I don't begin by a conclusion at all and I don't end by making a final and unalterable one...,' he wrote in his 'Afterthoughts', and therefore, till sufficient evidence is in, it behoves each of us to make a personal assumption.[1]

In his influential work, Roger Penrose has gone farther. And he has been more specific. The brain is not just a computational entity, he has argued. A non-computational element enters our understanding. It is in quantum processes that physics encounters non-computability, he pointed out. At what scale does non-computability occur? At the Planck scale—10^{-33} cm. Hence, the consciousness that is fundamental must occur at this fundamental level. Where in the brain could operations at this scale take place? At the suggestion of an anaesthesiologist, Stuart Hameroff, Penrose zeroed in on microtubules—the scaffolding within the neurons. This is the component and level 'which has a reasonable chance of isolating large-scale quantum effects', he reasoned, because the environment within the nerves themselves has too much going on. 'Mine is a version of the Sherlock Holmes argument,' he was to concede twenty-five years later, 'which I admit is a weak argument—that is to say that once you have eliminated everything else, what remains must be the truth, no matter how improbable.'[2]

Were these propositions to get adequate empirical confirmation someday, it would be a major advance, of course—though, some will argue, it would still leave the question open. The 'hard problem' has been to explain how consciousness erupts from purely physical components of the brain and their interactions. To affirm that consciousness arises from quantum phenomena—whether these occur in the microtubules or somewhere else in the brain—would still leave us with that very question: How does consciousness arise from these phenomena? Nor would it solve the age-old question: Are physical entities and their interactions all there is to consciousness?

Among spiritual and religious leaders, the Dalai Lama has taken an intermediate, open position. Sometimes it seems to him that all consciousness must have a physical basis, he says, adding that he doesn't really know! His long-term translator reminds us that, even as he maintains that all consciousness must have a physical basis, the Dalai Lama says that—in the light of recent developments in physics, for example—what is 'material', what is 'physical' may have to be thought through again. It may be that very subtle forms of energy underlie very subtle forms of consciousness. Not everything physical is material, Evan Thompson points out while recounting these observations of the Dalai Lama. Fields and forces are physical, he writes, but they are not material.[3]

We come to a fork here. Some neuroscientists and, of course, several New Age writers argue, and in this they come close to our mystics, that even if we were eventually able to fully identify the physical components and processes that trigger consciousness, we would not have got to know what consciousness is. On rubbing dry pieces of wood or striking two stones, we get fire, they say. But fire is not wood or stone, nor is it the rubbing together of those things. Getting to know the physical components and interactions will not even settle the question whether consciousness is a product of the brain or whether the brain is a sort of radio that receives it from elsewhere, they maintain. To conclude that consciousness is just a product of the inner workings of the brain would be like getting to know the wires and transistors of a radio or television set and concluding that they are creating the voice or picture, a prominent neuroscientist writes; a prism lets white light through, he points out, and the light gets dispersed into so many beautiful colours, but the prism is not the source of the light.[4] Some of them, in particular the New Age thinkers, maintain that consciousness either originates elsewhere or that it pervades the universe, and that we, as the shamans say they do, just plug into it as if through an antenna.[5]

Others argue that such positions arise merely from the current incompleteness of our knowledge regarding the brain and its functioning. They maintain that the 'hard problem' will just evaporate as knowledge advances. Consciousness is not *correlated with*, it is not even *caused by* processes within the brain. It *is* those processes. A leading authority in the field, Paul Churchland, asks us to recall what has happened to several counterparts of the 'hard problem' in physics. Something—an entity in itself, an unknowable entity—called 'vision' was thought to enable us to see and feel the sensations associated with seeing. But it now turns out that seeing is just a pattern of activations of neurons in specific parts of the brain—and one pattern of activations gives us the sensations that the object is red, another that it is green. Nor is that the end of the sequence within the brain: indeed, it is just the beginning; once the brain has determined whether the object is red or green, a series of other regions—the ones that evaluate a tomato that is still green or has turned red—are activated. And that activates memories as well as emotions triggered by our having eaten a red or a green tomato in the past ... All this happens in an instant, and it is the totality of these activations that gives us, indeed which is the feeling of red or green in that context. 'Electromagnetic waves don't cause light,' Churchland points out, 'they're not correlated with light; they are light. That's what light is. Similarly with sound: a sound of middle C isn't correlated with a compression wave train of 263 Hz.[6] It is a compression wave train with that frequency. And the feeling of warmth from a coffee cup isn't something that's correlated with mean molecular kinetic energy; it's identical with the mean molecular kinetic energy of the molecules in the cup.'[7] Hence, these scientists maintain, one day we will have a complete account of the neural processes that occur when we become conscious, and those processes will be the consciousness we have been looking for.

The Natural Explanations

Enormous advances have been made in the last century towards finding natural explanations for what we do and think, for the emotions that sweep us—explanations that focus on what happens in the brain. The search for these explanations has been accelerated manifold by the advances in brain-imaging techniques during the last forty to fifty years. And piles of studies have been conducted to ascertain what happens in the brain in different circumstances. What happens in the brain as we become conscious/aware? What happens in the brain as we go into deep sleep; what happens as we dream; what happens as within the dream we become aware that we are dreaming; what happens in the condition that is acquired by much, much greater effort—when, during dreamless sleep, we become aware that we are now in deep, dreamless sleep, a sort of 'lucid deep sleep'; what happens in the brain as we awaken, as we meditate, as our attention shifts...? Which components or regions of the brain get activated; electrical waves of how many cycles per second occur in different states? Does the fact that a stimulus has arrived at the crest or the trough of autonomous electrical rhythms in the brain make a difference to the probability and intensity of the stimulus breaking into our awareness? What happens as we direct our attention inward and shut out external sensory stimuli? What changes take place as a result of austerities and isolation and sensory deprivation in the chemical and electrical activity in the brain? What role do the neurotransmitters play? What role do the lesser studied astrocytes play? Piles of investigations have focused on each of these questions.

Another set of studies has attempted to reverse-engineer the processes. They have started from the experiences that have been reported by long-term, accomplished meditators and those who have had peak experiences. For instance, these personages have almost uniformly reported that the sense of time evaporates, that the boundaries between themselves and the rest of the universe blur and ultimately vanish, that they are filled with unalloyed bliss, and compassion, and so on. Neuroscientists have learnt from investigations conducted in other contexts about the areas which are primarily implicated in delineating the boundaries between us and the world, in the perception of time, in highly charged emotional experiences, etc. They have compared these findings with what can be observed about activity in the brains of accomplished meditators. Starting from the other direction, they have examined some observable features of the brains of long-term meditators and delineated how these differ from the same components and rhythms in the brains of non-meditators; as well as of those who seek to obtain the same sort of experiences through other devices—like ingesting some drugs.

The results are reported in a wide array of books and papers in neuroscience journals. Among the results from these studies that strongly confirm the insights of our saints, three have a direct bearing on the topics at which we have been glancing.

THREE CONFIRMATIONS

First, the studies document beyond any doubt that spiritual practices and pursuits greatly alter the relative strength of neuronal connections as well as the rhythms of their firing. The practices perceptibly change 'the amount of real estate' in the brain that is devoted to different functions. These results document what the sages have been saying for centuries, that the mind can be altered by working on the mind. It now turns out that the brain—as a physical organ—also can be altered by working on the mind, an alteration that will have further consequences for the way the mind works in the next moment or round. They also confirm that working on the body entails major changes in the brain as well as the mind. A lemma of this latter set of results is that the sorts of extreme austerities that our saints had practised—Sri Ramana for three-and-a-half years, Sri Ramakrishna for twelve years—would have had drastic effects on their brains and minds, and, one can surmise, could have triggered some of the experiences that we have observed earlier in the book.

The second feature that stands out is that consciousness/ awareness is the result of processes within the brain—for instance, as we shall see in a moment, from incessant exchanges between the cortex and the relay station, the thalamus; or, more accurately, consciousness is the state that the brain reaches by processes within the brain. We become conscious of or aware of the sensory input, that input is not the consciousness or awareness. Something may be before our eyes for long and we may not be conscious of it: neuroscientists point to 'change blindness' as an example. You can demonstrate it to yourself by switching on to YouTube: a basketball game is in progress; you are asked to count the number of baskets the team in white is scoring; as you are keeping your eyes on the ball and the players in white, a gorilla walks across the court, and you don't notice it. There is the other demonstration that is just as often cited—'binocular rivalry'. A different image is presented before each eye. The brain does not merge them into one composite image—it switches from one image to the other. Or the same image remains before our eyes for long, but our perception of it changes from moment to moment—you would have seen illustrations of the Necker cube: the outlines of a transparent cubic box, with a dot. One moment the dot seems to lie *inside* the box, the next *outside* it. There is the opposite phenomenon too: 'blindsight'. A person has lost his sight because of an injury; he does not consciously 'see' an object. He does not 'see' the word 'downpour'; but when some words are read out to him subsequently, he is more likely to pick a word that goes with the word 'downpour'—say 'umbrella' or 'flood'. That suggests to neuroscientists that he has become aware of the original word—'downpour'—without being conscious of the fact that he has become aware of it. This phenomenon is seen most dramatically in the case of split-brain patients, patients in whose brains the 200-odd million connections between the two hemispheres—the corpus callosum—have had to be sundered so as to prevent intractable epileptic convulsions from spreading from a focus in one hemisphere to other, distant parts of the brain. An instruction is placed within the visual field of, say, the right hemisphere—that is, on his left side. He does not 'see' it, but he acts on it. He may even go so far as to maintain that someone else has done the deed using his limbs. In all these instances, the stimulus is present, sometimes it has registered within the person's brain, but he is not conscious of it. Our sages downplay the significance of sensory inputs, and ask us to focus instead on activities within our brains.

The third confirmation that comes through is their emphasis on the fact that consciousness, indeed all life, is a continuum. It isn't that consciousness is either present or not. But that it is present or absent in degrees of gradation—in plants, trees, single-cell entities, animals and humans. Some types of mushrooms glow so as to attract animals which in turn will accelerate pollination; sea anglerfish glow to attract prey; fireflies glow to attract mates.[8] Sunflowers turn towards the sun. Plants sense each other as well as the environment. Members of a single species of plants or trees, for example, develop entirely differing rhythms depending on the environment in which they happen to be—depending on the amount and temporal distribution of rainfall, for instance. Trees seem to have 'memory'. Without formal 'brains', they seem to do exactly what our brains do—integrate enormous amounts of information. They shift attention to the new variable that has appeared and is going to be significant to their well-being. They are able to locate hosts as well as prey. Studies point to electrical activity in the roots, to commands that are sent out from here to the elongation zone. They produce chemicals that act as hormones and neurotransmitters. To alert their kind in the neighbourhood, they release chemicals which are the equivalent in the plant world to a scream...[9]

Only instinct? Automatic, unthinking, non-reflective reflex actions? No awareness?

A Humble, Single-cell Organism

Consider next the humble slime mould. *Physarum polycephalum*, as it is known, is a single-cell amoeba-like organism. Each cell subsists by itself. In 2000, Toshiyuki Nakagaki of the Hokkaido University, and his colleagues, placed a blob of these cells at one point on a map of Tokyo. They placed food at thirty-six points, corresponding to cities in the Tokyo area that are connected by the Tokyo rail system. At first, the slime mould maximized the area it was covering in its search for food. But soon, to recall the scientists' account in *Science*, the spread was 'resolved into a tubular network linking the discovered food sources through direct connections, additional intermediate junctions (Steiner points) that reduce the overall length of the connecting network, and the formation of occasional cross-links that improve overall transport efficiency and resilience'. Within twenty-six hours, the slime mould had fanned out, formed tubular connections and recreated the Tokyo rail network! Nor was that the end. The scientists knew that slime mould avoids bright light. They replicated the obstacles—mountains, waterbodies—by placing light sources of varying intensity in their place. 'This,' the scientists wrote, 'yielded networks with greater visual congruence to the real rail network.' The conclusion of the scientists tells the tale:

> Our biologically inspired mathematical model can capture the basic
> dynamics of network adaptability through iteration of local rules
> and produces solutions with properties comparable to or better

than those of real-world infrastructure networks. Furthermore, the model has a number of tunable parameters that allow adjustment of the benefit/cost ratio to increase specific features, such as fault tolerance or transport efficiency, while keeping costs low. Such a model may provide a useful starting point to improve routing protocols and topology control for self-organized networks such as remote sensor arrays, mobile ad hoc networks, or wireless mesh networks.[10]

No awareness? No intelligence? No striving towards a goal?

And remember, all this was accomplished by a variety of cell which usually subsists alone, acting together with cells of its kind, and without any central director, or central brain. Indeed, we would be hard put to find a counterpart to our brain in the single cell, to say nothing of a collection of them.

At about the same time, Nakagaki and others conducted another exercise with slime mould. A blob of the mould was placed at the entrance of a maze. At two exits, food was placed. At first the mould spread itself almost throughout channels of the maze. But soon, the extensions that had reached a dead end shrank while more and more cells accrued to the extensions that had reached the food. The experiment was repeated several times. Every time, of the four possible paths, the path that was the shortest (it was about a fifth shorter than the others) was selected. The scientists concluded that 'this simple organism has the ability to find the minimum length solution between two points in a labyrinth'.[11]

Still no awareness? No intelligence? No striving towards a goal?

Scientists in Britain put the organism through another task! They took the ten most populated urban areas in the United Kingdom and sought to find out what would be the optimal layout of transport links between these centres. They placed oat flakes at the location of the centres. They found that the network devised by the slime mould was isomorphic with the network of major motorways, with one exception—the motorway linking England with Scotland. As had happened in the original study of the Tokyo rail network, the researchers concluded, 'The results of the present research lay a basis for future science of bio-inspired urban and road planning.'[12]

We hardly need to be reminded about animals—the doggedness

with which the deer tries to flee the lion; the way a herd of buffalo returns and frees one of their own from a lion, and, indeed, tosses the lion into the air so high that it slinks away.[13]

No sense of 'self'? No sense of belonging? No sense of 'us' and 'them'? No 'consciousness'? No 'information processing'?

In short, when a scientist writes that animals do not have 'consciousness',* we must know that he is deploying a particular definition of 'consciousness' and concluding, by definition, that plants and trees and animals do not have consciousness, and humans do. Surely, we must adjust the criteria to the species that we are talking about.

So, plants, trees, single cells, animals, humans—a continuum.

BUT IF IT ISN'T THERE TO BEGIN WITH, HOW DOES IT ARISE?

But, even if we have nothing useful to say on 'consciousness' as something that pervades the universe and resides as a distinct entity in us, how does consciousness in the sense of awareness—in the sense of our being conscious of something, some person, some sensory input, even of ourselves—arise?

Components of our brain are said to be in 'unstable equilibrium'—a minuscule input from outside or a perturbation within can set of a cascade of neuronal firings. The components are perpetually engaged in chattering to each other. Some parts—the cerebellum, for instance, which used to be almost the entire brain of our mammalian ancestors, and sits at the back of our current brain—have connections that only go out to other parts. Most other parts have interconnections going to and fro. Some parts, in addition to the connections that they have to other parts of the brain, the constituents—neurons in the cortex, for instance—have a huge number of connections to other

---

*As a leading philosopher, Daniel Dennett did in his 1992 book, *Consciousness Explained*. He argued that only those who can use language are conscious, and, hence, animals and even pre-linguistic humans were *not* and are *not* conscious. On his reasoning, the essence of consciousness is being able to provide a narrative, and this can only be done by species that have the ability to use language. Moreover, the development of the ability to deploy language rewires the brain to be conscious.

constituents of the same part. As a result, neurons in the cortex are forever talking to other neurons in the cortex itself, much more so than they talk to neurons outside the cortex.

We look at the magnificent snow-covered Himalayas from Kausani. The scene does not enter our brain as a picture. It is not processed as a picture. It is not stored in long-term or short-term memory as a picture. As we noticed earlier, the scene is *represented*— as the pattern in which neurons have fired while we look at the mountains. The total picture is deconstructed, and parts of it, actually aspects of it, are sent to thirty different sites—the site that processes shapes, another that processes colour, etc. After being processed, the brain 'binds' the separate bits—they are brought together into a coherent representation. The representation is sent to other parts of the brain, for instance the limbic system, an assembly of components that, among other things, awakens us to the emotional significance of the scene. Assessing emotional significance necessarily entails that we bring up the memories with which the scene is associated. We now perceive the representation as one integrated experience. Sites that are responsible for our doing something in return are activated. If the action involves our saying something—calling out to a friend to see the magnificent mountains—the areas responsible for speech are brought into play. And so on.

All this happens incredibly fast, indeed almost simultaneously. Thus far, the brain is perhaps the fastest and most complex parallel processor. Second, this humungous volume of processing takes place without our being conscious of it—right up to the words that will spring up in our mind and which we will speak out as a coherent sentence. We would not have consciously searched out each word, nor would we have consciously threaded them into a sentence.

To grasp how all this happens will require a volume by itself. Here we may note just two or three facts about the brain and a few concepts that neuroscientists have developed.

The first fact to note about the brain, as we noted in another context also, concerns super-astronomical numbers. Just the cerebral cortex, Gerald Edelman and his associate Giulio Tononi tell us, has about *thirty billion* neurons and about *one million billion* connections or synapses. If we counted one synapse every second, it would take us *thirty-two million years* to finish counting them, they figure.

Given these connections, the number of possible neural circuits is *ten followed by at least a million zeros*, they write, and add, the total number of particles in the known universe is about 10 followed by seventy-nine zeros, i.e., 10^{80}.[14] And how unimaginably tightly they are packed! Diane Ackerman puts the point thus: 'In a dot of brain no larger than a single grain of sand, 100,000 neurons go to work at a billion synapses. In the cerebral cortex alone, 30 billion neurons meet at 60 trillion synapses a billionth of an inch wide'—sentences from which you will get an idea of how tightly together the neurons are packed and also of the range of numbers that leaders in the field report![15] Can you imagine something pulsating or 'firing' 800 to 1,000 times *per second*? But that is how many times, we are told, the central thalamus, a part we will encounter in a moment, fires when we are awake or dreaming.[16] Here is another figure from the books: a neuron receives signals from other neurons through its dendrites— it may have up to 10,000 of these; it sends out its message through its axon—this may be anywhere from a few millimetres to a metre long; but the electrochemical signal through the axon and synapse is just one of the media through which neurons spread messages. And neurons and their connections are just one element in the brain— indeed, they are just 15 per cent of the cells in our brain. Among the other types of cells—and they themselves are of many, many kinds—are glial cells which outnumber neurons anywhere from 6 to 1 to 15 to 1. The extraordinary functions that they perform are still being discovered.[17] And then there are chemicals, neurotransmitters, proteins of ever so many varieties, and many other substances...

The first point that emerges from these super-astronomical numbers is that for practical purposes, the combinatorial possibilities—the constellations of neurons that can form in response to an input, the patterns in which they can fire, and, therefore, the representational capacities of the brain—are almost endless. And it isn't just the neurons that fire which form a pattern at any moment; the ones that *don't* fire contribute just as much to the pattern that is formed—just as points of the paper that are left blank contribute to a drawing.

To maximize speed as well as to minimize the energy that is used—as it is, the brain uses a fifth of the energy that an average human consumes—neurons are grouped in what is called a 'small world' organization: neurons have massive numbers of connections to some neurons and a few to ones in other groups. This way the local group can process what it has received swiftly and send it over to the appropriate distant group for further work.

When an input arrives—whether it is something that our senses have perceived in the outside world or it is some spontaneous eruption within our brain—a coalition of neurons forms to process it. A leading cognitive psychologist, Bernard Baars, developed a concept that has been widely adopted. If the input is 'loud' enough, he said, or significant enough—for instance, for our emotions, given our past experiences—the initial constellation sends the processed input to the 'global workspace'. This 'workspace' is not a physical place or spot in the brain. It is an ensemble of neurons that have fired in a pattern. When a sensory input enters this workspace, it is as if it has been written on the blackboard of one of our old-fashioned classrooms. Just as whatever the teacher wrote on the blackboard became available to every student for further work, so also whatever enters the 'global workspace' becomes available to different regions of the brain for further processing—for being enjoyed, for being acted upon, for being stored in our memory, etc. These regions process it, each processing it for the aspect for which the region or component is primarily responsible.

The constellations of neurons are not fixed, however. A neuron or a set of neurons may fire in response to a particular input this moment, and be performing some other task the next. At the ensuing moment, the neuron may be silent even though the input is the same. It is because of this ceaseless flux that Edelman speaks of the 'dynamic core'—the ensemble is the 'core' because it is the primary focus for handling the input at this moment; it is 'dynamic' because it is ever-changing.

One other feature is central to the eruption of consciousness/ awareness—and that is 're-entry'. Edelman and his associate Giulio Tononi have drawn attention to 'meshwork of re-entrant connectivity' between the cortex and the thalamus, and between different regions in the cortex itself. Because of this meshwork of reciprocal pathways, they point out, 'Any perturbation in one part of the meshwork may be felt rapidly everywhere else. Altogether, the organization of the thalamocortical meshwork seems remarkably suited for integrating large number of specialists into a unified response.' The signalling is reciprocal, and not just a feedback from one periphery to some central source.[18] These rapid and reciprocal signals, signals that are processed simultaneously in several 'higher' parts, enable the brain to bind the different aspects of a sensory input into a unified experience. And that is consciousness.

'Four Signatures of Consciousness'

In an important paper published in 2003, Stanislas Dehaene, Claire Sergent and Jean-Pierre Changeux concretized the notion of the 'global workspace', and proposed a model of the neuronal processes and the neuronal assemblies that could be leading to information being sent into this workspace.[19] Over the next few years, a series of ingenious experiments confirmed their hypotheses. A decade later, Dehaene described them in a lucid book.[20]

We become conscious of an input or a thought when it, or the conclusion that has been reached after it has been processed in local centres, is 'broadcast' within the cortex and to other parts of the brain, Dehaene explains. A special set of neurons, the pyramidal neurons play a particularly important role in broadcasting the information. Relatively speaking, they are giant cells, and their axons criss-cross the cortex. Dehaene and colleagues found something as telling as it was specific. When an image is sped past us at less than one-third of a second, or when it is sandwiched between random, unrelated images and the interval during which it is shown is less than the critical one-third of a second, we do not 'see' it; but it registers on our unconscious—we accurately answer questions relating to the image. When the image is kept in view longer, we 'see' it consciously. The same interval proved critical in regard to sounds and patterns of sounds. What happens in the brain at that point?

Dehaene and colleagues discovered four 'signatures' of consciousness, that is, of information breaking through into our awareness. The first of these is a sudden ignition of parietal and prefrontal circuits, Dehaene reports, although the stimulus was exactly the same in the 'visible' and 'invisible' trials—that is, when the fleeting image was reported as having been 'seen' by the subject, and when the subject said that he had seen nothing—'in less than one-tenth of a second, between 200 and 300 milliseconds after the stimulus appeared, the recordings went from no difference at all to a massive all-or-none effect'.[21] Second, in the EEG recordings, conscious access appears as a late slow wave called the P3 wave, Dehaene reports. This wave appears about a third of a second after the stimulus has been presented. This slow and massive event is called the P3 wave because it is the third large positive peak after the stimulus appears, Dehaene explains, or the P300 wave because it often starts around 300 milliseconds. Tracking what is happening deep inside the brain with the help of electrodes reveals two further signatures: a late and sudden burst of high-frequency oscillations, and the synchronization of information exchanges across distant brain regions.

Dehaene's account has a host of riveting details. For our current concern, three specific points and one general point are relevant.

First, a sensory input or a thought, etc., generated internally is first processed locally by various assemblies of neurons. Once they come to a conclusion that it is significant, it is sent to the prefrontal and parietal areas. And from there, upon being simultaneously processed in those regions, it is broadcast far and wide. This sharing of information over wide areas of the brain is consciousness.

Second, at each successive step, to have rich information content what is broadcast must be both differentiated as well as integrated. Here, synchronization of firings of different sets of neurons is the key. Rather, the balance between their firing being fully synchronized and being fully random is crucial. If the neurons are firing in perfect synchrony, as in a massive convulsion, the information will be fully integrated but it will not have much content; if the firings are completely random—if neurons are behaving like molecules in a perfect gas—the data will be perfectly differentiated but not at all integrated, and, again, of little use for further processing.

Where in the Brain?

Third, while all agree that several regions of the brain are implicated in triggering consciousness, successive neuroscientists have hypothesized that one specific part of the brain or another plays a pivotal role in generating it. In the last scientific book that he wrote, the great neurophysiologist Wilder Penfield focused on a region encompassing the thalamus, basal ganglia and the upper part of the midbrain. He explained on the basis of his own surgeries that cellular inactivation of this region produces unconsciousness. Borrowing a phrase of Hughlings Jackson, he termed this area 'the highest brain-mechanism'. This rather than the cerebral cortex is the region that is responsible for the neuronal integrative action of the brain, Penfield felt. Proof of this, Penfield observed, lay in the facts that 'injury of a circumscribed area in the higher brainstem produces invariable loss of consciousness, and that the selective epileptic discharge, which interferes with function in this grey matter, can produce the unconsciousness (seen in epileptic automatism) without paralysis of the automatic sensory-motor control mechanism located nearby'. Penfield expressed the conclusion in unambiguous words, but he kept an open mind to what further investigations in the coming years would show: in indicating the region in a drawing, he ringed it with question marks.*[22]

As we saw, Dehaene and colleagues focus on pyramidal neurons in the cortex. Francis Crick and Christof Koch had long ago hypothesized that the key component was the claustrum—a thin elongated sheet of neurons under the neocortex. They reasoned that unless activity in the cortex of each hemisphere in itself and of both hemispheres taken together is coordinated, we would be buffeted by a cacophony. The claustrum seemed to them to be very well positioned, and with its extensive connections to different

---

*Of course, even while drawing attention to the probable role of this area, Penfield had emphasized that integration must be the outcome of several other areas also joining in. In his Maudsley lecture delivered twenty years earlier, he had observed, 'There is evidence ... that the most important area of integration is not to be found in association systems of the cortex, but in a more centrally placed area within the higher brainstem.... Hughlings Jackson assumed that such an area must exist. He called it the 'highest level', the place where final re-representation occurred. But it would be stupid of us to assume that he believed in independent function at any level. On the contrary, centrencephalic integration must be the outcome of synchronous central and cortical activity; activity in the brainstem and in those areas of the cortex of either hemisphere whose function is suited to the changing requirements of the moment. It seems likely that the temporal lobes are used simultaneously, as though in duplicate, for the purposes of recording the stream of consciousness.' Wilfred Penfield, 'The role of the temporal cortex in certain psychical phenomena', *The Journal of Mental Science*, Volume 101, July 1955, Number 424, pp. 451-65, at 458-60. The *Journal* was later subsumed in *BJPsych, The British Journal of Psychiatry*.

parts of the cortex well structured to act as 'the conductor of the orchestra'. In a recent experiment, surgeons found confirmation of their hypothesis. They were preparing a lady for surgery to deal with intractable epilepsy. They were able to switch off consciousness by electrically stimulating the claustrum, an outcome that led them to conclude that this single part of the brain may be vital for integrating disparate brain activity into a seamless experience of thoughts, sensations and emotions.[23]

Edelman assigned the critical role to the much more extensive thalamocortical system as a whole, and to the reciprocal connections in it, especially to the prefrontal and parietal cortex. These parts have more connections to each other than to other parts. When the relay station, the thalamus, suffers a lesion, the person's consciousness fades, he may even go into a vegetative state.

Nicholas Schiff, and following him, Patricia Churchland emphasized the role of a ribbon of neurons in the middle of the thalamus, called the intralaminar nuclei of the thalamus. This tiny stretch has connections going to and coming back from the top layer of every part of the cortex. By contrast, Churchland points out, the regions of the thalamus that relay information from the sense organs are *not* connected to all parts. She points to another clue that suggests that this ribbon of neurons plays a central part in conscious experience. 'During the awake and dreaming states,' she points out, 'neurons in the central thalamus fire in bursts at an unusually high rate—800 to 1,000 times per second (hertz), a remarkably energy-intensive behavior not seen anywhere else in the nervous system. They do not display the bursting pattern during deep sleep. The neuronal bursts of the central thalamus neurons track the aggregate wave pattern seen on the EEG that typifies the awake and dreaming states—20 to 40 hertz.' 'Collectively, here is what the clues suggest,' Churchland concludes, 'the ribbon of neurons that is the central thalamus is controlled by activity in the brainstem, and in turn regulates the cortical neurons to ready themselves for conscious business. Activity in this three-part arrangement—brainstem+central thalamus+cortex—is the support structure for being conscious of anything at all.'[24]

In an important paper dealing with the way in which anaesthetics may be inducing unconsciousness, Tononi, who collaborated with Edelman, and his co-authors focused on regions in the posterior parietal area, reasoning that when these regions are inactivated or their connections to the thalamus, or the connections within the cortex, are disrupted, the person becomes unconscious. The thalamus by itself may not be the switch of consciousness.[25] The vital role of the thalamus may spring from the fact that it is the relaying station, even for communication between cortical areas. This communication, and hence consciousness can be disrupted not just by the relay station being knocked out but also by a few of the long neuronal connections being disrupted. The very feature—'small world organization', with its numerous local connections and a few long-range connections—which makes for such efficient and energy-conserving processing may make the entire corticothalamic system very vulnerable. The focus of Edelman and Tononi had been on integration of discriminable information. And so, these authors focused not on one component or region of the brain as being the switch for consciousness but on the entire complex that comes into play for integrating diverse information to cause a conscious experience.[26]

As imaging techniques improve, neuroscientists are able to narrow down their search for the components and network connections that are critical for consciousness. Recall Penfield's tentative inference that the critical component would lie in the upper brainstem. In a recent exploration, eleven neuroscientists working together have found that within the upper brainstem, the pontine tegmentum, or the dorsal—upper—pons, could well be the critical component, and its connections to two cortical regions—the anterior insula and the pregenual anterior cingulate cortex—probably determine the difference between any sort of awareness and coma.*[27] They

---

*Because of the number of elements that are located within them as well as because of their extensive connections with other components and regions of the brain, both the pontine tegmentum and the anterior cingulate cortex are implicated in a wide range of functions. The former is involved, inter alia, in our processing information received from the senses, in our movements, in some autonomic functions such as breathing, in being alert and monitoring our environment. Apart from being vital in several autonomic functions such as keeping our blood pressure and heart rate within bounds, the latter is involved in paying attention, in the significance—emotional and otherwise—we attach to inputs or events and what we decide to do in response. As will be evident, each of these functions is in a sense a component of or a result of our being conscious.

examined thirty-six focal brainstem lesions. Twelve of these had resulted in coma. Twenty-four control lesions had not. Ten of the twelve lesions that had resulted in coma impacted a 2 mm^3 area in the pontine tegmentum. Injury to this component and disruption of the connections between it and a node in the anterior insula—this node includes the frontal portion of the claustrum, the component to which Crick and Koch had attached particular significance—and another node in the pregenual anterior cingulate cortex resulted in the patient slipping into coma. There is something particular about those two cortical regions also: they are among the primary sites of a special category of neurons, the scientists pointed out—VENs, the 'von Economo neurons'. These are found in just a few species, among which are humans. VENs are said to amalgamate and broadcast information across the brain through dendrites that spread through all six layers of the cortex.

In short, the precise region or component of the brain that is responsible for triggering consciousness remains still a matter of experimental exploration: some candidates have been proposed because once they are inactivated—through electrical stimulation or pressure arising from, for instance, a tumour, or any other cause—consciousness vanishes; others have been proposed because they have extraordinarily dense reciprocal connections with other parts of the brain. But while no conclusion has been reached, great advances have been made. And that general point impinges directly on what our saints said about consciousness and awareness, about thoughts and their witness. Much of what they thought and said about consciousness arose from their direct perception, of course, but also from what the state of knowledge was in their times. In fact, the mystery of consciousness, at least in the sense of awareness, is being peeled away a layer at a time, and with that some of their observations, at the least some of what they said in casual conversations can be assumed to have been products of the times.

An 'Emergent Property'

Once the brain, its components and processes reach a certain complexity, consciousness erupts as an 'emergent property'. The writings of neuroscientists are peppered with examples of such phenomena. 'Let's take electricity produced by a magnet moving through a coil of wire, which Faraday found in 1831,' Richard Gregory tells Susan Blackmore. 'You wiggle this magnet and, blow me, there's something utterly different happening: electricity!' Christof Koch reminds us that one or two molecules of H_2O are not enough, but you put zillions together at the right temperature and pressure, and wetness emerges. Single starlings do not produce the complex and delightful patterns in the sky that thousands of them, when flying together, do. Single ants do not build colonies and anthills; when their number reaches a critical minimum, they produce the most intricate cities. Life itself is an emergent property— none of the constituents of the original 'soup' had it; it emerged from the interactions of those constituents. The same holds for single neurons and the interactions of a billion of them.

There does not have to be a master planner. As the fetus grows, cells going merely by local information and local interactions make their way to distant and incredibly precise locations and, in association with other cells acting in a similar way, shape our complex bodies and brains. We see the same self-organizing ability in the functioning of markets, we see it every month in the evolution of the Internet. Language too would have emerged not because a Panini sat down and wrote down all the rules of communication. It would have emerged step by step as what each person had to communicate became more complex as well as more abstract—as he had to communicate information about categories, for instance, and not just single objects, as he had to talk about values—loyalty and betrayal—and not just events; and these needs would have arisen naturally as humans forayed farther afield and as they began living in larger groups.

Moreover, complex behaviour emerges from interactions of components which by themselves do very simple things: look at your laptop—it does many complicated things, and yet at the bottom its basic components are in just one of two states, 'on' or 'off'. Similarly, a neuron 'firing' or playing 'dormant', in association with a billion others living equally simple binary lives, comes to generate the miracles of our brain.

Furthermore, the property could not have been predicted merely by looking at or analysing the parts: to recall an example that is often used, the nature of the traffic jam at 9 a.m. on the highway to Gurgaon could not have been predicted by just looking at the car or even all the cars standing in the houses at 6 a.m. in Delhi; or even looking at their engines. Nor could consciousness and what it will accomplish have been predicted by looking merely at the neuron.

Nor can the property be reduced ex post facto to the components that gave rise to it. It cannot be deconstructed to the earlier level: fire cannot be reduced to or taken back to the condition in which the stones and neighbouring oxygen in the air were. Similarly, consciousness is not possible without the brain—and one consequence of that is: it will not survive once our brain ceases to function—but it is not reducible to the brain. A thought, an emotion cannot be deconstructed to yield the neurons and chemicals and neurotransmitters that went into its making. One side of the problem would be the reverse of 'the hard problem'—the latter being that of going from the physical components to the immaterial thought or emotion; the other is 'multiple realizability', or, to use Edelman's phrase, 'degeneracy'. A particular outcome can be realized by the activity of many, many different ensembles of neurons. As we cannot invariably associate a particular neuron with a particular thought or emotion, it would be that much more difficult to get from a composite result—an emotion that implicated millions of neurons—to the precise constellation that would always result in that emotion.

But Then How Did Nature Chance Upon It?

The weight of evidence favours the Darwinians. An organism faces a set of challenges in its immediate environment. Nature keeps trying myriad alternatives. When it chances upon one that works better in dealing with the challenge, it repeats it. And goes on repeating it till the alternative clearly is able to do the job better than its rivals. The organism then goes on repeating it till the alternative 'becomes second nature' to it, and is internalized. Daniel Dennett, a leading voice among evolutionary thinkers, puts the point with his usual felicity.

Nature works through endless cycles, he reminds us: seasons, day and night ... from atomic to astronomic ... up to the Darwinian cycles of reproduction and selection. He asks us to visualize a man long in the past who kept rubbing a branch on stone ... He seemed to be wasting time, to be going on doing something pointless ... One day that rubbing yields the head of an arrow. Those who had picked up the trick of imitation repeat what he was doing. The tribe gets an advantage over others ... The next man who kept rubbing wood on stone, eventually got to the handle of an axe ... Hence: repetition, practice, repetition, practice, repetition, imitation, repetition, Dennett explains—that is how nature works ... He recalls how in his book *Wetware*, the molecular and cell biologist Dennis Bray describes cycles in the nervous system:

> In a typical signaling pathway, proteins are continually being modified and demodified. Kinases and phosphatases work ceaselessly like ants in a nest, adding phosphate groups to proteins and removing them again. It seems a pointless exercise, especially when you consider that each cycle of addition and removal costs the cell one molecule of ATP—one unit of precious energy. Indeed, cyclic reactions of this kind were initially labeled 'futile'. But the adjective is misleading. The addition of phosphate groups to proteins is the single most common reaction in cells and underpins a large proportion of the computations they perform. Far from being futile, this cyclic reaction provides the cell with an essential resource: a flexible and rapidly tunable device.

'The word "computations" is aptly chosen,' Dennett writes, 'for it turns out that all the "magic" of cognition depends, just as life itself does, on cycles within cycles of recurrent, re-entrant, reflexive information-transformation processes, from the biochemical scale within the neuron to the whole brain sleep cycle, waves of cerebral activity and recovery revealed in the EEGs.'

Therefore, when confronting the apparent magic of the world of life and mind, a good rule of thumb, Dennett says, is: 'Look for the cycles that are doing all the hard work.'[28]

Conclusions

To summarize:

- We can say little about cosmic consciousness.
- As for the more mundane kinds of consciousness—the state in which a person is, consciousness of objects outside ourselves, of thoughts and emotions within our minds, of our selves—neuroscientists and specialists in other disciplines like psychology have gone far in accounting for them in terms of natural explanations.
- The origin of such forms of consciousness can also be accounted for in terms of Darwinian evolution.

14

The penultimate proof?

Necessity being the begetter of invention, the soul was bound to get invented. We dread death, and so we just had to devise something that would assure us that death is not destruction. We desperately want to continue our relationship with those we love, and so we just had to devise something that would enable us to believe that, even though they have died before our eyes, somehow they are round the corner. That they watch over us as they did when they were with us. That they will guide us at crucial moments. That it is just a matter of time before we are united with them once again.

Now, the body cannot provide such assurances. We see our own bodies decline. We have ourselves seen the bodies of our loved ones being buried or burnt.

So, it has to be something that 'fire cannot burn, nor water rot, nor wind dry'. And the only thing that can be beyond burning or wetting or drying is one that, *by definition*, never changes. Hence, the soul which, *by definition*, is what it is and will ever be what it is.

But do near-death experiences and even out-of-body experiences not point to an entity that is separate from the body? Did Sri Ramana himself not go through two near-death experiences in which he clearly saw that his 'Self' was altogether separate from his body, that it continued to abide, indeed to shine irrespective of what happened to his body?

SRI RAMANA'S TWO EPISODES

Let us return to the two instances during which Sri Ramana experienced that what was dying was his body, and not his 'Self'. At the time of the first instance, he is sixteen or seventeen years old. He is sitting alone in a room on the first floor in the house of his uncle. 'A great change in my life took place,' he was to tell his followers later. 'It was quite sudden.' He recalled, 'I seldom had any sickness and on that day there was nothing wrong with my health.' Now, that is the first point to bear in mind. He was not 'near-death' in any sense. Sri Ramana continued, 'But a sudden, violent fear of death overtook me. There was nothing in my state of health to account for it … I just felt, "I am going to die."'

'The shock of the fear of death drove my mind inward and I said to myself mentally, without actually framing the words: "Now death has come; what does it mean? What is it that is dying? This body dies." And I at once dramatized the occurrence of death.' He lay down with his 'limbs stretched out stiff as though rigor mortis had set in and imitated a corpse so as to give greater reality to the enquiry'. He held his breath, he said, 'and kept my lips tightly closed so that no sound could escape, so that neither the word "I" nor any other word could be uttered'. '"Well then," I said to myself, "this body is dead. It will be carried stiff to the burning ground and there burnt and reduced to ashes. But with the death of this body, am I dead? Is the body 'I'? It is silent and inert but I feel the full force of my personality and even the voice of the 'I' within me, apart from it. So I am Spirit transcending the body. The body dies but the Spirit that transcends it cannot be touched by death. This means I am the deathless Spirit."'

The after-effect of that experience was life-transforming. 'All this was not dull thought,' Sri Ramana noted; 'it flashed through me vividly as living truth which I perceived directly, almost without thought-process.' Here is another significant point: the experience was conclusive. It was experienced as a source of knowledge, as a source in itself of ultimate, irrefutable knowledge.

'"I" was something very real, the only real thing about my present state, and all the conscious activity connected with my body was centred on that "I",' Sri Ramana recalled. 'From that moment onwards the "I" or Self focused attention on itself by a powerful fascination. Fear of death had vanished once and for all. Absorption in the Self continued unbroken from that time on. Other thoughts might come and go like the various notes of music, but the "I" continued like the fundamental *sruti* note that underlies and blends with all the other notes. Whether the body was engaged in talking, reading, or anything else, I was still centred on "I". Previous to that crisis I had no clear perception of my Self and was not consciously attracted to it. I felt no perceptible or direct interest in it, much less any inclination to dwell permanently in it.'

To begin with, the experience was not what is today called a 'near-death experience'—on Sri Ramana's own telling, there was nothing that was wrong with his health that day. Second, the instance cannot be seen even as the conventional 'out-of-body' experience. There is no suggestion, for instance, of Sri Ramana feeling that he is viewing his body from a distance—certainly not from any height.

An idea, rather a feeling, a great fear seizes him—'I am going to die.' He enacts bodily death—he lies down; he stretches his limbs; he lies absolutely still; he holds his breath; he clenches his mouth shut so that not even a sound should escape. He now tells himself that his body has died, but that 'he', his 'Self' abides.

There is great fear to begin with, then an imagined death, and then an imagined resolution. The resolution is new to him—that his 'Self' abides his body's imagined death. But the notion that the 'Self' abides the body must have been at the time, as it is today, conventional, a common belief, a part not just of high advaita but also of the spiritual folklore of our religion and country.

The second episode differs from the first in several respects. The oil bath; the hot sun; the trudge up the hill; he feels 'tired and giddy'; the scene before him disappears, a bright white curtain is drawn across his line of vision; he stops walking lest he fall; he resumes walking, the giddiness recurs, he leans against the rock till it disappears; when the experience recurs a third time, he sits down near the rock. By now, the white curtain has completely shut out his vision, his head is swimming, and 'my blood circulation and breathing stopped'. His skin turns a 'livid blue'—'It was the regular death-like hue and it got darker and darker.' His companions think he has died.

Sri Ramana said that he clearly saw the discolouration of his skin, he felt his heartbeat and breathing stop. He felt his extremities become cold. He distinctly felt the clasp of his companion. 'My usual current of "Self-effulgence" (*Atma-sphurana*, Self-awareness) was continuing as usual in that state also,' he recalled. This time, 'I was not afraid in the least, nor felt any sadness at the condition of my body'. 'This state continued for some ten or fifteen minutes,' he told his devotees much later. 'Then I felt a shock passing suddenly through the body, circulation revived with enormous force, as also respiration; and there was profuse perspiration all over the body from every pore. The colour of life reappeared on the skin. I then opened my eyes, got up casually and said, "Let us go"...'

Unlike the first episode, this time Sri Ramana's body actually undergoes noticeable changes: the colour changes, his extremities become cold, his respiration and heartbeat stop. The episode as a whole may well have lasted for 'ten or fifteen minutes', but the last two features—the complete stoppage of breathing and the heart—could not have lasted for all of 'ten or fifteen minutes'—that would almost certainly have led to massive injury to the brain.

Two other features are just as important for the subject at hand. First, Sri Ramana remains fully conscious throughout the episode: he notices the change in the colour of his skin, he notices the stoppage of his heartbeat and breathing, he clearly notices the clasp of his companion's hand as well as which of his companions is clasping him; he notices their lamentation. He notices too that his 'Self-effulgence' is continuing just as it was irrespective of what is happening to his body. Second, notice that he does not view his body from any distance—not from a height, for instance: his angle of vision, as well as his 'Self' continue to be located in his real body. His experience is a 'first-person' experience, his perspective is a 'first-person' perspective; he does not feel that any of this is happening to someone else.

The episode was not an 'out-of-body' experience clearly. Nor did it have any of the ornate elements that near-death experiencers report.

A white-out can occur from a sudden fall in blood pressure—Parkinson's patients, as I know from looking after Anita, often experience a white-out, a grey-out or even a full blackout when they

get up suddenly, for instance. In Sri Ramana's case that day there
is the heat of the 10 a.m. sun, there is the body relaxed through an
oil bath, there is the trudge up the hill, the sudden feeling of being
tired and giddy, and then the white curtain that obscures the scene
from view ... Sri Ramana, as we have seen, attributed the episode to
the sort of fit he used to have—except that, as he stated, this time it
lasted longer.

Among the features that are significant in Sri Ramana's account
is one that will appear again in a while. And that is the way the
second episode concludes: 'Then I felt a shock passing suddenly
through the body, circulation revived with enormous force, as also
respiration; and there was profuse perspiration all over the body
from every pore. The colour of life reappeared on the skin...' As we
shall see, one of the persuasive analyses of near-death experiences
locates the elements that those going through one report to this
phase—'the late phase' when, because of the restoration of blood
availability and oxygen levels, the brain once again becomes active
across regions.

Wide Variations

What are today called 'near-death experiences' (NDEs) have been
reported for centuries, as have accounts of after-death journeys. The
events and encounters described in the *Vishnu Purana*, the bardo
states set out in the *Tibetan Book of the Dead*, the tortures in the
grave so graphically described by Islamic preachers are all instances.
In recent times, the books of Elisabeth Kubler-Ross, and even more
so books such as *Life After Life* by Raymond Moody—the book
has sold over thirteen million copies since it was published in
1975—the accounts of such a major influence on modern thought
as Carl Jung, of a philosopher of the prominence and outlook of
A.J. Ayer—a rationalist, an atheist, a logician, one who maintained
that propositions that could not be verified were 'meaningless'—the
accounts of such authorities of what they themselves experienced,
have brought wide acceptance to near-death experiences. NDEs
have become a widely accepted and widely reported phenomenon.
By now the 'standard' elements of such an experience are also well
known: the feeling that one is dying or is already dead; of being
separated from one's body—often, of viewing one's body from a

distance, most often from a vantage point near the ceiling; seeing what is being done by doctors or others to revive it; a tunnel of darkness with an ever-enlarging light at the end of it, and of moving rapidly through it—most often flying or being sucked towards the light; meeting deceased relatives and figures revered in one's culture and religion, including God; a panoramic review of one's life; the perception of crossing a border or threshold; a feeling of being enveloped by an unconditional, unquestioning love; of being 'one with the universe'; of having transcended space and time; a sense of great calm and peace; gaining knowledge of fundamentals—of reality, of the true nature of the universe; being told—by a relative, by an angelic figure—that one has to return as there are tasks that one has yet to accomplish; an extreme reluctance to return; being taken back—to the hospital room, for instance—and being forcefully thrust back into one's body. Those going through one are left in no doubt about the experience, they are certain it occurred, and about what occurred. They are said to be able to describe what was happening, who was doing what—for instance, in the operation theatre—during the time they were said to be clinically 'dead'. The experience transforms their perspective—they lose the fear of death, for instance—it changes their very lives.[1]

While such lists are common, and while they have been combined into a 'scale' also to reveal the 'depth' of the NDE, actually two scales, the experiences that are narrated by individuals show extreme variability. To begin with, only a minority of those who have actually been 'near death' report the experiences. Second, as we shall see in a moment, a number who have not been 'near death' report elements that figure in these standard lists. Third, among those who report the experience, the frequency with which each element is reported varies enormously: a useful exercise for the reader would be to locate a score of studies of near-death accounts, to list the elements of the experience as they have been reported in the studies, and to compile a frequency distribution of the elements.

To help him, here is a start. Generally, two indices are used to measure the 'depth' of an NDE. One was devised on the basis of the narratives of Raymond Moody and Kenneth Ring: it is known as the Weighted Core Experience Index (WCEI). The second is a modified version devised by Bruce Greyson whose work we will come across frequently in this chapter: it is known as the Greyson Near-death Experience Scale. Overall, only between 2 per cent and 13 per cent of cardiac survivors were recorded in different studies as having reported NDEs. The following two tables summarize what was reported by cardiac arrest survivors in three studies:

Table 14.1: Characteristics of near-death experiences as reported by 62 cardiac arrest survivors, according to the Weighted Core Experience Index (WCEI)

	Number of patients	Percentage of total
Awareness of being dead	31	50
Positive emotions	35	56
Out-of-body experiences	15	24
Moving through a tunnel	19	31
Communication with light	14	23
Observation of colours	14	23
Observation of a celestial landscape	18	29
Meeting with deceased persons	20	32
Life review	8	13
Presence of border	5	8

Source: A. Vanhaudenhuyse, M. Thonnard and S. Laureys, 'Towards a neuroscientific explanation of near-death experiences?', www.coma.ulg.ac.be?papers/vs/vanhaudenhuyse_NDE2010.pdf

Notice that in Table 14.1, 8 per cent of the survivors who had NDEs reported that they felt the 'presence of a border'; on the other hand, as many as 56 per cent of them reported feeling 'positive emotions.' Furthermore, Table 14.2 shows that in addition to variations in the frequencies in which individual elements were experienced, there is wide variation as between studies. Were your thoughts speeded up? None of the four in the study by Parnia and associates said 'Yes'; but 12, that is 44 per cent, in Greyson's study said 'Yes'. Did scenes from your past come back to you? Not one in the Parnia study said 'Yes', but 8, that is 30 per cent, in the Greyson study said so. Did you feel separated from your body? Two, that is half of Parnia's subjects, said 'Yes', while 12, that is 70 per cent, of Greyson's said so. In Table 14.1, the figure had been 24 per cent.

Table 14.2: Characteristics of near-death experiences according to the Greyson Near-death Experience Scale

	NUMBER OF CARDIAC ARREST SURVIVORS *(Figures in parentheses indicate percentages)*	
	Parnia et al., 2001 *(n = 4)*	*Greyson,* 2003 *(n = 27)*
Cognitive features		
Did time seem to speed up or slow down?	2 (50)	18 (66)
Were your thoughts speeded up?	0 (0)	12 (44)
Did scenes from your past come back to you?	0 (0)	8 (30)
Did you suddenly seem to understand everything?	1 (25)	8 (30)
Emotional features		
Did you have a feeling of peace or pleasantness?	3 (75)	23 (85)
Did you see, or feel surrounded by, a brilliant light?	3 (75)	19 (70)
Did you have a feeling of joy?	3 (75)	18 (66)
Did you feel a sense of harmony or unity with the universe?	2 (50)	14 (52)
Paranormal features		
Did you feel separated from your body?	2 (50)	19 (70)
Were your senses more vivid than usual?	2 (50)	4 (15)
Did you seem to be aware of things going on elsewhere, as if by extrasensory perception	2 (50)	3 (11)
Did scenes from the future come to you?	0 (0)	2 (7)
Transcendental features		
Did you seem to enter some other, unearthly world?	2 (50)	17 (63)
Did you seem to encounter a mystical being or presence, or hear an unidentifiable voice?	2 (50)	14 (52)
Did you come to a border or point of no return?	4 (100)	11 (41)
Did you see deceased or religious spirits?	1 (25)	7 (26)

Source: A. Vanhaudenhuyse, M. Thonnard, and S. Laureys, 'Towards a neuro-scientific explanation of near-death experiences?' op. cit. In the study of Parnia et al., sixty-three survivors of cardiac arrest were interviewed; seven reported memories of the period when they were unconscious; four reported NDEs. Greyson studied 1,595 cardiac survivors; of these twenty-seven scored more than 7 on his scale.

Were your senses more vivid than usual? Half of Parnia's subjects but only 15 per cent of Greyson's said 'Yes'. Did you seem to be aware of things going on elsewhere, as if by extrasensory perception? Half of Parnia's but only 11 per cent of Greyson's subjects said so. Did you come to a border or point of no return? All four in the Parnia study had experienced this border or point; only 41 per cent in the Greyson study. In Table 14.1, the figure had been one-twelfth, 8 per cent.

Is there a standard near-death experience?

INDIAN NDEs

Studies about NDEs of Indians show the same variability. Pasricha and Stevenson gave accounts of four cases.[2] They are as Indian as can be! Walking and being dragged to the point that 'my feet became useless', not flying through some tunnel. Yamaraja—'He looked dreadful and was all black. He was not wearing any clothes.' In another account, he is 'sitting on a high chair with a white beard and wearing yellow clothes'. His doots—rude and abusive, much like the government functionaries our villagers would be encountering. Chitragupta—the man who keeps the ledgers about all we do. In one case, two big pots of boiling water, except that there is no fire or firewood around. Yamaraja's hands are so hot that the water boils at his mere touch ... And the infernal mistakes of clerks—so much a part of our daily lives! Each of the four narrates that the person concerned—Yamaraja or, in one case, an old lady—told the footmen that they had made a mistake, and brought the wrong person. The first name of the person who had to be brought was the same as that of our subject, but he was of some other caste or from a neighbouring village. On one account Yamaraja's office looks very much like one of our government offices: 'There was an old lady sitting there. She had a pen in her hand, and the clerks had a heap of books in front of them...' (The man's wife told Pasricha and Stevenson that he had earlier told her that the person who had the pen in hand was a man, and not an old lady.) In another case, the 'senior official' who is berating the footmen for having brought the wrong man 'picked up a *lathi* ... with the intent to beat the lesser "employees" before they ran away'. And the concerns too are very much like the ones we drought-prone Indians would have! A Vasudev Pandey is dragged away by Yamaraja's footmen. When at last he reaches the court of

Yamaraja, the latter is furious. 'He said in a rage [to the attendants who had brought Vasudev], "I had asked you to bring Vasudev the gardener. Our garden is drying up. You have brought Vasudev the student..."'

Having set out the four cases, Pasricha and Stevenson said that 'the reports are typical of NDE cases that we have studied in India'. On all counts the settings were entirely Indian. And here is the table in which the two scholars summarized some of the constituents of the NDEs as reported by their sample of sixteen Indians and seventy-eight Americans:

Table 14.3: Comparison of Frequency of Features of Indian and American NDE Cases

Feature	Indian Cases (N=16)	American Cases (N=78)
(Figures in parentheses indicate percentages)		
Saw own physical body	—	51 (65)
Taken to 'other realm' by messengers	12 (75)	—
Saw deceased acquaintances	4 (25)	12 (15)
Saw 'beings of light' or religious figures	12 (75)	41 (53)
Passed on to 'man with book'	8 (50)	—
Reviewed own life; 'panoramic memory'	—	21 (27)
Sent back because of mistake; subject not 'scheduled' to die yet	10 (62)	—
Another person said to be due to die instead of subject	7 (44)	—
Apparently revived through thought of loved living persons or for other reasons and own volition	1 (6)	21 (20)*
Sent back by a loved one or an unknown figure, but not because of a mistake	—	15 (14)*
Brought back from 'other realm' by messengers	13 (81)	—
Residual marks on physical body after NDE	4 (25)	—

*In the computations for these figures a large number of American cases (N=106) was used.

Source: Satwant Pasricha and Ian Stevenson, 'Near-death experiences in India, A preliminary report', op. cit., p. 168.

How much more glaring can differences be? On some of the variables that differed prima facie, Pasricha and Stevenson suggested that at a deeper level the experiences may be similar: 'The idea of prematurity of death or "your time has not yet come" occurs in the cases of both cultures,' the authors observed, 'but the persons involved in sending the experient "back to life" differ'—Yamaraja among the Indians and deceased relatives among Americans.[3]

APPROPRIATION

There is a related problem—the predisposition of the recorders and analysts. While in much New Age writing the experiences are clubbed together under one label, the fact is that on closer scrutiny some of them could scarcely be fitted into the standard descriptions of NDEs. To consider just one instance, recall the reference earlier to the experience that the famous British philosopher-logician, A.J. Ayer, had and described. Spare a moment to glance at what he actually 'saw' when, as he wrote, he was 'dead'. Here is the relevant paragraph:

I was confronted by a red light, exceedingly bright, and also very painful even when I turned away from it. I was aware that this light was responsible for the government of the universe. Among its ministers were two creatures who had been put in charge of space. These ministers periodically inspected space and had recently carried out such an inspection. They had, however, failed to do their work properly, with the result that space, like a badly fitting jigsaw puzzle, was slightly out of joint. A further consequence was that the laws of nature had ceased to function as they should. I felt that it was up to me to put things right. I also had the motive of finding a way to extinguish the painful light. I assumed that it was signaling that space was awry and that it would switch itself off when order was restored. Unfortunately, I had no idea where the guardians of space had gone and feared that even if I found them I should not be able to communicate with them. It then occurred to me that whereas, until the present century, physicists accepted the Newtonian severance of space and time, it had become customary, since the vindication of Einstein's general theory of relativity, to treat space-time as a single whole. Accordingly, I thought that I could cure space by operating upon time. I was vaguely aware that the ministers who had been given charge of time were in my neighborhood and I proceeded to hail them. I was again frustrated. Either they did not hear me, or they chose to ignore me, or they did not understand me. I then hit upon the expedient of walking up and down, waving my watch, in the hope of drawing their attention not to my watch itself but to the time which it measured. This elicited no response. I became more and more desperate, until the experience suddenly came to an end.[4]

Can this account be clubbed with the near-death experiences described by those who had had one, experiences that are cited as proof of *Life After Life*? Quite the contrary: it is almost a textbook case of the ideas and names that had been part of a person's working life popping up at random when his brain and body were under stress, and his brain weaving them into a narrative ex post. And yet you will find it being held up as confirmatory evidence on website after website! 'Even notorious atheist has a Near-death Experience,' the believers proclaim.

The variations in the reported NDEs are so great that several analysts have concluded that there really is no standard list of elements, that there is no standard sequence to the 'near-death' experience, and that the standard pattern has been manufactured by authors like Moody, and that these authors have imposed on to the material they came across a consistency and coherence which was not there. Once the standard pattern or sequence has been put out, confirmatory bias kicks in: persons who may have an anomalous feeling will tend to interpret it as if it was one of the elements. In spite of such a proclivity kicking in, the variations remain glaring.

Authors like Moody just compiled report upon report with little scrutiny. But even if we were to examine individual cases for which adequate contemporary records are available, an entire volume would be required. A brief account of the questions that have been raised by just two or three authors about a single case, a case which is mentioned in almost every study of NDEs, will have to suffice to give a flavour of the questions that such accounts leave open.

A Famous Case

Almost every book that argues that near-death experiences are real points to the case of Pam Reynolds as proof. Ms Reynolds was an American singer. She developed a dangerous aneurysm close to the brainstem—the aneurysm was large, and it was very difficult to reach. The surgeon decided that the only way to save her life was through a drastic surgical procedure, 'hypothermic cardiac arrest': her body would be cooled to and kept at 10°C; her heart would be stopped; and, to prevent excessive bleeding, the blood would be drained from her head; the aneurysm would be dealt with thereafter. Her eyes were taped. And her ears were covered with earplugs—they had speakers to deliver a clicking sound to monitor her brain's response. Reynolds was just thirty-five then. The operation was a success. She lived to the age of fifty-three.

She was able to recall what had happened during the operation—including the sound of the drill that was used by the surgeon to drill two holes in her skull; the sound of the saw that was used to open her skull; the surgeon telling others that the artery he was planning to use for affecting the bypass was too narrow; a song that was being played, etc. What caught fire was her account of the time her heart had been stopped and her head drained of blood. It had almost all the elements that are associated with an NDE: sharpened awareness; light, towards which she was drawn; deceased relatives as well as others she had not known; peace and joy; being brought back against her will, and eventually being pushed back into her body.

Pam Reynolds narrated her experiences to a doctor, Michael Sabom, who wrote them in a book that created a sensation.[5]

Anaesthesia

When we come across accounts such as those of the Pam Reynolds case, the first thing we have to ascertain is what the condition of the person was. How near was the person to actually dying? Had the person been put under anaesthesia? Had medicines been administered to her or him? If so, which medicines? Was the person brain-dead? Had he or she slipped into a reversible coma? Into an irreversible coma? Into a vegetative state? Had the person actually died? For each of these conditions, the medical profession uses a series of criteria—there are more than a score for determining whether a person is brain-dead, for instance. Unfortunately, by speaking in terms of 'near-death experiences', most accounts just start on the premise that the person was 'near death'.

Several medicines that are given to persons trigger experiences similar to NDEs. Similarly, a person put under general anaesthesia may well have residual awareness. Indeed, this has led to legal cases against surgeons: the patient later reported that he heard the surgeon tell nurses and other doctors present during the operation X, Y and Z, and this has had a traumatic effect on his life since then; and from that follows a case for damages. As a result, in some cases an ingredient is injected along with the anaesthetic to ensure retrospective amnesia.

'Anaesthesia awareness' is a well-recognized state in the surgical profession. In rare cases, it has horrible consequences. The patient is to all intents and purposes completely unresponsive, to all appearances the anaesthetic has become fully effective. Yet the patient feels the pain that results from his skin, muscle and bones being cut up. He cannot communicate this horror to the surgeon, but he feels all the pain. It isn't just that the metabolism of the individual may be able to withstand a dose of the anaesthetic that knocks out another individual. Some types of anaesthetic may quieten some parts of the brain, and yet leave others receptive and reactive enough for the brain to register some inputs. In a telling paper, Tononi and his co-authors point out that 'although assessing loss of consciousness with verbal commands may usually be adequate, it may occasionally be misleading'. Unresponsiveness may occur without unconsciousness, they point out: we are unresponsive when we are dreaming because inhibition by the brainstem paralyses muscles. Similarly, some types of anaesthetics induce unresponsiveness by impairing those parts of the brain that are responsible for taking decisions to act—they point to ketamine, a drug to which we shall turn in a moment, as an example. Finally, a person may understand a command and yet not react because the anaesthetic has impaired his working memory—he does not carry out the action that the doctor asks him to perform because the demand is forgotten as soon as it has registered: they give the example of a patient whose arm is tied with a tourniquet before paralysis is induced—this way the hand can move while the rest of the body is paralysed. They point out that patients can sometimes carry out a conversation using their hands, but when they come out of anaesthesia they deny that they were ever awake. Thus, like unresponsiveness, 'retrospective oblivion is no proof of unconsciousness'.[6]

In short, the patient may still be conscious even though she or he has been administered anaesthesia to the point where she or he is no longer responsive, and even though later she cannot recall that she was at all conscious during that period.

AN EXTREME CONDITION

Anaesthesia apart, it is obvious that at least some parts of the brain must be active to not just have those experiences but also to etch them in the memories of the patient. Medical literature reports that the EEG readings of even persons in coma are not altogether flat: it is not that the brain of such patients have stopped functioning but that they have begun functioning in a particular way, a way that blocks out communication between certain areas, a way in which it blocks some parts from intruding on awareness.*

---

*In his informative book, *Consciousness and the Brain*, Dehaene gives us a glimpse into the brain of such patients. He writes, 'The EEG of coma patients is far from a flat line. It continues to fluctuate at a slow rate, producing low-frequency waves somewhat similar to those seen during sleep or anesthesia. Many cortical and thalamic cells are alive and active but in an inappropriate network state. Some rare cases even show high-frequency theta and alpha rhythms ("alpha coma") but with unusual regularity, as if large chunks of the brain, instead of showing desynchronized rhythms that characterize a well-functioning thalamic-cortical network, were invaded by exceedingly synchronous waves. My colleague the neurologist Andreas Kleinschmidt likens the alpha rhythm to the "brain's windshield wiper"—and even in the normal conscious brain, alpha waves are used to shut off specific regions, such as the visual area when we concentrate on sound. During some comas, much as in anesthesia with propofol (the sedative that killed Michael Jackson), a giant alpha rhythm seems to invade the cortex and wipe out the very possibility of a conscious state. Yet because the cells are still active, their normal coding may one day return. Comatose patients thus possess a demonstrably active brain.'

(Contd....)

As medical facilities have improved, in particular the techniques for handling severe traumas, hospitals in the USA and Europe have a very large number of patients who are in what is called the persistent vegetative state (PVS). In India, we have been awakened to the state by the condition to which either age or injury has reduced some of our prominent leaders. Metabolic activity in the brains of persons in a persistent vegetative state is seen to have reduced across the brain—often to 50 per cent or less of a normal brain. Almost invariably, patients in this state are treated, as the name of the condition implies, as being in the state of vegetables. There may be spontaneous recovery, of course, but, as they are in that 'persistent vegetative state', the assumption has been that, as activity across the brain has fallen abysmally, they are, in addition to being unresponsive, unaware. In an important investigation, Nicholas Schiff and colleagues studied five patients. The brains of the patients had suffered 'catastrophic' injuries. As a result, they had been in a persistent vegetative state from six months to twenty-five years. The patients exhibited some spontaneous, uncoordinated, random motor activity—the eyes moved occasionally, for instance. Schiff and colleagues focused on areas of the brain that would be correlated in normal brains with the kinds of unconscious behavioural movements that these five patients exhibited. The findings were as significant as they were unexpected. First, 'There were unexpectedly wide variations of resting cerebral metabolism accompanying the vegetative state in these five patients...' Second, yes, the general metabolic activity in the brains had indeed fallen disastrously—to less than 50 per cent of those with normal brains. But there were isolated areas in each of the five patients 'which retain anatomical integrity and remain active

---

Later in his book, Dehaene points to 'locked-in' brains as proof that 'an intact cortex and thalamus suffice to generate autonomous mental states', and that unfortunate persons with locked-in brains 'may continue to experience the full gamut of life's experiences'. In other cases, the patients are able to recognize a pattern as well as departures from it, Dehaene points out, it is just that they may not be able to communicate what they are feeling or wanting to do or wanting to be done: for these involve areas of the brain that are principally involved in language and memory and imagination. See Stanislas Dehaene, *Consciousness and the Brain: Deciphering How the Brain Codes Our Thoughts*, Viking, New York, 2014, pp. 204-08, 216-21.

in modular fashion that can support isolated but defined behavioural events'. The 'behavioural events' thus were not just random twitching. They were the result of the regions that were responsible for that kind of activity having remained intact in spite of the injuries that were correctly termed catastrophic in extent. This had a very important implication—that the brain is modular in nature. And that what had happened in the case of the five patients was that some of the modules did indeed continue to function but that they could not 'organize into meaningful patterns of sensorimotor integration'. Among the components of the brain on which Schiff and colleagues focused was that ribbon of neurons in the central thalamus, the intralaminar nuclei, which we have encountered earlier as being, in the reckoning of some neuroscientists, indispensable for awareness.[7] In a word, those who are taken to be in a vegetative state may not be altogether unconscious.

Four years had not passed and a breathtaking note was published in *Science* by neuroscientists from Britain and Belgium. A twenty-three-year-old lady had suffered a severe brain injury as the result of a car accident. She remained unresponsive even five months after the accident. A team determined that she fulfilled all the criteria set up under international guidelines to be considered as being in a vegetative state.

But then a surprising result emerged. Sentences were addressed to her, and her brain's responses were mapped using functional magnetic resonance imaging. 'Speech-specific activity was observed bilaterally in the middle and superior temporal gyri,' the neuroscientists reported, '*equivalent to that observed in healthy volunteers listening to the same stimuli.*' Next, sentences containing ambiguous words were addressed to her. Again, the response inside her brain was 'similar to that observed for normal volunteers'.

But did these responses show that the lady was conscious? After all, the neuroscientists reasoned, persons can learn when asleep, they can learn when they are under anaesthesia. Therefore, they put two tasks to the lady: imagine you are playing a game of tennis; second, imagine you are visiting each of the rooms in your house, starting from the front door. The appropriate brain areas lit up as she, who on all criteria was in a vegetative state, imagined performing each task—the supplementary motor area in response to the first one, and the parahippocampal gyrus, the posterior parietal cortex and the lateral premotor cortex in response to the second task. '*Her neural responses were indistinguishable from those observed in healthy volunteers performing the same imagery tasks in the scanner,*' the neuroscientists reported.

Here was a lady having suffered a severe brain injury, lying in a vegetative state for five months, and here she was responding to sentences spoken to her, and doing things she was asked to do. And not just that: as the neuroscientists noted, 'her decision to cooperate with the authors by imagining particular tasks when asked to do so represents a clear act of intention, which confirmed without any doubt that she was consciously aware of herself and her surroundings'.[8]

As is customary, questions were raised about statistical analysis, about whether the questions put to the lady in fact primed her to give a particular response, whether the response was a reflex action or a considered one, etc. In 2009, Laureys asked a patient who had been in a vegetative state for five years questions about his life and relatives. The patient was to imagine doing one task if the answer was 'yes', and another task if the answer was 'no'. The result was stunning: the patient answered five of the six questions correctly. The patient who had been on the 'do not resuscitate' list was moved to the 'not allowed to die' list. In 2010, the experiments were repeated on fifty-four patients who had been diagnosed as being in a vegetative or minimally conscious state. Five of them responded as the lady had in 2005-06. Four of these had been diagnosed as being in a vegetative state. Reviewing events preceding and following the 2005-06 experiments, a report in *Nature* quoted Owen as estimating that as many as 20 per cent of persons classified as being in a vegetative state are probably misdiagnosed; it reported that Nicholas Schiff, 'who weighs up the misdiagnosis a different way, goes further. Based on recent studies, he says around 40% of patients thought to be vegetative are, when examined more closely, partly aware'.[9]

As you can imagine, such findings have far-reaching, for some devastating, consequences. How well I remember the last days of my mother. She had begun to be struck by transient ischemia. Her speech would be affected, as would her ability to walk. But every time, she recovered quite well—in large part because of my father taking her through the paces, of recalling poems they both knew, of insisting that she complete the couplet, and so on. Eventually, there was a massive cerebral haemorrhage. We rushed her to the hospital. I started sleeping there. She had been central to so many lives. Our relatives came to visit her. After she had been a few days in the ICU, one night a doctor came up to me and said that her brain was not functioning, and that there was no prospect of recovery. She could be kept 'alive'—but she would not regain consciousness. On the other hand, if life support systems were switched off, she would be physically gone in three or four hours. I decided on behalf of everyone else—that the life support systems should be switched off.

Years later, I read about those in a vegetative state having residual awareness. And you can imagine what a trauma this has been since. Did I consign my dear and kind mother to death even though she was still aware?

The point of relevance for our current concern is that persons under anaesthesia or even impaired brain functioning may well be able to hear what the doctors are saying, that even persons in extreme states—of minimal consciousness and the vegetative state—may well have residual awareness.

THAT FAMOUS CASE

Just as the Pam Reynolds case is de rigueur for every account that seeks to establish that there is life after death, sceptics have examined every element of Reynolds's recollections.[10] No one has suggested that Pam Reynolds made up the narrative. She always said that she was just a musician and had nothing to say about what had caused her experiences or what they signified. The doubts that have been raised relate not to her truthfulness but to what could have happened medically. Among the doubts that have been raised, the following possibilities deserve special consideration—they have been listed by G.M. Woerlee, Michael Marsh and Evan Thompson:

- Reynolds was awake when she was wheeled into the operation theatre; the layout, the trolleys and monitors would have registered in her mind.

- Reynolds may have had her NDE well before her heart was stopped and her head drained of blood; she had been placed under general anaesthesia almost two hours prior to those steps, and, as we have noted earlier, 'anaesthesia awareness' is a well-established, though rare, phenomenon.
- That EEG readings have become flat does not imply cessation of brain activity.
- Reynolds may have 'recollected' the sound of the drill from similar drills used by dentists.
- Even if the earplugs were effective enough to shut out all sound, she could have heard the sound of the saw through bone conduction.
- As is the practice, indeed this was a legal requirement in the state (Arizona) at the time, the surgeon would have described to her what was going to be done to her; she would also have read about the procedures involved; what she 'saw' being done may have been what she recalled from what she had been told would be done.
- As we have noted, Reynolds narrated the experiences that she had during the time she was clinically 'dead' to Dr Sabom. But this was three years after the operation. She could have inadvertently 'filled in' details about the surgery and the operation theatre from what she picked up during this period.
- Dr Sabom set out the correspondence of Reynolds's NDE and what was happening during the operation—Reynolds was in the operation theatre for seven hours—three years after the event. 'Nothing in Reynolds's account of her journey through the tunnel to the light and her return to her body can establish that this experience happened during the period of hypothermic cardiac arrest,' Thompson writes. 'All we can reasonably infer, based on the events that she was able to accurately report, is that her out-of-body experience of the operating room happened before the cooling of her body began, and that her experience of hearing the Eagles song (which was really playing) happened after her body had been warmed, her heart had been restarted, the artificial respiration had been turned back on, and her brain was

active again (it's also possible that at this point, the white noise and clicking sounds presented to her ears had been terminated because her brainstem response no longer needed to be monitored).'[11]

- Woerlee also pointed out that Reynolds would have learnt about the decision to affect the bypass from the surgical reports; moreover, 'Pam Reynolds would have seen the wound for bypass tubing on the side other than that planned and explained beforehand.'

- Marsh pointed to the heightened sensitivity that each of us has to conversations relating to ourselves—in the cacophony of a party, someone mentions our name and our ears suddenly become aware of that particular conversation; that would be all the more so when questions involving our life and death are involved—as they would be in an operation theatre.

- Thompson also listed inaccuracies in her descriptions of, for instance, the surgical instrument, and omissions—things she could not but have seen had she really been seeing during the operation.[12]

Such instances can be multiplied. In short, individual reports leave many doubts. And the reports differ a great deal. They differ across individuals. And, what is just as telling, they differ across cultures.

Not 'the Same Under the Skin'

Elements of our religious and cultural beliefs of the groups into which we are born and in which we grow up seep deeply into our very nature—into our emotions, our memories, our reflexes. Growing up in a particular milieu, we would have internalized notions about so many intangibles—about love, the significance of events happening at the same time, about dying, about what lies beyond. As death approaches, or as we come to think it is imminent, these notions may well up—about those we have loved and whose love has sustained us, about incidents in our life, about death and what is going to happen soon ... And 'the great interpreter' weaves these disparate notions into a continuous, coherent 'near-death experience'. Several observers have remarked on the religio-cultural specificity of the visions one sees, indeed on how they differ from person to person: after all, if we are all 'the same under the skin', and if after death we are all going to the same place, how come the glimpses that we get during our NDEs of life-after-life are so dissimilar?

Notice, to begin with, that gods and prophets do not seem to cross over: Christians are liable to report seeing Jesus or Mary, Hindus the doots of Yama, Tibetan Buddhists the Buddha Amitabha or bodhisattvas. The personages are said to have merged back with God, they are said to have attained nirvana, they have crossed the cycle of birth and death, and yet they are still in human form. Not just that, they very closely resemble the images that are conventional in the religion and culture of the time and place. The sequence itself speaks to the strong tug of anthropomorphism: to begin with there is the light; that becomes the 'being of light', and that materializes into a conventional deity—Jesus or the Buddha or, indeed, God with the white flowing beard, the white flowing gown or cloak ... Incidentally, the same goes for the relatives whom the person encounters. In our religions, we are taught that each of us will have to go through lakhs of rebirths—as dogs, cats, birds, fish, depending on the deeds we have done, yet his deceased relatives, when he encounters them, are always humans, and of the same sex as they were when they were alive; their bodies would have been burned or would have decomposed in the graves, but they have the faces and posture and gait that they had when they were alive, indeed ever so often they are even wearing the very clothes that the person remembers them wearing when they were living. And, though disembodied and in another world, they always talk in the language of the person having the NDE!

To return to the Indian example, as the sixteen cases that Pasricha and Stevenson examined were from Uttar Pradesh and Rajasthan, Yamaraja, his emissaries, the 'employees' in his court all spoke in Hindi! And, invariably, it turned out that either the clerks in Yamaraja's court or his emissaries had made a mistake! The person was told that his/her time had not come, that a mistake had been made, and, therefore, he was brought back to earth and the body from which he had just been taken. The NDEs of Americans were, of course, different—they conformed more or less to the Moody model: tunnels and the rest. Pasricha and Stevenson, however, cautioned that too much must not be read into culture-as-a-determinant of the NDE thesis. The account may have been retrospectively interpreted in terms that conformed to internalized beliefs, they reasoned. Or, and this certainly was a novel suggestion, the prior beliefs may actually have affected what actually transpired after the person died. Finally, that while prima facie accounts of a constituent of the NDE may seem to differ, at a deeper level and on closer examination, they may actually be similar—a stretch, prima facie![13]

Nearly Dying in Thailand

This feature comes through most vividly in accounts published in popular literature.[14] Thai Buddhism, for instance, is laced with popular Hindu mythology—Yama, Indra, Brahma, heaven and hell, etc. Persons who report being dead and returning invariably report being visited by Yamadoots. They are then taken to other realms— mostly just flying, occasionally flying on a cloud, in one case flying on a glass table, in another being taken in an elevator. They are steered to halls where Yama sits with his book, weighing the good that the person has done against the ill that he has perpetrated. One of the returnees sneaks a look at Yama's book, and is surprised to see that it is written in Thai—instead of the sacred Pali that he expected. The doots are dressed alternately in the white robes that lay followers wear in Thailand, and black—in one case he is 'wearing ancient armor' and carrying a spear, in another three of them are wearing 'SE Asian style turbans'. The angels are bedecked in beautiful clothes, and exquisite jewellery.

The doots, in some cases angels, take them on tours of the chambers of hell, as well as the mansions of heaven. In the chambers of hell, souls of persons are being tortured for the sins they committed: the sins are graded in accordance with the conventional moral code, brought up to date, it would seem—killing animals, lying and slandering, taking heroin or opium, committing arson, rape, murdering or stealing, and the one for which the severest punishment is administered—sexual misconduct. The tortures are ones that will be familiar to readers of *Kalyan,* our mythological magazine: being cast into big copper pots of boiling water, being forcibly made to climb trees that have spikes of thorns, 'two hands long', sticking out, having their heads badgered with an iron hammer, being made to walk on hot coals, being chopped to pieces, being made whole again only to be chopped up again till their bad karma is exhausted, being made to drink acid.

In the mansions of heaven are all the things for which we pine here on earth: lush gardens, fragrant flowers, large rooms, servants, cool breeze ... Indra, Brahma—the latter is a bit forlorn: he says many of his rooms are empty as so few have done the merits that would entitle them to ascend to the level of heaven that he oversees.

Predictably, the ones who make it to heaven are ones who have looked after monks and who have made donations to monasteries; and those who have observed the Thai Buddhist rituals—one, a Chinese Thai on seeing the respective fate of groups, reports how during the NDE he at last wished that he had followed the Thai-Buddhist rituals rather than those traditional to the Chinese. Yama, his doots, as well as others advise the persons that if they want to avoid hell and come to heaven, they must look after monks, and make donations to monasteries, they must observe the rituals—including the life-extending ceremony for all the extra years that Yama has granted them.

Invariably, it turns out that here also the doots of Yama have made a mistake, and fetched the wrong man. They are ordered to take our man back—swiftly because the body will start decaying soon and then it will not be possible to return the man to his rotted body...

A Manicured Garden

Some of the features listed by Moody and Bruce Greyson as constituting the elements of an NDE are reported among the Japanese also, just as others are missing from the Japanese accounts.[15]

Out of the twenty-two, ten reported 'Feelings of peace and quiet'; thirteen reported 'Meeting "spiritual beings"'; sixteen reported 'Experiencing a heavenly place'; twelve reported 'Sensing a border or limit'; thirteen reported 'Subtle "broadening and deepening" of life'; and thirteen reported 'Elimination of fear of death'.

On the other hand, only three reported 'Ineffability'; only three reported 'Hearing themselves pronounced dead'; only one reported

'Hearing unusual noises'; only four reported 'Being "out of the body"'; only one reported 'Seeing a dark tunnel'; only three reported 'A bright light'; not one reported a 'Panoramic life review'—you will recall that the last three features are among the most frequent constituents of accounts in Western NDEs. Only one reported being in 'A realm of bewildered spirits'; none reported 'Experiencing a "supernatural rescue"'; not one reported 'Coming back "into the body"'; one acknowledged 'Frustration relating the experience to others'; only two reported 'Corroboration of events witnessed while "out of the body"'.

The differences do not end at the numbers. Often, while a Japanese may be reporting that he too had a particular experience—'sensing a border or limit,' let us say—what he says he saw at the border turns out to be entirely different. While Western NDErs are liable to report the border between this world and the one they entered during the NDE as 'a body of water, a gray mist, a door, a fence across a field, or simply a line', of the twelve Japanese who mentioned a border, ten had seen a river, a pond, and in one case a stone wall. Ohkado and Greyson recall a study of 700 Western NDE accounts: of them only nine referred to a river as a border. That goes for being in 'heaven' too: of the sixteen Japanese who referred to a heavenly place, thirteen recalled the place to be a flower garden, two recalled it to be a white world, one as a sky. Similarly, the journey that the person remembers undertaking is said often to have been on foot, while in Western NDEs the journey is a sort of 'swoosh'.

How Differences Are Treated

One feature of NDE analyses will bring a smile even as it will instruct. Analysts like Greyson, who are articulate advocates of taking NDEs seriously, have often to strain to read 'universal' themes into the accounts. As Ohkado and he point out in the present paper, in the original listing of the Moody-Greyson criteria, 'a bright light' was followed by the expression 'as a being of light'. But in analysing accounts this time round 'we omitted this qualification because, in Japanese NDEs, experiencers did not seem to sense any personality in the bright light that appeared comparable to the '"being of light" in Western NDEs'—even with this truncation of the criterion, recall that of the twenty-two persons only three had reported seeing 'a bright light'. Similarly, they tell us that one of the original criteria was 'a city of light'. They say that it was intended to refer to a heavenly place. 'The image of such a place may be "a city of light" to many Westerners,' they write, 'but it is not necessarily so to Japanese. For this reason, we replaced "a city of light" with "a heavenly place"...'

'A realm of bewildered spirits' and 'experiencing a "supernatural rescue"' also did not figure in the Japanese accounts, they record. Well, Ohkado and Greyson reasoned, they did not occur in the original list of Moody either—and that may suggest that these two elements 'are less frequently reported even in Western NDEs'—not that the elements may be occurring less frequently but that persons concerned may be reporting them less frequently! And then another leap: 'Taking into consideration the small number of Japanese NDEs that researchers have so far analysed, it may be that future investigators will eventually find these two elements in Japanese NDEs, as well.'

From that, a leap to a conclusion: 'To summarise, we found almost all the elements observed in the Western NDEs to have been present also in Japanese NDEs. Thus, Japanese NDEs appear to be phenomenologically very similar to Western NDEs.'

They trace the two or three glaring differences to differences in the religio-cultural background of the Japanese from the westerners. That the Japanese, when they report seeing the light do not associate it with a 'being of light' the way westerners do, they trace to the deeply rooted Christian tradition, 'God is light'. That westerners report being enveloped by love, and the Japanese seldom do, they attribute to the other equally deep Christian tradition, 'God is love'. And to the fact that the Japanese are reticent to express their love in verbal terms!

None of the twenty-two reported a 'panoramic life review'. That Ohkado and Greyson think is because in Eastern traditions the review of one's deeds is done by Yama, the god of death, or, his Japanese counterpart, Enma-Daio. That leaves no role for or need for self-review!

In the view of Ohkado and Greyson, underlying all the differences is the fact that the Japanese are not a religious lot now. But surely, in asserting this they are looking at 'being religious' through Western eyes. They are taking 'being religious' to mean observing the external rituals of an organized religion.

In sum, according to Ohkado and Greyson, Japanese NDEs contain almost all the elements of Western NDEs, and the two sets are 'phenomenologically very similar'. Furthermore, the differences in regard to the bright light and what to make of it, the heavenly place and that frequent feature of Western NDEs, 'the panoramic life review', these 'are accounted for by cultural differences'.[16]

The way this feature is explained away is that the universal elements of near-death experience are real, just that the specifics—a garden instead of a tunnel—are culturally influenced. In this explanation, the bright white light would be real but the figure of Jesus or Mary, of Khizr or the Buddha would be the result of the culture in which one has grown up. But this seems a bit of a dodge: after all, every feature is a specific—the white light is not universal, it a specific as far as the blind person is concerned.

In addition to the ones that have been listed, a feature would have become obvious. Scholars will go to some length to find reasons to minimize the significance of evidence that does not fit their predisposition.

Second, NDE accounts do not differ merely across cultures. As we have seen, even within one culture, the NDEs that people report are far from being uniform. When these accounts are written—as in Moody's book—the author presents a standardized sequence, a standard check-list, and thereby imposes coherence and consistency onto experiences which are, in fact, diverse. And when such standardized accounts become well-known in a culture—as the sorts of accounts we have summarized above would be among Thai Buddhists, for example—the person having even a few elements of the experience is liable to 'fill in' the rest; just as he is liable to forget or downplay any element that falls outside the standard, received template. This is not deliberate dishonesty. It is but the confirmatory bias that each of us has, that each culture has.

An Unsatisfactory Refutation

Athappilly, Greyson and Stevenson tested the culture-specificity of NDE accounts in an interesting way—and we should take note of their conclusion as it is contrary to what we have been tending towards.[17] Moody's book, *Life After Life*, was published in 1975. It had sold over 12 million copies by the time they were writing their paper—by now, as we noted, over 13 million copies have been sold. The accounts that he had put together had become folklore. The authors compared NDE accounts before 1975 and after: if cultural lore was affecting the accounts, the two sets of accounts should differ. They found that of the fifteen features that Moody had listed, only in regard to the tunnel was the frequency significantly higher. They decided that the tunnel was not central to the experience. One reason they gave was that this feature was observed in other circumstances also. But so were the other features! Moreover, the authors themselves noted that the sample size of their study was small—twenty-four accounts collected before 1975, and twenty-four after. They also noted that they had not investigated whether the accounts were accurate. And, finally, the coding categories in their data base were different from the fifteen features that Moody had listed. In the light of these limitations, listed by the authors themselves, for them to claim that their study established that 'These data challenge the hypothesis that near-death experience accounts are substantially influenced by prevailing cultural models,' was a leap in inference!

THREE CAUTIONARY TALES

A few steps back, and we will come across cautionary tales—of how easy it is to theorize on the basis of portmanteau variables like culture and religion.

Let us now take up a much-cited paper by the lead of the article that we have just glanced through, Allan Kellehear's 'Culture, biology, and the near-death experience, a reappraisal'.[18] Listing some differences to which we shall turn in a moment between near-death experiences of persons who belonged to what he called 'historic religions' and primitive peoples—that is, those who did not practise or adhere to 'historic religions'— Kellehear argued, 'It is toward the world of culture ... rather than biology alone, that we should turn to further our understanding of the NDE.' That some features of the NDE may occur in the case of persons from some cultures and not in the case of others, he argued, did not mean that those features were phantoms of fevered imagination. It could be that the element occurred across cultures, but was *interpreted* differently by persons from different cultural and religious backgrounds. Asked to describe 'Paris', a gourmet would describe it in one way and an architect in another way, Kellehear wrote. But that does not mean that 'Paris' does not exist.

Now, as we have seen, there certainly are differences in the reports of persons from different religious and cultural backgrounds. That much is easy to discern. But what the features are in each religion or culture to which one may ascribe the features that are particularly frequent in the NDEs of its members, well that is a fertile ground for theories and hypotheses!

Kellehear observed that two features that are found in NDEs of Christians, Hindus and Buddhists are the tunnel with a light at the end; and life review. These are *not* found—unless they are inferred by stretching the accounts—in the NDEs of primitive peoples. As we just noticed, other studies were to show that these were among the features that were *not* found in the recounting of Hindus and Buddhists—whether these be Hindu-Buddhists in Thailand or the 'irreligious' Buddhist-Shintos of Japan.[19]

Having observed that the two components—tunnel with a light at its end, and a life review—were present in one set and not in another, Kellehear advanced the argument that these two features may be the results of cultural, religious and technological environment in which the subjects had lived. That last variable—the 'technological environment'—was something that later studies had not quite detected; but for Kellehear the variable came to mind naturally. After all, he was contrasting the experiences of the presumably modern, in the sense of living in a modern technological environment, and 'primitive peoples'.

As for the tunnel, Kellehear noted that the cross-cultural feature seemed to be darkness; it is Western people having NDEs, he said, who describe that darkness as a tunnel. In their recounting, he reasoned, the experience of rushing through a tunnel may denote a period of prolonged suffering or difficulty, such as in the expression 'light at the end of the tunnel'. 'From a child's kaleidoscope through to the later experiences of gazing through telescopes, microscopes, and binoculars, Western people have grown accustomed to seeing strange new worlds through the dimness of tunnels,' he noted. What about the Japanese whose experiences Ohkado and Greyson were to be writing about twenty years later? Surely, they were as accustomed to looking through 'a child's kaleidoscope ... telescopes, microscopes, and binoculars'. How come, acculturated by these devices, they did *not* experience any tunnels? Second, Kellehear reasoned, 'Tunnels are also common images for the idea of transition, of traversing one side to another.' But for the Japanese—not quite the 'primitive peoples' Kellehear had in mind—walking through a manicured garden and boarding a boat for the other shore seemed to be 'the idea of transition, of traversing one side to another'.

Similarly, Ohkado and Greyson observed the singular *absence* of a life review among Japanese having a NDE, and we saw the same absence among the Thai. And Ohkado and Greyson had little difficulty in finding a 'reason' for the absence: in these religious and cultural traditions, Yamaraja or his equivalent Enma-Daio is the one who keeps an account of one's deeds—the task has been outsourced. Hence, they concluded, there is no call for the individual to be reviewing his life. Kellehear, on the other hand, found that life review is characteristic of persons from 'historic religions'. In primitive religions, he theorized, all are taken to be pure and inherently good. Historic religions place great emphasis on conduct, on guilt, on reaping consequences of what one has done, on transgressions. 'Historic religions are religions that actively appeal to the notion of conscience, and conscience places great importance on past thought and action in the process of self-evaluation ... Since these religions link death with conscience, and conscience with identity after death, it is little wonder that some kind of life-review takes place in near-death circumstances in people from these cultures,' Kellehear wrote. 'In a different world view altogether, aboriginal and Pacific cultures may not review their past personal life in search of a sense of identity ... the store of social experience is contained, not within the self, but rather within the animistic life of the physical world ... There is probably little personal use or social function in a life review for individuals from this type of society.' Buddhism is perhaps the religion most based on ethical conduct. The codes of the Shinto are both demanding and severe. And yet the Japanese do not report a 'life review' but Western Christians do!

Kellehear concluded that 'social circumstances play an influential role in the appearance or absence of certain features of NDE'—so far so good. But then a leap, 'in Western reports of a tunnel experience, this development materializes in the common shapes and symbols mentally associated with modernity and technology'. 'And the life review results from the fact that Christianity, Hinduism, Buddhism have cultivated an ethic of personal responsibility and conscience. This may be the chief influence behind the evaluative style of mental process near death. Life review in people of this cultural orientation is part of the general social and psychological process of identity formation, a task of ongoing personal importance in cultures with little or no regard for tribe or totem.' But again: the Shinto have great regard for tribe and totem, as do the Tibetans. And yet, no life review! Similarly, generally, 'primitive people' lived in small-group societies. Going against what the survival and welfare of that small group required could be fatal for the rest. All members of the group, therefore, would have watched each other's conduct assiduously— much more so than is done in the large anonymous conglomerations in which persons of 'historic religions' came to live. How can one just assume that for the 'primitive people' transgression by an individual was a matter of less importance, and, therefore, there was no impulse to review how one had lived as a member of the group?

Let us go back to the original paper of Pasricha and Stevenson. How did they account for the manifest differences in the NDEs of Indians and Americans?

Noting that there were 'marked differences' in the two sets, this is what they thought could account for them:

> We should remember, however, that if we survive death and live in an after-life realm, we should expect to find variations in that world, just as we find them in different parts of the familiar world of the living. A traveler to Delhi encounters dark-skinned immigration officials, who in many respects behave differently from the lighter skinned immigration officials another traveler may meet when arriving in London or New York. Yet we do not say that the descriptions of the first traveler are 'real' and those of the second traveler are 'unreal'. In the same way, there may be different receptionists and different modes of reception in the 'next world'

after death. They may differ for persons of different cultures. We are by no means the first persons to suggest that an after-death realm would have features influenced by the ideas, including beliefs and expectations, of living persons.[20]

And they invoked the *Tibetan Book of the Dead* to substantiate the proposition. 'Take it or leave it' is all one exclaims.

The same sort of logic goes for another difference. On dying, Indians are met by and taken away by the emissaries and footmen of Yamaraja. Americans are met by deceased relatives. But there is the common feature, Pasricha and Stevenson seem to argue: in both cases the person who dies is met! 'If we survive death, it would be entirely appropriate for us to be met at that crisis by another person,' they wrote. 'The variations in the persons of the "next world",' they explain, 'do not weigh against (or for) their reality'[21]—this time round, we must be thankful, I suppose, for that 'or for'!

ANOTHER STUDY OF INDIANS

Susan Blackmore's view was that NDEs are just the result of what happens in a dying brain. If NDEs differed across cultures, her thesis would be undermined: after all, our brains and its processes are the same whether we are Indian or American, and so the experiences that are triggered in a dying brain should be the same. The findings that Pasricha and Stevenson had reported undermined her thesis. She presented her counter-findings in a paper in the *Journal of Near-Death Studies*.[22]

She published an advertisement in *The Times of India* in November 1991 inviting persons who had had a close brush with death to contact her. She received ninteeen replies. She sent the nineteen a questionnaire in which she sought answers to the content of the experiences that they may have had at the time. That her anxiety was the physiological thesis she had advanced, and which she was later to develop in her influential book, *Dying to Live*,[23] was evident from the paper. The experiences reported by Satwant Pasricha and Ian Stevenson were 'dramatically different from the type of NDE first described by Raymond Moody,' she wrote. '... There were no tunnels, no bright lights, and no out-of-body experiences (OBEs) ...

This discrepancy might be used to argue against the universality of NDEs, and is particularly important for physiological theories.' And again: '... If this lack of tunnels in a different culture were confirmed, *it would provide evidence against the physiological theories.*' And yet again: '... By contrast, the physiological theories make a much clearer prediction, and *evidence of a cultural bias in tunnels would be evidence against them.*' 'For these reasons,' she wrote, 'I wanted to collect accounts of near-death encounters from India. The aim was to solicit accounts from people who had come close to death, without suggesting what experiences I was interested in, and to see whether any people spontaneously described tunnels and bright lights...'[24]

Of the nineteen, nine answered the questionnaire. Seven reported no experiences. Four reported experiences 'that were quite unlike the type of NDE described initially by Moody ... they included none of the classic components. These were strange dreamlike or hallucinatory experiences...' Eight respondents 'reported at least some elements of the classic NDE', Blackmore said.

And then came the crucial finding: 'In their initial letters, only six reported NDE-like experiences. Although very varied, these were clearly Moody-type NDEs, and most included elements at least comparable to the classic idea of a tunnel.'[25] Two giveaways in one sentence: '*Although very varied,*' and '*at least comparable to*'!

Blackmore reproduced verbatim the responses of six persons. Not one referred to a tunnel. Some talked of darkness, some of bright lights, but not one talked of a tunnel. Here was a thesis being father to evidence.

Blackmore noted some limitations of her study. Nevertheless, her conclusion was unambiguous: 'The Indian NDEs reported here include most of the key features of the classic Moody-type NDE and, although this sample is very small, the proportions experiencing tunnels, dark places, and lights are remarkably similar to those in previous studies. In other words, these features seem independent of the person's culture. This conclusion fits with what would be expected if these features are a product of brain physiology and are not dependent on culture.'[26]

Pasricha and Stevenson were cut to the quick. In a strongly worded response, joined by two others, they pointed to several lacunae in Blackmore's account.[27]

The sample was not representative of Indians as it was limited to the 'elite' readers of *The Times of India*. Not one respondent had talked of a tunnel: Blackmore had elicited that inference through leading questions. Her own thesis about the bright light in the tunnel being the result of the way that cells in the visual cortex are organized—'with many more cells devoted to the central area of the visual field, with the result that random firing would produce a much brighter impression in the center of the field of view, fading towards the periphery: in other words a tunnel pattern'—was refuted by the accounts she had herself given of what the respondents had told her: 'no respondents [sic] reported a bright impression in the center of their visual field,' Pasricha and Stevenson pointed out.

So far so good. But now their own thesis prodded them to say more! First, they adduced a questionable argument of Kellehear which we just encountered: the difference that 'historic religions' make. 'Historic religions, such as Christianity, Islam, or Hinduism, tend to occur in cultures of long-term settlement, where tunnels are common technological and architectural forms'—tunnels in Vedic India? In early Christianity? In fourteenth-century Islam? And are Buddhism and Jainism not 'historic religions' if Christianity, Islam and Hinduism are? 'In societies influenced by primitive religions, such as hunter-gatherer communities, tunnels may not be of common occurrence, and hence cultural significance.'

And then they were carried off to a criticism that spoke to their anger. 'The above points notwithstanding,' the four scholars wrote, 'Blackmore exaggerated the importance of these data by attaching percentage labels to single digit sample sizes. ... By lumping a single (and questionable) case of "tunnel" sensation with two other cases in which the subjects reported an experience of darkness, she permitted herself the claim that 38 per cent of her respondents could be counted as having had the tunnel experience. We direct the reader's attention to a percentage figure (38) that is over twelve times the actual sample number (3)! Considering that the effective size of this sample is eight persons, we consider the claim of 38 per cent (representing the dubious conflation of three somewhat different reports) to be an example of torturing data until they give you the answer you need.'[28]

Absolutely right. But what had Pasricha and Stevenson done

in their original paper? Their effective sample size was sixteen persons. And yet, as the table that has been reproduced from their article earlier shows, they too attached percentage figures to absolute numbers as low as '1', '4', '4', '7', '8'!

THIS-WORLDLY EXPLANATIONS

Near-death experiences that persons report are not transcendental experiences, they do not prove that there is *life after life*, nor that there is a tunnel which we swoosh through to be united with the Being of Light or our deceased relatives. The experiences are very much of *this* world. They are the result of what happens inside the brain in specific circumstances—either psychological or physiological.

The fear that we are dying may seize us suddenly—either because we think that we are in imminent danger of dying: we may or may not be; or because our body and brain have been dealt an injury which has actually brought us close to death. Of course, in the latter case death may be instantaneous—we have been struck by a bullet or an explosive. There won't be any chance of our having any extended experience in such circumstances. But in the cases where persons report passing through tunnels, etc., the approach to death—where this occurs at all—is gradual: the heart stops, oxygen availability to the brain falls ... Doctors tell us that in such a circumstance the brain can continue to function more or less normally for up to ten seconds, that cells in it begin to die if oxygen intake does not resume for around a minute; that the brain can rarely revive if oxygen intake is not resumed to normal levels within three or, at the extreme, five minutes. It is during these varying intervals that changes occur in the brain, and these in turn cause the sorts of experiences that are taken to be 'near-death experiences'.

Second, there seems to be general agreement that we should not look for just one explanation for all the elements of an NDE. In all probability, different elements are triggered by different factors. The different frequencies in which these different elements occur in the case of individuals themselves indicate that the elements are severable, that the continuous narrative which the experiencers report is an ex post construct. Moreover, there is the modular organization of the brain itself. True, as we have noticed time and again, parts of the brain are connected to other parts by innumerable dendrites and axons, and happenings in one part of the brain can be transmitted to other parts by 'a cascade' of chemicals and neurotransmitters. Accordingly, an injury to or dysfunction in one part of the brain is liable to set off a cascade that envelops several other parts—as happens in an epileptic seizure. But not all parts are connected to all other parts. So, it is entirely possible for some parts to keep functioning even as others have been compromised. With its functioning impaired, or being restored in a disorderly fashion the brain tries to make sense of fragments. As it does in our dreams, it discerns patterns, it weaves a story out of unconnected, even random firings. Hence the ex post narrative of an NDE.

As one can imagine, when a person is wheeled into a hospital in a 'near-death' condition, or he falls into that condition in an ICU, doctors concentrate on saving him. They are scarcely in a position to be examining the activity in his brain so as to tally it with the experiences that he may report later—for at that time they will almost never know that he is having an NDE. Similarly, often persons have NDEs when they are completely out of the reach of medical equipment and expertise—in a supersonic plane, on a mountain top, in a car smash. For this reason, among others, inferences about what factors may be triggering which element of the NDE are drawn from knowledge gained from persons placed in circumstances other than being 'near-death'.

Several of the inferences have been drawn from what has been learnt from neurological studies of the brain in general. Thus, for instance, neuroscientists have discovered that the amygdala is implicated when we are seized by panic and intense fear. From this it is inferred that when the fear that we are about to die seizes us, the amygdala would have got involved. Having learnt that after the initial panic a great calm descends, that at some point even bliss envelops the person, psychologists and neuroscientists looking for this-worldly explanations conclude that it must be the calm that descends when we surrender to the inevitable, or that the calm and bliss occur when we realize that the danger has passed.

Believers in the proposition that NDEs testify to a transcendental reality, to a *life after life*, seize upon this feature and proclaim that these inferences are just hypotheses, that they are merely *suggestive*, that they only indicate what *may* be happening in the brain and how that *may* be linked to the experience that the subject is reporting. True, but if it is clear that the amygdala is implicated when a person with a normally functioning brain is gripped by fear, what is the reason to believe that it would *not* be implicated when a brain under great stress is seized by panic or fear? Taken together, the evidence, gathered though it is from the brain in other circumstances, builds an almost complete case for the proposition that NDEs are *this*-worldly reactions of the brain undergoing great stress—stress that may have been triggered by a wide array of factors ranging from depletion of oxygen availability to intense fear.

Help from Aerospace

Clues can be had by examining circumstances other than 'near-death' in which persons report experiences that have elements similar to the NDE. We need not recall the explorations of Wilder Penfield and the experiments of Olaf Blanke and others as we have already glanced through them. In the experiments of Blanke and his associates, as we saw, the out-of-body experience as well as the experience of a presence nearby were generated both by stimulating specific points in the brain and by non-invasive methods. Wilder Penfield elicited a very wide range of experiences—of being out of one's body, of talking to relatives and friends who were not present, of hearing 'heavenly music', of floating, of being 'half here and half not here'. So many of the expressions that the patients used are well-nigh indistinguishable from NDEs. In the present context, to supplement the point that emerges from those experiments and explorations— namely, that elements of the NDE can be elicited in persons who are not near death by a range of means—it will be enough to recall just one set of experiments.

That pilots could lose consciousness at certain altitudes and also when their aircraft were accelerated suddenly to great speeds had been a problem since the end of the First World War. The problem grew as the aircraft became capable of gaining higher and higher speeds in shorter and shorter bursts. Pilots began to be put in centrifuges to simulate the effects of sudden and rapid acceleration. The pilots would lose consciousness as blood drained away from the brain and pooled in their abdomen and extremities: the state came to be called G-LOC, the loss of consciousness induced by sudden acceleration.[29] James Whinnery, a professor of chemistry, worked on these studies for long, and wrote a series of monographs and papers reporting results obtained from around 1,000 episodes of G-LOC that were induced in centrifuges over a period of sixteen years.[30]

The persons who were put through the experiments were completely healthy. In fact, the majority of them were fighter pilots 'who, on the average, represented the extreme of self-confidence and self-control, frequently under conditions of extreme and even life-threatening situations in aerial combat'.[31]

Unless a person is wearing a specially designed suit to prevent the blood from draining from his brain towards his abdomen and legs, etc., the heart is less and less able to supply blood to the brain as the acceleration exceeds +5Gz. Six seconds into the acceleration, the person would lose consciousness. On an average, he would remain unconscious for twelve seconds. Again on the average, losing and recovering consciousness would cover twelve to twenty-four seconds. On regaining consciousness, the pilot would feel incapacitated, a bit confused and disoriented for about twelve seconds. 'A lot happens in a very short time over the course of the loss and recovery of consciousness,' Whinnery wrote. And this is where the parallels start.

First and foremost, half of the subjects did not immediately recognize that they had suffered loss of consciousness, and were shocked to see the videotape that had been recorded of them going through the acceleration. 'Many subjects automatically, and essentially uncontrollably, attempted to fill in their void by confabulation,' wrote Whinnery in words that could scarcely be improved as we weave disjointed elements into a continuous and coherent NDE.[32]

Second, 'The most common symptoms associated with exposure to +Gz stress are related to alterations of vision,' Whinnery found. 'As the perfusion pressure to the eye falls during exposure to +Gz stress, the most distal circulation within the retina is compromised first, producing loss of peripheral vision,' Whinnery pointed out. 'As the +Gz level increases further [as the acceleration increases further], the visual field contracts to produce what is known as *tunnel vision*. This results when perfusion pressure is enough to supply only the small area where the central retinal artery enters the eye. Finally, when the perfusion pressure is so low that no blood flow to the retina occurs, *blackout*, or complete loss of vision, results.' 'If the rate of onset of +Gz is gradual,' Whinnery added, 'then the progression of visual symptoms from "grayout" (loss of peripheral vision) to tunnel vision to blackout can be observed.'[33] We will turn in a moment to what Whinnery called 'dreamlets' that many of the pilots experienced. For the moment we may just note his observation that like other effects—like myoclonic jerking of the extremities—the tunnel vision was also likely to be incorporated into the dreamlet and 'could logically be interpreted as coming out of the darkness of a tunnel or perhaps [into] bright sunlight.'

Third, 'A sense of floating is one of the most frequently reported symptoms associated with G-LOC experiences,' Whinnery found. 'It is commonly associated with autoscopy, automatic movement, paralysis, a sense of dissociation, and,' and here we come to the fourth point relevant for our present concern, 'being pleasurable enough to result in the individual not wanting to be disturbed. Overall, the majority of individuals consider the G-LOC experience not only pleasurable, but euphoric. Much less frequently, on the other hand, an occasional individual does find the experience to be disagreeable and frustrating.'[34] Two parallels there: the sense of floating, and the pleasure to the point of euphoria from which the individual does not want to be disturbed.

Fifth, 'although not a common occurrence', the subjects had out-of-body experiences. The longer the G-LOC episodes lasted, and especially when these were repeated—say, after fifteen minutes—the more likely was the subject to have an out-of-body experience. 'The individual walking down a hallway immediately after a centrifuge exposure became aware not only that he was walking down the hallway, but also that he was above and behind himself, watching his own body walking,' Whinnery noted. 'The duality persisted for approximately three minutes before the experience ended with what was described as a reintegration process with his body.'[35]

Whinnery traced these out-of-body experiences, and this feeling that one was viewing the body from a distance to the loss of sensory input—one of the things that is a precursor to NDEs: 'Loss of sensory input to the nervous system essentially produces a de-afferentation.

Loss of motor output eliminates the effective link of the nervous system with the remainder of the organism, or de-efferentiation, the net result being a perception of nervous system detachment or dissociation and the sensation of floating or being out of, and not connected to, the body.'[36]

The sixth feature was very important—it dovetailed directly into NDEs, and to the brain's confabulations. Thirty-five to 40 per cent of the pilots reported having what Whinnery termed 'dreamlets'. Once again, the more severe the ischemia, the more memorable the dreamlet characteristics turned out to be. The dreamlets met the criteria of dreams, Whinnery pointed out, 'including emotional intensity, detailed sensory imagery, illogical content and organization, uncritical acceptance, and difficulty in remembering once it is over'. Indeed, the correspondence with NDEs went further: 'The dreamlets are vivid and frequently include family members and close friends. They commonly have beautiful settings and their content includes prior memories and thoughts of significance to the individual. We might describe the dreamlets as being very memorable, when they are remembered; they have a significant impact on individuals who experience them, and remain crystal clear for years after they occur. There is a very strong urge in most individuals to try to understand and explain what they experienced.'[37]

We have come across the proposition earlier that several aspects of the NDE weave into the narrative prior beliefs, associations, etc. Whinnery found the exact same feature in what the pilots remembered of what they were experiencing during the G-LOC period. By comparing the last act that they executed before loss of consciousness, Whinnery noticed that memory was compromised shortly before unconsciousness overtook the pilot. On the other side, he found that memory returned before the return of consciousness. The result has a direct bearing on narratives of NDE: 'The fact that mnestic processes in general return also provides the compendium of the individual's prior thoughts, experiences, and ideas that can be incorporated into the experience.'[38]

Finally, Whinnery wrote, many of these psychological alterations persisted for several hours following the G-LOC episode.[39]

In summary, after reviewing the reports of 1,000 G-LOC episodes, Whinnery concluded that the NDE and the G-LOC experiences were 'remarkably similar'.

The major characteristics of G-LOC experiences that are shared in common with NDEs include tunnel vision and bright lights, floating sensations, automatic movement, autoscopy, out-of-body experiences, not wanting to be disturbed, paralysis, vivid dreamlets of beautiful places, pleasurable sensations, psychological alterations of euphoria and dissociation, inclusion of friends and family, inclusion of prior memories and thoughts, the experience being very memorable (when it can be remembered), confabulation, and a strong urge to understand the experience.[40]

And that the differences between them were because of differences in the severity of the insult to the brain. Furthermore, he noted, like NDE, what transpired during G-LOC were a 'vivid reality to those who have them', and that 'Both G-LOC and the NDE are usually very significant events that can result in subsequent behavior modification'.[41]

Whinnery's explanation for the experiences during G-LOC were very similar to explanations neurologists give for NDEs. The G-LOC experiences are a result of 'the complex integration of all psychophysiologic inputs and memory existing within the nervous system during various stages of functional neurologic capability,' he wrote, and that some of illogical associations, etc., might be resulting from the fact that 'some of the sensory input may be received when the nervous system is only partially functional and therefore may be processed in a nonstandard manner'.[42]

How much closer can the correspondence be?

And yet believers in the transcendental testimony of NDEs tried to underplay it. Yes, Whinnery's evidence did suggest that hypoxia had a role in the experiences, Greyson acknowledged, only to add that Whinnery had cautioned that his model 'does not explain *all near-death phenomena*,' that the G-LOC effects may be used to differentiate the elements that occur because of the onset of unconsciousness from those that are unique to NDEs.[43] But this is to set up and knock down a straw man. And critics set up such straw men by demanding that every other circumstance that is put forward as generating some aspects of the NDE must in fact account for each and every feature of the latter. Mario Beauregard evades the remarkable parallels by another device. He acknowledges that some features of NDEs do occur as a result of hypoxia in G-LOC. But, he says, 'the main characteristics' of the G-LOC experiences are impaired memory of events preceding onset of consciousness, confusion, and disorientation upon coming out of the episode; and that these are the opposite of NDEs.[44] Are these the 'main characteristics' that emerged even on Whinnery's own telling?

A 'MODEL'

Ever since NDEs became the subject of popular books and culture, attempts have been made to collate information about which constituents of the brain and which processes are liable to be implicated in generating the experiences.[45]

Twenty five years ago, two Chilean scientists, Saavedra-Aguilar and Gomez-Jeria, proposed a model bringing together processes and parts of the brain to suggest what might be triggering NDEs.[46] A glance at their model will do both: it will acquaint us with the role that constituents of the brain play, and it will also give us a glimpse of how inferences have necessarily to be drawn.

Assume a person has suffered a traumatic event—a cardiac arrest. Consequences will be triggered in two dimensions at once: at the physiological plane, the availability of blood and, therefore, of oxygen to his brain will be compromised; at the psychological level, his mind too would be put to great stress. The initial intense pain subsides, and the dread is replaced by a feeling of being detached and, soon enough, by euphoria. Complex auditory and visual hallucinations follow: noises; the tunnel, flying through it, and here there is a substantial change in the position of his body— most NDEs occur when the person is lying down, but in flying or rushing through the tunnel, he would be ascending at a steep angle; bright lights changing into the Being of Light; distortion of time and space—the feeling that he is in a place 'beyond time', that he is 'one with the rest of creation'; 'life review'; the return to the body; making sense of the experiences, and eventually narrating them to others.

Next, let us see which parts of the brain are involved in which of these events and experiences: the 'limbic system' in general because of the high emotional salience of the experiences; the amygdala in particular because of the dread. The vestibular system because of the reorientation of the body that is experienced. The hippocampus because of the autobiographical memories that would be implicated in the 'life review'. The temporoparietal junction because, as we have seen from the later experiments of Blanke, that is where diverse sensory inputs are integrated, and it is the dysfunctions in this part that trigger misperceptions of all kinds, including that of where one is. The 'great interpreter' would certainly come in to stitch fragments together into a consistent narrative, as would the language system when the person tries to string the experiences together and articulate them to others. And so on.

Having identified the components of the brain that would be involved in each of the experiences, the scientists would delineate the sequence by which the trauma and that sudden fall in the availability of blood and oxygen would cascade from one part to another through the mutual connections of parts of the brain—as an epileptic seizure does. And there are the crucial experiential components in the episode: the intense pain abates, the dread is replaced by acceptance, by peace, even by euphoria, the illogicalities and bizarre connections. These would be made possible by endorphins and other substances being released in much greater magnitudes by the brain itself to meet and counter the extreme stress to which it has been subjected; and by the imbalances in neurotransmitters that would have occurred as the injury cascaded through the brain.

Saavedra-Aguilar and Gomez-Jeria related the components of the NDE to the parts and neurotransmitters that are liable to be implicated, and presented a sort of timeline of the way the cascading insult and the experience would unfold. Their model focused on four factors in particular: 'the temporal lobe dysfunction, hypoxia/ ischemia, stress, and the neuropeptide/neurotransmitter imbalance'. If they were putting the model together today, in all probability they would be more specific in emphasizing the significance of the temporoparietal junction, the vestibular system, and the 'great interpreter' module which, as we saw, Gazzaniga surmises, is located in the left hemisphere.

Components

While many disparate factors and regions get implicated in generating specific elements of the NDE, there seems to be wide agreement on the role of one factor and one region. The factor on which most neurologists seem to agree is the diminution in the availability of oxygen that was almost the focal point of Whinnery's findings. And the region on whose crucial role most agree is the temporoparietal junction—the region where inputs from several senses are processed and integrated. The 'mismatched integrations' in this region of inputs from our vestibular, visual, tactile and proprioceptive systems—the systems that give us our sense of balance, of a scene, of what we feel by touch, of our position in space in relation to other entities—are what give rise to feelings of being elsewhere, of being out of one's body, of hearing 'heavenly music', and so on.

A promising suggestion has been made by Michael Marsh. With a host of arguments, he maintains that the NDE does not occur so much in 'the early phase' when the brain is undergoing the insult as in 'the late phase' when it is getting back to its normal functioning. The experience, he argues, is undergone in the final moments preceding the abrupt resumption of awareness or consciousness, its disparate elements occur in the disordered return to normality. 'The experience is not about dying,' Marsh says, 'but of a vigorous return to life and hence a re-appropriation by the brain of its former functional competence.'[47]

Marsh points to a telltale difference. Features describing *early-phase* events contrast markedly with those occurring during the *late phase*, he points out. In the former, the experient is quite indifferent to leaving his mourning relatives; he has no difficulty going through or flying over obstacles—doors, walls, glass, unopened windows. In the late phase, he is concerned about the duties that he has yet to complete, the relatives he has to look after. This contrast speaks to the growing influence of the prefrontal cortex, Marsh reasons, the part of the brain where moral decision making occurs. He no longer sees himself just flying over or through physical barriers; moreover, he is now seized by an increasing 'moral' pressure to discharge his earthly responsibilities or cares.[48] This vivid antithesis emphasizes the divide between a dreamlike fantasy world, Marsh says, and its progressive replacement by the incipient dawning of conscious reality.[49]

Marsh suggests the neurological counterpart of the experiences that occur in this 'late phase'. These terminal aspects of the extra-corporeal experience occur just as conscious reawakening occurs, he says, and point to a reactivation and recoupling of the lateral-orbital frontal cortex, and dorso-lateral prefrontal cortex. Other parts of the brain, he writes, having generated their own subconscious mentation which, like dream states, is somewhat bizarre, illogical and incongruous, are now being told by the prefrontal cortex, as it fully recovers its own controlling influences and critical faculties, 'stop all this fantasy; wake up—it's time to get going'. 'The overwhelming moral coercion to return to earth and attend to one's responsibilities is consistent with the re-establishment of critical pathways from the frontal lobes to other parts of the cortex, thalamus and related structures,' he writes. 'And the abrupt termination of the event, coincident with the reappearance of conscious volition, would then be consistent with the full reconstruction of frontal lobe activity.'[50]

Understandably, the quest is far from over. Various hypotheses have been proposed for explaining specific elements of the near-death experience. To recount the suggestions that have been made to account for each and every element of the NDE will take us too far afield. As an illustration let us take up one element.

That Dreadful Fear, and the Peace That Descends

Sri Ramana, as we have seen, approached death with perfect equanimity—to the very end he was consoling devotees; to the very end he was reiterating his conviction that he was not the body and that they were distraught only because they were identifying him with the body; to the very end he remained compassionate and concerned—insisting that, in spite of the strain that doing so was putting on him, the small window through which devotees could see him must not be shut. Sri Ramakrishna Paramahamsa fretted as the end approached and as the pain wracked him—at times, with the innocence of a child, he would be imploring the doctor to see how the pain could be lessened, how the cancer could be cured; at times he would be seeing a divine purpose in his being subjected to the cancer. To the extent that we will be conscious at that penultimate hour, most of us, so unlike Sri Ramana, are likely to be seized by a dreadful fear.

Earlier we have seen the reactions of persons who found themselves suddenly rushing into an accident—with an out-of-control truck hurtling towards them. They were seized by panic. And then just as suddenly a great calm descended into them. Many of them reported that it was as if they had moved away from the scene of the collision-in-the-making, and that they were viewing the scene from a distance. Psychologists see this as a defence against death. It may be denial of something we just do not want to confront. Or it may be the precise state of mind that will equip us better to deal with the danger. Two pioneers in the field, Eugene d'Aquili and Andrew Newberg, suggested that the hippocampus comes to play a pivotal role at such a time. As the intense arousal drive triggered by the life threat reaches maximal capacity, they argued, there is a 'quiescent spillover'. As the quiescent drive rises, the hippocampus is stimulated, and this leads to vivid, hyper-lucid, even blissful visions. 'The archetype of dissolution' is replaced by what they termed as 'the archetype of transcendent integration'. The lightning 'life review' d'Aquili and Newberg traced to the continued stimulation of the hippocampus—as it is intimately involved with memory.

The same frame of mind—'dissociation' is the word that psychologists use—may come over us even if the process is gradual. As the dread of approaching death reaches an apogee, quiescence breaks through, psychologists say—soldiers under fire in a battlefield report that sudden calm. The mind may react Ramana-like by distancing itself from the body completely: 'It is only that body lying down there which is dying,' the person near death may tell himself, 'not me.' The person still has a sense of 'self', but he has shifted it out of his body. On Marsh's premise that the NDE, including this deep calm, occurs in 'the late phase' as the brain is recovering its functions, it could be that the calm permeates one because of the subconscious realization that the danger has passed.

One set of explanations for experiences at this stage—of overpowering fear followed by calm—centres around the release of endorphins. Some have urged that we focus specifically on beta-endorphin and related peptides. These are released under stress, and they are known to block pain and induce pleasure. Their release would trigger the 'limbic lobe syndrome', and thereby account for the complex psychological manifestations that are reported in NDEs. In a much-noted communication, Jansen, who spent years working on ketamine, pointed out that almost all aspects of the near-death experience are reproduced by ketamine—'including a sense of ineffability, timelessness, that what is experienced is "real", that one is actually dead, a perception of separation from the body, vivid hallucination, rapid movement through a tunnel, and emerging "into the light"'. Drawing on the experiences that ketamine induces, he argued that we should look for an endogenous agent that has the same effect as ketamine, and he pointed to one such agent: excess glutamate which, among other substances, binds to the NMDA—the N-methyl-D-aspartate—receptor can kill neurons; like ketamine and its cousins, alpha endopsychosin binds to NMDA, and can thus prevent this from happening and shield neurons. During ischaemic attacks, there would be a massive release of endorphins and this in turn may be triggering the NDE.[51] Others have argued that while endorphins would work in the direction of inducing those experiences, they are not potent enough to account for them. Citing prior work, Susan Blackmore has countered this by arguing that the temporal lobe and the limbic system are known to be implicated in NDEs, and endorphins are known to lower the seizure threshold of these. Michael Sabom, whose account of the Pam Reynolds case we have glanced at earlier, discounted the role of an endorphin that had attracted much attention in this context, beta-endorphin, on the ground that it acts for a much longer period than the interval during which an NDE might be expected to have taken place. Still others have instead drawn attention to another neurotransmitter, serotonin, as the one that plays the vital role in inducing those experiences.

Greyson and others have remained unconvinced about the possible role of ketamine-like substances. They point out that several persons who have been administered the drugs have fearful experiences that contrast sharply with the blissful NDEs that are reported. Others counter by maintaining that in all probability fearful experiences are under-reported or under-recorded. These scholars point to a telling fact. A much higher proportion of NDEs reported during the Middle Ages included accounts of hell, of torture, they write. An overwhelming proportion of NDEs recorded or compiled now are beatific. The former, they point out, were recorded by the clergy. The latter are being recorded or compiled by New Age adherents—a much more optimistic lot![52]

There are other objections too. Marsh points to instances in which hallucinations triggered by the anaesthetic use of ketamine lasted for more than a year.[53] The users of drugs usually recognize that the experiences that they are having are illusory—this is in sharp contrast to persons having an NDE: they feel that the experience is 'more real than real'. Moreover, say the critics, drugs usually produce confusion while the NDEs are marked by hyper-clarity. But so many hallucinations are equally clear to the person having them— as I learnt at first hand, it takes a great deal of patient work over quite some time to convince the person affected that no record of Subbulakshmi is being played outside the window, that the 'singing' is inside the person's brain.

Other drugs—nitrous oxide, LSD, mescaline, etc.—are also said to trigger near-death experiences. And it is entirely likely that combinations of drugs that may be administered to a patient in an ICU, say, cause not just the oft-documented hallucinations but also various constituents of near-death experiences. As we have seen, the critics of tracing NDEs to drugs argue that ever so many persons who have *not* had any drugs report NDEs. Second, they say that while the hypotheses are suggestive, there is as yet no evidence that links them through dysfunctions of the brain to specific elements of NDEs.

Even among those who are agreed that NDEs are *this*-worldly phenomena, there are disagreements, or at the least differences in emphasis over the role of individual triggers as well as the nature of individual components of the NDEs. In her pioneering work, Susan Blackmore, whose book *Dying to Live*[54] had done much to advance the thesis that processes inherent to a dying brain could account for the experiences that others were looking upon as proof of life-after-death, had traced the tunnel-and-light experience to the way the visual cortex is organized. Many, many more cells are devoted to the centre of the visual field, she had pointed out, than to the periphery; as a result, even the random excitation of the cells will produce a tunnel effect—a bright light at the centre fading out towards the periphery.[55] Michael Marsh, on the other hand, has maintained that the experience of hurtling through the tunnel does not come from the primary visual cortex but is the result of dysfunction of the vestibular system which gives us the sense of balance and of our whereabouts in space.[56] Similar arguments have continued regarding hyper-carbia (the surge of carbon dioxide in the blood) and hypo-carbia (a fall in the level of carbon dioxide).

And so on.

In summary, by no means can one claim that the issue is settled. Perhaps a part of the difficulty arises from trying to explain every feature of NDEs in every case in terms of every single variable: NDEs of persons who had not been administered drugs could well have been caused by other—this-worldly—factors. Moreover, it may well be that the drugs do not explain NDEs in particular cases but that the mechanisms through which they act may be the ones through which NDEs may be occurring, and, therefore, what factors may be triggering those mechanisms should certainly be examined.

VARIABILITY

But what about one feature of NDEs to which we had referred when we were discussing the effects of culture and religion on the experiences that those near-death reported—namely, the fact that the experience varied so greatly from person to person? We had wondered then, how come, if we are all 'the same under the skin', the experiences differ so much between cultures and religions? Does the same question not arise when we consider physiological explanations? As the structure and processes of the brain are the same from person to person, if it is the physiology of a dying brain that accounts for NDEs, should the experiences not be the same? The answer seems to lie in the complexity of the brain itself. Given the billion cells and their trillion interconnections, the structures that may be compromised in the episode affecting one individual are certain to be complex, their connections with other parts are liable to be incredibly intricate. As a result, an insult is hardly a standard one, nor can its pattern of propagation be a standard one. Furthermore, while the overall organization of the brain and its processes in general are the same in us, each brain is unique. To start with, there are the anatomical differences—hardly a surprising fact, given the billion cells and trillion connections in that small space. And the smallest differences in the anatomy of two brains and their interconnections can result in huge cumulative differences in the ultimate effect from 'the same' injury. More than that, what a brain is at a particular moment—say, 'near-death'—is going to be influenced by the entire history of the individual: the experiences that he has had over a lifetime, the interests he has pursued, the beliefs he has acquired. In a word, his entire life history, and that surely is unique to the individual. When we glanced at studies about the plasticity of the brain we saw how much and how swiftly a brain is altered by an experience, a hobby, the effort to acquire a skill. We saw how substantially it can get changed even without our making any conscious effort to change it—as is the case when, one faculty being lost, the brain reapportions some of 'the real estate' that was devoted to that faculty to sharpen another faculty. How a person's brain will react to an injury will, therefore, depend on his entire life history, and, as this is unique to the individual, the experiences that he may have as death approaches or when he thinks he is near death will be unique. The Chilean scholars we encountered a short while ago drew a telling parallel in this regard. Their general finding was that 'the list of mental phenomena in TLE [temporal lobe epilepsy] and stereotaxic electrical stimulation of the temporal lobe *includes all the NDE phenomenology*'. And from this they drew their principal clue: 'Therefore,' they wrote, 'if NDEs share some characteristics of TLE phenomena, it does not appear too far-reaching that they may also share some common pathophysiological mechanisms.'

They listed a series of reasons to account for the person-to-person variability of temporal lobe epileptic seizures. To start with, the anatomical structures that are involved in the origin and propagation of the seizures are very many, each of them—like the limbic system—is complex, and their connections to other parts are both extensive and intricate. Second, one determinant of the course that the seizure will take is the personal history of the individual—his personal biography in episodic memory as encoded in the limbic system, they wrote. Third, they pointed out, 'the origin of the seizure and the spread of the after-discharge can vary from subject to subject and from time to time'. Fourth, citing earlier work, they recalled, 'it is difficult to determine "whether the patient's verbal report represents a sufficiently accurate description of what he or she actually experiences, or whether a rather vague sensation is being elaborated on"'. Finally, 'it has been shown that amnesia occurring during medial temporal lobe paroxysms can be highly variable, ranging from normal memory to complete amnesia, implying recall of different types of mental phenomena by different individuals...'[57] Quite the kind of reasons, with but a little modification, would help account for the wide variations in NDEs![58] Thus, on this matter the fact that the NDEs differ is an argument that works in favour of a physiological explanation, not against it.

In Summary

First, as we saw, the two episodes of Sri Ramana did not have the elements of either an out-of-body or a near-death experience.

Second, of course, the matter is far from settled. And that can hardly be a surprise—after all, questions such as whether there is 'life after life', questions such as what happens once we die have been with mankind for eons. And it *is* true that many of the explanations that are in the field to account for NDEs are at this state of knowledge suggestive, many of them set out what *could* be happening. Empirical evidence is yet to establish them firmly. But the cumulative effect does seem to be heavily in favour of the proposition that NDEs are *this*-worldly phenomena, and are triggered by responses of the brain to severe stress—whether psychological or physiological.

The way forward would seem to involve three points at the least. First, and Marsh recalls the suggestion to this effect that Dr Paul and Linda Badham made thirty-five years ago, playing cards, pictures of unique sites, etc., should be placed at strategic places—on top of almirahs, for instance—in operating theatres and ICUs. This will enable a record to be built of the number of persons who were near death, who reported floating to the ceiling, and who could later accurately describe the cards, pictures or other objects that had been placed at vantage points.[59] Second, the report of the person who claims to have had an NDE should be recorded with meticulous care—maximum care being taken that the prior beliefs or expectations of the recorder do not colour the account. Third, whenever we hear of a child who 'remembers her previous life', the report should be examined meticulously: by independent observers meeting the child, by noting down what the child herself says, not what her parents and other adults say she says, by visiting the family that she says was hers in her previous birth and scrupulously checking out the details she has narrated, etc. The same goes for reports of other miraculous events. For instance, now and then we hear of monks or yogis who have died but whose bodies do not decay for weeks on end. We must ascertain the respects in which the body did not decay; what the ambient temperature and humidity of the place was when this happened, etc.

Contrast these elementary requirements with the paper we have encountered earlier, the one about NDEs in India by Pasricha and Stevenson. The two were gathering information about instances of reincarnation—a subject on which Stevenson had written the much-noticed book, *Twenty Cases Suggestive of Reincarnation*.[60] People would gather around them in the village, and while they were examining the report that they had heard about a child remembering her previous life, say, someone would ask, 'Are you people also interested in persons who die and recover?' That is how they got to eighteen cases. Of these, information on two turned out to be too scanty. Of the remaining sixteen, they interviewed the subject in ten, and a first-hand informant in five. 'We admitted the 16th case into the series,' they wrote, 'because the informant, although a second-hand witness, had learned about the case within the day, or a few days at most of its occurrence from the subject herself.' Of the six not interviewed, three had died and three were not available.

Not just that. In the four cases that formed the subject of their paper, 'The median interval between the NDE's occurrence and our first investigation of the case', they wrote, 'was approximately 14 years.' The interval was forty-five years, thirty years, six years, and five or six years respectively.[61] What would memory, as well as the telling and retelling not do on a matter so significant in village life as what happened to them after they had 'died'?

Finally, the question of whether there is 'life after life' is an empirical one—it is not one to be settled by belief or faith or religion. Why react with such vehemence when evidence suggests that reports of NDEs are clearly influenced by the culture and religion in which the experient has grown up? True, the neurological evidence is not yet complete. But why not consider with greater equanimity the evidence that *has* accumulated from situations in which the brain has suffered a major injury? How can one reject a hypothesis that explains some or even just one element of NDEs on the ground that it does not account for all the elements?

15

Is everything *really* unreal?

As the Self alone is, everything else is a chimera. For Sri Ramana, this is a matter of direct perception, of immediate, overwhelming direct experience. The problem is us. To explain this truth to persons like us who have not had that conclusive experience, he has to give a reason or two, he has to rely on analogies. And this is where problems arise.

ALL IN THE MIND, ALL NOTHING BUT A THOUGHT

'What is the goal of this process?' a devotee asks.

'Realising the Real,' Sri Ramana says.

What is the nature of the Reality?

The Maharshi answers:

(a) Existence without beginning or end—eternal.

(b) Existence everywhere, endless, infinite.

(c) Existence underlying all forms, all changes, all forces, all matter and all spirit. The many change and pass away (phenomena), whereas the One always endures (noumenon).

(d) The one displacing the triads, i.e., the knower, the knowledge and the known. The triads are only appearances in time and space, whereas the Reality lies beyond and behind them. They are like a mirage over the Reality. They are the result of delusion.[1]

As nothing else is without beginning or end; as nothing else is everywhere; as nothing else is infinite; as nothing else 'underlies' everything else, every change; as nothing else displaces the triads, and as, by definition, the Self is all this and does all this, it is Reality, it alone is Reality.

Thus far, it all seems a tautology:

- Reality is X, Y, Z.
- The Self is X, Y, Z.
- And so, the Self is Reality.
- Furthermore, nothing else is X, Y, Z.
- Hence, nothing else is Reality.

But then comes a leap: 'Reality' becomes the conventional 'real'. And so, from 'Self is Reality', we are hurled to 'The Self alone is real'. From 'Nothing else is Reality' we are hurled to 'Everything else is unreal ... The Self alone exists, nothing else exists ... everything else is a phantom of the mind...'

The affirmations are as elusive as they are frequent.

'The world is made up of five kinds of sense perceptions and nothing else,' the Maharshi declares in *Reality in Forty Verses*. 'And those perceptions are felt as objects by the five senses. Since through the senses the mind alone perceives the world, is the world other than the mind?'[2] True, we may perceive the world through five senses—though even that is not strictly the whole picture: the mathematician or physicist perceives, or at least comprehends the universe, step by step, through purely mental abstractions and reasoning also and not just through the five senses; true, what the five senses perceive is then processed in the mind—the mind here being 'what the brain does' as Pinker would have us believe; but from that does it follow that the world is nothing but the mind? How does the fact that I perceive the world through the mind negate the world? Yes, the *perception I have of the world* is in my mind, but from that how do we conclude that the world is in my mind, that the world is nothing but the mind?

Not just the world, on the same reasoning, time and space too are just in the mind. The Maharshi says in *Reality in Forty Verses*: 'Without us there is no time nor space. If we are only bodies, we are caught up in time and space. But are we bodies? Now, then and always—here, now and everywhere—we are the same. We exist, timeless and spaceless we.'

Again, in response to a lady's persistent questions about how the world could be a phantasm, about how it could be completely unrelated to us, and after leading the lady to 'Only remain still and see', the Maharshi tells her, 'Nothing is perceived in deep sleep ... All these are seen only after waking; only after thoughts arise the world comes into being; what can it be but thought?'[3]

Again the reason that we have encountered earlier: 'Nothing is perceived in deep sleep.' But, again, that has to do with what we perceive of the world, not with the world itself.

In a variant, a little later the Maharshi tells an inquirer, 'The world is only spiritual. Since you are identifying yourself with the physical body, you speak of this world as being physical and the other world as spiritual. Whereas, that which is, is only spiritual.' But is that so because 'that which is' has been defined in a particular way? Could one say instead, 'The world is only *energy*. Since you are identifying yourself with the physical body you speak of this world as being physical...'?

The Maharshi puts the point across through a simile he uses often: 'The mirror reflects objects; yet they are not real because they cannot remain apart from the mirror,' he observes. True, the *reflections* cannot remain without the mirror; but do the *objects* that are reflected also cease to exist when the mirror is not there? We cannot exist without food or air or water. But does that mean that we are only food, air, water? 'Similarly, the world is said to be a reflection in the mind as it does not remain in the absence of mind.' Does, in the absence of the mind, the world not remain for the person in question or does it not remain intrinsically?

But wouldn't there have to be a real object—the universe—in order for it to be reflected in the mind? the Maharshi says, voicing the question that would naturally spring in our minds. His answer is: 'This amounts to an admission of the existence of an objective universe. Truly speaking, it is not so.' But that is an obiter dicta! What would be wrong a priori with 'an admission of the existence of an objective universe'?

The universe is like the world we see in our dreams, and has no more objective existence, Sri Ramana teaches. And then follows an affirmation that leads straight to the unknown. The universe is created by vasanas that are latent in our mind, he says, 'Just as a whole tree is contained potentially in a seed, so the world is in the mind.'

But the seed is a product of the tree. So, the tree must have existed for the seed to be produced, the Maharshi agrees. 'So [for the vasanas to have formed in our minds] the world also must have been there for some time.' 'The answer is, No!' he says with emphasis. The vasanas in our minds have been occasioned by previous births, and the minds that existed in each round: 'There must have been several incarnations to gather the impressions which are remanifested in the present form. I must have existed before as I do now.' But that only leads to the usual infinite regress. And, in this case, it implies that there must have been a world in which the previous births occurred, and the vasanas were formed.

'The straight way to find an answer,' he continues, 'will be to see if the world is there. Admitting the existence of the world I must admit a seer who is no other than myself. Let me first find myself so that I may know the relation between the world and the seer. When I seek the Self and abide as the Self, there is no world to be seen. What is the Reality then? The seer only and certainly not the world. Such being the truth the man continues to argue on the basis of the reality of the world. Whoever asked him to accept a brief for the world?'[4]

Not quite fair! We were merely asking a question—in fact, it so happens, that in this instance, the Maharshi himself was asking the question on our behalf—and had not taken up any brief on behalf of the world.

The Maharshi continues: you are just like a person in a cinema who appears to be watching the world. Neither you nor the world that you are watching is any more real than the cinema show. But that is just a simile. It is not a reason. It is not evidence.

How can the universe be merely a thought? The thought is in the mind. The mind is in the brain. The brain is in this skull. How can the whole universe be contained inside this small skull, a professor of philosophy asks.

But what is the mind, the Maharshi asks in turn, and explains:

The world is seen when the man wakes up from sleep. It comes after the 'I'-thought. The head rises up. So the mind has become active. What is the world? It is objects spread out in space. Who comprehends it? The mind. Is not the mind, which comprehends space itself space (*akasa*)? The space is physical ether (*bhootakasa*). The mind is mental ether (*manakasa*) which is contained in transcendental ether (*chidakasa*). The mind is thus the ether principle, *akasa tattva*. Being the principle of knowledge (*jnana tattva*) it is identified with ether (*akasa*) by metaphysics. Considering it to be ether (*akasa*) there will be no difficulty in reconciling the apparent contradiction in the question. Pure mind (*suddha manas*) is ether (*akasa*). The dynamic and dull (*rajas and tamas*) aspects operate as gross objects, etc. Thus the whole universe is mental.

That reasoning would turn on what we understand 'ether' to mean. Is it space, as in this passage? Is it air? Is it some form of energy? And also on the level of disaggregation at which we are to consider the entities. Even if we take it on faith that the mind, brain, body, world, universe are all the same at the level of photons and electrons or some even subtler level, would they be the same at some grosser form of aggregation also?

FROM DREAMS TO WARS

The Maharshi makes another attempt to explain the matter. A man has walled and locked himself up. He goes to sleep, and yet a whole world appears to him in his dream. From where has the world and all the goings-on in it entered? Surely, they have erupted only in his brain. 'How does it [the sleeper's brain] hold this vast country in its tiny cells?' the Maharshi asks. 'This must explain the oft-repeated statement that the whole universe is a mere thought or a series of thoughts.'

But surely there are many other explanations for the man having a dream, and what he 'sees' and experiences in it. And many other inferences can be drawn from the fact that a dream world has appeared to him in sleep than the inference that the entire universe is just a thought. And how does the proposition that 'the whole universe is a mere thought or a series of thoughts' follow from the dream having come up in spite of a man having walled and locked himself? Once again, a proposition turns on definitions. The waking state is a dream; hence, the world seen in the waking state is no more real than the world seen in a dream. Similarly, the dream occurs in one's head; the dream world is, therefore, in one's head; the waking state is a dream; hence, the world in the waking state is in one's head.

But I have a toothache, a devotee complains. Is it only a thought? Why, then, can I not think it away?

If we think other thoughts, the toothache will not be felt, the Maharshi responds—that is, of course, true as we saw from our review of experiments on alleviating pain via the mind. But does the fact that I can lessen the severity of the ache mean that the ache was just a thought to begin with? What about the tooth infection that led to the pain? Is that also just a thought?

Reinforcing the point, the Maharshi says that if we fall asleep, the toothache will not be there. What about the toothache that keeps the person from falling asleep? In any case, here too the analogy rests on the definition with which we started: Only that is Reality which is always present, specifically in the three states of waking, dreaming and deep sleep; as the toothache disappears in deep sleep, it is not Reality. And from that the leap that we encountered earlier: As the toothache is not Reality, it is not real.

SOME OTHER WORD?

At the moment the Sino-Japanese war is going on, a devotee says. (The exchanges are taking place in February 1938, and you will recall the horrendous cruelties that were a regular feature of that war.) If it is just imagination, why does Sri Bhagavan not imagine the contrary and end the war?

'The Bhagavan of the questioner is as much a thought as the Sino-Japanese war,' the Maharshi exclaims.

Everyone laughs.

And the question remains unanswered.[5]

Later, another lady reports that she is troubled: she is in the world, and there are wars in it. Does Self-realization remove discontents? Can it put an end to wars?

Are you in the world, or is the world in you? Sri Ramana asks. The lady says she doesn't understand, the world is certainly around her. The Maharshi responds, 'You speak of the world and the happenings in it. They are mere ideas in you. The ideas are in the mind. The mind is within you. And so the world is within you.'

Even if I do not think about the world it is still there, the lady persists. Do you mean that the world is apart from your mind and that it can exist in absence of the mind? Sri Ramana asks. 'Did the world exist in your deep sleep?'

And we are back in the same loop. The lady says that she may not be aware of the world when she is in deep sleep but others who are awake see it. But that is something you have learnt from others after you have woken up, Sri Ramana points out. 'So you speak of waking knowledge and not of sleep experience,' he continues. 'The existence of the world in your waking and dream states is admitted because they are the products of the mind. The mind is withdrawn in sleep and the world is in the condition of a seed. It becomes manifest over again when you wake up. The ego springs forth, identifies itself with the body and sees the world. So the world is a mental creation ... Did you not create a world in your dream? The waking state is also a long-drawn-out dream,' the Maharshi says.

The world in your dream is a creation of your mind. The waking state is a dream. Therefore, the world you experience and perceive in your waking state is also a creation of your mind. That is the sequence once again.

But the lady persists: If I kick a stone, that hurts my foot; and that injury tells me that the stone exists and so does the world.

Does the foot say there is the stone? Sri Ramana asks.

No, I say, responds the lady.

And we are back on familiar terrain: 'Who is this "I"?' Sri Ramana asks. Not the body ... Not the mind ... Hence, the Self ... Search the Self ... To realize the Self is happiness...

But how can one be happy when there are wars going on?

'Is the cinema screen affected by the scene of fire burning or the sea rising?' the Maharshi asks in turn. 'So it is with the Self.'[6]

Should the word be 'inconsequential' rather than 'unreal'? Should we be saying that from the lofty heights of the ones who have realized the Self, wars and the like are inconsequential? Or that they just do not exist and are mere creations of the mind? But we anticipate.

Nor is the matter limited to toothaches and a foot hitting the

stone and wars. Time and space too are nothing but creations of the
mind, they too are just in the mind. One cannot hope to measure
the universe and phenomena, Sri Ramana tells devotees, because the
objects are mental creations: 'The universe is only an object created
by the mind and has its being in the mind. It cannot be measured
as an exterior entity. One must reach the Self in order to reach the
universe.'[7] Now, there may be some *ultimate* sense in which the
universe cannot be comprehended except by an inward effort. But at
a level short of that ultimate one, physicists and astronomers have
continued to make advances in comprehending the universe and the
phenomena in it as 'exterior entities'.

As exchanges continue, birth, death, Wagner's music, every
single thing turns out to be nothing but the creation of the mind
of the questioner. And the Maharshi affirms again and again that
there is absolutely no difference between the dream and the waking
states—except that the perception of time is different: in a dream we
fly through years in minutes. That is all. There is no other difference.
And from this, he advances the proposition that nothing we perceive
or experience during our waking state is any different, it is not any
more real than what we experience or perceive during a dream.[8]

SHORT OF THE SELF, WHAT COULD THE PROPOSITIONS SIGNIFY?

The questions that the devotees and visitors asked were the obvious
ones that would come to mind. It is also evident that on occasion
the answers that were given did not really answer the questions.
Sometimes the great authority and aura of the Maharshi ended the
exchanges. But most often the exchange ended because the Maharshi
steered the conversation back to the here and now, to what that
particular questioner needed to do here and now. As we have noticed
earlier, he was loath to expend time in abstruse discussions, and he
certainly did not want devotees to waste their time in debating, to
pluck a phrase, 'how many angels can stand on a pinhead'. He would
answer a few questions but quite swiftly bring the questioner back
to what she or he must be doing next. And to what the questioner
could do. Why debate wars and the like about which you cannot
do anything? Why not focus on what *you* can do—directing your

attention inward, inquiring who 'you' are? That was his general attitude.

The first, and probably the basic, point underlying his statements was a different perspective. The world is real for both the ajnani as well as the jnani, he said. But there is a difference:

> To those who do not know and to those who do, the world is real. But to those who do not know, Reality is bounded by the world; while to those who know, Reality shines formless as the ground of the world. Such is the difference between them.[9]

And there is another sense in which the world and the happenings in it are different for the jnani. The experience that envelops the jnani, and the state in which he lives thereafter are so overwhelming that everything else seems *inconsequential*. I do feel that this word better conveys the essence of many of the statements that the Maharshi made to devotees than the word that is customarily used, 'unreal'. Recall his response to the lady who asked how one could be happy when wars were going on: 'Is the cinema screen affected by the scene of fire burning or the sea rising? So it is with the Self.' The logic is: As the world and what is happening in it do not affect the Self, *from the point of view of the Self*, they are false, they just do not exist. Similarly, one day as he and Devaraja Mudaliar are talking about mithya and satyam, Sri Ramana remarks:

> He who sees the Self, sees only the Self in the world also. To the *jnani* it is immaterial whether the world appears or not. Whether it appears or not, his attention is always on the Self. It is like the letters and the paper on which the letters are printed. You are wholly engrossed with the letters and have no attention left for the paper. But the *jnani* thinks only of the paper as the real substratum, whether the letters appear on it or not.[10]

In other words, the jnani's attention is focused on the Self, and on the Self alone. To him 'it is immaterial whether the world appears or not'. I had earlier recalled a statement of Sri Ramakrishna to the same effect. '...I go into a strange mood while thinking of the Lotus Feet of God. The cloth on my body drops to the ground and I feel something creeping up from my feet to the top of my head. *In*

that state I regard all as mere straw…'[11] In the same vein, Kapali
Sastri, a scholar who had the good fortune to delve deep into the
Maharshi's teachings, remarked in his introduction to *Ramana Gita*,
'Just as to a man who is awake when he is thinking about one thing
one-pointedly, at that time he has no concept of existence or non-
existence of other things, as he has no occasion to remember and
take note of other things, likewise, as the person established in the
form of the Self is aloof from the universe, for him it can be said that
the world is false…'[12]

The most dramatic illustration of this transformed perspective
was provided by the final days of Sri Ramana. His end, as that of
Sri Ramakrishna, was excruciatingly painful—the cancerous tumour
began the size of a lemon, it was surgically removed; it grew back
the size of an orange, and was again surgically removed; the third
time, it erupted with a vengeance, eventually becoming the size of
a cauliflower, eyewitnesses reported. Devotees were distraught. Sri
Ramana refused another bout of surgery. He remained his serene
self, as if the pain and illness were happening to someone else on
that proverbial cinema screen. In fairness to the reader, I must record
that that is not the way in which Sri Ramakrishna contended with
his final illness, that fatal cancer in the throat. He was alternately his
benign self, anxious to impart all he had to his disciples, and a child
flailing against pain.

Unreal in the Sense That…

Three facts can be accepted straightaway. First, we do not experience
the world directly. It is refracted to us through our senses. As a result,
it is not merely what we see. And it is not entirely what we see.

That the world is not merely what we see is evident from the
fact that there is so much that we cannot perceive through our
senses. There are wavelengths of light that we cannot see. There are
sounds that are audible to other species but which we cannot hear.
We cannot see or touch or smell atoms and electrons and protons.
We cannot perceive so much of what our own brain does—from
processing sensory inputs to the myriad tasks our unconscious
executes day and night.

That the world is not entirely what we experience with our
senses is also evident. It is an 'illusion'—it is not as if the world is

not there at all but that it is not what it seems to our senses. That this is so is illustrated by the scores of optical and auditory illusions that you can find on scores of websites by clicking on to the Internet. And there cannot be much surprise in this. After all, as evolutionists tell us, our senses developed to give us that representation of the world which will help us survive—an approximate representation if that will do. They did not develop so as to provide the most accurate theories about that world.

Nor is it just a matter of our senses not being perfect lenses. Once the input has been received, it is processed. We see an ambiguous-shaped cloud or a weave of the carpet, and our brain reads a face in it. Apart from everything else, history comes in. Our brains are affected by each experience—synapses are formed, some connections are strengthened, others die out. Thereby, every input is in a sense processed and interpreted by a new brain. Over a lifetime, the same sensory input will be interpreted in so many dissimilar ways. And the way the world appears to us will naturally be affected by the instrument we use. When my eyes have got covered with cataracts, a scene will seem very different from what it appeared when they were young and clear. This room, Ajit Kembhavi, one of our leading astronomers, pointed out one day as he came to visit our home, would appear very different if we used an ordinary camera from what it would seem if we X-rayed it. And what it would seem will be greatly affected by scale, Kembhavi continued: it would look very different if I were atom-sized than it would if I were tall as the Eiffel Tower.

As Long as He Is Immersed in the World, You Just Have to Say It Is a Delusion

These caveats are evident, and important. And yet they do not quite account for the ubiquitous use of the word 'unreal'. Is there some other reason that Sri Ramakrishna and Sri Ramana may have used it so often, and in so many different contexts? I think there is, and we have it in Sri Ramana's own words.

In her straightforward, reverential *Letters from Sri Ramanasramam*, Nagamma Suri records that one day a new visitor to the ashram asked the Maharshi something in English. She could

not follow the question as she did not know English. But Sri Ramana
replied in Tamil, and this is what he said:

> The question arises: It is said that Brahman is real, and the world
> an illusion; again it is said that the whole universe is an image of
> Brahman. How are these two statements to be reconciled? *In the
> sadhak stage, you have got to say that the world is an illusion.*
> There is no other way, because when a man forgets that he is the
> Brahman, and deludes himself into thinking that he is a body in
> the universe which is filled with bodies that are transitory, and
> labours under that delusion, *you have got to remind him that the
> world is unreal and a delusion.* Why? *Because, his vision which has
> forgotten its own Self is dwelling in the external material universe
> and will not turn inward into introspection unless you impress
> upon him that all this external, material universe is unreal.* When
> once he realizes his own Self, he will come back to look upon the
> whole universe as Brahman. There is no universe without his Self.
> *So long as a man does not see his own Self which is the origin of
> all, but looks only to the external world as real and permanent,
> you have to tell him that all this external world is an illusion. You
> cannot help it.* Take a paper. We see only the script, and nobody
> notices the paper on which the script is written. The paper is there,
> whether the script on it is there or not. To those who look upon the
> script as real, you have to say that it is unreal, an illusion, since it
> rests upon the paper. The wise man looks upon both the paper and
> script as one. So also with Brahman and the universe.[13]

A complete answer as to why Sri Ramana was so insistent that we
see the world as unreal. He did so because we are so insistent on
seeing only the external world as real.

If I may transpose to a more general context the conclusions that
I had set out in *Mother's Heart* in the context of suffering:

- To some extent the affirmations are a device—to draw us back
  from what is outside us to that which is inside, especially to
  what goes on in our mind;
- In part, the matter turns on how 'Reality' is defined;
- Statements that the world, our bodies, our pain are all
  'mental projections' are intended not to deny their reality as

much as to continually focus our attention on the principal instrument at hand—namely, our mind;

- The sages and our scriptures reiterate this perspective—of what is real and what is just a projection of the mind—incessantly because, as Osborne notes, their objective is not to set up a theoretical system but to steer us to what must be done here and now;

- From the mystics' vantage point, of course, everything seems trivial, almost inconsequential; but, as exemplified in the lives of Sri Ramakrishna and Sri Ramana, and in spite of what they tell devotees, even they felt deeply the pain of others, and did an enormous lot to comfort them. And, while they said the world was unreal, they ate, they taught, they composed hymns, they fell ill, Sri Ramakrishna loved luchis, Sri Ramana walked fourteen kilometres around a hill that by those statements did not exist in reality, they teased and laughed...

16

Their pristine example

The boys have started visiting Sri Ramakrishna. But they are boys. For them as yet he is an eccentric. They argue among themselves— about what he says, about what he is. They have heard that he cannot even touch money, that he is repelled by it. One day, when he is out of his room, they slip a coin under his mattress. As Sri Ramakrishna returns, he goes to his cot. He has barely sat down that he shoots up as if an electric current has shocked him. The boys feel ashamed to have to put him to a test.

On another occasion, under similar circumstances, Swami Premananda sees a person secretly slip money under the mattress; when Sri Ramakrishna returns to the room, he is not able to even approach the bed.[1]

1885: Sri Ramakrishna is taken to the festival at Panihati. At the festival, crowds gather around him. He dances in ecstasy. He is offered five rupees by the manager of the festival. He does not accept the money. The manager secretly gives the money to Rakhal, Swami Adbhutananda who was with Sri Ramakrishna at the time, tells us. Rakhal buys mangoes and a packet of sweets for Sri Ramakrishna with the money. When Sri Ramakrishna learns of this, he is angry with Rakhal, and warns him: 'Never do anything like that again. Your acceptance means my acceptance. A monk must be like the birds and not lay things up for the future.'[2]

'Once when the Master was sick,' Swami Adbhutananda tells us in the same account, 'Doctor Mahendranath Paul came to see him. Before leaving, he gave five rupees to Ramlal Dada for the Master. The Master did not know this. That night he tossed and turned in bed. I fanned him for a long time, but still he was restless. Finally, he said to me: "Please call Ramlal. That rascal must have done something—otherwise why am I not able to sleep?" It was then one or two o'clock in the morning. As soon as Ramlal Dada arrived, the Master said: "You rascal. Go and return the money to the man who gave it to you in my name." Then Ramlal Dada told the Master the whole story. That very night I accompanied him to Mahendranath Paul's house, where he roused the doctor from his sleep and returned the money.'[3]

A Marwari businessman, Lakshminarayan, sees the soiled coverlet on Sri Ramakrishna's bed. He offers to put ten thousand rupees in a bank account so that Sri Ramakrishna's expenses may be met. Sri Ramakrishna falls unconscious, Swami Turiyananda tells us. The businessman says that he will give it to Hriday who is looking after Sri Ramakrishna so that he may have money for Sri Ramakrishna's expenses. 'Oh no!' Sri Ramakrishna exclaims. 'He will accept it in my name, and I can't bear the thought of possessing money!' 'Ah, I see,' says the businessman as if to tease and corner him. 'You have not yet overcome the idea of acceptance and rejection.' 'No, I haven't,' Sri Ramakrishna replies. Swami Nikhilananda reports that as the businessman was not yielding to argument, Sri Ramakrishna cried out, 'O, Mother, why dost Thou bring such people here, who want to estrange me from Thee?' Sri Ramakrishna later said, 'At the offers of Mathur and Lakshminarayan, I felt as if somebody was sawing through my skull.'[4]

Sri Ramakrishna requests Mahendranath to bring two pieces of cheap cloth that he can use for drying himself after a bath. Mahendranath brings two pieces of unbleached and two pieces of washed cloth. Sri Ramakrishna has him take back the washed pieces. You see, I cannot store anything for the future, he tells Mahendranath.[5]

That is a point that is brought into relief in instance after instance—not just that he had overcome all desire for worldly things but, in addition, that he could not store things up on the assumption that they may come in handy someday.

The final illness has set in. A doctor has come to examine Sri Ramakrishna. Sri Ramakrishna is telling him that medicines do not agree with him, that his system is different. 'Well, what do you think of this?' he asks the doctor to illustrate the difference. 'When I touch a coin my hand gets twisted; my breathing stops. Further, if I tie a knot in the corner of my cloth, I cannot breathe. My breathing stops until the knot is untied.'* He asks for a coin and places it in his hand. 'When Sri Ramakrishna held it in his hand, the hand began to writhe with pain,' Mahendranath recorded. 'The Master's breathing also stopped. After the coin had been taken away, he breathed deeply three times and his hand relaxed. The doctor became speechless with wonder to see this strange phenomenon...'

'I get into another state of mind,' Sri Ramakrishna explains to the doctor. And continues,

It is impossible for me to lay up anything. One day I visited Sambhu Mallick's garden house. At that time I had been suffering badly from stomach trouble. Sambhu said to me: 'Take a grain of opium now and then. It will help you.' He tied a little opium in a corner of my cloth. As I was returning to the Kali temple, I began to wander about near the gate as if unable to find the way. Then I threw the opium away and at once regained my normal state. I returned to the temple garden.

One day at Kamarpukur I picked some mangoes. I was carrying them home. But I could not walk; I had to stay standing in one place. Then I left the mangoes in a hollow. Only after that could I return home. Well, how do you explain that?[6]

His aversion for things worldly was absolute. And it extended to everything, not just money. Once, Mathur gave him an expensive shawl. 'He took it cheerfully,' Swami Nikhilananda wrote, 'and like a boy showed it to others.' But soon, his mind went to the evil temptations that the shawl could lead him into. He threw the shawl on the ground, 'and began to trample and spit on it. Not content

---

*Among his disciples, rules like not tying a knot, not locking a door or cupboard became strict observances: for tying something up in a knot in one's clothing would mean that one was regarding that thing as somehow precious, that one had an attachment to that thing; locking a door meant that there was something one wanted to hide.

with this, he was about to burn it when someone rescued it.' The same sort of thing happened another day. He had gone to Hriday's house. He came out to leave. He was wearing a scarlet silken cloth, had a gold amulet on his arm, and his mouth was crimson from chewing paan. People had gathered to see him. But they see me every day, he said. Why have so many gathered? he inquired. Hriday said that they had come to see him specially because he looked so handsome in that particular dress. That was enough to shock Sri Ramakrishna. 'What, people crowding to see a man! I won't go. Wherever I may go, people will crowd like this.' 'He returned to his room and took off the robe in utter disgust,' Swami Nikhilananda tells us. 'In spite of the entreaties of Hriday and others, he would not go out that day...'[7]

This aversion cost him an invitation once! He had gone to meet the father of Rabindranath Tagore, Devendranath Tagore—rich, father of eight children, the moving spirit and leading light of the Brahmo Samaj, with a retinue of attendants, an aristocrat, learned, but, in Sri Ramakrishna's discerning eye, vain, and one given to both—religion and this world.

'At the outset I noticed a little vanity in Devendra,' Sri Ramakrishna remarked later. 'And isn't that natural? He had such wealth, such scholarship, such name and fame! Noticing that streak of vanity, I asked Mathur: "Well, is vanity the outcome of knowledge or ignorance? Can a knower of Brahman have such a feeling as, 'I am a scholar; I am a *Jnani*; I am rich?'"'

They converse for a long time. Devendranath tells Sri Ramakrishna that he must come to their Brahmo festival. Sri Ramakrishna demurs. 'That, depends on the will of God,' he says. 'You can see the state of my mind. There's no knowing when God will put me into a particular state.' Devendranath insists: 'No, you must come. But put on your cloth and wear a shawl over your body. Someone might say something unkind about your untidiness, and that would hurt me.' 'No,' Sri Ramakrishna says. 'I cannot promise that. I cannot be a *babu*.' Devendra and Mathur, who has taken Sri Ramakrishna to the house, laugh.

'The very next day Mathur received a letter from Devendra forbidding me to go to the festival,' Sri Ramakrishna told his devotees later. 'He wrote that it would be ungentlemanly of me not to cover my body with a shawl.' This time it was the devotees who laughed.[8]

TRIPLE LESSONS FOR US

Of course, Sri Ramakrishna had high regard for Devendranath Tagore, and many were the encomiums that he showered on him—on his scholarship and all. But what he said about Devendranath has triple lessons for us—for our glib belief that *we* are clever enough so that we will be able to combine both immersion in the affairs of the world and the inner quest; for the way we convince ourselves over the years that we are advancing on the path; and, for the way we judge men to be great, including, and especially the godmen to whom we flock.

A deputy magistrate has come to visit Sri Ramakrishna. They are involved in animated exchanges. They are talking about affairs of the world, and of the inner search. Sri Ramakrishna is explaining the difficulties of combining the two. As if to suggest that Sri Ramakrishna is positing an impractical ideal, the magistrate remarks, 'I can tell you truthfully, sir, that not more than six or seven persons like you have been born since the creation of the world.' 'How so?' Sri Ramakrishna asks. 'There certainly are people who have given up everything for God. As soon as a man gives up his wealth, people come to know about him. But it is also true that there are others unknown to people. Are there not such holy men in upper India?'

The magistrate says, 'I know of at least one such person in Calcutta. He is Devendranath Tagore.'

'What did you say?' Sri Ramakrishna demands. 'Who has enjoyed the world as much as he? Once I visited him at his house with Mathur Babu. I saw that he had many young children. The family physician was there writing out prescriptions. If, after having eight children, a man doesn't think of God, who will? If, after, enjoying so much wealth, Devendranath hadn't thought of God, people would have cried shame upon him.'

A person butts in: 'But he paid off all his father's debts.'

'Keep quiet! Don't torment me any more,' Sri Ramakrishna cuts them short. 'Do you call anyone a man who doesn't pay off his father's debts if he is able to? But I admit that Devendranath is infinitely greater than other worldly men, who are sunk in their worldliness. They can learn much from him.' 'There is an ocean of difference between a real all-renouncing devotee of God and a householder devotee,' Sri Ramakrishna continued. 'A real *sanyasi*, a real devotee who has renounced the world, is like a bee. The bee will not alight on anything but a flower. It will not drink anything but honey. But a devotee leading the worldly life is like a fly. The fly sits on a festering sore as well as on a sweetmeat. One moment he enjoys a spiritual mood, and the next moment he is beside himself with the pleasure of "woman and gold".'[9]

Years pass. Keshab Chandra Sen has come to visit him. Sri Ramakrishna is alerting him to the impossibility of immersing oneself in devotion even as one is immersed in affairs of the world.

'Keshab, once I went to your temple,' Sri Ramakrishna tells him. 'In the course of your preaching I heard you say, "We shall dive into the river of devotion and go straight to the Ocean of *Satchidananda*." At once I looked up (at the gallery where Keshab's wife and the other ladies were sitting) and thought, "Then what will become of these ladies?" You see, Keshab, you are householders. How can you reach the Ocean of *Satchidananda* all at once? You are like a mongoose with a brick tied to its tail. When something frightens it, it runs up the wall and sits in a niche. But how can it stay there any length of time? The brick pulls it down and it falls to the floor with a thud. You may practise a little meditation, but the weight of wife and children will pull you down. You may dive into the river of devotion, but you must come up again. You will alternately dive and come up. How can you dive and disappear once for all?'

Keshab asks: 'Can't a householder ever succeed? What about Maharshi Devendranath Tagore?'

'Twice or thrice the Master repeated softly, "Devendranath Tagore—Devendra-Devendra" and bowed to him several times,' we learn in *The Gospel*.

'Let me tell you a story,' Sri Ramakrishna says. 'A man used to celebrate the Durga Puja at his house with great pomp. Goats were sacrificed from sunrise to sunset. But after a few years the sacrifice was not so imposing. Then someone said to him, "How is it, sir, that the sacrifice at your place has become such a tame affair?" "Don't you see?" he said. "My teeth are gone now." Devendra is now devoted to meditation and contemplation. It is only natural that he should be, at his advanced age. But no doubt he is a great man.'[10]

As the vices desert us, the aphorist says, we convince ourselves that we have become virtuous. That won't do, Sri Ramakrishna warns us.

His Humility

Sri Ramakrishna's aversion towards worldly honours was no less than for money, fancy clothes, and other worldly trinkets. Indeed, the aversion had lodged in his subconscious, it had become his second nature. You will recall how a disciple who was sleeping in the room once found Sri Ramakrishna pacing up and down in the dead of night. 'At every turn he spat on the floor, remarking in a tone of utter disgust, "Fie! I spit on it! I don't want it, take it back, Mother! Don't tempt me with this trifle."' When Sri Ramakrishna regained some awareness, he told the disciple, 'At dead of night I suddenly awoke from sleep to find the Divine Mother approaching me with a basket in Her hand. She held it out to me and asked me to accept the contents, which were mine. At a glance I found that the Mother had brought me worldly honours. They looked so hideous that I turned my face in disgust and prayed to Her to take back Her allurements. Thereupon, She disappeared with a smile.'[11]

Nor was all this just a shrinking away from worldly things. There was the positive side—utter humility. So sincere and spontaneous was it that it disarmed everyone. The Brahmos were a proud lot—after all, they were the bearers of the 'New Dispensation'. They would not bow before Sri Ramakrishna. But every time they came to him or Keshab Chandra Sen came, Sri Ramakrishna would spontaneously greet them with deep bows. Soon, they, including Keshab were touching the ground with their foreheads when they came into Sri Ramakrishna's presence! A Muslim notable and his companions came to call on Sri Ramakrishna. This is how the distinguished gentleman described what happened:

> When we arrived, Sri Ramakrishna was not in his room. We waited
> for him at the Panchavati. When Sri Ramakrishna came there,
> Ram Babu bowed down to him. We decided not to bow down, as

according to our religious tradition, we are not supposed to bow down to anyone other than Allah. We were, however, willing to pay proper respect to him. But as soon as he came near he bowed down to us. We were puzzled and were compelled to bow down to him.[12]

'We saw with our own eyes the incarnation of perfect humility,' Swami Premananda wrote. 'When the beggars finished their meals at the Dakshineswar temple garden, the Master carried their dirty leaf-plates on his head. And in order to eradicate any sense of superiority over the untouchable sweepers, he cleaned the toilets of the temple garden with his long hair...'[13]

AND TODAY?

Today we have godmen presiding over empires—of money, of real estate. We have godmen adding prefixes upon prefixes to their name. We have godmen on whose behalf the boast is carefully orchestrated about the throngs that flock to them. We have godmen who make sure that everyone notices the VIPs who come and sit at their feet. We have godmen whose real accomplishment is that they can outdo the best advertising guru and event manager.

And not just godmen. We have temples that are known by the amount of money that they garner per day. We have idols whose power is judged by the number of diamonds that are studded in their crowns.

Do you remember what happened when Guru Nanak reached the Jagannath temple at Puri to pray, and, disconcerted by the ostentation, left to pray under the open sky? There he sang that beautiful aarti:

Gagan mein thaal
Rav chand deepak baney
Taarka mandal janak moti
Dhoop malyaan lau pavan jhavro kare
Sagal banraye phulwant jyoti
Kaisi aarti hoye Bhavkhandan teri aarti ...

The sky is the platter
The sun and moon the lamps
And the stars the jewels
Sandalwood's fragrance is the incense
The wind is the flywhisk
And all the trees in the forest are Your flowers
How wonderful an aarti, O Lord, is Your aarti...

But the godmen and the controllers of temples and *maths* alone are not responsible for the resulting debasement. *We* are. Most often because of our desperation, often because of our greed. We are stricken by an illness, someone dear to us is stricken. We are desperate, and look for miracles. We flock to the latest godman. Often we just want a boost in our careers, we want a project to succeed, a business deal is stuck and we want it to turn in our favour. How I remember what a guru told me when, desperate, I was visiting him for help with Anita's condition. 'Do you know...?'—he asked as he raised his gaze in the direction of a big businessman who was sitting nearby. 'The other day, I told him, "Ask for anything. I will give you *anything* you ask for today." And do you know what he asked me to do? Can you even guess? He said, "Guruji, a godown-full of cotton bales is lying. I have not been able to sell them for a year. Bless me so that those bales get sold." Here I was, prepared to give him anything, *anything at all*. And what did he want—that I sell his bales!'

We don't even notice the incongruity. We pride ourselves at the weight of gold in the ornaments that we have donated for the idol. And simultaneously we sing that beautiful aarti of Sri Guru Nanak.

JUDGING THEM, JUDGING OURSELVES

The Buddha said—not about some sundry godmen, but about himself—do not accept something because I have said it; test it on the anvil of your experience. Both in the Buddhist tradition as well as in that of Hinduism—for instance, in regard to being initiated into sanyas—the teacher as well as the aspirant were to assess each other for *twelve years*.

That implied both things: that each must judge the other, and that she or he must do so over an extended time—for, after all, the two were not to judge each other by what the person said, but by her or his conduct. And while that conduct too could be faked for a short while, it could not be faked over twelve years.

That is sound practice. We must judge those to whom we flock; we must judge our own motivation.

Is the guru a person of spiritual attainments? Or is his hallmark worldly success?

Is he known for miracles? For the empire he has built? For the numbers that flock to him? For the VIPs who sit at his feet?

Does he lead us into an inner-directed search? Or does he lure us with promise of worldly boons?

Does he cause us to strive on our own? Or does he make us progressively more dependent on him?

Does he just spin words? Maya, Brahman, Ananda, Satchidananda … Does his conduct accord with what he urges us to do? Is he addicted to being reverenced even as he hectors us to erase our egos?

Has the conduct of those who have been with him for long become exemplary? Or do they 'do what businessmen just have to do in the world today' and, as a Tibetan text says, look to him to wash away their sins with water? Are they buying, and is he selling indulgences?

Even more important, and ever so much easier to do, we must be watchful of our own motives.

Have we gone to him so as to advance on an inner search? Or have we gone to secure some mundane goal—through his blessing or through the contacts we will make, especially with those VIPs at the sangat?

As conspicuous religiosity is but a variant of conspicuous consumption, have we gone to him to be seen by others as being pious?

Has despair carried us to him?

The Pristine Standard

We must hold the guru/godman as well as ourselves to the highest standard. Ever so often when a godman is exposed for what he is, I hear the cry go up, 'It is all a Christian conspiracy.'

Firstly, so what if the exposure has come about as the result of a conspiracy? The question is, 'Are the charges correct or not?'

Second, it is vital that these personages measure up to the highest standard—to the Ramakrishna–Ramana standard. The one 'pearl of great price' that we have, the one treasure that our culture can still give to the world is what our rishis discovered about the inner-directed search. And these persons are either the bearers of that treasure or ones trading in it. When they stray from the strictest standard, they don't just fool a few persons, they endanger that singular tradition.

As for us, we too must remember that that tradition is about the inner-directed search. Ever so often, we depart from that search. We flock to these persons for miracles. But, as Gandhiji said, there are no miracles contrary to the laws of nature. If we do come across an occurrence that is incomprehensible, we should look for the natural explanation and see how far that will carry us before lunging for the supernatural one.

Beyond this futile search for miracles, as far as the inner-directed search is concerned, if I may be so bold as to report my own experience, the vicissitudes of life are an adequate guru. We do not need the godmen of today. The ups and downs of our lives hurl us this way and that. As they buffet us, we have but to observe our mind, and we would have put them to work.

THE GREAT MYSTICS

As for the great mystics who have been the occasion for the book, there are three conclusions.

The real miracle in their case was their goodness, their compassion, the complete consistency of their teachings and their life. Their sterling qualities must not discourage us. Of course, we cannot even dream of being like them. But, as we were taught at school in the context of Gandhiji, we can strive to be ten-paisa Ramakrishnas–Ramanas.

Second, many of the peripheral experiences that were reported about these great mystics, and which are often taken to be marks of their divinity, were incidentals. There are probably several this-worldly explanations for those phenomena.

Finally, their real attainment was the peak, mystic experience. Having set the peripherals aside, we are better prepared to try and understand that experience.

So, should we begin?

Notes

1. THEIR MESMERIC POWER

1. The preceding incidents are reproduced almost verbatim from Swami Saradananda, *Sri Ramakrishna, The Great Master,* Original in Bengali, *Sri Ramakrishna Lilaprasanga,* 1914, Translated by Swami Jagadananda, Sri Ramakrishna Math, Mylapore, Chennai, 1952, Sixth Edition, 1978, pp. 1040-42, 1044, 1086-88, 1146-48. Henceforth, *The Master.* This biography was first published in 1914. In his *The Life of Ramakrishna,* Romain Rolland, wrote, 'Saradananda, who died in 1927, was on terms of intimacy with Ramakrishna and likewise possessed one of the loftiest religious and philosophical minds in India. His biography, unfortunately unfinished, is at once the most interesting and the most reliable.' Romain Rolland, *The Life of Ramakrishna,* 1929, Advaita Ashram, Calcutta, Eighth Edition, 1970, pp. 33-34. Unless otherwise specified, all sentences that have been italicized, have been italicized by the author.

2. For this episode, *The Life of Swami Vivekananda by His Eastern and Western Disciples,* Prabuddha Bharat Office, Mayavati, Almora, 1914, Volume I, pp. 415-22.

3. Ibid., pp. 427-28.

4. *The Life of Swami Vivekananda by his Eastern and Western Disciples,* Prabuddha Bharat Office, Mayavati, Almora, 1914, Volume II, Chapter LXV, 'Ramakrishna or Pavhari Baba', in particular pp. 94-96.

5. Munagala S. Venkataramiah, *Talks With Sri Ramana Maharshi,* Sri Ramanasramam, Tiruvannamalai, 1955/2006, pp. 534-35. Henceforth, *Talks.*

6. A. Devaraja Mudaliar, *Day By Day With Bhagavan,* Sri Ramanasramam, Tiruvannamalai, 1968/1989, pp. 105-07.

7. Nagamma Suri, *Letters from Sri Ramanasramam,* Sri Ramanasramam, Tiruvannamalai, 1970/2006, pp. 371-72.

8. Cf. my *Missionaries in India,* ASA, New Delhi, 1994, pp. 134-35, 148-49.

9. 'Try to be mindful, and let things take their natural course,' the great Thai teacher taught in words that could be a literal description of Sri Ramana. 'Then your mind will become still in any surroundings, like a clear forest pool. All kinds of wonderful, rare animals will come to drink at the pool, and you will clearly see the nature of all things. You will see many strange and wonderful things come and go, but you will be still. This is the happiness of the Buddha.' Cf. *A Still Forest Pool, The insight meditation of Achaan Chah,* compiled by Jack Kornfield and Paul Breiter, Theosophical Publishing House, Wheaton, Illinois, 1985/2001, p. vi.

10. Just so that no one takes that to be a real contrast, here is a passage about Sri Ramana from Arthur Osborne: 'The initiation by look was a very real thing. Sri Bhagavan would turn to the devotee, his eyes fixed upon him with blazing intentness. The luminosity, the power of his eyes pierced one, breaking down the thought-process. Sometimes it was as though an electric current was passing through one, sometimes a vast peace, a flood of light. One devotee has described it: "Suddenly Bhagavan turned his luminous, transparent eyes on me. Before that I could not stand his gaze for long. Now I looked straight back into those powerful and wonderful eyes, how long I cannot tell. They held me in a sort of vibration distinctly audible to me." Always it was followed by a feeling, the indubitable conviction, that one had been taken up by Sri Bhagavan, that henceforth he was in charge, he was guiding ... The initiation by silence was equally real. It entered into those who turned to Sri Bhagavan in their hearts without being able to go bodily to Tiruvannamalai. Sometimes it was given in a dream, as with Natesa Mudaliar.' Arthur Osborne, *Ramana Maharshi and the Path of Self Knowledge,* Sri Ramanasramam, Tiruvannamalai, 1997, 2004 edition, pp. 171-72.

11. Mahendranath Gupta, *The Gospel of Sri Ramakrishna,* Translated from the Bengali by Swami Nikhilananda, Sri Ramakrishna Math, Mylapore, Madras, 1944/1974, p. 113. Henceforth, *The Gospel.*

12. *The Gospel,* passim, for instance pp. 27, 88, 212, 304, 636-47, 760.

2. THE REAL MIRACLE

1. Recalled in Michael S. Gazzaniga, *Who's In Charge? Free Will and the Science of the Brain*, HarperCollins, New York, 2011, p. 10.
2. Swami Chetanananda, *How to Live with God: In the Company of Ramakrishna*, Advaita Ashram, Kolkata, 2009, p. 507.
3. *The Master*, Swami Jagadananda (tr.), Sri Ramakrishna Math, Chennai, 1952/2008. See, for instance, p. 866 where he writes about the effects of Sri Ramakrishna having taken on the sins of others; see pp. 832-33 for the effects of overexertion and sleeplessness as being the causes of the disease.
4. For these and other examples, see Swami Chetanananda, *How to Live with God: In the Company of Ramakrishna*, pp. 158-63.
5. Ibid., pp. 158, 161-62, 504, 508, and the various sources cited there.
6. Jawaharlal Nehru, *The Discovery of India*, The Signet Press, Calcutta, 1946, pp. 77-78.
7. Vaikunthanath Sanyal's *Sri Sri Ramakrishna Lilamrita*, cited in Swami Chetanananda, *How to Live with God: In the Company of Ramakrishna*, pp. 162-63.
8. Dalai Lama, *The Universe in a Single Atom: The Convergence of Science and Spirituality*, Harmony Books, New York, p. 9.
9. Ibid., p. 13.
10. Evan Thompson, *Waking, Dreaming, Being: Self and Consciousness in Neuroscience, Meditation, and Philosophy*, Columbia University Press, New York, 2015, Kindle, loc. 2236-52.
11. So as not to cause offence, and so as not to get sidetracked into an unnecessary controversy, in this as well as the preceding paragraph, I have withheld the name of the great mystic and his books from which the expressions are taken.
12. On all this, see William James, *The Varieties of Religious Experience, A Study in Human Nature, Being the Gifford Lectures on Natural Religion Delivered at Edinburgh in 1901-1902*, The Modern Library, New York, 1902/1929, pp. 3-26.
13. William James, *The Varieties of Religious Experience*, pp. 413-14.
14. Ibid., pp. 414, 417-18.
15. Ibid., pp. 494-95.
16. Ibid., pp. 266-74.
17. Ibid., p. 285.

3. 'O, THE STATE IN WHICH I WAS...'

1. *The Master*, op. cit., pp. 74-75, 142-43.
2. Ibid., pp. 75, 92-93; Swami Nikhilananda, *Life of Sri Ramakrishna*, Foreword by Mahatma Gandhi, Advaita Ashrama, Kolkata, Eighteenth Reprint, 2011, p. 34 onwards.
3. *The Master*, pp. 249-50; also Swami Nikhilananda, *Life of Sri Ramakrishna*, pp. 88, 89.
4. Introduction by Swami Nikhilananda in Mahendranath Gupta, *The Gospel Sri Ramakrishna*, 'Bible Edition', Sri Ramakrishna Math, Mylapore, Madras, 1981/1986, p. 13; *The Master*, op. cit., p. 184.
5. *The Gospel*, op. cit., pp. 796-97.
6. Ibid., for instance, pp. 205, 405.
7. *The Gospel*, 'Bible Edition', Sri Ramakrishna Math, Mylapore, Madras, 1981/1986, pp. 13-14; *The Master*, op. cit., pp. 190-92.
8. *The Master*, op. cit., pp. 191-92.
9. Swami Nikhilananda, *Life of Sri Ramakrishna*, pp. 83-84.
10. *The Master*, op. cit., p. 353.
11. Swami Nikhilananda, *Life of Sri Ramakrishna*, pp. 158-60.
12. *The Master*, op. cit., pp. 503-05.
13. Ibid., p. 542.
14. *The Gospel*, op. cit., p. 45.
15. Ibid., p. 169.
16. Ibid., at several places, for instance, pp. 93, 266, 554.
17. A. Devaraja Mudaliar, *Day to Day With Bhagavan*, op. cit., pp. 241-43.
18. Nagamma Suri, *Letters from Sri Ramanasramam*, Volumes I and II, and *Letters from and Recollections of Sri Ramanasramam*, D.S. Sastri (tr.), Sri Ramanasramam, Tiruvannamalai, Fifth Revised Edition, 2006, pp. 115-16.
19. B.V. Narasimha Swami, *Self-Realization, The Life and Teachings of Sri Ramana Maharshi*, Sri Ramanasramam, Tiruvannamalai, 1931, 1993 Edition, p. 43. Henceforth, *Self-Realization*.
20. Ibid., p.47.
21. Ibid., p.48.
22. Ibid., p. 49; K. Swaminathan, *Ramana Maharshi*, op. cit., p. 14.
23. *Self-Realization*, op. cit., p. 52.
24. A. Devaraja Mudaliar, *Day to Day With Bhagavan*, pp. 282-83.
25. Nagamma Suri, *Letters from Sri Ramanasramam*, pp. 391-92.
26. *Self-Realization*, op. cit., pp. 52-58.
27. A. Devaraja Mudaliar, *Day to Day With Bhagavan*, p. 122.

28. Nagamma Suri, *Letters from Sri Ramanasramam*, p. 389.
29. A. Devaraja Mudaliar, *Day to Day With Bhagavan*, p. 207.
30. Arthur Osborne, *Ramana Maharshi and the Path of Self Knowledge*, Sri Ramanasramam, Tiruvannamalai, 1997, 2004 Edition, pp. 44-45.
31. *The Master*, op. cit., pp. 832-33.
32. Swami Ramakrishnananda in *Ramakrishna As We Saw Him*, Swami Chetanananda (ed. and tr.), Advaita Ashram, Calcutta, 1993, pp.141-60, pp. 154-55.
33. For a quick introduction to apnoea and its types, see, for instance, National Institutes of Health, http://www.nhlbi.nih.gov/health-topics/topics/sleepapnea.
34. A leading neurosurgeon, one of the pioneers in India of Deep Brain Stimulation, currently director of the Sree Chitra Tirunal Institute for Medical Sciences and Technology, Thiruvananthapuram.
35. Leonardo Vintini, *Epoch Times,* 5 May 2008.
36. A non-profit organization and campaign established in 1938 for raising funds to combat polio. Later it enlarged its mandate to help alleviate other ailments also.
37. https://www.youtube.com/watch?v=4MT8ekBGyM4.
38. But it is not clear that this downward spiral had that much to do with the hours of going without sleep: he was implicated in a scandal of playing songs in return for gifts. Writing in *New York Times*, years later, Thomas Bartlett listed hallucinations of other kinds too that Tripp experienced: '... While Tripp somehow managed to keep it together during broadcasts, off the air he was experiencing wild hallucinations. He saw mice and kittens scampering around the makeshift studio. He was convinced that his shoes were full of spiders. He thought a desk drawer was on fire. When a man in a dark overcoat showed up, Tripp imagined him to be an undertaker and ran terrified into the street. He had to be dragged back inside.' Thomas Bartlett, 'The stay-awake men,' *New York Times,* 22 April 2010.
39. Lt Cdr John J. Ross, 'Neurological findings after prolonged sleep deprivation', *Archives of Neurology,* Volume 12, April 1965, pp. 399-403, at 399-400. For ease of reference, I have italicized the number of days since the commencement of the vigil.
40. Ibid., p. 400.
41. 'More than a decade ago it was found that total sleep deprivation in rats leads to death. (They normally live from two to three years.),' we learn. 'These animals show weight loss despite greatly increased food consumption, suggesting excessive heat loss. The animals die, for reasons yet to be explained, within 10 to 20 days, faster than if they

were totally deprived of food but slept normally.' Jerome M. Siegel, 'Why we sleep', *Scientific American,* November 2003, pp. 92-97, p. 94.

42. On this, Helen Thomson, BBC Future, 7, 20 July 2015.

43. The condition is described in various publications dealing with sleep. For the foregoing, Ann Finkbeiner, 'Awake asleep: Insomniac brains that can't switch off', *New Scientist,* 2969, 14 May 2014, http://www. newscientist.com/article/mg22229690.400-awake-asleep-insomniac-brains-that-cant-switch-off.html.

44. For arresting accounts see, for instance, Niels C. Rattenborg, 'Do birds sleep in flight?', *Naturwissenschaften,* September 2006, Number 93, pp. 413-25; and Sam Ridgway et al., 'Dolphin Continuous Auditory Vigilance for Five Days', *The Journal of Experimental Biology,* 2006, Volume 209, Number 18, pp. 3621-28.

4. A BRIEF DIVERSION

1. See, for instance, Lyn M. Goff and L. Roediger III, 'Imagination inflation for action events', *Memory and Cognition,* 1998, 26 (1), pp. 20-33; and Isabel Lindner, Gerald Echterhoff, Patrick S.R. Davidson and Matthias Brand, 'Observation Inflation: Your Actions Become Mine', *Psychological Science* 2010, 21 (9), pp. 1291-99; originally published online, 5 August 2010.

2. Among studies that have exercised the greatest influence in this regard are numerous papers by Elizabeth Loftus, and her book, *Eyewitness Testimony, Civil and Criminal,* Fourth Edition, LexisNexis, 2007; see also Barbara Tversky and George Fisher, 'The problem with eyewitness testimony', *Stanford Journal of Legal Studies,* April 1999, and Gary L. Wells and Lisa E. Hasel, 'Eyewitness Identification: Issues in Common Knowledge and Generalization', in *Beyond Common Sense, Psychological Science in the Courtroom,* E. Borgida and S.T. Fiske (eds), Wiley-Blackwell, 2007.

3. Ulrich Neisser, 'John Dean's memory: A case study', *Cognition,* 1981, Volume 9, pp. 1-22; also Leonard Mlodinow, *Subliminal: The Revolution of the New Unconscious and What It Teaches Us About Ourselves,* Allen Lane, Penguin, London, 2012, pp. 56-58.

4. Michael Sweeney, *Brain: The Complete Mind, How It Develops, How To Keep It Sharp,* National Geographic, Washington. DC, 2009, pp. 59-60.

5. I will continue to use the name as it is spelled in the accounts of Sacks and Sweeny; the name might have been Bhagwanti.

6. Oliver Sacks, *The Man Who Mistook His Wife for a Hat, and Other Clinical Tales,* HarperCollins, New York, 1970/1985.
7. Ibid., pp. 153-55.
8. Private communication.
9. *The Master,* op. cit., pp. 935-37.
10. Shailendranath Dhar, *A Comprehensive Biography of Swami Vivekananda,* Vivekananda Kendra Prakashan, Madras, Second Edition, 1990, p. 800. Christopher Isherwood maintained that Max Müller's reservations on this count were exaggerated and misplaced: Christopher Isherwood, *Ramakrishna and His Disciples,* Advaita Ashram, Calcutta, Fifth Impression, 1986, e.g., pp. 22-23.
11. Swami Vivekananda, *The Complete Works of Swami Vivekananda,* Advaita Ashram, Calcutta, Eleventh Edition, 1978, Volume IV, p. 359; 'Studiously avoiding all miracles' emphasized in the original; emphasis in the other two sentences added.
12. The nickname by which another disciple, Mudaliar was known.
13. Swami Vivekananda, *The Complete Works of Swami Vivekananda,* Advaita Ashram, Calcutta, Eleventh Edition, 1979, Volume V, pp. 52-54.
14. Ibid., pp. 54-55.
15. Max Müller had contributed a brief sketch to a journal, and had been criticized by Christian missionaries for being carried away by accounts regarding Sri Ramakrishna.
16. Swami Vivekananda, *The Complete Works of Swami Vivekananda,* Volume VI, p. 364.
17. Sri Ramanasramam, Tiruvannamalai, 1997, 2004 edition.
18. National Book Trust, Delhi, 1975.
19. This caveat was brought home to me forcefully when, for other reasons, I read Peter W. Kaplan and Robert S. Fisher (eds), *Imitators of Epilepsy,* Second Edition, Demos Medical Publishing, New York, 2005.

5. Deities, celestial beings, ghosts

1. *The Master,* op. cit., pp. 134-35. Also, *The Gospel,* at several places, for instance, pp. 93, 881, 926.
2. *The Gospel,* op. cit., at several places, for instance, pp. 93, 885.
3. *The Master,* op. cit., pp. 71, 138-39.
4. Ibid., pp. 73-74.
5. Swami Nikhilananda, *Life of Sri Ramakrishna,* op. cit., pp. 193-94.

6. *The Gospel*, 'Bible Edition', Sri Ramakrishna Math, Mylapore, Madras, 1981/1986, pp. 14-15.
7. Ibid., p. 28.
8. *The Master*, p. 279-80.
9. Ibid., p. 281.
10. Sri Chaitanya.
11. *The Gospel*, p. 108.
12. Ibid., p. 815.
13. Ibid., pp. 324-25.
14. Ibid., p. 312.
15. Ibid., p. 417.
16. Ibid., p. 789.
17. The drumstick.
18. *The Gospel*, pp. 817-18.
19. Ibid., pp. 817-19.
20. Swami Nikhilananda, *Life of Sri Ramakrishna*, p. 154.
21. *The Gospel*, pp. 754-55.
22. *The Master*, p. 788.
23. Ibid., pp. 800-01.
24. *The Gospel*, p. 785.
25. Ibid., p. 899.
26. *The Master*, op. cit., pp. 398-99.
27. Ibid., pp. 442-43.
28. Ibid., pp. 235-38.
29. Ibid., pp. 935-37.
30. *The Gospel*, pp. 503-06; *The Master*, pp. 278-79.
31. *The Gospel*, p. 485.
32. Ibid., p. 93.
33. Cf. *The Master*, pp. 511-12; also Swami Nikhilananda, *Life of Sri Ramakrishna*, pp. 117-18.
34. *Talks*, p. 383.
35. Ibid., pp. 127-28
36. A. Devaraja Mudaliar, *Day by Day With Bhagavan*, Sri Ramanasramam, Tiruvannamalai, 1952, 1989 edition, pp. 278-79.
37. Nagamma Suri, *Letters from Sri Ramanasramam*, Tiruvannamalai, 1970/1985, pp. 501-03.
38. *Self-Realization*, pp. 11-12.
39. *The Gospel*, p. 115.
40. Ibid., p. 209.
41. Ibid., p. 386.
42. Ibid., pp. 511-17.

43. Ibid., p. 324.
44. For the states mentioned in this paragraph, Swami Nikhilananda, *Life of Sri Ramakrishna*, pp. 187-191, 199; *The Master*, pp. 382-83. For the rest, as mentioned, *The Gospel*.
45. On these, and similar observations of Sri Ramakrishna, *The Gospel*, pp. 659-60, 755, 199, and elsewhere; and *The Master*, op. cit., pp. 755-62.
46. *The Master*, pp. 534-35.
47. Ibid., pp. 534-36, 755-62.
48. Swami Chetanananda, *How to Live with God, In the Company of Ramakrishna*, Advaita Ashram, Kolkata, 2009, p. 504, and the references to *Srimau Katha* given therein. That last incident, of the umbrella being closed, contains a cautionary tale. Having read about the incident in the Swami Chetanananda volume, I wanted to get to the original book, *Srimau Katha*. Monks of the Ramakrishna Mission located a copy. I sent the full passage to my friend P.K. Basu for translation. His reading differed completely from that of Swami Chetanananda. Basu said that the preceding sentences referred to a devotee of Sri Ramakrishna having died. In the context, the word 'chhaati' meant 'chest' not 'umbrella', and the word 'bojano' meant 'stopped' not 'closed'. And so, the passage actually meant that when Sri Ramakrishna heard that the chest of his devotee had stopped— that is, when he had stopped breathing—he went into samadhi. Not wanting to doubt what Swami Chetanananda had written, I sent the alternative translation to him. He replied that, indeed, the sentence must be read in context, and that the context was clear. That scarcely settled the matter! What was the context that was so clear? That the devotee had died or that the umbrella had been closed? I requested friends in Kolkata to go back to the monks. They stood by the umbrella!
49. *The Master*, pp. 367-68.
50. For illustrative references, my *Does He Know a Mother's Heart? How suffering refutes religions*, HarperCollins *Publishers* India, NOIDA, 2011, pp. 233-35.
51. For a fetching account of the steps by which this happens, Bruce M. Hood, *Supersense: Why We Believe in the Unbelievable*, HarperOne, San Francisco, 2009.
52. *The Master*, pp. 203-04, 703-04.
53. As on every other ailment, the literature on musicogenic epilepsy is also quite large. A few short contributions, two brief reviews and a book as incisive as it is delightful will suffice for our purposes. The

first is an essay by a pioneer in this field (as well as others)—he began writing about it in the late 1930s—included in a book edited by him: M. Critchley, 'Musicogenic Epilepsy', in *Music and the Brain*, M. Critchley and R.A. Hensen (eds), Heinemann, London, 1977, pp. 344-53; the contribution in the same volume by D. Scott, pp. 354-64; H.G. Wieser, Hansjorg Hungerbuhler, et al., 'Musicogenic Epilepsy: Review of the Literature and Case Report with Ictal Single Photon Emission Computed Tomography', *Epilepsia*, 1997, Volume 38, Number 2, pp. 200-07; J.C.M. Brust, 'Music and the Neurologist: A Historical Perspective', *Annals of the New York Academy of Science*, 2001, Number 930, pp. 143-52; Peter W. Kaplan, 'Musicogenic Epilepsy and Epileptic Music: A Seizure's Song', *Epilepsy and Behavior*, 2003, Volume 4, pp. 464-473; and, of course, Oliver Sacks, *Musicophilia, Tales of Music and the Brain*, Alfred A. Knopf, New York, 2007.

54. Oliver Sacks, *Musicophilia, Tales of Music and the Brain*, p. 50.
55. Ibid., p. 67.
56. Ibid., p. 68.
57. Ibid., pp. 69-70.
58. Ibid., pp. 72-73.
59. Ibid., p. 72.
60. Wilder Penfield and Phanor Perot, 'The Brain's Record of Auditory and Visual Experience: A Final Summary and Discussion', *Brain*, Volume 86, Part 4, December 1963, pp. 596-696, at p. 639.
61. For general accounts, see Oliver Sacks, *Hallucinations*, Picador, London, 2012; Michael Shermer, *The Believing Brain: From Ghosts and Gods to Politics and Conspiracies—How We Construct Beliefs and Reinforce Them*, Times Books, New York; and T.M. Luhrmann, *When God Talks Back: Understanding the American Evangelical Relationship with God*, Vintage, Random House, New York, 2012. See also, R.K. Siegel, 'Hostage Hallucinations: Visual Imagery Induced By Isolation and Life-threatening Stress', *Journal of Nervous and Mental Disease*, 1984, Volume 172, Number 5, pp. 264-72.

6. 'The collyrium of love'

1. *The Master*, p. 340.
2. Ibid., pp. 294-95; as well as Swami Nikhilananda, *The Life of Sri Ramakrishna*, pp. 138-41.
3. Swami Nikhilananda, *Life of Sri Ramakrishna*, op. cit., p. 142-43.
4. *The Master*, pp. 217-18.
5. *The Gospel*, pp. 626-27.

6. *The Master*, pp. 327-331.
7. Ibid., pp. 327-36.
8. Ibid., p. 365.
9. Ibid., pp. 414-16.
10. Ibid., pp. 416-17.
11. For instance, in an important paper, Herbert Moller made out the case that in parts of western Europe during the eleventh and twelfth centuries, 'affective mysticism' arose in areas from which there had been pronounced emigration, a process in which far more males than females had left the regions, and thereby male-to-female ratios had fallen to abnormally low levels. Cf. Herbert Moller, 'The social causation of affective mysticism', *Journal of Social History*, Vol. 4, No. 4, Summer 1971, pp. 305-38.
12. Herbert Moller, op. cit., pp. 306, 309, 319, 328, 330, 333.
13. Introduction by Swami Nikhilananda, *The Gospel*, 'Bible Edition', Sri Ramakrishna Math, Mylapore, Madras, 1981/1986, pp. 5-6.
14. Ibid., p. 12; also *The Master*, pp. 180-82.
15. Swami Nikhilananda, *Life of Sri Ramakrishna*, pp. 52, 58, 64-65.
16. *The Master*, pp. 503-05.
17. Ibid., p. 542.
18. Ibid., pp. 631-32.
19. Ibid., pp. 193-94.
20. Introduction by Swami Nikhilananda, *The Gospel*, 'Bible Edition', p. 14.
21. *The Gospel*, p. 106.
22. Ibid., p. 23.
23. *The Master*, p. 408.
24. *The Gospel*, p. 79.
25. Ibid., p. 177.
26. Ibid., p. 291.
27. Swami Nikhilananda, *Life of Sri Ramakrishna*, pp. 188, 401, 415.
28. *The Gospel*, p. 229-30.
29. Ibid., p. 735.
30. Ibid., p. 736; see also p. 537.
31. T.M. Luhrmann, *When God Talks Back: Understanding the American Evangelical Relationship with God*, Vintage, Random House, New York, 2012.
32. The website of Professor Diana Deutsch, deutsch.ucsd.edu, is a fine place to start as it has examples of the illusions she has created and also leads the visitor to other sites.

7. 'A YOUNG SANYASIN LOOKING LIKE ME WOULD EMERGE FROM
   MY BODY AND INSTRUCT ME IN ALL MATTERS...'

1. *The Master*, p.232.
2. Swami Nikhilananda, *Life of Sri Ramakrishna*, Advaita Ashram,
    Kolkata, 1924/2011, p. 89.
3. *The Master*, pp. 233-34.
4. Swami Chetanananda, *Ramakrishna As We Saw Him*, Advaita
    Ashram, Calcutta, 1990/1993, and *How to Live with God, In the
    Company of Ramakrishna*, Advaita Ashram, Kolkata, 1997/2009.
    And from Swami Nikhilananda, *Life of Sri Ramakrishna*, Foreword
    by Mahatma Gandhi, Advaita Ashram, Kolkata, 17th impression,
    2008.
5. *The Master*, pp. 385-86.
6. Ibid., pp. 611-13.
7. As mentioned in the text, these instances, which are set out in a series
    of writings of Sri Ramakrishna's direct disciples and companions,
    are taken from Swami Chetanananda's two anthologies of those
    accounts, *Ramakrishna as We Saw Him*, pp. 30-31, 209-10, 227,
    56-57, 127, 154, 131, 254-55; and *How to Live With God, In the
    Company of Ramakrishna*, op. cit., pp. 72-81.
8. *Self-Realization*, op. cit., pp. 105-07.
9. Ibid., pp. 79-80. Narasimha Swami's account of the particular incident
    in the text was based on the Tamil poem that Pillai had composed
    describing his relations with Sri Ramana.
10. Nagamma Suri, *Letters from and Recollections of Sri Ramanasramam*,
    D.S. Sastri (tr.), Sri Ramanasramam, Tiruvannamalai, Fifth revised
    edition, 2006, p. 25.
11. A. Devaraja Mudaliar, *Day by Day With Bhagavan*, Sri
    Ramanasramam, Tiruvannamalai, 1952, 1989 edition, p. 269.
12. *Self-Realization*, p. 104.
13. Arthur Osborne, *Ramana Maharshi and the Path of Self-Knowledge*,
    Sri Ramanasramam, Tiruvannamalai, 1997/2008, pp. 57-58.
14. Nagamma Suri, *Letters from Sri Ramanasramam*, D.S. Sastri (tr.),
    Sri Ramanasramam, Tiruvannamalai, 1962, 1970 editions; First
    combined edition, 1970, reprint 2006, pp. 228-30.
15. Cf. Arthur Osborne, *Ramana Maharshi and the Path of Self-
    Knowledge*, Chapters 17 and 18, '*Mahasamadhi*' and 'Continued
    Presence', pp. 214-234; K. Swaminathan, *Ramana Maharshi*, National
    Book Trust, Delhi, 1975, Chapter VII, 'Ramanasramam: Power of the
    Presence', pp. 52-62.

16. Cf. J. Yamamoto, K. Okonogi, S. Yusimura, 'Mourning in Japan', *American Journal of Psychiatry,* 1969, Number 125, pp. 1660-65.

17. W. Dewi Rees, 'The hallucinations of widowhood', *British Medical Journal,* 1971, 4: pp. 37-41.

18. A. Grimby, 'Bereavement among Elderly People: Grief Reactions, Post-Bereavement Hallucinations and Quality of Life', *Acta Psychiatrica Scandinavica,* 1993, 87: 72-80.

19. P.C. Horton, *Solace: The Missing Dimension in Psychiatry,* Chicago University Press, 1981; for a brief discussion of imaginary companions, see M. O'Mahony, K. Shulman and D. Silver, 'Roses in December: Imaginary Companions in the Elderly', *Canadian Journal of Psychiatry,* March 1984, 29, pp. 151-53.

20. Hermann Buhl, *Nanga Parbat Pilgrimage: The Lonely Challenge,* Baton Wicks, London, The Mountaineers, Seattle, 2001/2008.

21. As I have mentioned in the text, all this is but the sheerest summary of the last two chapters in Hermann Buhl's hair-raising, *Nanga Parbat Pilgrimage,* pp. 298-350.

22. Cf. Frank Smythe, *Camp Six: An Account of the 1933 Everest Expedition,* Hodder and Stoughton, London, 1937; and his, *The Adventures of a Mountaineer,* J.M. Dent and Sons, London, 1949. The account is summarized in several books that deal with both mountaineering as well as the Third Man phenomenon.

23. Charles Clarke, 'On surviving a bivouac at high altitude', Communication to *British Medical Journal,* 10 January 1976, pp. 92-93.

24. Chris Bonington, email to Suman Dubey, 24 November 2012.

25. Judie Ketteler, 'The Third Man Factor, Invisible Guardians: Angels or a Brain Function?', *AOL Health,* 27 August 2009, interview with John Geiger.

26. Shahar Arzy, Moshe Idel, Theodor Landis, Olaf Blanke, 'Why Revelations Have Occurred On Mountains?: Linking Mystical Experiences and Cognitive Neuroscience', *Medical Hypotheses,* Elsevier, 2005, Volume 65, pp. 841-45. We will come back to this contribution and the authors' hypotheses in a little while.

27. Shackleton's account of the expedition is justly famous, and figures in almost every study of the third-man phenomenon. His original account is now available as an eBook also under The Gutenberg Project from which the passage above is taken: Ernest Shackleton, *South! The Story of Shackleton's Last Expedition, 1914-17,* originally published in 1919; Gutenberg edition, 2004, p. 221. In point of fact, Shackleton did embark on another expedition, this time to

circumnavigate Antarctica, in September 1921. But he suffered a heart attack in Rio de Janeiro. Nevertheless, he pressed on, only to die in South Georgia—the very island that he had reached on the earlier expedition in the 20-foot wooden lifeboat, braving hurricanes and the rest, and then traversed on foot in search of help.

28. In the paper that set off these investigations ('Idea of a presence', *Acta Psychiatrica Neurologica Scandinavica*, Vol. 30, 1955; reproduced in MacDonald Critchley, *Divine Banquet of the Brain and Other Essays*, Raven Press, New York, 1979), the British neurologist, MacDonald Critchley, examined the experience of shipwreck survivors and explorers. For many instances, see John Geiger, *The Third Man Factor: Surviving the Impossible*, Penguin, Toronto, 2009, referred to earlier.

29. See, for instance, Gilles Fenelon, Thierry Soulas, Laurent Cleret De Langavant, Iris Trinkler, Anne-Catherine Bachoud-Levi, 'Feeling of presence in Parkinson's disease', *Journal of Neurology and Psychiatry*, 2001, Volume 82, Number 11, pp. 1219-24. Those suffering from psychosis or schizophrenia often feel the presence of another; indeed, so many of them project agency on to another, feeling that some outside force or being is in control and is doing or making them do what, in fact, they are doing. As Critchley had noted, the feeling of presence that psychotics and schizophrenics experience had formed the basis of the original 1913 paper by Jaspers.

30. Peter Suedfeld and Jane S.P. Mocellin, 'The "Sensed Presence" in Unusual Environments', *Environment and Behavior*, January 1987, Vol. 19, No. 1, pp. 33-52, at 45-46.

31. The same thing occurs in regard to spots that are caused by lesions in the retina or the primary visual cortex—'scotomas'; and in regard to 'scotomas' that are artificially created: for ingenious experiments that show this, V.S. Ramachandran and R.L. Gregory, 'Perceptual filling-in of artificially induced scotomas in human vision', *Nature*, 1991, pp. 350, (6320), 699-702. As Ramachandran and Gregory showed, the blind spot is filled in not just by what is immediately around it, but also by mobilizing the patterns from 'the remote surround'.

32. As on everything else, the literature examining the physiological and psychological dimensions of the third man phenomenon is considerable. The following will suffice to illustrate the sorts of factors that scholars of medicine and psychologists have advanced as likely explanations: the original piece by MacDonald Critchley, 'Idea of a Presence', *Acta Psychiatrica Neurologica Scandinavica*, Volume 30, 1955; the informative review paper, Peter Suedfeld and Jane

S.P. Mocellin, 'The "Sensed Presence" in Unusual Environments', *Environment and Behavior,* January 1987, Volume 19, Number 1, pp. 33-52; John Geiger, *The Third Man Factor: Surviving the Impossible,* Penguin, Toronto, 2009; Judie Ketteler, 'The Third Man Factor, Invisible guardians: angels or brain function?', *AOL Health,* Interview with John Geiger, 27 August 2009; Shahar Arzy, Moshe Idel, Theodor Landis, Olaf Blanke, 'Why Revelations Have Occurred on Mountains?: Linking Mystical Experiences and Cognitive Neuroscience', *Medical Hypotheses,* Elsevier, 2005, Volume 65, pp. 841-845; and a much earlier paper, Tore Nielsen, 'Felt Presence: Paranoid Delusion or Hallucinatory Social Imagery?', *ScienceDirect, Consciousness and Cognition,* Elsevier, 2007, Volume 16, pp. 975-83.
33. Once again I will leave out the references that the authors mention.
34. Suedfeld and Mocellin, op. cit., pp. 47-48.
35. *The Master,* pp. 231-32.

8. 'I SUDDENLY FELT MY BODY CARRIED UP HIGHER AND HIGHER...'

1. *Self-Realization,* op. cit., pp. 94-95.
2. For descriptions of the history of G.A., the anatomy of her brain, the operation, and her experiences during that period, Wilder Penfield and Theodore Rasmussen, *The Cerebral Cortex of Man: A Clinical Study of Localization of Function,* Macmillan, New York, 1950, pp. 174-75; Wilder Penfield and Herbert Jasper, *Epilepsy and the Functional Anatomy of the Human Brain,* Little, Brown and Company, Boston, 1954, pp. 326-31; see also, Wilder Penfield and Theodore C. Erickson, *Epilepsy and Cerebral Localization: A Study of the Mechanism. Treatment and Prevention of Epileptic Seizures,* Charles C. Thomas, Springfield, Illinois, 1941, pp. 122-23, 261-65. The operation was a complete success, and G.A. grew up to be working full-time. Sixteen years after the operation, as the new edition of the Penfield and Jasper book was being completed, they were able to report that G.A. was married, had a family of children and had not had any major seizure—'Only the occasional tingling in her left arm reminds her of her former seizures.' Penfield and Jasper, op. cit., p. 329.
3. Wilder Penfield, 'The role of the temporal cortex in certain psychical phenomena', *The Journal of Mental Science,* July 1955, Volume 101, Number 424, pp. 451-65, at 458-60. This journal was later subsumed in *BJPsych, The British Journal of Psychiatry.*

4. The angular gyrus is located near the temporal lobe, and is implicated in processing sensory information pertaining to our bodies. Like other components of the brain, it is involved in a host of other functions also: speech, memory, processing auditory and tactile sensory inputs, etc.

5. Olaf Blanke, Stephanie Ortigue, Theodor Landis and Margitta Seeck, 'Stimulating Illusory Own-Body Perceptions: The Part of the Brain That Can Induce Out-of-body Experiences Has Been Located', *Nature*, Vol. 419, 19 September 2002, p. 269.

6. Olaf Blanke and Shahar Arzy, 'The Out-of-body Experience: Disturbed Self-processing at the Temporo-Parietal Junction', *Neuroscience Update*, 2005, Volume 11, Number 1, pp. 16-24.

7. On all this, A. Selimbeyoglu and J. Parvizi, 'Electrical Stimulation of the Brain: Perceptual and Behavioral Phenomena Reported in the Old and New Literature', *Frontiers in Human Neuroscience*, 2010; 4; 46; 1-11.

8. B. Lenggenhager, M. Mouthon and O. Blanke, 'Spatial aspects of bodily self-consciousness', *Consciousness and Cognition*, 2009, 18 (1), 110-17.

9. Ibid., p. 115.

10. Wilder Penfield and Phanor Perot, 'The Brain's Record of Auditory and Visual Experience: A Final Summary and Discussion', *Brain*, Volume 86, Part 4, December 1963, pp. 596-696.

11. Ibid., p. 635.

12. Ibid., pp. 637-38.

13. Persinger has written over 300 papers, and several among those who have worked with him have written several papers of their own about his work. The reader will get an adequate sampling of his ideas and experiments from his book, *The Neuropsychological Bases of God Beliefs*, 1987; M.A. Persinger, 'Religious and mystical experiences as artifacts of temporal lobe function: a general hypothesis', *Perceptual and Motor Skills*, 1983, 57, pp. 1255-62; M.A. Persinger, 'Vectorial cerebral hemisphericity as differential sources for the sensed presence, mystical experiences and religious conversions', *Perceptual and Motor Skills*, 1993, 76, pp. 915-30; as an example of what seems to be shooting and then drawing the bullseye where the bullet has hit the target, M.A. Persinger, 'The Sensed Presence Within Experimental Settings: Implications for Male and Female Concept of Self', *The Journal of Psychology*, 2003, 137(1), pp. 5-16; the reader will find a useful account of Persinger's work in a YouTube video by an associate of his who worked with him for years, Todd Murphy, www.jps.net/ brainsci/

14. The precise configuration of the fields that is generated, how the pattern for their pulsation is derived from the pattern in which the amygdala pulsates, how the coils are activated alternately, etc., are described in several publications of Persinger and his associates.

15. http://www.webofstories.com/play/susan.blackmore/13—Susan—Blackmore—Scientist—Michael Persinger and the God Helmet—Web of Stories.

16. Cf. vimeo.com/54557808—Persinger vs. Dawkins: the God Helmet on Vimeo.

17. Todd Murphy's Forum, 'Richard Dawkins—Alcohol and the God Helmet don't mix—Dr. M.A. Persinger's blog', Posted on 30 May 2015.

18. Jack Hitt, 'This Is Your Brain on God: Michael Persinger Has a Vision—The Almighty Isn't Dead, He's an Energy Field. And Your Mind Is an Electromagnetic Map To Your Soul', *Wired,* 1 November 1999.

19. P. Granqvist, M. Fredrikson, P. Unge, A. Hagenfeldt, S. Valind, D. Larhammar and M. Larsson, 'Sensed Presence and Mystical Experiences Are Predicted By Suggestibility, Not by Application of Transcranial Weak Complex Magnetic Fields', *Neuroscience Letters,* 2005, 379, 1-6, Elsevier, ScienceDirect.

20. L.S. St. Pierre, M.A. Persinger, 'Experimental Facilitation of the Sensed Presence Is Facilitated by the Specific Patterns of the Applied Magnetic Fields, Not by Suggestibility: Re-Analysis of 19 Experiments', *International Journal of Neuroscience,* 2006, Volume 116, pp. 1079-96.

21. M. Larsson, D. Larhammar, M. Fredrikson and P. Granqvist, 'Reply to M.A. Persinger and S.A. Koren's Response to Granqvist et al', *Neuroscience Letters,* 2005, Volume 380, pp. 348-50.

22. Shahar Arzy, Margitta Seeck, Stephaie Ortigue, Laurent Spinelli and Olaf Blanke, 'Induction of an Illusory Shadow Person', *Nature,* Vol. 443/21, September 2006, 'Brief Communications', p. 287.

9. SANGAT AND SUGGESTIBILITY

1. M.T. Orne, 'On the Social Psychology of the Psychological Experiment: With Particular Reference to Demand Characteristics and Their Implications', *American Psychologist,* 1962, Volume 17: pp. 776-83.

2. T.X. Barber and D.S. Calverley, 'An Experimental Study of "Hypnotic" (Auditory and Visual) Hallucinations', *Journal of Abnormal and Social Psychology,* 1964, Volume 68, Number 1, pp. 13-20.

3. R. Lange, J. Houran, Timothy M. Harte and R.A. Havens, 'Contextual Mediation of Perceptions in Hauntings and Poltergeist-like Experiences', *Perceptual and Motor Skills*, 1996, 82: pp. 755-62.

4. J. Houran and R. Lange, 'Diary of Events in a Thoroughly Unhaunted House', *Perceptual and Motor Skills*, 1996, 83, pp. 499-502.

5. R. Lange and J. Houran, 'Context Induced Paranormal Experiences: Support for Houran and Lange's Model of Haunting Phenomena', *Perceptual and Motor Skills*, 1997, 84: pp. 1455-58.

6. M.T. Orne, 'On the Social Psychology of the Psychological Experiment: With Particular Reference to Demand Characteristics and Their Implications', *American Psychologist*, 1962, 17, 776-83.

7. R. Lange and J. Houran, 'The Role of Fear in Delusions of the Paranormal', *The Journal of Nervous and Mental Disease*, 1999, 187 (3): pp. 159-66.

8. Of his numerous publications and TV shows, and videos on YouTube, *Paranormality: Why We See What Isn't There*, Pan Macmillan, London, 2011, is especially relevant to our current topic.

9. Richard Wiseman, Caroline Watt, Emma Greening, Paul Stevens and Ciaran O'Keefe, 'An Investigation into the Alleged Haunting of Hampton Court Palace: Psychological Variables and Magnetic Fields', *The Journal of Parapsychology*, 2002, 66: pp. 387-408.

10. Richard Wiseman, Caroline Watt, Paul Stevens, Emma Greening and Ciaran O'Keefe, 'An Investigation into Alleged "Hauntings"', *British Journal of Psychology*, 2003, 94: pp. 195-211.

11. For a telling report on this phenomenon, Tanya L. Chartrand and John A. Bargh, 'The Chameleon Effect: The Perception-Behavior Link and Social Interaction', *Journal of Personality and Social Psychology*, 1999, Volume 76, Number. 6, pp. 893-910.

12. Solomon E. Asch, 'Studies of Independence and Conformity: I. A Minority of One against a Unanimous Majority', *Psychological Monographs: General and Applied*, Volume 70, Number 9, Whole Number 416, 1956; pp. 1-70.

13. The experiment is perhaps the most famous one in sociology. It was replicated in 2009 in a less stringent form. Of the numerous writings on the experiment, see in particular Stanley Milgram, 'Behavioral study of obedience', *The Journal of Abnormal and Social Psychology*, Vol. 67, Number 4, 1963, pp. 371-78; Stanley Milgram, *Obedience to Authority*, Harper Perennial, New York, 1974. In the years that followed, numerous criticisms erupted. A major critical study was done by an Australian journalist: Gina Perry, *Behind the Shock Machine: The Untold Story of the Notorious Milgram Psychology Experiments*,

Scribe Books, New York, 2013. For a defence of Milgram and his work, T. Blass, *The Man Who Shocked the World: The Life and Legacy of Stanley Milgram*, Basic Books, New York, 2004, and the website that Blass runs; for a review, including that of Perry's critique, Augustine Brannigan, 'Stanley Milgram's Obedience Experiments: A Report Card 50 Years Later', Springer, Science+Business Media, New York, Published on-line, 9 October 2013, http://www.ucalgary.ca/justice/files/justice/brannigan_milgram_society2.pdf.

14. Stanley Milgram. *Obedience to Authority*, Harper Perennial, New York, 1974, p. 15.
15. Oscar Wilde, *The Picture of Dorian Gray*, 1891.
16. *Talks*, op. cit., Volume II, p. 277.
17. Ibid., pp. 290-91.
18. Ibid., pp. 369-70.
19. *Talks*, Volume III, pp. 439, 441.
20. Nagamma Suri, *Letters from Sri Ramanasramam*, Volumes I and II, and *Letters from and Recollections of Sri Ramanasramam*, D.S. Sastri (tr.), Sri Ramanasramam, Tiruvannamalai, Fifth revised edition, 2006, pp. 228-230.
21. A. Devaraja Mudaliar, *Day by Day With Bhagavan*, Sri Ramanasramam, Tiruvannamalai, 1952, 1989 edition, p. 13.

10. MIND>BRAIN>BODY>MIND>BRAIN>...

1. Three arresting books will suffice to introduce the subject, and will be of special interest to those who have to look after persons affected by brain injuries: Sharon Begley, *Train Your Mind, Change Your Brain: How a New Science Reveals Our Extraordinary Potential to Transform Ourselves*, Ballantine Books, New York, 2007; Norman Doidge, *The Brain that Changes Itself: Stories of Personal Triumph from the Frontiers of Brain Science*, Penguin, New York, 2007; and Norman Doidge, *The Brain's Way of Healing, Remarkable Discoveries and Recoveries from the Frontiers of Neuroplasticity*, Penguin, New York, 2015.
2. Donald O. Hebb, *The Organization of Behavior: A Neuropsychological Theory*, John Wiley, 1949, Kindle 2008.
3. Sharon Begley, *Train Your Mind, Change Your Brain*, p. 54.
4. Ibid., pp. 87-88.
5. R. Christopher DeCharms, K. Christoff, G.H. Glover, J.M. Pauly, S. Whitfield and J.D. Gabrieli, 'Learned Regulation of Spatially Localized Brain Activation Using Real-Time Functional MRI', *Neuroimage*, November 2004, 21, pp. 436-43.

6. R. Christopher DeCharms, Fumiko Maeda, Gary H. Glover, David Ludlow, John M. Pauly, Deepak Soneji, John D.E. Gabrieli and Sean C. Mackey, 'Control over Brain Activation and Pain Learned By Using Real-Time Functional MRI', *Proceedings of the National Academy of Sciences of the United States of America,* Vol. 102, No. 51, 20 December 2005, pp. 18626-31.

7. He got the Nobel Prize in 1972 for Medicine or Physiology.

8. Gerald M. Edelman and Giulio Tononi, *A Universe of Consciousness: How Matter Becomes Imagination*, Basic Books, 2000, p. 149.

9. For telling accounts of the effectiveness of hypnosis in treating a person with 'fish skin disease'—'a congenital disease appearing at birth or shortly thereafter in which a thick, black, horny layer of skin, inelastic and subject to painful lesions, covers part or even all of the body'—eczema, allergies, warts, and a range of other ailments, see, Mario Beauregard, *Brain Wars: The Scientific Battle over the Existence of the Mind and the Proof That Will Change the Way We Live Our Lives*, Harper One, New York, 2013, pp. 109-11; for several studies on the usefulness of hypnosis in treating a variety of ailments, see *The International Journal of Clinical and Experimental Hypnosis*.

10. Michael Grosso, Emily Williams Kelly, Edward F., Kelly, Adam Crabtree and Alan Gauld, *Irreducible Mind: Toward a Psychology for the 21st Century,* Rowman and Littlefield, New York, 2007, Kindle edition, loc. 4409, 4417, 44413, 4658-67, 4788, 4829, 4834, 4839, 4913-15, 4918.

11. Laurence Buelens, 'My Voice Goes with You', research.eu, April 2010, No. 63, pp. 26-29. As illustrations of evidence of the use and effectiveness of hypnosis in a variety of procedures, see, for instance, S.A. Lambert, F.P. Bolton, 'The Effects of Hypnosis/Guided Imagery on the Postoperative Course of Children', *Journal of Developmental and Behavioural Pediatrics*, October 1996, Volume 17, Number 5, pp. 307-10; M. Meurisse, E. Hamoir, et al., 'Bilateral Neck Exploration Under Hypnosedation: A New Standard of Care in Primary Hyperthyroidism?', *Annals of Surgery,* March 1999, Volume 229, Number 3, pp. 401-08; M.H. Mauer, K.F. Burnett, et al., 'Medical Hypnosis and Orthopedic Hand Surgery: Pain Perception, Post-Operative Recovery and Therapeutic Comfort', *Journal of Clinical and Experimental Hypnosis*, April 1999, Volume 47, Number 2, pp. 144-61—an especially interesting contribution as those undergoing hand surgery often feel a great deal of pain in the days following the operation; E.V. Lang, E.G. Benotsch, L.J. Fick, S. Lutgendorf, M.L. Berbaum, K.S. Berbaum, H. Logan and D. Spiegel, 'Adjunctive

Non-Pharmacological Analgesia for Invasive Medical Procedures: A Randomized Trial', *The Lancet*, April 2000, Volume 355, pp. 1486-90. For two accounts in the popular press: Michael Waldholz, 'Altered States: Hypnosis in Mainstream Medicine', *The Wall Street Journal*, 7 October 2003; Lesley Alderman, 'Using Hypnosis to Gain More Control Over Your Illness', *The New York Times*, 15 April 2011.

12. The precise manner in which the effect—for instance, in the lowered perception of pain—is accomplished and which components of the brain, and which neurotransmitters play a decisive role in securing the result remain as yet open questions: some argue that changes in brain activity prevent information about pain from reaching the higher cortical areas which are responsible for perceiving pain; others that hypnosis activates the downward pain-inhibiting paths. See for instance, Laurence Buelens, 'My Voice Goes with You', research. eu, April 2010, No. 63, pp. 26-29, cited earlier; and in particular the informative review article by A. Vanhaudenhuyse, S. Laureys and M.E. Faymonville, 'Neurophysiology of Hypnosis', *Clinical Neurophysiology,* October 2014, Volume 44, Number 44, pp. 343-53.

13. L.A. Cobb, G.I. Thomas, D.H. Dillard, K.A. Merendino and R.A. Bruce, 'An Evaluation of Internal-Mammary-Artery Ligation By a Double-Blind Technic', *New England Journal of Medicine*, May, 1959, Volume 260, Number 22, pp. 1115-18. During a discussion about the trend in hospitals to order unnecessary tests and even operations, a leading physician drew my attention to the fate of this procedure as well as the one relating to the knee that is considered next. I later saw that the procedures and how they had proved no better than sham surgeries had been mentioned in passing by others also, for instance, by Joe Dispenza in his books.

14. E.G. Dimond, F. Kittle and J. Crockett, 'Comparison of Internal Mammary Artery Ligation and Sham Operation for Angina Pectoris', *The American Journal of Cardiology*, April 1960, pp. 483-86.

15. J.B. Moseley, K. O'Malley, N.J. Petersen, T.J. Menke, B.A. Brody, D.H. Kuykendall, J.C. Hollingsworth, C.M. Ashton and N.P. Wray, 'A Controlled Trial of Arthroscopic Surgery for Osteoarthritis Of The Knee', *The New England Journal of Medicine*, July 2002, Volume 347, Number 2, pp. 81-88.

16. Alexandra Kirkley, Trevor B. Birmingham, Robert B. Litchfield, J. Robert Giffin, Kevin R. Willits, Cindy J. Wong, Brian G. Feagan, Allan Donner, Sharon H. Griffin, Linda M. D'Ascanio, Janet E. Pope and Peter J. Fowler, 'A Randomized Trial of Arthroscopic Surgery for

Osteoarthritis of the Knee', *The New England Journal of Medicine*, September 2008, Volume 359, Number 11, pp. 1097-1107.

17. The Western Ontario and McMaster Universities Osteoarthritis Index: WOMAC.

18. R. Sihvonen, M. Paavola, A. Malmivaara, A. Itälä, A. Joukainen, H. Nurmi, J. Kalske and T.L.N. Järvinen, 'Arthroscopic Partial Menidectomy Versus Sham Surgery for a Degenerative Meniscal Tear', *The New England Journal of Medicine*, December 2013, Volume 369, Number 26, pp. 2515-24.

19. C.R. Freed, R.E. Breeze, N.L. Rosenberg, S.A. Schneck, E. Kriek, Jianxin Qi, T. Lone, Ying-bei Zhang, J.A. Snyder, T.H. Wells, L.O. Ramig, L. Thompson, J.C. Mazziotta, S.C. Huang, S.T. Grafton, D. Brooks, G. Sawle, G. Schroter and A.A. Ansari, 'Survival of Implanted Fetal Dopamine Cells and Neurologic Improvement 12 to 46 Months After Transplantation for Parkinson's Disease', *The New England Journal of Medicine,* Volume 327, Number 22, November 1992, pp. 1549-54.

20. C.R. Freed, P.E. Greene, R.E. Breeze, Wei-Yann Tsai, W. DuMouchel, R. Kao, S. Dillon, H. Winfield, S. Culver, J.Q. Trojanowski, D. Eidelberg and S. Fahn, 'Transplantation of Embryonic Dopamine Neurons for Severe Parkinson's Disease', *The New England Journal of Medicine*, March 2001, Volume 344, Number 10, pp. 710-19.

21. On the foregoing, Gina Kolata, 'Parkinson's Research Is Set Back by Failure of Fetal Cell Implants', *The New York Times*, 8 March 2001.

22. For the following, C.W. Olanow, C.G. Goetz, J.H. Kordower, A.J. Stoessl, V. Sossi, M.F. Brin, K.M. Shannon, G.M. Nauert, D.P. Perl, J. Godbold and T.B. Freeman, 'A Double-Blind Controlled Trial of Bilateral Fetal Nigral Transplantation in Parkinson's Disease', *Annals of Neurology*, September 2003, Volume 54, Number 3, pp. 403-14.

23. For the following, C. McRae, E. Cherin, T.G. Yamazaki, G. Diem, A.H. Vo, D. Russell, J.H. Ellring, S. Fahn, P. Greene, S. Dillon, H. Winfield, K.B. Bjugstad and C.R. Freed, 'Effects of Perceived Treatment on Quality of Life and Medical Outcomes in a Double-Blind Placebo Surgery Trial', *Archives of General Psychiatry*, Volume 61, April 2004, pp. 412-20; and corrigendum, *Archives of General Psychiatry*, Volume 61, June 2004, p. 627.

24. See, for example, F. Benedetti, C. Arduino, S. Costa, S. Vighetti, L. Tarenzi, I. Rainero and G. Asteggiano, 'Loss of Expectation-related Mechanisms in Alzheimer's Disease Makes Analgesic Therapies Less Effective', *Pain,* 2006, Volume 121, pp. 133-44. The study (of twenty-eight patients with Alzheimer's disease) showed that the placebo effect in alleviating pain was indeed reduced; in addition, that the

effect was reduced not so much by global cognitive impairment as by the pattern of impaired connectivity: the placebo effect was especially weak in the case of patients in whom connectivity of the prefrontal lobes was reduced, and thereby the communication of the placebo and the expectations from the prefrontal lobes to the rest of the brain would be lessened.

25. A. Katsnelson, 'Experimental Therapies for Parkinson's Disease: Why Fake It?', *Nature*, 2011, Volume 476, Issue 7359, pp. 142-44. She cites two instances of cell implants that were abandoned because the effects did not differ significantly from those of sham surgery, although the persons who had received the implants continued to be better long after the implants.

26. For one such exercise which sought to identify the brain network modulations that are particularly differentiable in the case of placebo-susceptible persons, J.H. Ko, A. Feigin, P.J. Mattis, C.C. Tang, Y. Ma, V. Dhawan, M.J. During, M.G. Kaplitt and D. Eidelberg, 'Network Modulation Following Sham Surgery in Parkinson's Disease', *The Journal of Clinical Investigation*, July 2014, Volume 124, Number 8, pp. 3656-66.

27. For instance, Penelope J. Hallett, Oliver Cooper, Damaso Sadi, Harold Robertson, Ivar Mendez and Ole Isacson, 'Long-term Health of Dopaminergic Neuron Transplants in Parkinson's Disease Patients', *Cell Reports*, June 2014, Volume 7, Number 6, pp. 1755-61.

28. J.H. Ko, A. Feigin, et al., op. cit.

29. B. Klopfer, 'Psychological Variables in Human Cancer', *Journal of Projective Techniques*, Volume 21, Number 4, December 1957, pp. 331-40.

30. The sequence narrated originally by Klopfer is cited often: see, for instance, Norman Doidge, *The Brain's Way of Healing: Stories of Remarkable Recoveries and Discoveries*, op. cit.; Joe Dispenza, *You Are the Placebo: Making Your Mind Matter*, Hay House, 2014.

31. Bruno Klopfer, op. cit., pp. 337-39.

32. Luana Colloca, Leonardo Lopiano, Michele Lanotte and Fabrizio Benedetti, 'Overt Versus Covert Treatment for Pain, Anxiety, and Parkinson's Disease', *The Lancet, Neurology*, November 2004, Volume 3, Number 11, pp. 679-84.

33. A path-breaking study in 2001 uncovered the surprising fact that it is not just the placebo, but in addition *the expectation of improvement*, independently of the actual improvement, that triggers the brain to release more of its own dopamine into the striatum of the Parkinson's patients—the area that consists of the caudate and the putamen;

these together provide inputs into the basal ganglia which, through its connections with other parts of the brain—the frontal lobe, the extra-pyramidal motor system—is partly responsible for initiating movement and modulating it, and it is in the synapses of this network, among others, that dopamine levels fall among Parkinson's patients: more endogenous dopamine was released precisely in the synapses of the damaged nigrostratial dopamine system. (Cf. R. de la Fuente-Fernandez, T.J. Ruth, V. Sossi, M. Schulzer, D.B. Calne and A.J. Stoessl, 'Expectation and Dopamine Release Mechanism of the Placebo Effect in Parkinson's Disease', *Science*, 2001, 293: 1164-66.) A study by Wager and colleagues indicated how in response to pain and the anticipation of pain, activity in two regions of the brain— one that actually processes pain, and one that evaluates inputs—was correlated. Furthermore, it showed that anticipation of pain triggered opioid release in the midbrain. And, finally, that *different* regions of the brain became active as the pain advanced: from anticipation of pain activating potentially opioid-containing regions of the midbrain, to the anterior cingulate showing lowered responses early in the pain, and then the contralateral thalamus and insula showing decreases only after the pain had persisted for a while. (T.D. Wager, J.K. Rilling, E.E. Smith, A. Sokolik, K.L. Casey, R.J. Davidson, S.M. Kosslyn, R.M. Rose, and J.D. Cohen, 'Placebo Induced Changes in fMRI in the Anticipation and Experience of Pain', *Science*, 2004, 303, pp. 1162-67.) Similarly, palpable differences have been observed between patients with good and bad motor performance as the stimulus to the subthalamic nucleus has been decreased or increased and they were primed to expect worsening or improvement of motor performance. (A. Pollo, E. Torre, L. Lopiano, M. Rizzone, M. Lanotte, A. Cavanna, B. Bergamasco and F. Benedetti, 'Expectation Modulates the Response to Subthalamic Nucleus Stimulation in Parkinsonian Patients', *Neuro Report*, 2002, Volume 13, pp. 1383-86.) Activity levels even at the level of individual neurons differ depending on whether the patients are or are not susceptible to the placebo effect. (F. Beneditti, L. Colloca, E. Torre, M. Lanotte, A. Melcarne, M. Pesare, B. Bergamasco, and L. Lopiano, 'Placebo-responsive Parkinson's Patients Show Decreased Activity in Single Neurons of Subthalamic Nucleus', *Nature Neuroscience*, 2004, Volume 7, pp. 587-88.) On all this see the instructive review piece by Mario Beauregard, 'Effect of mind on brain activity: Evidence from neuroimaging studies of psychotherapy and placebo effect', *Nordic Journal of Psychiatry*, 2009, 63: pp. 5-16, which led me to the preceding articles, and from which the extremely abbreviated account in the text has been given.

34. Norman Doidge, *The Brain's Way of Healing*, op. cit., Chapter 2.

35. *The Master*, op. cit., pp. 253-54.

36. Ibid., p. 332. As we have noticed earlier, there were a few other incidental explanations also for the cancer, including a curse by his brother many, many years earlier; however, this—the taking on the ill-karma of others—was the most prominent one.

37. Ibid., pp. 332-33.

11. 'A God-realised man behaves sometimes like a madman...'

1. *The Gospel*, op. cit., p. 115.

2. Ibid., p. 294.

3. Commission on Definitions and Classifications of the International League Against Epilepsy, 'Proposal for Revised Clinical and Electroencephalographic Classification of Epileptic Seizures', *Epilepsia*, 1981, 22, pp. 489-501.

4. *The Master*, op. cit., pp. 310-11.

5. On the foregoing, in addition to the 1981 Report of the Commission on Definitions and Classifications of the International League Against Epilepsy cited earlier, see the informative paper by Chrysostomos P. Panayiotopoulos, 'Typical Absence Seizures and Related Epileptic Syndromes: An Assessment of Current State and Directions for Research', *Epilepsia*, 2008, 49 (12), pp. 2131-42; and the simple descriptions on websites of the Mayo Clinic and similar organizations.

6. For the foregoing, *Epilepsia*, 1981, 22, pp. 489-501, at pp. 496-97.

7. Fyodor Mikhailovich Dostoyevsky, *The Idiot*, trans. Eva Martin, 1868, http://www.gutenberg.org, pp. 208-11.

8. For the following, see the various and overlapping papers of one of the principal researchers into ecstatic seizures, Fabienne Picard, Department of Neurology, University Hospital and Medical School of Geneva, and A.D. Craig of the Barrow Neurological Institute, Phoenix, Arizona. In particular, Bjorn Asheim Hansen and Eylert Brodtkorb, 'Partial Epilepsy with "Ecstatic" Seizures', *Epilepsy and Behavior*, 2003, Volume 4, pp. 667-73; A.D. Craig, 'How Do You Feel—Now? The Anterior Insula and Human Awareness', *Nature Reviews/Neuroscience*, 2009, Volume 10, pp. 59-70; Fabienne Picard and A.D. Craig, 'Ecstatic Epileptic Seizures: A Potential Window on the Neural Basis for Human Self-Awareness', *Epilepsy and Behavior*, 2009, Volume 16, pp. 539-46; Fabienne Picard and Florian Kurth, 'Ictal Alterations of Consciousness During Ecstatic Seizures', *Epilepsy*

and Behavior, 2014, Volume 30, pp. 58-61; Markus Gschwind and Fabienne Picard, 'Ecstatic Epileptic Seizures: A Glimpse into the Multiple Roles of the Insula', *Frontiers in Behavioral Neuroscience*, 2016, Volume 10, published online 17 February 2016. As an example of an earlier study that traced such seizures also to the temporal lobe, see F. Cirignotta, C.V. Todesco and E. Lugaresi, 'Temporal Lobe Epilepsy with Ecstatic Seizures (So-called Dostoyevsky Epilepsy)', *Epilepsia*, 1980, Volume 21, pp. 705-10.

9. In their 2013 paper, Picard and Kurth added accounts of two more patients to those of these five. Those two reinforced evidence along the same lines: c.f., Picard and Kurth, op. cit.

10. Picard and Craig, op. cit., p. 540.

11. Ibid., p. 541.

12. Hansen and Brodtkorb, op. cit., p. 672.

13. Gschwind and Picard (2016), op. cit., pp. 88-89.

14. Hansen and Brodtkorb, op. cit., p. 671.

15. Ibid., pp. 669, 671; Gschwind and Picard, op. cit., p. 89.

16. Gschwind and Picard, op. cit.

17. Hansen and Brodtkorb, op. cit., pp. 668, 669, 671; Gschwind and Picard, on-line 2016, op. cit.

18. Gschwind and Picard, *Epileptologie*, 2014, 31, pp. 90-92.

19. *The Gospel*, op., cit., pp. 205, 405; and passim.

20. *The Master*, op. cit., pp. 541-43.

12. THE SELF IN THE HEART

1. *Talks*, op. cit., p. 271.

2. Ibid., pp. 201-02.

3. Ibid., p. 6.

4. Ibid., pp. 269-70.

5. Ibid., pp. 376-77.

6. Ibid., p. 579.

7. Ibid., p. 478.

8. Ibid., pp. 22-23.

9. Ibid., p. 55.

10. Ibid., p. 174.

11. Ibid., p. 201.

12. Ibid., p. 210.

13. Ibid., p. 377.

14. Ibid., p. 576.

15. Ibid., p. 579.

16. Arthur Osborne, *The Collected Works of Sri Ramana Maharshi*, Sri Ramanasramam, Tiruvannamalai, 1979, pp. 57.
17. Ibid., p. 58.
18. Ibid., 64.
19. Ibid., p. 92-93.
20. Ibid., p. 94.
21. Ibid., p. 216-17.
22. Ibid., p. 367.
23. Ibid., p. 126.
24. Ibid., p. 2. Sri Ramana cited the slokas in his pithy work *Reality in Forty Verses*. The two slokas in the Malayalam work *Ashtanga Hridayam* are: 'Between the two paps, below the chest, above the stomach, there are six organs of various colours. Of these, one, looking like a lily bud, is the Heart, at two digits' distance to the right of the centre ... Its mouth is closed. Within its cavity is seated a heavy darkness, filled with all desires; all the great nerves are centred there; the home it is of breath, mind, light of knowledge.' Ibid., pp. 125-26.
25. His biography by Narasimha Swami to which we have turned on several occasions earlier.
26. *Talks*, p. 383.
27. Ibid., p. 93.
28. Ibid., p. 403.
29. Ibid., p. 539.
30. Tiziano Terzani, *One More Ride on the Merry-go-Round*, Harper Element, NOIDA, UP, 2016, p. 83.
31. *Talks*, pp. 33-34.
32. Ibid., pp. 358-60.
33. Ibid., p. 451.
34. Ibid., p. 488.
35. Ibid., pp. 198-99, 468, 531; only a few of the many citations that can be given are cited for illustrative purposes.
36. Ibid., pp. 98, 274-75.
37. Ibid., pp. 270-71.
38. Ibid., p. 217.
39. Ibid., pp. 198, 319-20, 478.
40. Ibid., p. 265.
41. Ibid., pp. 196-97.
42. Ibid., pp. 79, 271.
43. Ibid., pp. 268-69.
44. Ibid., pp. 5-6.
45. Ibid., pp. 8-9; the sequence is set out on several occasions, see, for instance, Ibid., pp. 51, 79.

46. Ibid., pp. 561-66. As the same sorts of questions are asked again and again, Sri Ramana explains the distinction between the three states many times over—that one entity alone subsists in each of them, that the way to apprehend that one reality is 'Self-inquiry', for instance, Ibid., pp. 270-71.

47. Ibid., p. 275.

48. The conditions are well-known, and are often mentioned. For instance, they are listed—in a different context—by Evan Thompson, *Waking, Dreaming, Being: Self and Consciousness in Neuroscience, Meditation, and Philosophy*, Columbia University Press, New York, 2015, Kindle, loc. 3953.

49. Bruce Hood, *The Self Illusion: Who Do You Think You Are?*, Constable, London, 2011, pp. 4, 7.

50. Douglas Hofstadter, *I Am a Strange Loop*, Basic Books, New York, 2007.

51. Ibid., p.102.

52. Diane Ackerman, *An Alchemy of Mind: The Marvel and Mystery of the Brain*, Scribner, New York, 2004, p. 136.

53. Bruce Hood, *The Self Illusion*, p. 21.

54. Ibid., p. 59.

55. Olaf Blanke, 'Out-of-body experiences, consciousness and cognitive neuroprosthetics', TED Talks, YouTube, 2013.

56. As on other questions, the literature on these and related issues is vast. The reader will find four accounts to be as arresting as they are instructive: Douglas Hofstadter, *I Am a Strange Loop*; Michael S. Gazzaniga, *Who's In Charge? Free Will and the Science of the Brain*, Ecco, HarperCollins, New York, 2011; Bruce Hood, *The Self Illusion: Who Do You Think You Are?*; and Antonio Domassio, *Self Comes to Mind: Constructing the Conscious Brain*, William Heinemann, London, 2010.

57. Mark Johnston, *Surviving Death*, Princeton University Press, New Jersey, 2010.

58. Ibid., pp. 14-15, 49.

59. Ibid., pp. 139-40.

60. A.D. Craig, 'How Do You Feel—Now? The Anterior Insula and Human Awareness', *Nature Reviews/Neuroscience*, January 2009, Volume 10, pp. 59-70. The hypothesis and the evidence in support of it have been elaborated in subsequent papers by Craig, Fabienne Picard and Markus Gschwind. In addition to Craig's paper, see Fabienne Picard and A.D. Craig, 'Ecstatic Epileptic Seizures: A Potential Window on the Neural Basis for Human Self-Awareness',

Epilepsy and Behavior, 2009, Volume 16, pp. 539-46; Fabienne Picard, 'State of Belief, Subjective Certainty and Bliss as a Product of Cortical Dysfunction', *Cortex*, 2013, Volume 49, pp. 2494-500; Fabienne Picard and Florian Kurth, 'Ictal Alterations of Consciousness During Ecstatic Seizures', *Epilepsy and Behavior*, 2014, Volume 30, pp. 58-61; Markus Gschwind and Fabienne Picard, 'Ecstatic Epileptic Seizures: A Glimpse into the Multiple Roles of the Insula', *Frontiers in Behavioral Neuroscience*, 2016, Volume 10, published online 17 February 2016.

61. A.D. Craig, op. cit., p. 65.
62. Ibid., p. 67.
63. Ibid., p. 68.
64. For the following, see Fabienne Picard, 'State of Belief, Subjective Certainty and Bliss as a Product of Cortical Dysfunction', *Cortex*, 2013, Volume 49, pp. 2494-2500. Published online, 23 January 2013.
65. Ibid., p. 2495.
66. Ibid., p. 2496.
67. On the preceding, ibid., pp. 2494-2500.

13. But what about consciousness?

1. Wilder Penfield, *The Mystery of the Mind: A Critical Study of Consciousness and the Human Brain,* Princeton University Press, New Jersey, 1975. The position runs through the book; the specific sentences used in the text are from pages 62-63, 79, 81, 103, 113.
2. In Susan J. Blackmore, *Conversations on Consciousness*, OUP, New York, 2005, Kindle edition, loc. 3782-855; also loc. 2566 for Hameroff's account of the basic notions and how he and Penrose came upon the thesis.
3. Evan Thompson, *Waking, Dreaming, Being: Self and Consciousness in Neuroscience, Meditation, and Philosophy,* Columbia University Press, New York, 2015, Kindle edition, loc., 1763, 2212, 2268-69.
4. Mario Beauregard, *Brain Wars: The Scientific Battle over the Existence of the Mind and the Proof that Will Change the Way We Live Our Lives,* Harper One, New York, 2013, p. 10.
5. Several contributions to *The Oxford Handbook of Psychology and Spirituality*, Lisa J. Miller (ed.), Oxford, 2012, approximate this position; for instance, Gary E. Schwartz, 'Consciousness, Spirituality, and Postmaterialist Science: An Empirical and Experiential Approach', at pp. 584-97.

6. 'Hz': Hertz—that is, cycles per second.
7. Paul Churchland in Susan J. Blackmore, *Conversations on Consciousness*, op. cit., loc. 1157.
8. Tara Subramaniam's summary of research by Japanese and Russian scientists, *The Indian Express*, 10 July 2016, p. 16.
9. In India we remember the discoveries of Sir J.C. Bose. And most of us would have read Peter Tompkins and Christopher Bird, *The Secret Life of Plants*, Perennial Library, 1989. For a brief and interesting summary of the research bearing on trees, Anil Ananthaswamy, 'Roots of Consciousness', *New Scientist*, 6 December 2014, pp. 34-37.
10. Atsushi Tero, Seiji Takagi, Tetsu Saigusa, Kentaro Ito, Dan P. Bebber, Mark D. Fricker, Kenji Yumiki, Ryo Kobayashi and Toshiyuki Nakagaki, 'Rules for Biologically Inspired Adaptive Network Design', www.sciencemag.org, *Science*, Volume, 327, 22 January 2010.
11. Toshiyuki Nakagaki, Hiroyasu Yamada and Agota Toth, 'Maze-solving by an Amoeboid Organism', *Nature*, Volume 407, 28 September 2000, p. 470, www.nature.com.
12. Andrew Adamatzky and Jeff Jones, 'Road Planning with Slime Mould: If Physarum Built Motorways It Would Route M6/M74 through Newcastle', arXiv:0912.3967[nlin.PS]
13. As one of numerous examples that are just a click away, see 'Battle at Krueger Park', http://www.youtube.com/watch?v=LUDDY68kM
14. Gerald M. Edelman and Giulio Tononi, *A Universe of Consciousness: How Matter Becomes Imagination*, Basic Books, New York, 2000, p. 38.
15. Diane Ackerman, *An Alchemy of Mind: The Marvel and Mystery of the Brain*, Scribner, New York, 2004, p. 41.
16. Patricia S. Churchland, *Touching a Nerve: Our Brains, Our Selves*, W.W. Norton, New York, 2013, p. 235.
17. Glial cells were long neglected because neuroscientists were relying on electrodes to record electrical signals, and glial cells do their work—including listening in to what neurons are signalling and extensive communication among themselves—without emitting electrical signals. For a glimpse into the many functions they execute, see R. Douglas Fields, *The Other Brain: The Scientific and Medical Breakthroughs That Will Heal Our Brains and Revolutionize Our Health*, Simon and Schuster Paperbacks, New York, 2009.
18. Edelman developed the proposition in several elegant books such as *Wider Than the Sky: The Phenomenal Gift of Consciousness*, Yale University Press, 2004; and *Second Nature: Brain Science and*

Human Knowledge, Yale University Press, 2006. The sentences in the text are from Gerald M. Edelman and Giulio Tononi, *A Universe of Consciousness: How Matter Becomes Imagination*, Basic Books, New York, 2000, pp. 44-45.

19. Stanislas Dehaene, Claire Sergent and Jean-Pierre Changeux, 'A Neuronal Network Model Linking Subjective Reports and Objective Physiological Data During Conscious Perception', *Proceedings of the National Academy of Sciences*, 2003, 100, pp. 8520-25.

20. Stanislas Dehaene, *Consciousness and the Brain: Deciphering How the Brain Codes Our Thoughts*, Viking, New York, 2014.

21. Ibid., p. 124.

22. Wilder Penfield, *The Mystery of the Mind: A Critical Study of Consciousness and the Human Brain*, Princeton University Press, New Jersey, 1975, pp. 38, 47-48, 56, 63-64, 83.

23. *New Scientist*, 20/27 December 2014, p. 33.

24. Patricia S. Churchland, *Touching a Nerve: Our Brains, Our Selves*, W.W. Norton, New York, 2014, pp. 234-36.

25. They observe, inter alia, '...thalamic activity does not decrease with all anesthetics. Ketamine increases global metabolism, especially in the thalamus ... Other anesthetics can significantly reduce thalamic activity at doses that cause sedation, not unconsciousness ... the metabolic and electrophysiological effects of anesthetics on the thalamus of animals are abolished by the removal of the cortex ... By contrast, after thalamic ablation, the cortex still produces an activated EEG, ... suggesting that the thalamus is not the sole mediator of cortical arousal, nor perhaps is it the most direct one. In patients with implanted brain electrodes undergoing a second surgery to place a deep brain stimulator, the cortical EEG changed dramatically the instant the patients lost consciousness ... However, there was little change in thalamic EEG activity until 10 minutes later. Conversely, in epileptic patients, during REM sleep (usually associated with dreaming) the cortical EEG was activated as if awake, but the thalamic EEG showed slow wave activity as if asleep ... Thus, the effects of anesthetics on the thalamus effect may represent a readout of global cortical activity rather than a consciousness switch, and thalamic activity may not be a sufficient basis for consciousness.' Michael T. Alkire, Anthony G. Hudetz, and Giulio Tononi, 'Consciousness and Anesthesia', *Science*, 7 November 2008; 322 (5903), pp. 876–880.

26. Ibid.

27. D.B. Fischer, A.D. Boes, A. Demertzi, H.C. Evrard, S. Laureys, B.L. Edlow, H. Liu, C.B. Saper, A. Pascual-Leone, M.D. Fox and

J.C. Geerling, 'A Human Brain Network Derived from Coma-Causing Brainstem Lesions', *Neurology* 87, 4 November 2016. The paper describes in addition several other findings. For instance, unexpectedly the scientists found that 'this arousal-promoting brainstem region was relatively left-lateralized'. 'This finding,' they noted, 'runs counter to conventional wisdom that a lesion must destroy midline or bilateral brainstem tissue to impair consciousness'; therefore, while listing several possible reasons for left-laterization, they suggested that the finding 'should be interpreted with caution and requires replication in larger cohorts'.

28. Daniel Dennett, 'Cycles', in John Brockman, (ed.), *This Will Make You Smarter,* Harper Perennial, New York, 2012, pp. 170-73.

14. THE PENULTIMATE PROOF?

1. By now even the published accounts run into hundreds. Two volumes will suffice as they bring together many accounts and cull out elements and patterns, and give an overview of the subject from the point of view of those who believe that these experiences testify to something beyond our mundane life: Janice Miner Holden, Bruce Greyson and Debbie James (eds), *The Handbook of Near-death Experiences: Thirty years of Investigation*, Praeger, Santa Barbara, CA, 2009; and P.M.H. Atwater, *The Big Book of Near-death Experiences: The Ultimate Guide to What Happens When We Die*, Hampton Roads, Charlottesville, VA, 2007.

2. Satwant Pasricha and Ian Stevenson, 'Near-death Experiences in India, A Preliminary Report', *The Journal of Nervous and Mental Disease*, 1986, Volume 174, Number 3, pp. 165-70.

3. For a study that strained to show that NDEs of Indians had all the standard features, in particular the tunnel and bright light, see the discussion below about Susan Blackmore's paper, 'Near-death Experiences in India: They Have Tunnels Too', *Journal of Near-Death Studies,* Summer 1993, Volume 11, Number 4, pp. 205-17.

4. A.J. Ayer, 'What I Saw When I Was Dead', *Sunday Telegraph,* 28 August 1988. See also, the 'Postscript to a postmortem' he wrote a few months later: http://archive.spectator.co.uk/article/15th-october-1988/13/postscript-to-a-postmortem.

5. Michael B. Sabom, *Light and Death: One Doctor's Fascinating Account of Near-Death Experiences*, Zondervan, Grand Rapids, MI, 1998.

6. Michael T. Alkire, Anthony G. Hudetz and Giulio Tononi, 'Consciousness and Anesthesia', *Science*, 7 November 2008, Volume 322, Number 5903, pp. 876-80. That the auditory awareness of a patient may still be present under anaesthesia and that this may enable him to gather what is being said during the period is commented upon often by scholars examining NDEs. For instance, Michael N. Marsh, *Out-of-Body and Near-Death Experiences: Brain-state Phenomena or Glimpses of Immortality?*, OUP, Oxford, 2010, p. 31-32.

7. Nicholas D. Schiff, et al., 'Residual Cerebral Activity and Behavioural Fragments Can Remain in the Persistently Vegetative Brain', *Brain*, 2002, 125, pp. 1210-34.

8. Adrian M. Owen, Martin R. Coleman, Melaine Boly, Mathew H. Davis, Steven Laureys, John D. Pickard, 'Detecting Awareness in the Vegetative State', *Science*, Volume 313, 8 September 2006, p. 1402.

9. For events preceding and following this set of experiments, see David Cyranoski, 'Neuroscience: The Mind Reader', *Nature*, 13 June 2012, http://www.nature.com/news/neuroscience-the-mind-reader-1.10816; and Roger Highfield, 'Reading the Minds of the "Dead"', *Mosaic@ Future*, BBC, 22 April 2014.

10. Among the latter, the following are indeed worth reading: G.M. Woerlee, 'An Anaesthesiologist Examines the Pam Reynolds Story', *The Skeptic*, 2005, Volume 18, Numbers 1-2; 'Could Pam Reynolds Hear?', *Journal of Near-Death Studies*, Vol. 30, pp. 3-25; 'Pam Reynolds Near Death Experience', http://neardth.com/pam-reynolds-near-death-experience.php; accessed on 27 July 2016; Michael N. Marsh, *Out-of-Body and Near-Death Experiences: Brain-state Phenomena or Glimpses of Immortality?*, OUP, New York, 2010 [Kindle edition, pp. 19-26]; and Evan Thompson, *Waking, Dreaming, Being: Self and Consciousness in Neuroscience, Meditation, and Philosophy*, Columbia University Press, New York, 2015, Kindle edition. These bring together many of the doubts listed in the text.

11. Evan Thompson, op. cit., loc. 6347.

12. Ibid., loc. 6367-70.

13. S. Pasricha and I. Stevenson, 'Near-death experiences in India: A preliminary report', *Journal of Nervous and Mental Diseases*, March 1986, Volume 174, Number 3, pp. 165-70.

14. Cf. 'Eleven Thai near-death experiences', https://www.shaktitechnology.com/bkknde.htm. Retrieved 5 August 2016.

15. A few studies set out accounts of Japanese NDEs. A two-volume compilation of 243 such accounts is also available, though I have not been able to obtain an English translation. For purposes of the next

few paragraphs, just one review will suffice: Masayuki Ohkado and Bruce Greyson, 'A Comparative Analysis of Japanese and Western NDEs', *Journal of Near-death Studies*, Summer 2014, Volume 32, Number 4, pp. 187-98. This paper is based on accounts of twenty-two people. These were intensively interviewed by an intrepid journalist, Tachibana Takashi, who also authored the two-volume study. Ohkado and Greyson noted that Tachibana had acknowledged that of the 243 cases recorded in the two-volume study, he had investigated only fifteen in detail.

16.   As noted earlier, the foregoing is based on Ohkado and Greyson, op. cit.

17.   Geena K. Athappilly, Bruce Greyson and Ian Stevenson, 'Do Prevailing Societal Models Influence Reports of Near-Death Experiences? A Comparison of Accounts Reported Before And After 1975', *The Journal of Nervous and Mental Disease*, Volume 194, Number 3, March 2006. Bruce Greyson devised the sixteen-point questionnaire that is used to determine whether or not an experience is an NDE. Ian Stevenson wrote the well-known book, *21 Cases Suggestive of Reincarnation*.

18.   *The Journal of Nervous and Mental Disease*, 1993, Vol. 181, 148-56.

19.   It isn't altogether surprising that a participant in the debate like Bruce Greyson treats the absence of some elements—in this case, life review or panoramic memory—in disparate ways in two different papers: he pointed to the absence of a life review to discount the similarities between NDEs and the experiences in G-LOC of Whinnery's subjects; and in his paper with Ohkado, he explained away the absence of life review among the Japanese by attributing it to their having forsaken religion! Contrast, Bruce Greyson, 'Near-death experiences: clinical implications', *Review of Clinical Psychiatry,* Sao Paulo, 2007, Volume 34, Supplement 1, and the joint paper with Ohkado.

20.   Satwant Pasricha and Ian Stevenson, 'Near-death Experiences in India: A Preliminary Report', *Journal of Nervous and Mental Disease*, 1986, Volume 174, Number 3, pp. 165-70, at p. 169.

21.   Ibid.

22.   Susan J. Blackmore, 'Near-death Experiences in India: They Have Tunnels Too', *Journal of Near-Death Studies*, Volume 11, Number 4, Summer 1993, pp. 205-17.

23.   Susan J. Blackmore, *Dying to Live: Science and the Near-death Experience*, London: Grafton. 1993.

24.   Susan J. Blackmore, 'Near-death Experiences in India: They Have Tunnels Too', op. cit., pp. 206, 207.

25. Ibid., p. 210.
26. Ibid., p. 216.
27. Allan Kellehear, Ian Stevenson, Satwant Pasricha and Emily Cook, 'The Absence of Tunnel Sensations in Near-death Experiences from India', *Journal of Near-Death Studies*, Winter 1994, Volume 13, Number 2, pp. 109-13.
28. Ibid., pp. 111-12.
29. The 'z' in the 'Gz' that occurs in the following text refers to the force acting vertically from head-to-feet in contrast to it acting horizontally from back-to-front or across the shoulders.
30. The reader will find two of his papers and one that he co-authored sufficient for our present purpose: E.M. Forster and James E. Whinnery, 'Recovery of Gz-induced Loss of Consciousness: Psychophysiologic Considerations', *Aviation Space and Environmental Medicine*, 1988, Volume 59, pp. 517-22; James E. Whinnery, 'Acceleration-induced Loss of Consciousness: A Review of 500 Episodes', *Archives of Neurology*, 1990, Volume 47, pp. 764-76; and James E. Whinnery, 'Psychophysiologic Correlates of Unconsciousness and Near-death Experiences', *Journal of Near-Death Studies*, Summer 1997, Volume 15, Number 4, pp. 231-58. As the last paper deals directly with the subject at hand, in the following paragraphs, I will confine myself to it.
31. Ibid., p. 237
32. Ibid., p. 236. 'Confabulation': Fabricating Memories or Reading into Them What Is Not There.
33. Ibid., p. 238. Italics in the original.
34. Ibid., p. 239.
35. Ibid., p. 242.
36. Ibid., p. 242-43.
37. Ibid., pp. 244-45.
38. Ibid., p. 241.
39. Ibid., p. 242.
40. Ibid., p. 245.
41. Ibid., pp. 245, 247-48, 255-56.
42. Ibid., pp. 247-48.
43. Bruce Greyson, 'Biological Aspects of Near-death Experiences', *Perspectives in Biology and Medicine*, Autumn 1998, 14, https://muse.jhu.edu/article/401393/pdf, accessed 25 May 2014; Bruce Greyson, 'Near-death Experiences: Clinical Implications', *Archives of Clinical Psychiatry*, Sao Paulo, 2007, Volume 34, Supplement 1.
44. Mario Beauregard, *Brain Wars: The Scientific Battle over the Existence*

of the Mind and the Proof That Will Change the Way We Live Our Lives, Harper One, New York, 2013.

45. It would take us too far afield to review all the hypotheses that have been advanced, and the evidence that has been adduced tracing each element of NDEs to some dysfunction or process or part in the brain. Apart from the few papers that are cited in the text, the following two books will give the reader a flavour of the suggestions that have been put forth as well as objections to them. I found Michael N. Marsh, *Out-of-Body and Near-Death Experiences: Brain-state Phenomena or Glimpses of Immortality?*, OUP, New York, 2010, to be a comprehensive and informative treatment of the subject; for a spirited statement of the opposing point of view, Mario Beauregard, *Brain Wars: The Scientific Battle over the Existence of the Mind and the Proof That Will Change the Way We Live Our Lives*, Harper One, New York, 2013. And so will the following contributions in scholarly journals: Susan J. Blackmore, 'Near-death experiences', *Journal of the Royal Society of Medicine*, February 1996, Volume 89, pp. 73-76; Dean Mobbs and Caroline Watt, 'There is nothing paranormal about near-death experiences: How neuroscience can explain seeing bright lights, meeting the dead, or being convinced you are one of them', *Trends in Cognitive Sciences*, October 2011, Volume 15, Number 10, pp. 447-49. For representative reactions to the Mobbs and Watt paper, and to get a glimpse of the passions that arguments on the subject spark, see the discussion between Alex Tsakiris and Janice Holden, Skeptiko.com, Interview Number 164. See also Janice Holden, Bruce Greyson and Debbie James, (eds), *The Handbook of Near-Death Experiences: Thirty Years of Investigation*, Praeger, Santa Barbara, CA, 2009; Bruce Greyson, 'The Psychodynamics of Near-death Experiences', *The Journal of Nervous and Mental Disease*, 1983, Vol. 171 (6), pp. 376-81; Bruce Greyson, 'Biological Aspects of Near-death Experiences', *Perspectives in Biology and Medicine*, Autumn 1998, 14; Bruce Greyson, 'Near-death Experiences: Clinical Implications', *Archives of Clinical Psychiatry,* Sao Paulo, 2007, Volume 34, Supplement 1, http://dx.doi,org/10.1590/S0101-60832007000700015. It has been argued that the out-of-body experience and the NDE should not be seen as two separate, unconnected experiences but as parts of a continuum. Hence, clearly the extensive literature on out-of-body experiences is also relevant—from the experiments of Wilder Penfield to those of Olaf Blanke and his colleagues, and several others. But as these have been dealt with elsewhere in the book, I am not listing the papers

here. Of course, others who discern a transcendental dimension to NDEs dispute the relevance of the responses to electrical stimulation. They argue that the kinds of reactions that Penfield reported—hearing music, hearing voices, talking with living friends who are elsewhere— are never reported in NDEs, for instance, Bruce Greyson, 'Near-death Experiences: Clinical Implications', op. cit.

46. Juan C. Saavedra-Aguilar and Juan S. Gomez-Jeria, 'A Neurobiological Model for Near-death Experiences', *Journal of Near-Death Studies*, Summer 1989, Volume 7, Number 4, pp. 205-22.

47. Michael N. Marsh, *Out-of-Body and Near-Death Experiences: Brain-state Phenomena or Glimpses of Immortality?*, OUP, New York, 2010. This theme runs through the book; see in particular, Chapter 4.3, pp. 88-91.

48. Michael N. Marsh, op. cit, pp. 86, 89.

49. Ibid., p. 91.

50. Ibid., p. 89. Marsh lists some differences between NDEs and the dreams that we have. But then draws suggestive parallels: 'Despite such strictures, the very distinctive parallels between certain dream-state modes and ECE must be considered. Firstly, the twilight mentation of sleep-onset hypnogogic [the phase in which we are drifting into sleep] reveries not only involves perception of vivid visual and auditory imagery, but the acquisition of "complete knowledge" and "all-knowing states" that is typically representative of NDE narratives. Of further relevance to NDE ... are the intrusive vestibular influences of flying, rapid acceleration, being propelled through a tunnel, or being wrenched out of the body. Secondly, identical motor/vestibular phenomenology attends the REM dream state: indeed flying over water, or falling from a great height, are almost universal features of this type of unconscious mentation, accompanied by formed panoramic coloured vistas, sounds of music, chimes or bells, and sequences of highly affective content and meaning. Thirdly, hypnopompic [the phase in which we are coming out of sleep] dream-offset events usually occur during the shorter periods of sleeping following subjects' first morning awakenings. The dream content is extremely vivid, while the awakening is often accompanied by an abrupt "startle" reaction, such as the perception of a noise, typically a ringing (telephone or door) bell or a knock on the door...' For the instructive discussion, Ibid., pp. 152-57.

51. Karl Jansen, 'Near Death Experience and the NMDA Receptor', *British Medical Journal*, 24 June 1989, Vol. 298, No. 6689, p. 1708. In the book that we have encountered earlier, *Surviving Death*, Mark

Johnston adds to the elements of the NDE that users of ketamine report. This horse tranquilizer produces out-of-body experiences, Johnston reports, the view from the ceiling, the tunnel, as well as the light towards which one travels. The person is sure that his soul has left the body and that he is viewing the body from the ceiling. But in fact his body is animated, Johnston says: those who are attending on him see him vomiting, drooling, mumbling inarticulately, and carrying on conversations based on the scene *in front* of his eyes. Cf. Mark Johnston, *Surviving Death*, Princeton University Press, New Jersey, 2010, pp. 135-36.

52. Maurice Rawlings, *Beyond Death's Door*, Sheldon Press, London, 1980; Maurice Rawlings, *To Hell and Back*, Thomas Nelson Publishers, Nashville, 1993; Carol G. Zaleski, *Otherworld Journeys: Accounts of Near-Death Experience in Medieval and Modern Times*, OUP, New York, 1987; cited in Eugene d'Aquili and Andrew B. Newberg, *The Mystical Mind: Probing the Biology of the Religious Experience*, Fortress Press, Minneapolis, 1999, p. 65.

53. Michael N. Marsh, *Out-of-Body and Near-Death Experiences: Brain-state Phenomena or Glimpses of Immortality?*, OUP, Oxford, 2010; for an extended discussion about possible roles of endorphins, ketamine and NMDA receptors, see Chapter 9.1, in particular pp. 179-82.

54. Susan Blackmore, *Dying to Live: Near-death Experiences*, Prometheus, Buffalo, NY, 1993.

55. Susan J. Blackmore, 'Near-death Experiences', *Journal of the Royal Society of Medicine*, February 1996, Volume 89, pp. 73-76.

56. Michael N. Marsh, *Out-of-Body and Near-Death Experiences: Brain-state Phenomena or Glimpses of Immortality?*, OUP, Oxford, 2010, Chapter 9.2.

57. Juan C. Saavedra-Aguilar and Juan S. Gomez-Jeria, 'A neurobiological model for near-death experiences', *Journal of Near-Death Studies*, Summer 1989, Volume 7, Number 4, pp. 205-22, at pp. 208-09.

58. Compare Marsh's conclusion in regard to the variability of NDEs: 'Given the widely varying biological circumstances under which each brain recovers, every descriptive narrative offered by NDE subjects is idiosyncratically fashioned, reflective of the memories and lifelong impressions unique to each professing individual. These aberrant mental images are not culled from any other-worldly journey but as a thorough-going, this-worldly event, occasioned by the reawakening to conscious-awareness of a brain subjected in ~80 per cent of subjects to major antecedent circulatory/hypoxic insult. The return to

conscious-awareness can only be envisioned as a chaotic process of reperfusion and re-oxygenation, terminating abruptly as conscious-awareness fully re-emerges from the world of subconscious, dream-like mentation.' Michael N. Marsh, op. cit., p. 259.

59. Marsh also noted that five years of observation by a researcher had not yielded a single case in which the close-to-death experient had been able to report the cards, etc., that had been placed at the vantage points. Michael N. Marsh, *Out-of-Body and Near-Death Experiences*, p. 124.

60. Ian Stevenson, *Twenty Cases Suggestive of Reincarnation*, University Press of Virginia, Charlottesville, 1966, second revised and enlarged edition, 1974.

61. Satwant Pasricha and Ian Stevenson, 'Near-death Experiences in India: A Preliminary Report', *Journal of Nervous and Mental Disease*, 1986, Volume 174, Number 3, pp. 165-70, at 166-67.

15. IS EVERYTHING *REALLY* UNREAL?

1. *Talks*, Sri Ramanasramam, Tiruvannamalai, 1955/2006, pp. 29-30. There are other formulations, of course. For instance, in answer to questions on another occasion, Sri Ramana says, 'Reality is that which transcends all concepts, including that of God. Inasmuch as the name of God is used, it cannot be true. The Hebrew word *Jehovah* = (I am) expresses God correctly. Absolute Be-ing is beyond expression.' Ibid., p. 106. As I have dealt with aspects of the question earlier in *Does He Know a Mother's Heart?*, HarperCollins, NOIDA, 2011, some of the points made here and passages adduced figure in that book also.

2. Arthur Osborne, *The Collected Works of Sri Ramana Maharshi*, Sri Ramanasramam, Tiruvannamalai, 1979, p. 116.

3. *Talks*, p. 285.

4. Ibid., pp. 412-13.

5. For the preceding exchanges, Ibid., pp. 426-27.

6. Ibid., pp. 465-69.

7. Ibid., pp. 462-64.

8. The relevant passages are recounted in *Does He Know a Mother's Heart?*, HarperCollins, NOIDA, 2011.

9. Arthur Osborne, *The Collected Works of Sri Ramana Maharshi*, p. 117.

10. A. Devaraja Mudaliar, *Day By Day With Bhagavan*, Sri Ramanasramam, Tiruvannamalai, 1968/1989, p. 266.

11. *The Gospel*, p. 879.

12. *Sri Ramana Gita: Being the Teachings of Bhagavan Sri Ramana Maharshi composed by Sri Vasishtha Ganapati Muni with Sanskrit Commentary Prakasha of Sri T.V. Kapali Sastriar,* Sri Ramanasramam, Tiruvannamalai, 1998/2006, p. 40. Ganapati Muni was the 'premier disciple' of Sri Ramana. After the *Ramana Gita* had been composed and gone over, when a question was asked, Sri Ramana would often ask the seeker to look up the answer in this book. Kapali Sastri was a well-known scholar in his days—he was equally devoted to Sri Ramana and Sri Aurobindo.

13. Nagamma Suri, *Letters from Sri Ramanasramam,* Sri Ramanasramam, Tiruvannamalai, 1970/1985, p. 94.

16. THEIR PRISTINE EXAMPLE

1. Swami Premananda in *Ramakrishna: As We Saw Him*, Swami Chetnananda [ed.], Advaita Ashram, Calcutta, 1990/1993, p. 103.

2. Ibid., pp. 83-84.

3. Ibid., p. 89. Mahendranath Gupta reports the incident in Sri Ramakrishna's own words. 'Is it for your aunt?' Sri Ramakrishna asked Ramlal—that is, for Sri Sarada Devi. When he is told that the money had been given for his expenses, 'At first I thought I should use it to pay what I owed for my milk,' Sri Ramakrishna said. 'But will you believe me? I had slept only a little when I suddenly woke up writhing with pain, as if a cat were scratching my chest.' See, *The Gospel*, op. cit., pp. 226, 543.

4. Swami Turiyananda in *Sri Ramakrishna: As We Saw Him*, op. cit., p. 203. Swami Nikhilananda, *Life of Sri Ramakrishna*, Advaita Ashram, Kolkata, 1924/2011, p. 242.

5. *The Gospel*, pp. 609.

6. Ibid., p.831.

7. Swami Nikhilananda, *Life of Sri Ramakrishna*, pp. 93-94, 241.

8. *The Gospel*, p. 619.

9. Ibid., p. 478.

10. Ibid., p. 1022.

11. Swami Nikhilananda, *Life of Sri Ramakrishna*, op. cit., p. 154.

12. Cf. Swami Chetnananda, *How to Live with God: In the Company of Ramakrishna*, Advaita Ashram, Kolkata, 1997/2009, p. 184.

13. Swami Premananda in *Ramakrishna as We Saw Him*, op. cit., p. 111.

Index

Acknowledgements

The subject dealt with in this book is, in a sense, a natural subject for Indians. Yet little has been written on it. In fact, our libraries do not have even the basic journals and books that deal with such subjects. Nor do they feel that they should have them. Dr P.N. Tandon, one of the pioneers of neurosurgery in India, once told me that he had offered his collection of books, journals and papers—the collection of a lifetime spent in neurosciences, a collection that included difficult-to-get books that Theodore Erickson had turned over to him—to an institution with which he had himself been closely associated. No one had taken up the offer.

For this reason, I had to turn to my friend, the distinguished scholar Arvind Sharma even for such basic material as some of the books of Wilder Penfield. I am grateful to him. Most of all, I had to tax my good friend Philip Oldenburg. Throughout, as is his nature, he has been most helpful. I would just have to send him an email, and he would send me the papers that I had tried to hunt down in our libraries. Philip helped me with the same generosity as he has always helped his students. I am most grateful to him.

I had to turn to others also for checking facts and propositions. I am grateful to them all, in particular to Dr P.N. Tandon, who pointed me in the right direction at various turns.

And finally, my grateful thanks to Dr Ambarish Satwik, distinguished doctor and scholar; to Rakesh Sinha, executive editor of the *Indian Express*; and to Shantanu Ray Chaudhuri, executive editor at HarperCollins, for going through the draft manuscript and suggesting improvements. And to Rajinder Ganju for typesetting the book.